MW00583743

HISTORICAL DICTIONARIES
OF LITERATURE AND THE ARTS
Jon Woronoff, Series Editor

1. *Science Fiction Literature*, by Brian Stableford, 2004.
2. *Hong Kong Cinema*, by Lisa Odham Stokes, 2007.
3. *American Radio Soap Operas*, by Jim Cox, 2005.
4. *Japanese Traditional Theatre*, by Samuel L. Leiter, 2006.
5. *Fantasy Literature*, by Brian Stableford, 2005.
6. *Australian and New Zealand Cinema*, by Albert Moran and Errol Vieth, 2006.
7. *African-American Television*, by Kathleen Fearn-Banks, 2006.
8. *Lesbian Literature*, by Meredith Miller, 2006.
9. *Scandinavian Literature and Theater*, by Jan Sjåvik, 2006.
10. *British Radio*, by Seán Street, 2006.
11. *German Theater*, by William Grange, 2006.
12. *African American Cinema*, by S. Torriano Berry and Venise Berry, 2006.
13. *Sacred Music*, by Joseph P. Swain, 2006.
14. *Russian Theater*, by Laurence Senelick, 2007.
15. *French Cinema*, by Dayna Oscherwitz and MaryEllen Higgins, 2007.
16. *Postmodernist Literature and Theater*, by Fran Mason, 2007.
17. *Irish Cinema*, by Roderick Flynn and Pat Brereton, 2007.
18. *Australian Radio and Television*, by Albert Moran and Chris Keating, 2007.
19. *Polish Cinema*, by Marek Haltof, 2007.
20. *Old-Time Radio,* by Robert C. Reinehr and Jon D. Swartz, 2008.

Historical Dictionary of Old-Time Radio

Robert C. Reinehr
Jon D. Swartz

*Historical Dictionaries of
Literature and the Arts, No. 20*

The Scarecrow Press, Inc.
Lanham, Maryland • Toronto • Plymouth, UK
2008

SCARECROW PRESS, INC.

Published in the United States of America
by Scarecrow Press, Inc.
A wholly owned subsidary of
The Rowman & Littlefield Publishing Group, Inc.
4501 Forbes Boulevard, Suite 200, Lanham, Maryland 20706
www.scarecrowpress.com

Estover Road
Plymouth PL6 7PY
United Kingdom

Copyright © 2008 by Robert C. Reinehr and Jon D. Swartz

All rights reserved. No part of this publication may be reproduced, stored
in a retrieval system, or transmitted in any form or by any means, electronic,
mechanical, photocopying, recording, or otherwise, without the prior permission
of the publisher.

British Library Cataloguing in Publication Information Available

Library of Congress Cataloging-in-Publication Data

Reinehr, Robert C.
  Historical dictionary of old-time radio / Robert C. Reinehr, Jon D. Swartz.
    p. cm. — (Historical dictionaries of literature and the arts ; no. 20)
  Includes bibliographical references.
  ISBN-13: 978-0-8108-5780-3 (hardback : alk. paper)
  ISBN-10: 0-8108-5780-4 (hardback : alk. paper)
  1. Radio broadcasting–United States–History–Dictionaries. 2. Radio programs–
United States–History–Dictionaries. I. Swartz, Jon David. II. Title.
PN1991.3.U6R45 2007
384.540973'03–dc22   2007021375

⊗ᵀᴹ The paper used in this publication meets the minimum requirements of
American National Standard for Information Sciences—Permanence of Paper
for Printed Library Materials, ANSI/NISO Z39.48-1992.
Manufactured in the United States of America.

Dedicated to our brothers, Bill Reinehr and
George Swartz, fans of old-time radio

Contents

Editor's Foreword *Jon Woronoff*   ix

Acknowledgments   xi

Preface   xiii

Acronyms and Abbreviations   xv

Chronology   xvii

Introduction   1

THE DICTIONARY   11

Bibliography   293
    Overview   293
    Published Books and Monographs   296
    Published Articles and Reports   303
    Unpublished/Privately Published Works 303
    Internet Sources and CDs   304

About the Authors   305

Editor's Foreword

Once upon a time for the younger generation, but not so long ago for their parents and grandparents, at almost any moment of the day and evening tens of millions of Americans would be tuned in to one or another of literally hundreds of programs on the radio. Indeed, from 1926–1960, radio was not only a very popular media, it was the most important source of entertainment and information in the United States . . . until it was supplanted by television. That period is now known as the golden age of radio, which it certainly was then, and old-time radio (OTR), which it has become. OTR is admittedly gone, but it is hardly forgotten and it is still worthwhile to take a closer look to see just why it was so popular and what it offered its listeners, inevitably a mixture of good, bad, and indifferent, but also a mix that provided something for everyone.

This *Historical Dictionary of Old-Time Radio* takes on a very broad phenomenon, with many different facets, aesthetic, technical, and organizational. Just how rich and varied OTR was quickly becomes clear simply from glancing through, and then more carefully reading, the dictionary section with a broad array of entries on programs of all sorts: soap operas and situation comedies, mysteries and westerns, quiz shows and drama anthologies, sports and music, news and information. Other entries present some of the countless persons involved, who brought the programs to life, whether by actually performing, or behind the scenes, or writing and producing. And yet others explain major technological innovations and the role of the networks. The introduction puts this all in a broader context and the chronology traces the key events from year to year. The selected bibliography is there to take this journey down memory lane even further for any who want to know more.

This volume was written by two outstanding authorities on OTR, Robert C. Reinehr and Jon D. Swartz. Dr. Reinehr is emeritus professor of psychology at Southwestern University at Georgetown Texas, where Dr. Swartz was associate dean and Brown professor of education and psychology. In their professional capacities, they have collaborated in writing several books and monographs, and alongside this, they are keen fans of old-time radio and boast impressive collections of OTR programs, premiums, and other memorabilia. They have also collaborated in this field, producing among other things a major reference work, *Handbook of Old-Time Radio: A Comprehensive Guide to Golden Age Radio Listening and Collecting*. This latest historical dictionary takes their collaboration a step further and provides a useful tool for scholars and researchers and also numerous fans—like you and I—of old-time radio.

Jon Woronoff
Series Editor

Acknowledgments

Hundreds of people have helped us since we started systematically to collect materials about the golden age of radio nearly thirty years ago. For the most part, the individuals who contributed to this book are those whose works we have cited in our bibliography. Of particular help in this current effort were Jim Harmon, Ben Ohmart, and David S. Siegel, all enthusiastic fans of old-time radio.

Preface

Old-time radio is a very broad topic, involving thousands of programs, performers, and other individuals, as well as dozens of terms that are more or less specific to radio. The size of the topic has made it necessary to limit the size of dictionary entries in order to keep the volume to a reasonable size. For readers interested in more-detailed information about a given program or personality, we have included a comprehensive bibliography.

It has also been necessary to restrict the number of programs and individuals listed. We have tried to limit our coverage of programs to the most popular or best known of those that appeared on the major networks, but there were also some popular programs that were heard by very large audiences, although appearing only on regional networks, and we have included these programs and some of the personalities associated with them.

The choice of programs and personalities to be included has, of necessity, been somewhat arbitrary. Essentially every well-known show business personality appeared on radio at some time. Aside from those whose primary identity and fame was in radio, many were stars in other fields, and their radio work was only a sideline. Others divided their time between radio and other fields, or after a radio career became primarily motion picture or television performers. We have chosen to include those whose radio careers seemed to us extensive enough to justify their identity as radio personalities, although they might be well known in other entertainment fields.

The names of programs can be a source of confusion to readers because programs often existed under several names. In the earliest days of radio, no commercials were allowed and no products could be named or mentioned. As a workaround to this constraint, programs often carried the sponsor's name in the title, a habit that continued long after the prohibition against commercials had been lifted. In addition, programs were often referred to by the name of the major performer, rather than by the show's actual name, and programs themselves were sometimes surprisingly casual about names, referring to themselves by one name when signing on and by another when signing off. Cross-indexing the hundreds of titles thus involved would have expanded the text beyond reasonable limits, so programs have generally been listed by the name in most frequent use at the time.

The historical development of network radio involved hundreds of technological developments and patent complications, which in turn involved many government entities and major corporations. For the purpose of the dictionary entries, we have provided a capsule version of the history of each major network, but the development of the networks was so labyrinthine and complex that events are sometimes difficult to understand out of context. We have included a somewhat more detailed version of that development in the Introduction, and the reader may find it necessary to refer to that section if something in the dictionary entry is confusing or unclear.

Acronyms and Abbreviations

ABC	American Broadcasting Company
AFI	Air Features Incorporated
AFM	American Federation of Musicians
AFRA	American Federation of Radio Artists
AFRS	Armed Forces Radio Service
AT&T	American Telephone and Telegraph
CBS	Columbia Broadcasting System
FBI	Federal Bureau of Investigation
FCC	Federal Communications Commission
FRC	Federal Radio Commission
GE	General Electric
MBS	Mutual Broadcasting System
NBC	National Broadcasting Company
OTR	old-time radio
OWI	Office of War Information
RCA	Radio Corporation of America
UIB	United Independent Broadcasters

Chronology

1900 Marconi sends first transoceanic radio message from England to Canada.

1904 John Fleming develops the "Fleming valve," a modification of the Edison incandescent light bulb that allows the bulb to act as a rectifier.

1906 Reginald Fessenden broadcasts music and speech from his transmitter at Brant Rock, Massachusetts. Lee De Forest develops the first version of the audion, a vacuum tube that can amplify radio signals.

1907 De Forest broadcasts phonograph records from a naval ship to shore installation and demonstrates broadcast of music from a shore-based transmitter in New York.

1909 Charles Herrold and his students in San Jose, California, begin regularly scheduled broadcasting from the radio station at his college.

1912 The U.S. government begins regulation of radio, restricting transmissions to licensed stations.

1916 Westinghouse begins productions of radios and later produces radios under contract to the government during World War I.

1917 Federal government assumes control of all radio transmissions for the duration of World War I and only authorized experimental stations are allowed to continue operation.

1919 Wartime restrictions are lifted and Frank Conrad begins scheduled broadcasts from his station outside of Pittsburgh, Pennsylvania. Radio Corporation of America (RCA) established by General Electric (GE), American Telephone and Telegraph (AT&T), and Wireless Specialty Apparatus Co., later joined by Westinghouse in 1921.

1920 KDKA makes historic first broadcast of returns from presidential election of 1920 and continues scheduled broadcasting thereafter.

1921 Westinghouse hires first full-time announcer for KDKA and establishes three new stations, in Newark, Boston, and Chicago. U. S. Government establishes broadcasting service and issues regulations to govern broadcasters. Westinghouse produces its first popularly priced radio receiver, the Aeriola. First broadcast produced by RCA, heavyweight championship match between Dempsey and Carpentier. Five broadcast stations on the air by December. WJZ broadcasts World Series baseball game.

1922 WEAF New York begins operation as first station in AT&T network. By September, 537 radio stations are broadcasting. 100,000 radio receiving sets produced during year.

1923 Paired broadcasting by AT&T network begins with WEAF New York and WNAC Boston broadcasting simultaneous programs. Some 500,000 radio receiving sets are produced nationwide.

1924 AT&T network produces first transcontinental broadcast. AT&T broadcasts presidential address over 23-station network in fall of year. More than 3 million radio sets in use in U.S. and over 1400 broadcast stations in operation.

1925 AT&T operates network of 26 stations by the end of the year. RCA begins Radio Group network, with WJZ as flagship station.

1926 National Broadcasting Company (NBC) created by RCA for the purpose of purchasing AT&T network and managing all of the radio broadcast holdings of RCA. AT&T network sold to NBC, renamed NBC-Red, Radio Group network renamed NBC-Blue.

1927 United Independent Broadcasters (UIB) begins broadcasting in January. UIB is renamed Columbia Broadcasting System (CBS) and sold to William S. Paley. CBS begins broadcasting in September with 16 stations. Federal Radio Commission (FRC) assigns frequencies and power levels to all stations.

1929 RCA acquires the Victor Talking Machine Company and changes name to RCA Victor. Government files antitrust suit against RCA, forces GE and Westinghouse to sell their interest in the company.

Amos 'n' Andy, possibly the most popular radio program of all time, debuts on NBC.

1933 First broadcast of *The Lone Ranger* on WXYZ, Detroit, on a regional network that later became a part of the Mutual Broadcasting System.

1934 Mutual Broadcasting System formed by a coalition of four large stations in Chicago, Detroit, Cincinnati, and New York. Federal Communications Commission (FCC) is formed to replace FRC.

1936 H. V. Kaltenborn makes remote broadcast from battlefield in Spain during civil war. Mutual Network incorporates Don Lee Network and Colonial Network.

1937 *The Guiding Light*, a daytime soap opera, first appears on NBC. It later moves to television and is still appearing in 2007.

1938 *Mercury Theatre on the Air* presents Orson Welles' production of H. G. Wells' "War of the Worlds" and causes a sensation because some listeners truly believed that Martians were invading.

1939 Radio news reported to be the primary source of news for 25 percent of Americans.

1940 NBC Red and Blue networks grown to a total of more than 200 stations, Mutual to more than 160 stations. After FCC investigation, RCA forced to sell one of the two NBC networks because of antitrust concerns.

1942 Office of War Information (OWI) created to control media coverage of World War II, Elmer Davis appointed director. More than 75 percent of Americans report that radio is their primary source of news.

1943 NBC Blue Network sold to the American Broadcasting System and renamed the American Broadcasting Company (ABC). "Sorry, Wrong Number" first performed on *Suspense*, later to be repeated seven more times.

1944 More than 57 million radios in U.S. homes.

1945 With the end of World War II, many news commentators turn to social activism and oversight of government activities.

1950   More than 90 million radios in use in U.S., but television use is growing rapidly, with 103 television stations broadcasting, and more than 5 million television sets in use.

1953   NBC produces *Weekend*, the first of the magazine-format programs that all networks would later introduce in an effort to retain listeners as most radio programming migrates to television. More than 300 television stations in operation; television sets in 25 million U.S. homes.

1955   NBC *Monitor* begins, remaining on the air until 1975, ultimately broadcasting for more than 20,000 hours, more than any other program in history.

1960   On 25 November, the last of the CBS daytime soap operas leave the air.

1962   Last episodes of *Suspense* and *Yours Truly, Johnny Dollar* are broadcast, considered by many authorities to signal the end of the Golden Age of Radio.

Introduction

In the old-time radio era, radio was the dominant medium of its day, as popular and ubiquitous as television is today. It was amazingly varied in the types of programming offered, with a broad cast of characters and some programs that were so popular that virtually everyone was familiar with them. Recorded versions of these programs are still extremely popular today, and are widely available, both from commercial outlets and from hobbyists, as well as being heard over satellite radio and on many local stations. Behind the production of these programs, however, was a complex technological and financial infrastructure that had to be developed virtually from scratch, in a world unaccustomed to the rapid communication and technological marvels that we take for granted today. The following is a brief summary of this development.

A HISTORICAL OVERVIEW OF RADIO NETWORKS

The terms *old-time radio* and *golden age of radio* are used more or less interchangeably by most authorities and both terms refer to the relatively brief period from 1926, when the **National Broadcasting Company (NBC)** first began network broadcasting, until approximately 1960, by which time most radio network entertainment programs had been terminated and television had become the dominant communication medium in the United States. During the period of old-time radio, radio was dominated, although not entirely controlled, by the four major networks: NBC, the **Columbia Broadcasting System (CBS)**, the **Mutual Broadcasting System (MBS)**, and the **American Broadcasting Company (ABC)**.

In its most basic form, a network is simply a collection of stations that coordinates broadcasting so that a program is broadcast at the same time over more than one station. Network programs had to be delivered to each station in the network so that each of the many transmitters could broadcast the network programs simultaneously, which presented a very significant technological challenge in early network broadcasting.

In addition to the technical problems, complex and expensive legal issues were involved in the creation of network broadcasting. Because the hundreds of patents that had been secured during the development of broadcast technology were in the hands of many different individuals and companies, the development of radio stations was more or less uncontrolled; stations sprang up all over the nation, and no two stations used exactly the same equipment or followed exactly the same policies. In order to develop the infrastructure necessary for coordinated nationwide broadcasting, this hodge-podge of equipment, patents, policies, and investors had somehow to be brought together into coherent business structures and the networks were the business entities formed for this purpose. NBC was the first of the four major networks to appear, beginning broadcasting in 1926; CBS began broadcasting the next year. The Mutual network appeared in 1934, and ABC, which was created by the renaming of an already existing network, in 1943.

PRE-NETWORK RADIO BROADCASTING

Radio was originally promoted as a wireless telegraph, primarily for communication between two stations, and transmissions consisted only of Morse code. That the signal could be heard by listeners to whom it was not directed was a convenience in certain situations (SOS calls from ships, for example) but was seen as a corollary benefit; the primary purpose of a radio station was to communicate with some other specific station. Radio telegraphy of this sort was being experimented with as early as 1897 and was in general use by about 1910.

After the development of the Fleming Valve in 1904, the vacuum-tube concept was further developed by **Lee De Forest**, an American inventor. In 1906, De Forest produced the audion, a type of tube that would today be called a triode, utilizing three elements rather than the two used in the Fleming Valve. This modification allowed the tube to perform several functions not possible with a two-element tube, including amplification of a radio signal. The audion was originally so crude and unreliable as to be little more than a curiosity, but further development of the concept by scientists other than De Forest, most notably

Edwin Armstrong, made vacuum tubes of the audion type much more functional and radio became increasingly capable of transmitting voice and music, rather than just the dots and dashes of radio telegraphy.

Voice transmission had actually been demonstrated as early as 1900, when **Reginald Fessenden**, from a site on Cobb Island, near Washington, D.C., had broadcast a few words from his transmitter to a receiver a mile away. By Christmas Eve of 1906 he was able to produce what some authorities cite as the first radio broadcast, playing "O Holy Night" on his violin and having his wife sing some Christmas carols. The development of the audion allowed the inexpensive amplification of radio signals and made transmission of voice and music more feasible. De Forest himself placed a transmitter on a naval vessel in 1907 and broadcast phonograph records from the ship to shore stations. Soon thereafter, he gave several demonstrations in New York, broadcasting programs of opera music from a land station to an audience of reporters. By 1909, Charles Herrold, who owned a college of Wireless and Engineering in San Jose, California, was making regularly scheduled broadcasts of music from a station at his college.

There was no regulation of radio transmitters in the United States until 1912, so amateur operators were free to set up transmitters of any type, and there was a great deal of experimentation with radio transmission. With the adoption of federal licensing, this freedom was somewhat restricted, but experimentation in radio was still quite active until 1917 when the United States entered World War I. At that time, all stations were taken over by the United States Navy and non-authorized stations were forbidden. The development of new equipment by authorized experimental stations was encouraged, however, and all patent infringement suits were prevented by government edict. The result was a dramatic upsurge in technical advancement and innovation. In 1919, the wartime restrictions were lifted, and widespread experimentation by amateur operators resumed, now taking advantage of the improvements in technology that had occurred during the war, although most operators still thought of radio as a point-to-point medium: the ability to transmit voice and music only caused them to view radio as a wireless telephone, rather than as a wireless telegraph.

The operator of one of the experimentally oriented amateur stations was **Frank Conrad**, who, in addition to being an enthusiastic radio amateur, was also the assistant chief engineer at Westinghouse, located in Pittsburgh, Pennsylvania. Conrad's station was located in Wilkinsburg, about five miles outside of Pittsburgh. He had been very active in the development of broadcasting equipment during the war, working from designated experimental stations both at his house and at the Westinghouse factory, and ultimately held more than 200 radio-related patents. Almost as soon as the war was over, Conrad was back on the air with his own personal transmitter, his station being licensed as a "special land station" some months before other amateurs were allowed to resume operation.

Incorporation of the new radio telephony capacity allowed stations to communicate more freely, but most amateur transmissions consisted primarily of operators describing their location and the equipment they were using. Dr. Conrad was bored with this kind of conversation, and decided on the evening of 17 October 1919, to place a microphone before the speaker of his phonograph and to play phonograph records for a period of time, for the enjoyment of anyone who might care to listen.

Conrad's early programming was very successful within the range of his transmitter, which included the Pittsburgh metropolitan area. Following is an excerpt from *The Radio Amateur News* of January 1920:

> Listening by means of wireless telephone to a selection of music played by a phonograph has become the Saturday evening amusement of 400 owners of wireless receiving sets living in Pittsburgh, Pa., and environs. Several weeks ago Frank Conrad, who has a private laboratory at Penn avenue and Peebles street, took his phonograph over to his wireless telephone transmitter, put on a record and started the music. That started the concerts. Every Saturday night since 400 ears have been glued to wireless telephone receivers, listening to Conrad's renditions. Conrad stated that he is using four vacuum valves to transmit the music, and employs a spark transmission of 900 cycles frequency. The music is heard, it is said, in exactly the tones rendered by the phonograph record.

The broadcasts continued into the summer of 1920, and H. P. Davis, a Westinghouse executive, noticed an ad in a Pittsburgh newspaper stating that a local department store was selling radio receivers that could pick up the music that Conrad was broadcasting. This suggested to Davis that there might be a profitable market for moderately priced radio receivers if sufficient programming were available. He proposed that the company experiment with the possibility of furnishing programming to a larger audience than that reached by Conrad's transmitter. He thought that broadcasting the results of the presidential election of 1920 would afford an excellent opportunity for Westinghouse to estimate the attraction of broadcasting to a broad listening audience.

It was not until mid-October that the project was approved and a license application submitted, leaving very little time to prepare the equipment for an Election Day broadcast. One of the buildings in the Westinghouse complex in East Pittsburgh already had a radio transmitter on its roof, and it was decided to modify this installation for the historic broadcast. The preparations were hurried, and some compromises had to be made, but by Election Day, a shed housing a 100-watt transmitter was in place on top of the building and the necessary communication connections were established. The studio was just a single room that accommodated the transmitting equipment, a turntable for records, and the broadcast staff, which consisted of an announcer, an engineer, and a telephone line operator. Included in the Election Day broadcast was an appeal to listeners to report reception: "Will anyone hearing this broadcast please communicate with us, as we are anxious to know how far the broadcast is reaching and how it is being received."

Reception reports were received from more than 1,000 listeners and from distant points, and the Westinghouse executive suite decided both to continue the broadcasts and to go forward with the production of popular-priced radio receivers.

The station began a regular nightly broadcast schedule that proved to be very successful in promoting the sale of the Westinghouse receivers. In January 1921, to meet the demands of the growing program service, Westinghouse hired their first full-time announcer, **Harold W. Arlin**, a young electrical engineer. For the first few months of operation, there was no need for a real studio because programming consisted of announcements read by the announcer, phonograph records played from the transmitter shack, and programs originating from churches, theaters, hotels, or other remote points. In May, a large tent was erected next to the transmitter shack, which, with the addition of drapes and acoustical board, served as a studio until a more permanent studio could be built.

Westinghouse later established three additional broadcasting stations: WBZ near Boston, KYW Chicago, and WJZ Newark, each sending out programs for about an hour each night. There was a growing sense of excitement as broadcasting activities increased and in December the Department of Commerce formally established a broadcasting service and issued regulations to govern its activities. In the following year, there was an almost unbelievable boom in radio broadcasting, with hundreds of new stations appearing. By the end of 1922, there were more than 500 commercial radio stations on the air in the United States and shortly thereafter, networks began to develop.

DEVELOPMENT OF THE NETWORKS

At the onset of World War I, radio transmission in the United States was primarily for business purposes and was dominated by American Marconi, a company that was owned primarily by British investors. During World War I, the entire radio industry was placed under government control, with the Department of the Navy playing the largest governmental role, because of the essentially maritime nature of much of commercial broadcasting.

After the war, radio stations were returned to their owners, but the Navy Department still wanted to avoid foreign control of U.S. international communications, and in mid-1919 was able to influence the government to apply pressure on American Marconi to sell their holdings to an American company. At the same time, the government convinced General Electric (GE) that they should make an offer for these holdings. GE was selected because it was a large manufacturer of electrical equipment, including a type of transmitter that seemed likely to become dominant in international radio communications.

Because neither GE nor any other manufacturing company had a corporate structure well suited for the management of radio stations, GE combined with several other large companies to form a new corporation for this purpose, the **Radio Corporation of America (RCA)**; to this corporation the radio assets of American Marconi were sold for the purpose of placing their management in American hands. The new corporation purchased all the foreign-held stock of American Marconi as well as all assets of the corporation.

Initially, the partners in RCA were General Electric, American Telephone and Telegraph (AT&T), and a manufacturing company called Wireless Specialty Apparatus Company; these three companies were joined in 1921 by Westinghouse. Among them, the four companies held almost every worthwhile patent in radio, and manufactured most of the commercial radio equipment produced in the United States, as well as having strong connections with overseas radio companies. In addition, almost immediately after it was formed, RCA began to buy up the radio-related patents that were not already owned by its constituent members. By the middle of the 1920s, RCA controlled much of the technology of radio broadcasting.

RCA was initially seen primarily as a sales agent for the equipment produced by the parent companies, since the sale of radio equipment was at the time the only source of revenue in the radio industry. It was agreed that Westinghouse would produce 40 percent of the radios sold by RCA, and that General Electric would produce 60 percent; RCA did not at that time have any production facilities and did not produce any equipment itself. For Westinghouse, this was simply a more efficient way of continuing the company's interest in the production of such receivers because, like GE, it was primarily a manufacturing company and did not have a retail sales force or a large dealer network. They had already begun production of the **Aeriola** line of popularly priced radios and, after joining the RCA group, continued to market these radios under their own name until 1922, after which they were sold as RCA radios. Being the sole source of the Westinghouse and General Electric radios immediately placed RCA in a prominent position in the radio receiver market.

RCA was always alert to the acquisition of companies that might be in competition with them and in 1929 had an opportunity to purchase the Victor Talking Machine Company. General Electric and Westinghouse loaned RCA $32 million dollars for that purpose, and RCA combined with the new acquisition to form RCA Victor. The Justice Department felt that the already-dominant position of RCA in radio was now becoming a threat to competition. Later that same year, the Justice Department filed an antitrust suit, demanding that GE and Westinghouse be separated from RCA Victor. The separation agreement was finally completed in 1932, and RCA Victor was an independent company thereafter.

In addition to its role as purveyor of equipment produced by its parent companies, RCA was aggressive in the pursuit of other business opportunities, and entered the broadcasting business early in the company history. The RCA broadcast debut was the heavyweight championship fight between Jack Dempsey and Georges Carpentier on 2 July 1921. The broadcast, like the earlier Westinghouse broadcast of the 1920 presidential returns, was a great success, and the radio boom of the next year expanded RCA sales of Westinghouse and GE radio receivers into a national market.

At about the same time, the introduction of amplification systems for telephone lines had caused AT&T to experiment with sending speeches and reports of current events to distant points, where multiple listeners could listen on loudspeakers. It was only a short step from that to using telephone lines to connect radio broadcast stations. In late 1921, an AT&T company memo outlined the creation of a national radio network, centered around station WEAF in New York. The network was to consist of a group of stations that would charge for broadcast time, just as AT&T charged for telephone time.

WEAF began operation in August 1922 and the first simultaneous broadcast of a program from WEAF and WNAC Boston was on 4 January 1923. There was continuous paired broadcasting over WEAF and WMAF, another Boston station, during the summer of 1923. More stations were added rapidly, and, in 1924, AT&T produced a transcontinental broadcast by including KPO San Francisco in the network. In the fall of that year, a presidential address was broadcast over a 23-station network. By the end of 1925, AT&T was operating a network of 26 stations.

RCA responded by forming the **Radio Group Network**, centered on WJZ, Newark, one of the four original Westinghouse stations. Because AT&T would not allow them to use their telephone lines to connect the stations, the Radio Group had to use telegraph lines, which were not well suited to the task, and they encountered many technical problems getting the network established.

Although AT&T was skilled at the technical aspects of establishing a network, by 1925, it was becoming apparent that their corporate structure was not well suited to the operation of a broadcast network. They accordingly decided to sell all their radio assets and to revert to leasing telephone lines, which was their primary business. They agreed to sell the AT&T network to RCA and to allow them to use AT&T telephone lines to connect their stations.

RCA recognized that a different company structure was going to be required to meet the demands of network broadcasting and a new corporation, the **National Broadcasting Company (NBC)**, was created for the purpose of operating the combined assets of the two existing networks. In 1926, NBC purchased WEAF and the associated AT&T network and combined it with the Radio Group Network that was already owned by RCA. The original AT&T chain was renamed the NBC Red Network, with WEAF continuing as the flagship station. The smaller Radio Group Network was renamed the NBC Blue Network, with WJZ as the flagship station. The formation of the NBC networks was announced in September 1926 and the first broadcast under the NBC name followed on 15 November of that same year. New stations were added rapidly. By 1928, NBC was operating 56 stations; by 1940, the number had grown to more than 200 stations nationwide.

Although the two NBC networks were supposedly equal, and each did eventually have over 100 stations, NBC Red was, in fact, the more important and carried most of the better established and more profitable programs. The Blue network carried many of the sustaining programs and the newer programs. The Red/Blue designations were said to be derived from the color of marking pens used to delineate network connections on maps at the NBC headquarters. The distinction between networks was not apparent to listeners and stations did not always make it clear to which of the two NBC networks they belonged.

The executives at RCA were not the only people to recognize the commercial potential of broadcast radio, nor the only ones to see the need for a network structure to fund and direct broadcasting activities. A number of regional networks soon appeared. In 1927, one of these, the **United Independent Broadcasters (UIB)** was formed in New York. An arrangement was made with the Columbia Phonograph Company to form another corporation, the Columbia Phonograph Broadcasting System, which was to handle sales for the UIB network.

Broadcasting began in January 1927, only two months after NBC's initial broadcast, with the UIB contracting to pay each of the 16 network stations $500 a week for 10 hours of air time. It was soon apparent that the sales unit could not sell enough advertising to cover this cash drain, and because capitalization was inadequate, the network was near collapse after only a few months. The Columbia Phonograph Company then withdrew from the venture and sold all its capital stock to UIB, which was renamed the **Columbia Broadcasting System (CBS)**.

CBS began broadcasting on 18 September 1927, with 16 stations in the network. WOR Newark was the flagship station, although construction was still incomplete (the first control room was in the men's room). A little over a year later, WOR was replaced as the flagship station by WABC, New York. Like NBC, the CBS network grew very rapidly; by 1938, it consisted of more than 100 stations.

The third of the four major radio networks did not begin until 1934, and was organized very differently from NBC and CBS. The **Mutual**

Broadcasting System was a working agreement among independently owned stations, with all member stations maintaining considerable autonomy. By the end of 1940, there were 160 stations in the Mutual network. Mutual later went through a long series of changes in corporate ownership, until the use of the Mutual name was finally discontinued in 1999.

The **American Broadcasting Company (ABC)** did not exist until 1943 and it was not a newly created network, but simply a new name for a network already in existence. In 1940, the Federal Communications Commission (FCC) issued a "Report on Chain Broadcasting" after having conducted hearings for several years. The report found that RCA, the parent company of NBC, was using the NBC Blue Network to stifle competition with the NBC Red Network. The FCC ordered that no license should be issued to any station belonging to a company that maintained more than one network, essentially forcing RCA to divest itself of one of its networks. RCA protested, and appealed to the courts, but the FCC ruling was upheld and RCA elected to sell the NBC Blue Network, the less valuable of their two networks.

In October of 1943, the NBC Blue Network was sold to a corporation headed by Edward Noble, the owner of Life Saver candies, and was renamed the *American Broadcasting Company*. Network operation continued with very few changes apparent to listeners, although the new management instituted many policy changes over the course of the next several years.

It was not long before many changes were necessary in all the networks, because the growth of television was as explosive as the growth of radio had been only 30 years before. In 1948, there were about 350,000 television sets in the United States and 27 television stations were in full operation. Only two years later, in the fall of 1950, there were more than 5 million television sets and 103 television stations; by 1953, there were television sets in more than 25 million homes, and more than 300 TV stations in operation.

Popular radio programs migrated to television, and in the end, network radio returned to being a series of brief news broadcasts throughout the day, with local sponsors and local news added by affiliate stations. Radio still had the capacity to provide rapid in-depth coverage of breaking news on a national and international level, but network radio reporting was commingled with television news and network radio existed primarily as an adjunct to television.

The Dictionary

– A –

A & P GYPSIES (THE). A very early **musical program** first heard over WEAF in New York in the days before any network radio existed, *The A & P Gypsies* was later carried by NBC from 1926 until 1936. Headed by Russian-born violinist Harry Horlick, The Gypsies began as a small string ensemble that played Hungarian and Russian folk songs as well as Gypsy music. Over the years, the number of musicians and the repertoire broadened until the program featured a 26-piece orchestra playing all types of popular music. Top singers of the time appeared as guests on the program and the orchestra dressed in Gypsy costumes for every performance. The orchestra and program were named for the sponsor, The Atlantic and Pacific Tea Company.

A. L. ALEXANDER'S MEDIATION BOARD. The Mediation Board was a panel of educators and social workers that offered advice to people who appeared before them to relate their personal problems, often domestic difficulties or marital discord. Heard from 1943 to 1950, it was an outgrowth of a previous program, *Goodwill Court*, that had offered legal advice but had been forced to leave the air because the New York Supreme Court refused to allow any lawyers to give legal advice over the air. Alexander, who acted as moderator of both programs, had been a divinity student, an actor, and a reporter before beginning a radio career as an announcer. He later created the *Court of Human Relations* for television and, in 1940, published a collection of poems, *Poems That Touch the Heart*, that has sold more than 650,000 copies and is still in print.

ABBOTT & COSTELLO SHOW (THE). Although best known as movie comics, making more than 30 films together, the famous com-

11

edy team of **Bud Abbott** and **Lou Costello** appeared on radio for many years, headlining their own show from 1940–1949. Abbott and Costello were vaudeville performers who did slapstick skits, some of which became famous comedy routines; and their radio program was primarily a collection of these skits, with brief musical interludes. A television version of the program was seen from 1952 to 1954. From 1947 to 1949, they also hosted a Saturday morning radio program for children, *The Abbott and Costello Children's Program*, conducting games and quizzes and presenting child performers.

ABBOTT, BUD (1895–1974). William "Bud" Abbott was the straight-man half of the Abbott & Costello comedy team. Abbott was working in the box office of a vaudeville theater in 1929 when **Lou Costello** was booked as a performer. Costello's straight man was taken ill and Abbott took his place. The two men worked together in vaudeville until forming a permanent partnership in 1936. The partnership was dissolved amicably in 1957, but in 1958 Abbott sued Costello for money allegedly owed him from their television program. Costello died before the suit was settled and although Abbott later tried to revive some of the old routines with new partners, he never was successful. He experienced considerable financial difficulties in his later years due to Internal Revenue Service (IRS) claims for large sums of back taxes.

ABE BURROWS SHOW (THE). Abe Burrows was a successful comedy writer who was writing for the *Joan Davis Show* when she invited him to conduct a show after the broadcast. These performances led to Burrows being given his own program on which he conducted interviews, did comedy monologues, and performed his own humorous musical compositions. First heard from 1947 to 1948, he returned in 1949 with a similar program called *Breakfast with Burrows*.

ABIE'S IRISH ROSE. A **situation comedy** based on a very successful play of the same name, *Abie's Irish Rose* first appeared as an episode on *The Knickerbocker Playhouse* and became so popular that it eventually replaced the original program. Heard from 1942 to 1944, the program centered around the family conflicts encountered when a Jewish boy married an Irish–Catholic girl in New York City. Sydney Smith and **Betty Winkler** were the first to play the parts of

Abie Levy and Rosemary Murphy; but they were later replaced by Richard Coogan and Mercedes McCambridge and then by several others. The same format was used for the later television program, *Bridget Loves Bernie*.

ACE, GOODMAN (1899–1982) and JANE (1905–1974). Goodman Ace and his real-life wife, Jane, were the stars of an early **comedy program**, *Easy Aces*, which consisted largely of conversation between them. Goodman Ace wrote the entire show; after it left the air, he became one of the highest-paid writers in radio and later in television. Jane played the part of his ditzy wife and was famous for her malapropisms, some of which became very well known, such as "Time wounds all heals" and "We're all cremated equal." In real life, she was extremely clever and was almost as funny when ad-libbing as when reading from the script. She and her husband met while in high school in Kansas City and were married in 1922.

ADAMS, MASON (1919–2005). Adams was a versatile actor who worked in theater, television, and radio. On radio, he played the title role on *Pepper Young's Family* from 1945 to 1959 and also appeared regularly on juvenile programs and science fiction anthology programs. He later received an Emmy nomination for his role as the managing editor on television's *Lou Grant*.

ADVENTURE PROGRAMS. Adventure programs were very popular on old-time radio (OTR), although titles are sometimes misleading; many of the programs with "Adventures of . . ." in the title are **Crime Programs** or **Juvenile Adventure Programs**, both of which are discussed separately.

A number of adventure programs were espionage shows of one sort or another. *I Was a Communist for the FBI* was based on the real-life adventures of an American agent who infiltrated the communist party organization in America. Although it was a syndicated program rather than a network production, it appeared on over 600 stations nationwide during the height of the communist scare of the early 1950s. *The Man Called X* featured an American intelligence agent who operated in exotic foreign settings; *Dangerous Assignment* was very similar. *Ned Jordan, Secret Agent* also worked to expose foreign agents and other enemies of the government; but he worked in the United States, using as a cover his everyday job as a railroad detective.

World War II was the setting for a number of espionage programs, the best known of which was *Counterspy*. The show was originally concerned with German and Japanese spy plots, but over the years evolved into a more general espionage thriller.

The non-espionage adventure programs varied widely, from the sea stories in *Voyage of the Scarlet Queen* to the romantic heroes of *Bold Venture* and *Café Istanbul*, who led adventurous lives in exotic settings. On *Box 13*, the protagonist was a retired newspaper reporter who advertised "Adventure wanted: will go anywhere, do anything."

The champion of all OTR adventure programs, however, was *I Love a Mystery*, which, in spite of the title, was not a mystery program but an adventure thriller about three partners in a detective agency. Jack, Doc, and Reggie roamed the world, engaging in exotic and often gory adventures. It is still one of the most popular, and most fondly remembered, of all OTR programs. Several years after ILAM left the air, *I Love Adventure* appeared, detailing the later exploits of these heroes. Both programs were written by **Carlton E. Morse**, who also wrote the long-running evening serial, *One Man's Family*. *See also* CRIME PROGRAMS, JUVENILE ADVENTURE PROGRAMS.

ADVENTURES OF ELLERY QUEEN (THE). A mystery program based on the stories written by Frederic Dannay and Manfred B. Lee, cousins who also wrote the scripts for the original radio version, *The Adventures of Ellery Queen* was first heard in 1939 as a 60-minute program. The format changed to 30 minutes the next year and remained so until the program left the air in 1948. Ellery Queen was a private detective without official police affiliation who was often called into cases by his father, a police inspector. The program had several unusual features, including a panel composed of experts or celebrity guests, who would speculate about the solution to the crime just before the last act began. The title role was played by several actors, but Hugh Marlowe was the first. Ellery's father was originally played by **Santos Ortega**.

ADVENTURES OF FRANK MERRIWELL (THE). There were two versions of this program, both of them **juvenile adventure pro-**

grams based on the character created in books by Burt L. Standish. The first version, heard in 1934, was a 15-minute continuation drama with Donald Briggs as Frank. The better-known version was heard from 1946 to 1949 as a 30-minute Saturday morning program, with each adventure completed in one episode. Frank Merriwell was a student at Yale in the late 19th century, a heroic figure both in athletics and in life situations, and the introduction of the program attempted to set the scene in the romantic past. Lawson Zerbe played Frank in this version, with Elaine Rost as his girlfriend, Inza Burrage.

ADVENTURES OF HELEN AND MARY (THE). See LET'S PRE-TEND.

ADVENTURES OF NERO WOLFE (THE). Based on the character created by Rex Stout, this 30-minute detective series featured a huge fat genius who solved crimes for very high fees. As in the books, he never left his house, leaving all the legwork and physical activity to his assistant, Archie Goodwin. Wolfe concerned himself primarily with eating and tending his orchids. The program first appeared as *The Amazing Nero Wolfe* in 1945–1946, with Francis X. Bushman in the title role. A later version in 1950–1951 starred Sidney Greenstreet as Wolfe and is sometimes listed as *The New Adventures of Nero Wolfe.*

ADVENTURES OF OZZIE AND HARRIET (THE). A **situation comedy** featuring the lives of the Nelson family, this program was originally titled *The Ozzie Nelson–Harriet Hilliard Show.* Ozzie Nelson was a popular bandleader and his wife Harriet was a vocalist in his orchestra. After appearing as musicians for several popular radio programs, they developed their own show, which ran from 1944 to 1954, and then moved the program to television, where it appeared until 1966 with very few changes in format or cast. Their sons, David and Ricky, were originally portrayed by actors Tommy Bernard and Henry Blair; but their boys began playing themselves in 1949, when David was 13 and Ricky was nine. Ozzie's neighbor Thorny was played by **John Brown**, and **Lurene Tuttle** played Harriet's mother.

ADVENTURES OF PHILIP MARLOWE (THE). A 30-minute detective drama based on the tough-guy private detective character created by Raymond Chandler, *The Adventures of Philip Marlowe* was first heard in the summer of 1947 with Van Heflin in the title role. After being off the air for a year, the program reappeared in 1948 starring **Gerald Mohr** as Marlowe and was heard until 1951. It was a more hard-boiled program than many of the other private detective shows of the time, containing few quips or quaint characters. The supporting cast was drawn from the best radio actors in Hollywood, with producer/director **Norman Macdonnell** often using actors who worked with him on other programs.

ADVENTURES OF SAM SPADE (THE). Although the program featured the San Francisco private investigator introduced by author Dashiell Hammett, the Sam Spade of radio was much different from the dour Spade portrayed by Humphrey Bogart in *The Maltese Falcon*. Heard from 1946 to 1951, the radio version of Spade was tough but witty and clever and the stories had a light touch; he referred to each case as a "caper." The programs revolved around Spade's dictation of case reports to his secretary, Effie, played by **Lurene Tuttle**, and always included his license number, 137596. **Howard Duff** played the title role from 1946 to 1950, at which time Stephen Dunne took over for a final season.

ADVENTURES OF SUPERMAN (THE). A **juvenile adventure program** based on the hero of DC comics, *The Adventures of Superman* was first heard in syndication on WOR, New York, in 1940, and appeared on the national network from 1942 to 1951. It was for many years a 15-minute program heard in the late afternoon, but, in 1949, the format was changed to 30 minutes and the program moved to Saturday morning. From 1943 to 1947, it was sponsored by Kellogg's Pep cereal and many premiums were offered. **Clayton "Bud" Collyer** starred as Superman, but his identity was kept secret until 1946, when he revealed his role in an interview for *Time* magazine. Jackson Beck was the narrator and also played several minor roles during the program's long run.

ADVENTURES OF THE THIN MAN (THE). A 30-minute crime drama detailing the adventures of retired private detective Nick Charles and his glamorous wife Nora, *The Adventures of the Thin Man* was based on the 1934 film starring William Powell and Myrna

Loy. The first stars of the radio show, **Les Damon** and **Claudia Morgan**, sounded so much like the film characters that many listeners found it hard to believe that the stars of the film were not performing. Several other actors later played Nick, but Claudia Morgan played Nora for the entire run, from 1941 to 1950. Nick Charles had married into upper-class New York society but remained friends with several colorful underworld characters to whom he often turned for information not available to the police. His rich and beautiful wife assisted him in solving crimes and the program featured witty, sophisticated dialogue similar to that heard on its competitor, *Mr. and Mrs. North*. The title of the program was changed in 1948 to *The New Adventures of the Thin Man*.

AERIOLA. The Aeriola, manufactured by Westinghouse, was the first factory-built, popularly priced receiver. First appearing in June of 1921, it was a crystal set (no tubes) and sold for $25, including earphones. The Aeriola Sr., an upscale receiver with a single vacuum tube, appeared in December of the same year and sold for $65. One-tube receivers are not very good at producing a signal strong enough to operate a speaker, so a two-tube version called the Aeriola Sr. Amplifier was introduced in March of 1922, and sold for $68. It later became part of the Radiola line of radios from RCA.

AIR ADVENTURES OF JIMMIE ALLEN (THE). A very early 15-minute **juvenile adventure program**, *The Air Adventures of Jimmie Allen* was broadcast in syndication from 1933 to 1936 and transcriptions of the original broadcasts were re-released in the summers of 1942 and 1943. Jimmie was a teenage pilot who flew dangerous missions around the world accompanied by his friend and mentor, veteran pilot Speed Robertson. The program was extremely popular: at one time, the Jimmie Allen Flying Clubs distributed the club newsletter to more than 600,000 members per week. The program was written by Robert M. Burtt and Wilfred G. Moore, both of whom had fought in World War I; Burtt had served with the Lafayette Escadrille. The same team later wrote radio's famous *Captain Midnight* series.

AIR FEATURES INCORPORATED (AFI). AFI was an organization that **Frank and Anne Hummert** formed in 1944 to make possible the assembly-line production of the many programs that they produced: primarily soap operas, but also crime detection and juvenile adventure programs. The Hummerts dictated or otherwise outlined plots, and dialogue scribes wrote the actual scripts that were used on the air. This procedure allowed the Hummerts to produce the scripts for more than four hours of network airtime daily.

AL JOLSON SHOW (THE). Al Jolson, whose real name was Asa Yoelson, was a vaudeville performer who sang in blackface, primarily songs about the South. He was often billed as "the world's greatest entertainer." Certainly, he was immensely popular long before radio; in addition to vaudeville, he starred in the world's first talking movie, *The Jazz Singer*, in 1927. He was the featured performer in several radio variety programs of various names, beginning with *Presenting Al Jolson* in 1932, and continuing with ***Shell Chateau***, ***The Kraft Music Hall***, *The Lifebuoy Program*, and *The Al Jolson Show*. All of the programs were sometimes referred to as *The Al Jolson Show*, and all consisted of Jolson singing popular songs, interspersed with comedy skits, and the performances of guest stars.

AL PEARCE SHOW (THE). Although virtually unknown today, Al Pearce was one of the most durable comics of the radio era, appearing on a series of programs of various names from 1934 to 1947. One of the characters he played in comedic skits was a timid door-to-door salesman named Elmer Blurt who would knock on doors and hope aloud that nobody would be home: "I hope, I hope, I hope." This became one of the most popular catchphrases of the time. Some of the other names under which his programs appeared included *Al Pearce and His Gang*, *Watch the Fun Go By*, *Fun Valley*, and *Here Comes Elmer*. *See also* COMEDY PROGRAMS.

ALBERT, EDDIE (1906–2005). Although best known as a television and movie actor, Eddie Albert, who real name was Edward Albert Heimberger, was very active in radio in the 1930s and 1940s. He discontinued the use of his surname because announcers frequently announced it as "Hamburger." He headlined *The Eddie Albert Show*, *Eddie Albert Songs*, *Rain and Sunshine*, and a daytime light **music program** called *The Honeymooners*, where he and Grace Bradt did vocal duets. A remarkable individual, he graduated from the University of Minnesota and then worked as a circus trapeze artist before turning to dramatic work. He was a much-decorated hero in World War II, serving in the Navy as a lieutenant. A talented singer, dancer, and pianist, much of his radio work was music-related, although he later became exclusively an actor, usually in comedic roles.

ALDRICH FAMILY (THE). A long-running 30-minute **situation comedy** that first appeared in 1939 and continued with brief interruptions until 1953, *The Aldrich Family* centered around the bumbling of 16-year-old Henry Aldrich and relationships with his family and friends. The program was created and written by Clifford Goldsmith, based on his Broadway play, *What a Life*. It was first heard as a series of skits on *The Rudy Vallee Show* and later on *The Kate Smith Hour*. The introduction was famous, with Henry's long-suffering mother calling "Hen-reee! HEN-ry Aldrich! The role of Henry was originated on the stage by **Ezra Stone**, who played the role on radio for much of the run, although he was replaced by several other actors from 1942 to 1945, while he served in the Army.

ALLEN, FRED (1894–1956). One of the best-known and most-durable comedians of the radio era, Fred Allen, whose real name was John Florence Sullivan, began in vaudeville as a juggler. He and his wife, **Portland Hoffa**, appeared on radio on a **comedy program** that began in 1932 and continued under various names for nearly 20 years. He was considered to be one of the great natural humorists of his day and wrote much of the material for his own programs. He and Jack Benny had a long-running pseudo-feud that provided a great deal of comedic material for both. Allen was also known for mocking network executives, at a time in history when such activity was unwelcome; he was once cut off the air as he began a network satire. He made many guest appearances and his intelligence and wit made him popular as a panelist on *Information, Please* and similar programs.

ALLEN, GRACIE (1902–1964). The daughter of vaudevillians, Gracie Allen began performing as a child. In 1922, she met **George Burns** and they formed the comedy team of *Burns and Allen*. They were married in 1926, and starred in vaudeville before becoming regular radio performers in 1932. Gracie, who was portrayed as scatterbrained and brash on stage, was rather shy and self-conscious in private life. She retired in 1958 to concentrate on being a homemaker and gardener.

ALLEN'S ALLEY. A popular feature of *The Fred Allen Show*, Allen's Alley was added to the program in 1942, after the show had been on the air under various names for many years. Each week, Allen and his wife, Portland Hoffa, would stroll through an imaginary neighborhood, asking the various residents for commentary on the news of the day. The characters changed over the years, but some of them became very well known, including Mrs. Nussbaum (played by Minerva Pious), Titus Moody (played by Parker Fennelly), and Senator Claghorn (played by Kenny Delmar). The stroll down the alley was usually preceded by the question, "Shall we go?"

AMECHE, DON (1908–1993). Ameche, whose real name was Dominic Amici, first appeared on radio as the host on such dramatic series as *Grand Hotel* and *The First Nighter*. He later emceed *The Edgar Bergen–Charlie McCarthy Show* and teamed with Frances Langford in a series of comedic matrimonial sketches called *The Bickersons*, which was later spun off as a separate show. He was popular in movies and television as well, winning an Oscar at age 75.

AMECHE, JIM (1915–1983). The younger brother of Don Ameche, Jim started his career playing the title role in the extremely popular **juvenile adventure program**, *Jack Armstrong, the All-American Boy*. He sounded a great deal like his older brother and had a long career in radio, starring in *The Silver Eagle*, another juvenile serial, and serving as announcer on *Amos 'n' Andy*, as well as on several other programs.

AMERICAN BROADCASTING COMPANY (ABC). From 1926 until 1943, there were two *National Broadcasting Company* **(NBC)** networks: NBC Red and NBC Blue. In 1940, the Federal Communications Commission (FCC) found that the **Radio Corporation of America (RCA)**, the parent company of NBC, was using the NBC Blue Network to stifle competition with the NBC Red Network, and RCA was forced to divest itself of one of the two networks. RCA elected to sell the Blue network, the less valuable of the two; and, in 1943, it was sold to the American Broadcasting System, a corporation formed for the purpose of making the purchase. The NBC Blue Network was renamed the American Broadcasting Company (ABC) and network operation continued with very few changes apparent to either employees or listeners. Member stations, newspapers, and magazines were sometimes slow to use the new name of the network.

The change of network names led to the renaming of several important stations. WABC New York, the flagship station for CBS, was renamed WCBS; and WEAF New York, the flagship station for the NBC Red Network, was renamed WNBC. In 1953, ABC's New York flagship station, WJZ, assumed the abandoned call letters, WABC. ABC gradually morphed into the television network of today.

AMERICAN FEDERATION OF RADIO ARTISTS (AFRA). A labor union formed in 1937 to improve the compensation and working conditions of radio performers, the AFRA included performers from all types of programs, although many of the union leaders came from the soap operas or other daytime programs. The organization later became the American Federation of Television and Radio Artists, which is still in existence. Membership in 2005 was over 80,000.

AMOS 'N' ANDY. One of the most popular programs in the history of radio, *Amos 'n' Andy* was a **situation comedy** based on the experiences of two African-American men from Harlem who owned the Fresh Air Taxi Company, so named because its only taxi had no windshield. The two main characters were played by two white men, **Freeman Gosden** and **Charles Correll**, who did the voices of many other characters, as well as doing all the writing for the show. Heard on the network from 1929 to 1960, it first appeared as a 15-minute program heard daily at 7:00 P.M. and was, at one time, so popular that in many towns across the nation, movie theaters would interrupt the showing of movies to play the program through the theater sound system. In 1943, the show changed to a 30-minute weekly format and, in 1954, the situation comedy was replaced with *The Amos 'n' Andy Music Hall,* on which Gosden and Correll played popular records and did short Amos 'n' Andy skits.

ANDREWS, ROBERT HARDY (1903–1976). Andrews was an ex-journalist who was writing serial fiction for magazines when, in 1931, he was recruited by **Frank and Anne Hummert** to write a very early soap opera called *The Stolen Husband*. The program was not a success, but both Andrews and the Hummerts learned from the experience and Andrews later wrote several very successful soap operas, including *Betty and Bob* and *Just Plain Bill*, as well as *Skippy*, a popular children's program of the early 1930s. Andrews was a workaholic whose production was fantastic; he normally wrote more than 100,000 words a week.

ANSBRO, GEORGE (1915–). Although occasionally appearing as an actor, George Ansbro was primarily an announcer, narrator, and newscaster. He was the announcer on *Young Widder Brown* for 18 years and in addition to announcing for other soaps, music programs, and dramatic series, his weekly news series, *FBI Washington,* ran for 25 years. When he retired in 1990, he had been employed in network radio for 59 years. In 2000, he published a book of his recollections, *I Have a Lady in the Balcony*.

ARCHIE ANDREWS. A teenage **situation comedy** based on the comic strip by Bob Montana, *Archie Andrews* resembled *The Aldrich Family* in format, although noisier and more clearly aimed at a juvenile audience. Archie was portrayed as a typical hyperactive, bumbling teenager and he and his friends were involved in ridiculous situations of various kinds. First heard from 1943 to 1944 as a daily 15-minute program, it later changed to a 30-minute weekly format and was broadcast until 1953, often in a Saturday morning time slot. The title role was played by many different actors, although Jack Grimes was the first Archie and Bob Hastings is perhaps the best-remembered. Jughead Jones, Archie's best friend, was played by Harlan Stone Jr. for much of the long run.

ARDEN, EVE (1912–1990). Although she appeared in more than 100 movies and received an Academy Award nomination in 1945, Eve Arden is best remembered as high school English teacher Connie Brooks in the radio (and later, television) **situation comedy**, *Our Miss Brooks*. Born Eunice Quedens, she began performing on the Broadway stage in 1934 and first made her mark in radio as one of the lead performers in the *Sealtest Village Store*.

ARLIN, HAROLD W. (1896–1986). Harold Arlin was the first announcer hired by ground-breaking station **KDKA**, Pittsburgh, and is thought by some authorities to have been the first professional radio announcer. Arlin did the first broadcast of a professional baseball game when he broadcast the game between Philadelphia and Pittsburgh on 5 August 1921 (over KDKA); the next day, he did the first broadcast of a tennis match as well, broadcasting the Davis Cup match between Australia and Great Britain. That fall, he did the first broadcast of a football game, a game between Pitt and West Virginia. On 30 August 1972, he again broadcast a few innings of a baseball game on KDKA as his grandson, Steve, pitched for the San Diego Padres against the Pittsburgh Pirates.

ARMED FORCES RADIO SERVICE (AFRS). Early in 1942, President Franklin D. Roosevelt created the Office of War Information (OWI) for the purpose of coordinating information gathering, and this agency also became responsible for all short-wave radio stations that beamed their signals to other countries. The AFRS was a division within the OWI created for the purpose of supervising programming for servicemen overseas. The AFRS produced programs specifically for military audiences and also established a transcription unit that recorded many popular commercial programs and shipped the recordings to military transmitters overseas for re-broadcast. Many old-time radio (OTR) programs available today are from these transcriptions, which were of high quality.

ARMSTRONG, EDWIN (1890–1954). Armstrong was an American electrical engineer and one of the most prolific inventors of the radio era. He was responsible for some of the most important developments in radio, including the regenerative circuit, the superheterodyne receiver, and FM radio. Outside the laboratory, Armstrong was involved in a years-long legal struggle to defend his inventions as corporate entities and other inventors contested and sometimes stole his patents. In despair over his defeats in the courtroom, Armstrong committed suicide by jumping from the window of his 13th floor apartment in New York City. His widow continued his patent fights and ultimately won a major financial victory in 1967.

ARMSTRONG OF THE SBI. *See JACK ARMSTRONG, THE ALL-AMERICAN BOY.*

ARMY HOUR (THE). Heard from 1942 to 1945, *The Army Hour* was a 60-minute public-service program written and produced each Sunday afternoon during World War II by Army personnel using the **National Broadcasting Company (NBC)** production facilities in Los Angeles. The production was very complex, involving dramatizations, interviews, and live broadcasts from overseas, sometimes from the scenes of battles. The announcer was **Ed Herlihy**, but almost the entire stable of NBC announcers worked on the program from time to time. The program was reduced to 30 minutes in July of 1945 and was last broadcast on 11 November of that year.

ARTHUR GODFREY TIME. Heard from 1945 to 1972, *Arthur Godfrey Time* was one of the longest-running programs in the history of daytime radio. It was a morning variety program hosted by **Arthur Godfrey**, who introduced musical numbers and sometimes sang, often while playing the ukulele. Music was provided by the Archie Bleyer orchestra and the cast of regular performers at various times included The McGuire Sisters, Pat Boone, The Chordettes, and Julius La Rosa. Godfrey was extremely informal and folksy, sometimes poking fun at sponsors or network executives and sometimes making appreciative comments about products that were not advertised on the program. His show was very popular; at one time, it was estimated that it had as many as 40 million listeners each week. There was considerable controversy in October of 1953, when, without warning, Godfrey fired Julius La Rosa on the air and fired bandleader Archie Bleyer immediately after the program was over. He said that La Rosa had shown a "lack of humility." Bleyer was a partner with La Rosa in a recording company. Godfrey later fired many other people involved with the show, including writers, the producer, and some of the most popular performers. The program continued on the air for many years after, but Godfrey's image was damaged and his popularity declined.

ARTHUR GODFREY'S TALENT SCOUTS. A 30-minute weekly talent-search program heard from 1946 to 1956, *Arthur Godfrey's Talent Scouts* presented several young musical performers each week and asked the studio audience to select the winner. Winners were invited to appear on ***Arthur Godfrey Time*** for three days the following week. The national exposure was extremely valuable to young performers; if Godfrey liked them, they might even become regulars on his daily program. The Chordettes (who later recorded the hit song "Mr. Sandman") were perhaps the best known of the winners.

ARTHUR TRACY, THE STREET SINGER. This 15-minute musical program originally appeared from 1931 to 1933, and was called simply *The Street Singer*, with an unidentified voice as the singer. Public demand led to the identification of Arthur Tracy as the singer and to the program being billed with his name as part of the title. The program was off the air for several years in the mid-1930s while Tracy performed in England, but had two more short runs in 1940 and 1942.

ATWATER KENT AUDITIONS (THE). Programs showcasing the talent of little-known performers were popular during early radio, and this program—sometimes billed as *The National Radio Auditions*—was one of the earliest. Heard from 1927 to 1932 and sponsored by Atwater Kent radios, it conducted a nationwide series of competitions judged by audience response and expert opinion. The first finals, held in December of 1927, brought the finalists to New York City, where Fox Movietone Newsreels covered it. The grand champion received $5,000 and a period of study at a leading conservatory.

ATWATER KENT HOUR (THE). A very early 60-minute program of classical and semi-classical music heard from 1926 to 1931 and again briefly in 1934, the *Atwater Kent Hour* featured stars of the Metropolitan Opera, backed by a symphony orchestra conducted by Josef Pasternak. Sponsored by Atwater Kent radios, the show was extremely popular; in 1930, it finished behind only ***Amos 'n' Andy*** and ***The Rudy Vallee Hour*** in popularity. Although there were only two 60-second commercials during the entire 60-minute program, Atwater Kent required that its name appear at least 12 times during the rest of the program, so acts were referred to as "The Atwater-Kent Quartet" or "The Atwater Kent Symphony Orchestra." Many of the naïve listeners in the very early days of radio believed that they had to have an Atwater Kent radio in order to receive the program, although the company never suggested that such a thing might be true.

AUDIENCE-PARTICIPATION PROGRAMS. There were several very durable daytime audience-participation shows and the champion of all these was *The Breakfast Club*, which appeared on weekdays at 9:00 A.M. from 1933 until 1968, long after most other network radio programs had disappeared. Similar in format, although usually appearing in the afternoon, was *House Party*, which **Art Linkletter** hosted for 22 years. The most popular and best-remembered feature of the program was a series of short, unrehearsed interviews that Linkletter conducted each day with children from the studio audience. Another popular daytime program, *Queen for a Day*, asked female audience members to tell their fondest wishes; a panel then chose which contestant to reward with fulfillment of her wish as well as new clothing, dinner, and a night on the town.

There were also some popular evening audience-participation programs. *Truth or Consequences*, which first appeared in 1940, asked unanswerable questions and then required contestants to perform outrageous stunts as a penalty for having failed to answer correctly; *People Are Funny* appeared in 1942 and was very similar. **Ralph Edwards**, who created and hosted *Truth or Consequences*, later did the same with another human-interest program, *This Is Your Life*, on which the life of a well-known personality was reviewed in the presence of the featured individual, with guest appearances by people from his or her past. *See also* QUIZ PROGRAMS.

AUDITION PROGRAMS. Audition programs were often broadcast by networks to test the waters before they undertook to produce a regular series of shows. These programs appeared once or twice but might or might not be adopted for regular network broadcasting, or might appear with casts different than those of the audition programs. Often these "trial" programs are not identified as such in the catalogs of dealers who sell recordings of old-time radio programs and it is possible to confuse them with the regular broadcasts of programs appearing under the same name.

AUNT JENNY'S TRUE-LIFE STORIES. A 15-minute daily serial drama heard from 1937 to 1956, this program is sometimes listed as *Aunt Jenny's Real Life Stories*. Each day, Aunt Jenny welcomed listeners into her kitchen in the fictitious town of Littleton, where she would do some cooking using her sponsor's product (Spry Shortening) and would then introduce the chapter for the day. Unlike most **soap operas**, where plots were often very extended, each story lasted only from Monday through Friday. Both the writers and most of the actors in the stories changed frequently during the long run, but Aunt Jenny was originally played by Edith Spence and later by Agnes Young.

AUTRY, GENE (1907–1998). Autry was born on a ranch near Tioga, Texas, and was taught to sing at age five by his preacher grandfather so that he could be used in the church choir. After working on the ranch during his childhood and adolescence, Autry began working as a railroad telegrapher and—encouraged by comments from Will Rogers, who happened to hear him sing—began singing on station KVOO in Tulsa, Oklahoma. He made his first record in 1929 and then performed on WLS Chicago in 1930. He starred in **Gene Autry's Melody Ranch** for 17 years (1940–1956) while maintaining a hugely successful movie career, appearing in some 90 films. He wrote more than 250 songs, many of which he recorded, and starred in television as well as on radio and in the movies. *See also* WESTERN PROGRAMS.

– B –

BABBITT, HARRY (1913–2004). Babbitt was a vocalist and featured performer on *Kay Kyser's Kollege of Musical Knowledge*. He also appeared on *Kay Kyser's Surprise Party* and in the late 1940s starred in his own 15-minute program, *The Harry Babbitt Show*. During the early days of television, he appeared with Steve Allen, was a part of *Bandstand Review*, and from 1953 to 1954 hosted his own program, *Glamour Girl*, a daytime **audience-participation program**. He remained active after retirement and, in the 1980s, reorganized the **Kay Kyser** orchestra for concert tours under his direction. As late as 1997, he appeared at the University of New Mexico's "Battle of the Big Bands II," where he led the Big Band Alumni Orchestra.

BABY SNOOKS SHOW (THE). A 30-minute **situation comedy** heard from 1944 to 1951, *The Baby Snooks Show* starred comedienne **Fanny Brice** as a mischievous seven-year-old girl who lived with her "Daddy," Lancelot Higgins (played by Hanley Stafford) and "Mommy Higgins" (played by Arlene Harris). Her little brother

Robespierre was played by Leone Ledoux. Originally created as a stage character on the *Ziegfeld Follies,* Snooks first appeared on radio on the *Ziegfeld Follies of the Air* in 1936 and later moved to the variety program *Good News* and then to *Maxwell House Coffee Time*, where she remained until getting her own program in 1944. The program was still popular in 1951, when Brice died of a cerebral hemorrhage.

BACKSTAGE WIFE. One of the earliest and longest-running of the many **soap operas** produced by **Frank and Anne Hummert**, *Backstage Wife* was the story of Mary Noble, a sweet young girl from Iowa who married Larry Noble, a handsome Broadway actor. Larry was pursued by scheming women and Mary was herself pursued upon occasion, which caused the jealous Larry to indulge in angry outbursts. The program was on the air from 1935 to 1959 with several changes of networks and several different actors playing the leading characters.

BACKUS, JIM (1913–1989). James Gilmore Backus had one of the most famous voices ever heard on radio. A graduate of the American Academy of Dramatic Arts in 1933, he appeared on a number of popular radio programs during the 1940s, including *The Alan Young Show*, on which he originated his famous role of the fabulously rich Hubert Updike, the Third. On television, he achieved even greater fame as another rich man modeled on the Updike character, Thurston Howell III, on *Gilligan's Island*. In movies, he was the voice of the nearsighted Mr. Magoo of cartoon fame, and occasionally worked as a serious actor, playing James Dean's ineffective father in the classic movie *Rebel without a Cause*. Backus published his autobiography in 1965, *Only When I Laugh*.

BAER, PARLEY (1914–2002). Baer is best remembered for his role as Chester Proudfoot on radio's *Gunsmoke*, although he was featured on many other radio programs, including *The Count of Monte Cristo*, *Honest Harold*, and *Tales of the Texas Rangers*. After radio, he moved to television and played a variety of supporting roles, including the insurance agent on *The Aldrich Family*, Mayor Stoner on *The Andy Griffith Show*, Ozzie's neighbor Darby on *The Adventures of Ozzie and Harriet*, and Don Rickles' boss on *The Don Rickles*

Show. Baer was also the voice of Ernie, the original Keebler Cookie elf, in TV commercials. In addition to his radio and TV work, Baer appeared in a variety of character roles in motion pictures during the 1950s and 1960s.

BAILEY, JACK (1907–1980). Bailey began his professional career as a carnival barker, jazz musician, and tent show director. On the radio, he hosted *County Fair*, and was the long-time emcee of the immensely popular daytime show ***Queen for a Day***, first on radio and then on television. For a time, *Queen for a Day* was the top-rated daytime TV program. Bailey also starred in a movie based on the program in 1951. At one time, he did the voice of the cartoon character Goofy in Walt Disney cartoons. Bailey was also emcee of the TV programs *Place the Face* and *Truth or Consequences*.

BAILEY, MILDRED (1907–1951). The sister of Al Rinker, one of **Bing Crosby**'s partners in The Rhythm Boys, Mildred Bailey was known as Radio's Rockin' Chair Lady. She took her last name from an early short-lived marriage, and was one of the first big-band vocalists. Her style of singing impressed Paul Whiteman, and he featured her on his early broadcasts. In 1936, she was voted the "most compelling chanteuse" in a swing contest at the Imperial Theatre in New York. By 1939, she was a regular on *Benny Goodman's Swing School*. Her first show under her own name was a 30-minute, late-night musical program originally called *The Mildred Bailey Revue* and then *Music till Midnight*.

BAKER, KENNY (1912–1985). Born Kenneth Laurence Baker in Monrovia, California, Baker made his radio debut in 1930 as a crooner on a local Long Beach, California, station. He later won a radio contest and appeared in movies, where he played juvenile leads. **Jack Benny** heard him at the Cocoanut Grove in Los Angeles, and added him to his network program in 1935. Baker stayed with Benny until 1939, when he left to join **Fred Allen**. He later became the vocalist on *Blue Ribbon Town*, sponsored by Pabst Blue Ribbon Beer, and then hosted *Blue Ribbon Time*, also sponsored by Pabst. During the same period, he was heard regularly on ***Glamour Manor***, a comedy–variety program on which he played the hapless manager of the Glamour Manor Hotel. Baker made frequent guest appearances on other radio programs and hosted his own syndicated program, *Sincerely, Kenny Baker*, a 15-minute program heard in 1945. In 1944, he was voted radio's top tenor. Baker also appeared in supporting roles in motion pictures throughout the 1940s, and co-starred in the long-running Broadway musical, *One Touch of Venus*.

BAKER, PHIL (1896–1963). A comedian and accordionist, Baker came to radio from vaudeville, where he had partnered with **Ben Bernie**. He gained his first national exposure on radio thanks to **Rudy Vallee**, and in 1932 appeared on *The Beechnut Hour*. In 1933, he was given his own network program, *The Phil Baker Show*. In 1941, he took over as host of *Take It or Leave It*, a popular **quiz program**, remaining with it until 1947. In 1948, he hosted *Everybody Wins* on CBS, another quiz program. Baker retired in 1955 and moved with his Danish-born wife to Copenhagen, where he died in 1963.

BAND REMOTES. Music was a huge part of radio programming throughout the period of old-time radio. One of the earliest and easiest ways to program music was simply to take a microphone to ballrooms, hotels, restaurants, or any other place where musicians might be appearing. Hundreds of these live programs were broadcast from what were referred to as remote locations, and they might be heard at any time of the day or night. After network radio had been in operation long enough to develop some schedule routines, most were heard after 11 P.M. Much of late-night network broadcasting consisted of such programs and virtually every popular band or orchestra in the United States appeared at one time or another, as did many that were not well known. Although the sound quality of a remote broadcast might not be quite as good as if the broadcast were from a studio, the music was often better; musicians were working in a familiar environment with the comfort and support of audience feedback. The programs were extremely important to the bands of the day, enabling them to promote their records and to improve the market value of the band; some authorities credit the remote broadcasts for the development of the Big Band Era in popular music.

BANKS, JOAN (1918–1998). One of the busiest actresses on radio during the 1940s, Banks began her career in radio immediately after graduating from Hunter College in New York and appeared with *Stoopnagle and Budd* before she began her work on daytime **soap operas** in 1938.

She starred on some, and had featured roles on many others, including *John's Other Wife, Portia Faces Life, Today's Children, Young Widder Brown, Joyce Jordan, M.D.*, and *Young Dr. Malone*. In the evenings, Banks worked on many other popular radio dramas, including *The Falcon, The Man Called X, My Friend Irma*, and *The Saint*. She met her future husband, actor **Frank Lovejoy**, on a radio program in 1941, and then appeared with him on *Blue Playhouse* in 1943 and *Deadline Drama* the next year. She also appeared with him on *This Is Your FBI* and *Nightbeat*. On television, she played Sylvia Platt, the man-hungry girlfriend of Ann Sothern, on *Private Secretary*.

BANNON, JIM (1911–1984). James Shorttel Bannon was born in Kansas City, Missouri, and, after working on local stations in Kansas City and St. Louis, did announcing and narration on a variety of network programs, including *The Joe Penner Show, The Great Gildersleeve*, and *The Adventures of Nero Wolfe*. Bannon enjoyed a career in movies during the 1940s and 1950s, and, for a short time, starred as Red Ryder in the western film series about this cowboy character. He also played Jack Packard in a trio of movies for Columbia based on the famous *I Love a Mystery* radio series. On television, he starred in *Adventures of Champion*, the Gene Autry-produced program about his famous horse. Bannon was married to the talented radio and television actress Bea Benaderet; their son Jack had a career as a stage and TV actor.

BARBER, RED (1908–1992). A play-by-play sportscaster known as "The Old Redhead," Barber began his announcing career with the Cincinnati Reds and ended it with the New York Yankees; but he was most identified with the Brooklyn Dodgers, for whom he broadcast from 1939 to 1953. He broadcast the first major league baseball game he ever attended, from Cincinnati when he was 26. In 1935, he broadcast baseball's first night game; in 1961, he called the game in which Roger Maris hit his 61st home run. Barber and fellow sportscaster Mel Allen were the first broadcasters honored by induction into baseball's Hall of Fame.

BARRY, JACK (1918–1984). Barry began in radio as an announcer on the famous *Uncle Don* **children's program** in New York City. In the mid-1940s, he and his friend Dan Enright (Ehrenreich) conceived the idea of putting children on a radio program for a general audience and the result was *Juvenile Jury*, hosted by Barry. On the show, bright children talked about life's little problems. Barry and Enright later produced *Life Begins at 80*, on which elderly people did much the same thing. The partners moved to television in the late 1940s and early 1950s, producing several game shows that Barry hosted. They were successful with *The Big Surprise* and *Twenty-One*, but the latter show was revealed to be one of the leading culprits in the scandals of the late 1950s, when the results of several shows were found to be rigged. All of Barry's shows were cancelled, and he was off TV for more than 10 years. In the late 1960s, he began working again on a succession of TV programs, the most successful of which was *The Joker's Wild*, a daytime quiz program. Barry hosted it until his death in 1984.

BARUCH, ANDRE (1908–1991). Born in France, Baruch came to the United States at the age of 13 and eventually became one of the more familiar voices on radio. He was spokesman for Lucky Strike cigarettes and the voice for U.S. Steel. He announced for a number of popular programs, including *Bobby Benson and the B-Bar-B Riders*, *Just Plain Bill*, *The Kate Smith Hour*, *The FBI in Peace and War*, and *Your Hit Parade*. He hosted television's *Masters of Magic* in 1949, and was the announcer of the television version of *Your Hit Parade* from 1950 to 1957. During 1954–1955, he was also a member of the broadcasting team for the Dodgers. Baruch was married to vocalist Bea Wain who appeared on *Your Hit Parade* during its early years on radio. He was inducted into the National Broadcasters Hall of Fame in 1979.

BAUKHAGE, H. R. (1889–1976). Hilmar Robert Baukhage was better known simply as Baukhage, the only name he used on the air. After graduating from the University of Chicago, he attended universities abroad, where he acquired a fluency in both French and German. While studying at the Sorbonne, he found employment as an assistant to the Paris correspondent of London's *Pall Mall Gazette*, and also filed stories for the Associated Press (AP). He returned to the United States in 1914 and joined the AP in Washington, D.C., covering the State Department and various embassies and legations. He was the first reporter to broadcast directly from the White House, anchoring the NBC broadcast from the Capitol on 7 December 1941 after the attack on Pearl Harbor. He was at the Reichstag when Adolph Hitler announced the invasion of Poland, and he announced the outbreak of World War II from Berlin. He hosted a 15-minute program called *Baukhage Talking*, and was the announcer and commentator for many important events, including Franklin D. Roosevelt's funeral service and the Nuremberg War Trials. He possessed a deep, slightly raspy baritone voice, with clear enunciation. Known as "Buck" to his friends, he won many broadcasting awards, including one from *Radio Life Magazine* as the most "listenable" commentator on the air. In addition to his ABC broadcasts, he also broadcast over Mutual after 1948, switching there full-time in 1951. *Baukhage Talking* reached more than 500 stations. *See also* NEWS PROGRAMS.

BAZOOKA. The Bazooka was a peculiar musical instrument consisting of two pieces of gas pipe fitted together and played by sliding one pipe in and out, using much the same principle as the trombone. It was invented by comedian **Bob Burns** and the name was later adopted by the Army for one of its first shoulder-mounted anti-tank weapons, which was actually a rocket launcher and bore only a superficial resemblance to the musical instrument.

BEEMER, BRACE (1902–1965). Radio's best-known **Lone Ranger** was the third person to play the part. Beemer was station manager and narrator of the program when Earle Graser, the man playing the Lone Ranger, was killed in a car accident in 1941. Beemer assumed the role and continued in it until the program ended on radio in 1954. At the age of 14, after an altercation with a ninth-grade teacher who lectured continually on the merits of Kaiser Wilhelm II's Germany, Beemer quit school and enlisted in the Army. He was subsequently attached to Colonel Douglas MacArthur's Rainbow Division of the American Expeditionary Force and fought in World War I. During the war, he was wounded three times, earned a Purple Heart, and carried shrapnel in his legs the rest of his life. After starring as the Lone Ranger for more than 13 years, Beemer took on the title role in *Sergeant Preston of the Yukon* for that show's last year (1954–1955). In 1986, Beemer was inducted into the National Broadcasters Hall of Fame.

BELIEVE IT OR NOT. Hosted by **Robert Ripley**, a cartoonist who produced a popular newspaper feature of the same name, *Believe It or Not* appeared from 1930 to 1948 and featured dramatizations of unusual events or facts. Over a 19-year period, Ripley and his collection of odd facts appeared in a wide variety of formats, varying in length from 1-minute to 30-minutes and sometimes appearing weekly, sometimes daily, sometimes as a portion of other programs, and sometimes as an independent program. Ripley was very creative, being among the first to do remote broadcasts, and his program sometimes did unprecedented things, such as broadcasting from mid-ocean.

BENNY, JACK (1894–1974). Born Benjamin Kubelsky, Jack Benny came to radio from vaudeville and made his radio debut on the *Ed Sullivan Show* on 29 March 1932. Benny was the star of many programs during his career, the titles often changing with the sponsors: all were also known and advertised as *The Jack Benny Program*. His programs appeared from 1932 to 1955, for a total run of 924 shows in 23 years; and repeats of his programs (*The Best of Benny*) were heard until 1958. His television program was broadcast from 1950 to 1965. Benny also starred in a number of motion pictures from 1929 to 1967, with most of his starring roles coming during the late 1930s and early 1940s. He was married to radio performer **Mary Livingston** from 1927, and was inducted into the National Broadcasters Hall of Fame in 1977.

BERG, GERTRUDE (1899–1966). Gertrude Edelstein Berg became famous on radio as the matriarch Molly Goldberg, star of *The Goldbergs*, which she also wrote. This 15-minute daily serial drama, originally called *The Rise of the Goldbergs*, was the story of a poor Jewish family in the Bronx. The show changed to a 30-minute format during 1949–1950, when it ran concurrently with a television version. She wrote, produced, and starred in the TV version, receiving an Emmy Award as Best Actress in 1950. Berg also wrote and starred in *House of Glass*, a 30-minute comedic serial drama, and wrote *Kate Hopkins, Angel of Mercy*, a **soap opera** heard from 1940 to 1942. After *The Goldbergs* ended its TV run in 1955, Berg starred on her own TV situation comedy, *The Gertrude Berg Show*, also known as *Mrs. G. Goes to College*. In addition to her radio and television work, Berg starred in vaudeville, on the Broadway stage, and found time to write books, including the *Molly Goldberg Cookbook* (1955) and *Molly and Me* (1961), her autobiography.

BERGEN, EDGAR (1903–1978). Ventriloquist Edgar John Bergen appeared on radio for nearly 20 years with his dummies Charlie McCarthy, Mortimer Snerd, and Effie Clinker, and won a special Academy Award for the creation of Charlie, at one time more famous than Bergen himself. Charlie cost $35 but helped pay Bergen's way through Northwestern University. After college, Bergen joined the vaudeville circuit in the United States and Europe and got his start on radio in 1936 when he appeared as a guest on *The Rudy Vallee Show*. *The Edgar Bergen–Charlie McCarthy Show*, under various sponsor-related titles, was on the air from 1937 to 1956. Bergen also acted in movies, and in 1956–1957 hosted the CBS television quiz show *Do You Trust Your Wife?* He was the father of actress Candice Bergen.

BERLE, MILTON (1908–2002). Born Mendel Berlinger in New York City in 1908, Berle was at one time the most famous comedian on television. His career began when he was five years old and spanned more than 80 years on stage, film, radio, and television. He also penned some 400 published songs. He had been a vaudeville head-liner in the early 1930s, and made his radio debut in 1934, doing guest appearances on *The Rudy Vallee Show*. He was host of the panel show *Stop Me If You've Heard This One* in 1939 and starred on *Three-Ring Time*, *Let Yourself Go*, and *Kiss and Make Up* before being given his own program, *The Milton Berle Show*, in 1947. His show moved to television in 1949 and lasted on TV until 1956. He was so well known after his TV career that he often appeared as him-self in movies. His film credits ranged from *The Perils of Pauline* in 1914 to *Let Me in, I Hear Laughter* in 1999. **Walter Winchell** once called him the "Thief of Bad Gags" because of his predilection for stealing jokes from other comedians.

BERNIE, BEN (1891–1943). A colorful orchestra leader, Bernie was born Bernard Anzelevitz and worked in vaudeville with **Phil Baker** before coming to radio in New York in 1923, with a band that had been assembled by Don Juelle. Called "The Old Maestro," Bernie was one of the first bandleaders to become active in radio and some authorities credit him with being the first person to have a radio theme song. Because of a well-publicized pseudo-feud with **Walter Winchell**, Bernie became known to millions of radio listeners. He starred in his own network program beginning 24 January 1930. Billed as *The Ben Bernie Show* and by several other names, his program appeared until his death in 1943. Bernie was known for his intimate chatter, fat cigars, and catchphrases. He greeted his fans with "Yowsah, Yowsah, Yowsah" and signed off each show with "pleasant dreams." For a brief period, 1938–1940, he also hosted *Ben Bernie's Musical Quiz* on CBS.

BETTY AND BOB. One of the first of the daytime **soap operas**, *Betty and Bob* was heard from 1932 to 1940. Produced by **Frank and Anne Hummert** and written by **Robert Hardy Andrews**, it was the story of a beautiful-but-poor secretary who married wealthy and handsome Bob Drake. Because of the marriage, Drake was disinherited by his father. The program was initially successful, but after a child was born to Betty and Bob, ratings dropped; it eventually left the air in 1940. **Don Ameche** was the original Bob, but an unusually large number of actors played the leading roles; there were eight different Bobs and five different Bettys during the eight-year run.

BETTY CROCKER MAGAZINE OF THE AIR (THE). One of the earliest and longest-lasting programs on radio, *The Betty Crocker Magazine of the Air* was a 15-minute program of recipes, cooking tips, and other homemaker information heard from 1926 to 1953; almost the entire period of old-time radio. The part of the fictitious Betty Crocker, General Mill's homemaking expert, was played by many different actresses during the show's long run. *See also* TALK AND INFORMATION PROGRAMS.

BETWEEN THE BOOKENDS. A 15-minute program of poetry readings, *Between the Bookends* was on the air from 1938 to 1955, with a brief interruption during 1944–1945 while host Ted Malone served as a war correspondent in Europe. The program was extremely popular with female listeners; some months, Malone received more than 20,000 letters from fans. Malone's real name was Alden Russell; he had not originally used his real name because he did not want to be associated with such a "sissy" program. He later published a series of very popular poetry anthologies.

BEULAH. Beulah originally appeared as the African-American maid on *Fibber McGee and Molly*, played by **Marlin Hurt**, a white man. The character was so popular that a spin-off program was created in 1945, originally called *The Marlin Hurt and Beulah Show*. Hurt played Beulah on this 30-minute situation comedy, as well as playing the part of Bill Jackson, her shiftless boyfriend. He died the next year and the show was re-created a year after his death with Bob Corley, another white man, as Beulah. That version lasted only six months, but the program reappeared on CBS later in 1947 as a 15-minute nightly serial drama with Hattie McDaniel in the title role. When McDaniel became ill in 1952, the title role was assumed by Amanda Randolph until the program left the air in 1954.

BICKERSONS (THE). A 30-minute **situation comedy** that originated in 1946 as a comic skit on *Drene Time*, *The Bickersons* later appeared on the *Old Gold Program*, and still later on *The Edgar Bergen–Charlie McCarthy Show*. **Don Ameche** and **Frances Langford** were featured as John and Blanche Bickerson, a quarrelsome husband and wife. Blanche often woke her husband, who snored, to confront him with her various complaints. Although the skit is well remembered, the show only appeared as an independent program during the summer of 1951, with Lew Parker playing the part of John.

BIG SHOW (THE). A 90-minute variety program with a budget that was reportedly the largest of any program on radio, *The Big Show* was hosted by Tallulah Bankhead. She was supported by **Fred Allen**, and the biggest names in entertainment appeared every week. The program was created by NBC in 1950 to fill the Sunday night prime-time slot left vacant when *The Jack Benny Program*, *The Edgar Bergen–Charlie McCarthy Show*, and other Sunday night NBC regulars moved to CBS. The reviews were generally good, but the ratings were not; and the program was discontinued after the second year.

BIG SISTER. A 15-minute **soap opera** that remained on the air from 1936 to 1952, *Big Sister* was the story of Ruth Evans, the oldest of three orphaned siblings, and her efforts to raise her younger brother and sister. The first Ruth was played by **Alice Frost**, but the role was subsequently held by four other actresses. The program inspired a spin-off, ***Bright Horizon***, which featured some of the same characters.

BIG STORY (THE). A 30-minute **drama anthology** program appearing on NBC from 1947 to 1955, *The Big Story* featured dramatizations of newspaper stories that had exposed the truth about murder, corruption, or racketeering. Most stories were about murders that had been committed some years before, thus avoiding any problems with pre-trial interference. The names of all the people involved were changed, except for the reporter and the paper for which he worked. At the end of each program, the featured reporter received a $500 award from the sponsor.

BIG TOWN. A 30-minute **crime program** based on the exploits of crusading newspaper editor Steve Wilson, *Big Town* was perhaps the best known of the newspaper-based crime programs, partly because the part of Steve was originally played by Edward G. Robinson, a major movie star of the day. Robinson played the part from 1937 to 1942, but the program continued until 1952, with Edward Pawley and later Walter Greaza in the role.

BILLIE BURKE SHOW (THE). This 30-minute **situation comedy** was heard on Saturday mornings from 1943 to 1946, starring comedienne Billie Burke. Burke was the widow of show business legend Florenz Ziegfeld, who considered her one of the 10 most beautiful women of all time. She is best remembered as Glinda, the Good Witch of the North in the movie *The Wizard of Oz*, but she was well established as a comedienne on Broadway and often took the part of a scatterbrained or foolish woman. On her own program, she portrayed a kindly woman of the sort who went out of her way to help others, becoming involved in complicated comic situations as a result.

BING CROSBY SHOW (THE). Like many other major stars, Bing Crosby, whose real name was Harry, appeared in a long series of programs over the years, most of them named for sponsors, although often referred to as *The Bing Crosby Show*. After hosting several other programs beginning in 1931, Crosby took over as the star of *The Kraft Music Hall* when Al Jolson left the program in 1935. Crosby remained there until moving to *Philco Radio Time* in 1946. He then moved to CBS in 1949 to star in *The Bing Crosby Chesterfield Show*, *The General Electric Show,* and some shorter programs until leaving the air in 1956. Most of his programs were 30-minute variety programs, although *The Kraft Music Hall* was 60 minutes until 1942. His programs were all similar, consisting of low-key humorous dialogues and skits interspersed with music. He kept many members of his supporting cast for almost his entire radio career, including announcer Ken Carpenter and bandleader **John Scott Trotter.**

BLANC, MEL (1908–1989). Melvin Jerome Blanc began as a musician, playing the violin, bass, and tuba with various bands in the Northwest. He made his radio debut at KGW Portland, Oregon, in 1927, then moved to Portland's KEX in 1931. While there, he built a reputation for the many voices he could create. In 1937, he signed a contract with Warner Brothers, for whom he was to create the voices of Bugs Bunny, Daffy Duck, Porky Pig, and countless others. His appearances on local Los Angeles programs led to an appearance on *The Joe Penner Show*, where he eventually became the voice of Penner's famous duck Goo Goo. Blanc became a regular on *The Jack Benny Program* in 1940, where he did several memorable characters and sound effects: Monsieur Le Blanc, Jack's violin teacher; Sy, the Mexican gardener; Benny's Maxwell automobile; and the railroad station PA announcer who announced: "Anaheim, Azusa, and Cuc----amonga!" Blanc also appeared on many other popular radio programs, including *The Judy Canova Show*. His own program, *The Mel Blanc Show*, also known as the *Fix-It-Shop* and *Mel Blanc's Fix-It-Shop*, was broadcast on CBS during 1946–1947. On television, he was a regular on *The Jack Benny Program* from 1950 to 1965, and supplied the voices of many characters on Saturday morning cartoon programs. He was also the voice of Twiki the robot on the Buck Rogers television series (1979–1981).

BLACK, FRANK (1894–1968). The musical director of the **National Broadcasting Company (NBC)** from 1933 to 1948, Black frequently led the NBC Symphony and the Symphony of the Air. From

1938 to 1944, he conducted the orchestra on *Cities Service Concerts*, NBC's long-running 60-minute concert music program. He also appeared on *RCA Radiotrons*, *The Palmolive Hour*, *The Jack Benny Program*, and *Harvest of Stars*. His last appearance as conductor was for singer **Jane Pickens** on her NBC show in the early 1950s.

BLONDIE. A 30-minute **situation comedy** based on the popular comic strip by Chic Young, the radio program was very much like the popular movies based on the strip. Most of the movie cast appeared on the radio program, including **Arthur Lake**, who played Dagwood Bumstead for the entire run (1939–1950). **Penny Singleton** played Blondie until 1949, when the role was assumed by Ann Rutherford and later by Lake's wife, Patricia Van Cleve. The program, like the comic strip and the movies, centered around the bumbling of Dagwood, who could not do anything right. It is best remembered for the opening, which featured Dagwood's anguished cry of BLONNNNNNDIEEE!

BLUE NETWORK. *See* NATIONAL BROADCASTING COMPANY.

BOB AND RAY SHOW (THE). **Bob Elliot** and **Ray Goulding** were both working at WHDH, Boston in 1946 when they began to do some impromptu comedic discussions on Elliot's morning disc jockey program. They were later asked to do a pre-game program before the broadcasts of the Boston Red Sox baseball games and began to do satires of radio serials. They were picked up by NBC in 1951 and for nearly 40 years appeared on various networks in a variety of formats, but always doing the same thing: comedic dialogue with little or no script, just reacting to each other's ideas. They later moved on to satires of television and of political figures and some of their comedic characters became very well known, appearing for many years.

BOB BURNS SHOW (THE). Burns, known as "The Arkansas Traveler" and "The Arkansas Philosopher," was from Van Buren, Arkansas, and had a style of philosophical humor similar to that of Will Rogers. He told audiences about his relatives in the Ozarks and played the **bazooka**, a musical instrument of his own invention. After six years with **Bing Crosby** on *The Kraft Music Hall*, Burns was given his own comedy–variety show in 1941. The program featured skits based on the fictitious experiences of a rustic who traveled the countryside doing good deeds of various sorts. Burns had introduced the character on the *Fleischmann Yeast Hour* in 1935. Originally called *The Arkansas Traveler*, the program was soon renamed *The Bob Burns Show* and ran until 1947.

BOB HAWK SHOW (THE). A 30-minute **quiz program** hosted by Bob Hawk, *The Bob Hawk Show* was an outgrowth of an earlier program, *Thanks to the Yanks*. Heard from 1947 to 1953 and sponsored by Camel cigarettes, the program used announcers with portable microphones to choose contestants from the studio audience. The prizes were substantial cash awards. The best remembered feature of the show was the Lemac quiz, in which winners were designated a "Lemac" (Camel spelled backwards) and serenaded with the congratulatory jingle "You're a Lemac now."

BOB HOPE SHOW (THE). Bob Hope's first regular radio program was *The Intimate Revue* in 1935, followed by *The Atlantic Family* in 1936 and *The Rippling Rhythm Revue* in 1937. He began his own program in the fall of 1938. The *Bob Hope Show* was a long-running **comedy program** heard from 1938 to 1955, usually as a 30-minute program, although there were some 15-minute versions late in the run. From 1938 to 1948, the program was sponsored by Pepsodent toothpaste and was called *The Pepsodent Show Starring Bob Hope*. The Hope program was one of the all-time hits on radio and became a Tuesday night standard on NBC for many years. Hope was supported by a cast of regulars who became well known in their own right, including comedian Jerry Colonna and singer **Frances Langford**. The program toured the world during World War II, appearing in every theater of war and at virtually every military base in the United States.

BOBBY BENSON AND THE B-BAR-B RIDERS. Originally titled *Bobby Benson's Adventures* or *Bobby Benson and The H-Bar-O Rangers*, and heard from 1932 to 1936, the early version of this **juvenile adventure program** featured a young hero who lived on the H-Bar-O ranch, named for the sponsor, H-O cereals. In the better-remembered later version, heard from 1949 to 1955, Bobby was the child owner of a ranch in South Texas, who struggled against rustlers, bandits, smugglers, and other villains. Bobby was played by several different actors, including Billy Halop, Ivan Curry, and Richard Wanamaker.

BOGUE, MERWYN A. (1908–1994). A comedian, cornet player, and singer, Merwyn A. Bogue was known on *Kay Kyser's Kollege of Musical Knowledge* as Ish Kabibble, a name he took from one of the songs in his act. He joined Kyser's band in 1931 and quickly became the band's comedian and most popular member. As Ish Kabibble, he combed his hair straight down over his eyebrows and sang novelty tunes such as "Three Little Fishes," which became a best-selling record. He stayed with the band when it moved to television in the late 1940s, but after the program's short TV run, he retired from show business.

BOLD VENTURE. A 30-minute **adventure program** appearing in 1951–1952, *Bold Venture* was written specifically for Humphrey Bogart, who played Slate Shannon, and Lauren Bacall, who played his ward, Sailor. Shannon was the owner of a seedy hotel in Havana, and also owned a boat, *The Bold Venture*, that played a part in many of the adventures. The program was produced in syndication in 1951 and sold to more than 400 stations nationwide. Unlike many radio programs of the time, it was done entirely on tape; there were no live performances.

BORDER RADIO. *Border radio* referred to the practice of broadcasting from a transmitter located in Mexico to avoid the restrictions on transmission power and advertising veracity required by the U.S. government. Although several stations were involved, the best known was XERA, located in a village that was then called Villa Acuna, across the border from Del Rio, Texas. A Kansas physician, **John R. Brinkley**, had made a fortune promoting some very questionable medical procedures over a small station that he owned in Kansas. When the Federal Communications Commission refused to allow him to increase the power of his station and other agencies of the government began to investigate his medical claims, he built a station just across the Mexican border and in 1931 began transmitting with 75,000 watts of power. Soon thereafter, his lobbyists in Mexico City succeeded in getting permission from the Mexican government to increase the transmission power to 500,000 watts, and the station could be heard virtually everywhere in the United States, sometimes simply drowning out local stations.

The programming was very colorful, including Dr. Brinkley's extreme medical claims, legendary disc jockey **Wolfman Jack**, and all sorts of astonishing ads, including one that offered autographed pictures of Jesus Christ.

Several other stations were opened along the border and Border Radio prospered for several years, but changes in the Mexican government and pressures from the U.S. eventually led to a reduction in transmission power and other legal difficulties for operators of border stations. The broadcasts went on for many years with reduced power, although the border stations were still very powerful and at night one or another of them could be heard almost everywhere in the United States. XERB in Tijuana became well known because of the 1973 movie *American Graffiti*, which used Wolfman Jack's program as background music.

BOSTON BLACKIE. An outgrowth of an earlier motion picture series, this 30-minute **crime program** featured a private detective working in New York, and starred Chester Morris, who had played Blackie on the screen. Blackie was tough, irreverent, and like many private detectives of the era, often made the police look bad. First appearing as a summer replacement on NBC in 1944, the program was later syndicated and appeared on many network stations from 1945 to 1950. The lead role was played by **Richard Kollmar** in the syndicated version.

BOSWELL SISTERS (THE). Connee [Constance] (1907–1976), Martha (1908–1958), and Vet [Helvetia] Boswell (1909–1988) were the most popular female singing trio before the Andrews Sisters and are considered by some to be one of the all-time great jazz vocal groups. Connee, who sometimes spelled her name *Connie*, was paralyzed from the waist down due to a childhood accident. The sisters played several musical instruments in addition to their singing: Connee played cello, saxophone, and guitar; Martha played piano; and Vet played violin, banjo, and guitar. In 1931, they signed with NBC to appear on *The Pleasure Hour*. In 1932, they were heard on *Music that Satisfies*, and, in 1934, they co-starred with **Bing Crosby** on *The Woodbury Radio Program*. The Boswells also appeared on their own network program for CBS from 1931 to 1933, and Connie appeared on her own program on ABC, *The Connie Boswell Show*, during

1943–1944. Many of their hit records were made with the Dorsey Brothers Orchestra. Both Vet and Martha retired from show business in 1936, but Connie went on to enjoy a solo career.

BOX 13. *Box 13* was a 30-minute **adventure program** featuring newsman-turned-author Dan Holiday, who sought adventure by placing an ad in the classified section of the newspaper that read "Adventure wanted—will go anywhere, do anything." He used the resulting adventures as material for his works of fiction. Holiday was played by film star Alan Ladd, and the program was produced in syndication by a company in which Ladd was part owner. The program appeared on the Mutual network in 1948–1949 and on many individual stations for some years after that.

BOYD, WILLIAM (1895–1972). William Boyd was a successful silent-film actor before he was chosen to star in the western movie *Hop-A-Long Cassidy* in 1935. The success of the film resulted in a long series of **Hopalong Cassidy** films (with the hyphens dropped from the name), the last released in 1946 and produced by Boyd himself. Boyd bought all rights to the Hopalong Cassidy character, and brought Hoppy and his horse Topper to radio in 1948. The radio program was first heard on Mutual and then on CBS, ending its run in 1952. A TV series, telecast from 1949 to 1951, resulted in a boom for the Hopalong character and the many products associated with the name. When Boyd sold the rights to the character in the late 1950s, it made him a multi-millionaire.

BRACKEN, EDDIE (1920–2002). Edward Vincent Bracken was primarily a film star who was educated at New York's Professional Children's School, and made an early start in show business, acting, and singing on stage and in vaudeville. As a child, he appeared in the "Our Gang" comedy shorts and following several juvenile roles on Broadway, he was signed by Paramount Pictures and made his first feature film, *Too Many Girls*, in 1940. At the height of his film career, he starred in his own radio program, *The Eddie Bracken Show*, on which he played the same kind of role that had made him popular in the movies: a well-intentioned bumbler who always made a mess of things. Bracken supported **Ezra Stone** in several episodes of *The Aldrich Family*, playing Henry Aldrich's friend Basil "Dizzy" Stevens.

Although he had derived considerable fame from his work in radio, television, and the movies, Bracken loved repertory theater and spent years starring in revivals and in touring company productions of plays that had been successful on Broadway. Bracken was inducted into the National Broadcasters Hall of Fame in 1996.

BRADLEY, JOE (CURLEY) (1910–1985). Born George Raymond Courtney in Oklahoma, Bradley was the most famous of the several actors to play **Tom Mix** on the popular **juvenile adventure program.** He was a former Oklahoma cowboy and Hollywood stuntman who started out in show business as a member of the Ranch Boys' trio, with Ken "Shorty" Carson and Jack Ross. Bradley took over the role of Mix on radio in 1944, and remained until the program left the air in 1950. Earlier, Bradley and the other Ranch Boys had sung the Ralston theme song/commercial and played dramatic parts on the program. After the Tom Mix show ended, Bradley starred in his own program, *Curley Bradley, The Singing Marshall.* Earlier, he had also appeared in several 15-minute music programs and on *Road to Danger*, a wartime series about two Army truck drivers. In 1952, he appeared in a western short feature titled *Singing Marshal* and later made many singing appearances on television.

BREAK THE BANK. A **quiz program** offering large payouts, *Break the Bank* appeared as a 30-minute program from 1945 to 1953 and then as a 15-minute program until 1955. Contestants were selected in pairs from the audience and answered a series of increasingly difficult questions for amounts ranging up to $500. Contestants who reached this level were offered the chance to answer one more question for the amount in "The Bank." Amounts not won by contestants were added to The Bank, which grew from week to week but was always at least $1000. Beginning in 1946, **Bert Parks** was the host, with **Bud Collyer** as announcer, although Collyer also played a very significant role on the program and was essentially a co-host.

BREAKFAST AT SARDI'S. A morning program originally featuring interviews with women who were having breakfast at Sardi's restaurant in Hollywood, *Breakfast At Sardi's* was hosted by Tom Breneman from its debut in 1942 until his death in 1948. For many years, there were two broadcasts daily; one at 8:00 Pacific Time for broadcast to the East Coast and another at 9:30 for live broadcast to western listeners. Both before and after Breneman's death, there were several changes in location, performers, and program name, the first being a name change to *Breakfast in Hollywood* in 1943. In 1945, the program moved from Sardi's to a restaurant owned by Breneman and was sometimes called *Breakfast with Breneman*, or *Welcome to Hollywood*. After Breneman's death, **Garry Moore** and others took over as host; but the program was never again as successful and finally left the air in 1954. *See also* AUDIENCE-PARTICIPATION PROGRAMS.

BREAKFAST CLUB (THE). The first and the longest running of the many breakfast programs that populated old-time radio, *The Breakfast Club* was on the air continuously from 1933 to 1968, with the same host and the same format on the same network. It was a 60-minute variety program broadcast from Chicago, heard six days a week until 1946 and then five days a week. **Don McNeill** hosted and the program was an amiable mix of music, interviews, silly games, and good-natured chit-chat. It was completely unrehearsed and unscripted throughout the entire run. *See also* AUDIENCE-PARTICIPATION PROGRAMS.

BREAKFAST WITH DOROTHY AND DICK. Dorothy and Dick were **Dorothy Kilgallen**, a Broadway columnist for a New York newspaper, and **Richard Kollmar**, a radio actor and producer. *Breakfast with Dorothy and Dick* was a morning talk program, with Dorothy and Dick discussing Broadway happenings and other current events. Their breakfast was served them during the program and their children sometimes appeared. Their canary was often heard chirping in the background and was considered an essential part of the show. It was not a network program, but the New York station on which it was broadcast was a 50,000-watt station and the program was widely heard, with an audience estimated at 20 million listeners daily. *See also* TALK AND INFORMATION PROGRAMS.

BRICE, FANNY (1891–1951). A vaudeville and revue star before she came to radio, Brice (born Fannie Borach) created one of the most famous and beloved characters of radio, "Baby Snooks." First created on the radio version of the *Ziegfeld Follies* on 29 February 1936, the Snooks character was a regular feature of *Good News* from 1937 to 1939. In 1939, the name of the program was changed to *Maxwell House Coffee Time*, and Snooks occupied a 15-minute **situation comedy** segment on this show until 1944, when *The Baby Snooks Show* first appeared on CBS. In later years, Brice was seldom seen out of character, usually appearing in public only as Baby Snooks.

BRIGHT HORIZON. A 15-minute daily **soap opera** appearing from 1941 to 1945, *Bright Horizon* was a spin-off of *Big Sister*, with Michael West, one of the characters from the earlier program, as the lead character. West had been a singer on *Big Sister*, and continued in that role on *Bright Horizon*, but he also had a degree in law and gradually became more involved in a law career, at one time considering a run for governor. **Richard Kollmar** was the first Michael West, later succeeded by **Joseph Julian**. The early episodes included the lead character from *Big Sister*, Ruth Evans Wayne, at that time played by **Alice Frost**. After leaving the air in July of 1945, the program was extended for a few months, with the name changed to *A Woman's Life*.

BRINKLEY, JOHN R. (1885–1941). John Brinkley was the controversial physician who was largely responsible for the establishment of **border radio**. After acquiring a degree from the Eclectic Medical University of Kansas City, which he earned in one month of study, he was granted a license to practice medicine in Arkansas and through reciprocal agreements was licensed to practice in five other states, including Kansas and Texas. He opened practice in tiny Milford, Kansas, where he later conceived the notion that sexual potency could be returned to older men by transplanting portions of goat gonads. He promoted this operation so successfully that he was able to build his own hospital and eventually his own radio station, from which his promotion of the operation became even more effective. The station won a gold cup in 1929 as the most popular radio station in America, and over 3,000 letters a day poured in—so many that Brinkley built a new post office for tiny Milford so that it could handle the mail. When his application to increase the power of his transmitter was denied, he decided to move his station to Mexico, where government supervision of both communications and medical practice was less stringent. He was extremely successful during most of the 1930s, but eventually pressure from the governments of both Mexico and the United States—as well as lawsuits from patients and medical organizations—forced the closing of much of the border enterprise. Brinkley died of a heart attack in San Antonio, still embroiled in litigation of various sorts.

BROADWAY IS MY BEAT. A 30-minute **crime program** heard from 1949 to 1954, *Broadway Is My Beat* featured Danny Glover, a tough New York City police detective whose beat included Broadway and Times Square. One of the first programs directed by **Elliott Lewis**, the show was distinguished by a noisy background intended to give the flavor of the busy city. Larry Thor played the part of Danny and his characterization, along with the nature of the crimes presented, gave the program a gritty, realistic flavor.

BROKENSHIRE, NORMAN (1898–1965). Brokenshire was one of the great announcers of radio's early days. Born the son of a Methodist minister in Canada, he came to the United States in 1918 and joined an artillery unit of the U.S. Army. While visiting New York in 1924, he answered an ad for announcers and he and three others were chosen from hundreds of applicants. The next year, he broadcast the first presidential inauguration ceremonies to be put on the air. He later became one of the leading announcers at CBS, announcing for *Music That Satisfies* and *Major Bowes' Original Amateur Hour*. A drinking problem interrupted his career for a number of years, but he made a comeback in the mid-1940s with U.S. Steel's *Theatre Guild on the Air*, before moving to television.

BROWN, HIMAN (1910–). Brown began his career as an actor, but after appearing briefly on *The Rise of the Goldbergs* in 1929, he turned to directing and producing; in 1933, he produced CBS's first daytime soap opera, *Marie, the Little French Princess*. During radio's golden age, he was involved as writer, director, actor, and/or producer with many popular programs, including *Inner Sanctum Mysteries*, *Bulldog Drummond*, and *The Adventures of the Thin Man*. He brought *The NBC Radio Theater* to the air in 1959; 15 years later, he tried to resurrect network radio drama with *The CBS Radio Mystery Theater*. Brown won the American Broadcast Pioneer Award, as well as a **Peabody Award** (for *Radio Mystery Theater*), and edited a collection of stories, *Strange Tales from CBS Radio Mystery Theater* (1976). He was elected to the Radio Hall of Fame in 1988.

BROWN, JOHN (1904–1957). A talented and versatile character actor, Brown is remembered today primarily as an important supporting actor on many popular programs during Radio's Golden Age: *The Life of Riley*, *My Friend Irma*, *The Adventures of Ozzie and Harriet*, and *A Date with Judy*. He appeared in many others, including *The Mel Torme Show*, which he also produced. Brown once estimated that he had appeared on more than 10,000 live radio broadcasts.

BRYAN, ARTHUR Q. (1899–1959). Bryan played supporting characters on several popular radio programs, and starred in a few. In addition, he was the voice of Elmer Fudd in the Bugs Bunny cartoons of the 1940s, and appeared as an actor or host on television programs in the late 1940s and early 1950s. His major radio work consisted of *Major Hoople*, *Fibber McGee and Molly* (as Doc Gamble), *The Great Gildersleeve* (as Floyd Munson, the barber), *The Milton Berle Show*, *Blondie*, and *Nitwit Court*. He also appeared on radio in dramatic parts, and, at times, worked as an announcer, writer, and producer as well as an actor.

BUCK ROGERS IN THE 25TH CENTURY. An early **juvenile adventure program** based on a popular comic strip, this 15-minute program was broadcast first from 1932 to 1936, with brief reincarnations in 1939, 1940, and during 1946–1947. It was a science-fiction thriller featuring the adventures of a young man who had been held in suspended animation as a result of an accident in a mine and who awoke 500 years in the future. In addition to the many futuristic devices that were a regular feature of the program, the brilliant scientist Dr. Huer also provided fantastic inventions that were often an important part of the plots. The first actor to portray Buck was Curtis Arnall, followed by several others; Edgar Stehli played Dr. Huer.

BULLDOG DRUMMOND. The dramatic opening of this 30-minute detective adventure show was well known: echoing footsteps, a foghorn blast, gunshots, and a police whistle. Drummond was a British investigator called "Bulldog" because he was relentless in the pursuit of criminals. After a few episodes in England, the setting was moved to the United States and the program was sometimes listed as *The American Adventures of Bulldog Drummond*. Several talented actors, including George Coulouris, **Santos Ortega**, and Sir Cedric Hardwicke played the part of Drummond. The program was heard from 1941 to 1949 and again briefly in 1954.

BURNS AND ALLEN SHOW (THE). **George Burns** and **Gracie Allen** met in 1922 when George appeared in vaudeville in a small town in New York. George was breaking up with his comedy partner. With Gracie, who had previous vaudeville experience, he formed the popular Burns and Allen comedy team. They married the following year and became highly successful in vaudeville, on radio and television, and in films. Their first permanent radio network job was on the *Robert Burns Panatela Program*, which they joined in the 1932 season, sharing the limelight with orchestra leader **Guy Lombardo**. The program was called *The Adventures of Gracie* from 1934 to 1936 and then renamed *The Burns and Allen Show* in 1936. Burns and Allen were on the air continuously from 1932 to 1950, at which time they moved their show to television.

BURNS, GEORGE (1896–1996). The straight man to **Gracie Allen**, George Burns was born Nathan Birnbaum in New York City. He started out in vaudeville as a singer in a children's quartet, later trying roller-skating and then comedy. In 1925, he met Gracie, with whom he formed the popular Burns and Allen comedy team. When Gracie retired in 1958, Burns carried on alone and became a Las Vegas headliner and famous nightclub comic. At age 79, he had an Oscar-winning performance in the motion picture, *The Sunshine Boys* (1975) and scored another movie success in 1977, playing the title role in *Oh God!* His success in films led to another TV show, *The George Burns Comedy Week*, which he hosted in 1985. He wrote two autobiographies: *I Love Her, That's Why* (1955), and *Living It Up, or They Still Love Me in Altoona!* (1976). *See also BURNS AND ALLEN SHOW.*

BYRD EXPEDITION BROADCASTS. Rear Admiral Richard E. Byrd was a world-famous aviator and polar explorer who flew over the North Pole (1926), across the Atlantic (1927), and over the South

Pole (1929). On a second expedition to the South Pole in 1933, he sent scientific reports to listeners in the United States by means of a complex shortwave hookup originating first from his ship, and later from his outpost at Little America. Sent to Buenos Aires, Argentina, the signal was then relayed to New York, where the live two-way communications between the expedition and newscasters in the studio were broadcast over the network. The reports were broadcast from 1933 to 1935, and were advertised variously as *Byrd Expedition Broadcasts*, *The Adventures of Admiral Byrd*, or simply as *Admiral Byrd*. The broadcasts were sponsored by General Foods, maker of Grape Nuts, selected by Admiral Byrd as "the breakfast food his men should eat to fortify themselves against the punishing cold and hardships of the Antarctic." Several premiums were offered, including a colored map that listeners could use to follow the expedition. Byrd wrote three autobiographies: *Skyward* (1928), *Little America* (1930), and *Alone* (1938).

– C –

CAFÉ ISTANBUL. Created specifically for Marlene Dietrich, *Café Istanbul* was a 30-minute **adventure program** that appeared only in 1952. Dietrich played Madam Madou, the hostess and singer at a café in Turkey that was a center of international intrigue. The next year, the program moved to a different network and was renamed *Time for Love*. The location was changed to San Francisco and Dietrich's character was renamed Diane La Volta, but the program was essentially the same.

CAMEL CARAVAN (THE). The *Camel Caravan* was the umbrella title of a long series of programs sponsored by Camel cigarettes. Sometimes the program was known primarily by the name of the featured performer, sometimes simply by the umbrella title. The program began in 1933 as a program featuring Glen Gray and the Casa Loma Orchestra, with Walter O'Keefe added for comedy. The next year, **Stoopnagle and Budd** were added. In 1936, Camel sponsored both *Benny Goodman's Swing School* and a comedy program, **Jack Oakie's College**, linking the two together and calling the entire hour *The Camel Caravan*. In 1938, Eddie Cantor was the star and later versions starred **Bob Crosby**, Xavier Cugat, Herb Shriner, **Jimmy Durante** and **Garry Moore**, and **Jack Carson**. Some versions were called *The Camel Comedy Caravan*. In various permutations, the program was on the air continuously until 1954.

CAN YOU TOP THIS? Heard on the network from 1942 to 1954, *Can You Top This?* was a comedy panel program on which three panelists told jokes, attempting to elicit greater laughs than a joke sent in by a listener. Veteran radio actor **Peter Donald** read the listener's joke and the audience's reaction to all jokes was measured by a "laugh meter," which was a decibel meter attached to the audience microphone, with the resulting readings displayed to the audience on a large dial. The three panelists were "Senator" Ed Ford, **Harry Hershfield**, and Joe Laurie Jr., all of whom were veterans of vaudeville. Hershfield and Laurie, in particular, did many dialects. Each listener whose joke was used on the air received a small cash prize (originally $5) and slightly more if the panel members could not "top" the joke.

CANOVA, JUDY (1916–1983). Singer and comedienne Juliette Etta (Judy) Canova originally performed as the youngest member of a family act, "The Three Canovas," that also included her brother Zeke and her sister Annie. They appeared on *The Rudy Vallee Show*, *The Edgar Bergen–Charlie McCarthy Show*, and *The Paul Whiteman Hour* before Judy was given her own program, *The Judy Canova Show*, beginning in 1943. The music for her theme song was written with her brother Zeke. Judy also starred in several movies; her screen debut, with her family, was in 1935 in Busby Berkeley's *In Caliente*. After an absence of nearly 20 years, she returned to the screen in 1976 in *Cannonball* (starring David Carradine). Judy's daughter Diana acted on television in the 1970s and 1980s.

CAPTAIN MIDNIGHT. Captain Charles J. "Red" Albright was called Captain Midnight because he returned from one of his World War I adventures at that hour. In this 15-minute **juvenile adventure program** heard from 1940 to 1949, he was a captain in the Secret Squadron, a secret government organization that fought evil all over the world. He fought all kinds of enemies, particularly the master criminal Ivan Shark; but after World War II began, he fought Nazis and Japanese both at home and abroad. He was aided by two young people, Chuck Ramsey and Patsy Donovan (later replaced by Joyce Ryan) and his master mechanic, Ichabod "Ikky" Mudd. The program was written by Robert M. Burtt and Wilfred G. Moore, who had earlier written *The Air Adventures of Jimmy Allen*. Sponsored by Ovaltine, the program began on the network as a replacement for *Little Orphan Annie* and was noted for the many premiums offered, just as was its predecessor. The program's club, called The Secret Squadron, at one time had more than a million members.

CARLON, FRAN (1913–1993). Frances Carlon entered radio doing commercials on *Amos 'n' Andy* and, beginning in 1933, appeared in many **soap operas**, including *Girl Alone*, *Woman of America*, *Lora Lawton*, *Ma Perkins*, *Our Gal Sunday*, *Today's Children*, and *The Story of Mary Marlin*, as well as playing reporter Lorelei Kilbourne on *Big Town*. She played the title role in the television version of *Portia Faces Life* and also acted on the stage, where she enjoyed a long run in the 1950s hit *Sunrise at Campobello*.

CARNEY, DON (1889–1954). "Uncle Don" Carney, whose real name was Howard Rice, was the idol of hundreds of thousands of children in the Northeast who listened to his early morning radio program, **Uncle Don**, over New York's WOR from 1928 to 1949. Although for many years accused of having said, when he thought he was off the air, "There! I guess that'll hold the little bastards!" he always denied it and radio historians have credited the infamous line to "Uncle Wip," the host of a children's show broadcast on WIP in Philadelphia. Under his real name, Rice appeared on several local radio programs including *Main Street Sketches*, *Romance Isle*, and *Cabin Door*.

CARRINGTON, ELAINE (1891–1958). Carrington came to radio from a background of writing for the stage, magazines, and movies and earned one of the largest salaries in radio in the late 1930s as a writer of **soap operas**. Her first popular soap opera was *Red Davis*, which later became *Pepper Young's Family*. She also wrote *When a Girl Marries* and *Rosemary*, among others. Carrington dictated her scripts, while acting out all the parts and was at one time estimated to have produced more than two billion words annually. She was a founder of the Radio Writers Guild, and once remarked that her secret was writing about things listeners could easily identify with.

CARSON, JACK (1910–1963). John Elmer Carson was a comedian known for his double takes and pained expression, who came to movies and radio from acting in vaudeville and stock companies. His first radio program was *The Signal Carnival* in 1941, a **comedy program** sponsored by Signal Oil, and his own program, *The Jack Carson Show*, was an outgrowth of this earlier program. With **Eve Arden**, he hosted the *New Sealtest Village Store* during 1947–1948, replacing Jack Haley as the store's proprietor. He appeared in scores of films from the late 1930s until the early 1960s and, in addition to his radio and movie work, during the early 1950s hosted such television programs as *All Star Revue* and *The U.S. Royal Showcase*. He considered himself an actor first and a comedian second, and played many serious roles in films.

CASEBOOK OF GREGORY HOOD (THE). A 30-minute **adventure program** heard from 1946 to 1950, *Gregory Hood* featured a San Francisco importer who was also an amateur private detective. Assisted by his sidekick Sandy, he traveled the world looking for rare items for his import business. Although it was basically a mystery program, the artifacts that he found always were interesting in their own right and usually had intriguing histories. Several popular radio actors played the part of Hood, including **Gale Gordon**, **Elliott Lewis**, and Jackson Beck. Anthony Boucher was one of the writers.

CASEY, CRIME PHOTOGRAPHER. A 30-minute **crime program** heard from 1943 to 1950 and then again in 1954–1955, *Casey, Crime Photographer* appeared under several names, including *Crime Photographer*, *Flashgun Casey*, and *Casey, Press Photographer*. Based on the stories by George Harmon Coxe, Casey was the crack photographer for *The Morning Express*, but he spent most of his time solving crimes, with reporter Ann Williams at his side. He hung out at the Blue Note Café and was friendly with the bartender, Ethelbert, to whom he related his various adventures. Although Matt Crowley and **Jim Backus** played the part before him, **Staats Cotsworth** is best remembered in the role of Casey. Several actresses played Ann Williams, but the longest lasting was **Jan Miner**, who took over the role in 1947. John Gibson played the role of Ethelbert, the Blue Note bartender, for the entire run of the show. There was a television version of the program in 1951–1952, called *Crime Photographer*, starring first Richard Carlyle and then Darren McGavin as Casey, with Jan Miner again cast as Ann Williams. A book about the character, *Flashgun Casey, Crime Photographer: From the Pulps to Radio and Beyond*, was published in 2005. Alonzo Dean Cole was one of the writers on the series.

CASS DALEY SHOW (THE). See *FITCH BANDWAGON.*

CAVALCADE OF AMERICA. Dedicated to dramatizing important events in United States history, this long-running 30-minute drama anthology was heard from 1935 to 1953, sponsored by Dupont for the entire run. During World War II, the program dramatized current events. Originally, the acting was by members of a prestigious repertoire company in New York, including many of the biggest names in radio. Later programs from Hollywood starred some of the biggest names in motion pictures. Writers were of a similar high quality; special projects were authored by various Pulitzer Prize winners and by such luminaries as Carl Sandburg and Arthur Miller.

CBS RADIO WORKSHOP (THE). See *THE COLUMBIA WORKSHOP.*

CHALLENGE OF THE YUKON. See *SERGEANT PRESTON OF THE YUKON.*

CHAMBER MUSIC SOCIETY OF LOWER BASIN STREET (THE). This unusual 30-minute program was heard from 1940 to 1944 and then appeared again briefly in 1950 and 1952. The music was swing or jazz and the announcements, delivered by **Milton Cross**, were tongue-in-cheek, with almost all musicians referred to as "Dr." or "Professor" in a parody of programs of serious music. Dinah Shore was one of the early singing stars, although there were several others after her.

CHANDLER, JEFF (1918–1961). Chandler, born Ira Grossel in Brooklyn, starred in dozens of action pictures and westerns during his movie career (twice playing Cochise on the screen) and being nominated for an Oscar in 1950 for one of these portrayals in the film *Broken Arrow*. On the radio, Chandler appeared in the title role on the crime drama, **Michael Shayne**, in the first network version of the series broadcast from 1948 to 1950; but he was best known for his role as Mr. Boynton, the shy teacher on *Our Miss Brooks*, opposite **Eve Arden**. During 1950–1951, he also made appearances on *Screen Director's Playhouse*, once again playing Cochise in the radio version of *Broken Arrow*. He died at the age of 42 of blood poisoning following surgery.

CHANDU, THE MAGICIAN. Like several other **juvenile adventure programs**, Chandu was actually only a network program for a short time, although widely heard on regional stations. There were two versions of the program, the first heard as a 15-minute program from 1932 to 1936 over various regional stations and briefly on Mutual, originally with Gayne Whitman in the title role. The program was revived in 1948 with Tom Collins in the title role, still as a 15-minute program. The format was changed to 30 minutes in 1949, and the program was aired on the Don Lee Network and then on Mutual during 1949–1950. Chandu was the name given Frank Chandler, an American agent who had learned magic from a yogi in India. He battled evil all over the world, but was often opposed by the master criminal Roxor. Many of the premiums offered on the later version of the program were magic tricks that children could learn to perform.

CHAPPELL, ERNEST (1903–1983). Chappell graduated from Syracuse University in 1925, and wanted to be a singer, but instead had a long and successful career on radio as an announcer and executive. For 17 years, he was the announcer for the American Tobacco Company's Pall Mall brand of cigarettes, and its spokesman on *The Big Story* (1947–1955). He also appeared on several other programs, including *The George Jessel Show*, *The Song of Your Life*, and *The Fabulous Dr. Tweedy*; and he was the host/narrator of *Quiet, Please*, which he also helped produce. Chappell served as announcer for the wartime newscasts of **Edward R. Murrow** and, at one time, coached Eleanor Roosevelt for her radio broadcasts.

CHARLIE CHAN. A detective program based on the stories by Earl Derr Biggers, featuring the famous Chinese detective, *Charlie Chan* was first heard as a 30-minute weekly program in 1932–1933, with Walter Connolly as Chan. From 1936 to 1938, it was a 15-minute daily serial, before returning to the 30-minute format during 1944–1945 with Ed Begley as Chan and Leo Janney as his Number One son. In late 1945, it appeared as a 15-minute program and in 1947–1948 then again as a 30-minute program. It is sometimes listed as *The Incomparable Charlie Chan* or *The Adventures of Charlie Chan.*

CHASE AND SANBORN HOUR (THE). The Chase and Sanborn Hour was the umbrella title for a long series of programs sponsored by Chase and Sanborn coffee, beginning in 1929 and continuing until 1948. The programs varied considerably, and the name of the program changed often, although it often contained the name of the sponsor, either in the title or in the announcer's introduction to the program. First heard as a 30-minute **music program** called *The Chase and Sanborn Choral Orchestra* from 1929 to 1931, it became a 60-minute program from 1931 to 1934, starring **Eddie Cantor** and called both *The Chase and Sanborn Hour* and *The Eddie Cantor Show.* The next year, it was renamed *The Opera Guild*, a **concert music** program hosted by **Deems Taylor**. In 1936, it became *Major Bowe's Original Amateur Hour*. In 1937, it became *The Edgar Bergen–Charlie McCarthy Show* and remained so for the last 10 years of its run.

CHEERIO. An unusual 30-minute program heard weekday mornings from 1927 to 1937, *Cheerio* featured Charles K. Field, who felt that his mission in life was to spread cheer and goodwill. He read poems, told stories, and played cheerful organ music while a small flock of canaries, who had their own microphone, chirped in the background. Field shunned publicity and lived on his private means, donating all his fees to charity. From 1937 to 1940, the program changed to a 30-minute weekly format; in 1936, there was a short-lived evening version called *Cheerio's Musical Mosaics.*

CHICAGO THEATER OF THE AIR (THE). A 60-minute **concert music** program heard from 1940 to 1955 on the Mutual network, *The Chicago Theater of the Air* presented operettas that had been rewritten for radio, attempting to retain all of the best known music and all of the essential elements of the plot within the constraints of a 60-minute presentation. The casts were large and the soloists came from major opera companies, including The Metropolitan Opera and The Chicago Civic Opera Company. The dramatic cast consisted of veteran radio actors working in the Chicago radio environment.

CHILDREN'S HOUR (THE). *See COAST-TO-COAST ON A BUS.*

CHILDREN'S PROGRAMS. Children's programs appeared early in the history of old-time radio, almost all of them being heard on Saturday morning or late on weekday afternoons. The Saturday morning programs were directed at younger children and a tradition of Saturday morning programming for children continued throughout the period of old-time radio, both on the networks and on local stations. As early as 1929, CBS produced a long-running Saturday morning children's program, *The Adventures of Helen and Mary*, which consisted of the fairy-tale adventures of two young girls. The name was changed to *Let's Pretend* in the late 1930s and **Nila Mack** wrote and directed the program until she died in 1953, the program continuing only one more year after her death.

Another popular Saturday morning children's program, *Smilin' Ed's Buster Brown Gang*, started in 1944 and had a very successful nine-year run before moving to television, where it was equally popular. It was hosted by Smilin' Ed McConnell, a veteran of both vaudeville and radio. The program was a good-natured mixture of stories, songs, and silly skits that young children loved.

The weekday afternoon children's programs were usually 15-minute serial adventure shows, with each episode ending in the traditional cliff-hanger manner. They are covered under **Juvenile Adventure Programs**.

CISCO KID (THE). Loosely based on the character in the O. Henry stories, The Cisco Kid was a Mexican adventurer who roamed the West, always helping the deserving, usually victimizing the rich and greedy. Cisco and his partner Pancho were more light-hearted than other heroes of juvenile westerns, often making jokes even while in very tense situations. Cisco was also almost the only juvenile hero to show much interest in women, often collecting a kiss from a beautiful senorita before riding off at the end of the program. First heard from 1942 to 1945 on Mutual, with Jackson Beck as Cisco, the program then moved to the Don Lee Network and to syndication with Jack Mather as Cisco and Harry Lang as Pancho. The program offered many premiums.

CITIES SERVICE CONCERTS. The title of this program refers to the sponsor, the Cities Service Oil Company, a large company with service stations nationwide (now CITGO). It was a **concert music** program that was heard on NBC for almost the entire period of old-time radio, first as a 60-minute program from 1927 to 1940 and then as a 30-minute program from 1940 to 1956. The show originally presented only instrumental music, but singers were soon added, including **Jessica Dragonette**, who was hugely popular and one of the greatest radio stars of the day. When her contract expired in 1937, she moved to CBS on the *Palmolive Beauty Box Theater* and was replaced by Lucille Manners, who remained on the program for the next 10 years. The program had several titles during its long run, including *The Cities Service Orchestra*, *Highways in Melody*, and *The Cities Service Band of America*.

CLARA, LU, AND EM. Sometimes cited as radio's first **soap opera**, *Clara, Lu, and Em* was the first network daytime serial, but it lacked many of the elements of a true soap opera and is perhaps best seen as an early antecedent of the soap opera. The program was essentially a dialogue between three gossipy women who discussed daily happenings in the neighborhood. The show originated as a sorority skit at Northwestern University, featuring three students: Louise Starkey, Isobel Carothers, and Helen King. They managed to get it on the air on WGN Chicago, where it eventually attracted enough listeners to be adopted by NBC in January of 1931. First heard at 10:30 at night, it moved to a daytime slot in 1932. Isobel Carothers died suddenly in 1936 and the other two women decided not to go on without her. An attempt was made to bring the program back on CBS in 1942 with Harriet Allyn taking Carothers' place, but it was not successful.

CLIQUOT CLUB ESKIMOS (THE). The Cliquot Club Eskimos are notable chiefly because they were one of the very first acts to appear on broadcast radio, first appearing several years before the creation of the networks. The Eskimos were originally a six-piece banjo ensemble, led by Harry Reser. As the program became more popular, a more conventional orchestra was substituted, although Reser, who played many instruments, was still featured. The orchestra was named for the sponsor, Cliquot Club Ginger Ale, which featured an Eskimo in its logo. After appearing on WEAF New York from 1923 to 1926, the Eskimos moved to the newly created NBC in 1926 and remained on that network until 1936.

CLOONEY, ROSEMARY (1928–2002). Rosemary and her sister Betty performed on local radio as the Clooney Sisters and then toured for three years with Tony Pastor's Orchestra from 1946 to 1948. When Betty decided to leave the act, Rosemary continued as a single, starring on the *Rosemary Clooney Show* from 1953 to 1955. She later worked with both **Bob Hope** and **Bing Crosby** on radio and television. She was twice married to Oscar-winning actor José Ferrer, and they had five children; two of their sons, Miguel and Rafael, became professional actors. A nephew, George Clooney, is an award-winning movie star. Her autobiography, *Rosie*, was published in 1982.

CLUB FIFTEEN. A 15-minute program that took its name from the length of the program, *Club Fifteen* was heard five nights a week from 1947 to 1952, and then three nights a week during 1952–1953. It is sometimes listed as *Bob Crosby's Club Fifteen* because **Bob Crosby** was the original star, although Dick Haymes took over in 1949–1950. Although only a 15-minute program, it presented major stars from the music business, among them The Andrews Sisters, Margaret Whiting, Jo Stafford, and Gisele MacKenzie.

CLUB MATINEE. A late afternoon **variety program** heard in both 60-minute and 30-minute formats, *Club Matinee* was originally hosted by **Ransom Sherman**. Heard six times a week from 1937 to 1941, then three times a week from 1941 to 1943, it is the program where **Garry Moore** got his start in 1939; and he eventually became a co-host with Sherman. Moore began on the program under his own name, Thomas Garrison Morfit, and one of the best-remembered features of the show was a contest to rename him; a woman from Pittsburgh won $50 by suggesting the name *Garry Moore*.

COAST-TO-COAST ON A BUS. Originally called *The Children's Hour*, *Coast-to-Coast on a Bus* was a **children's program** showcasing talented children. Hosted by **Milton Cross**, the program was also known as *The White Rabbit Line*, and was organized around an imaginary bus on which Cross was the conductor. The bus made many stops, each stop to pick up another young performer, who was introduced and who then performed. Heard in 60-minute, 45-minute, and 30-minute versions, the program was on the air Sunday mornings from 1927 to 1948. Many of the children who appeared later had distinguished careers as performers, including Ann Blyth, **Jackie Kelk**, and Risë Stevens.

COLGATE SPORTS NEWSREEL (THE). A long-running 15-minute program that dramatized events or personalities related to sports, *The Colgate Sports Newsreel* was hosted by **Bill Stern**, a famous sportscaster. Although not always completely accurate, the program was always melodramatic, with organ music, sound effects, and dramatic narration. It was heard from 1939 to 1956 and had a very large following. *See also* SPORTS BROADCASTS.

COLLINS, RAY (1889–1965). A former vaudeville performer and Broadway actor, Collins began on radio with roles on *The March of Time* in 1933. In 1939, he joined **Orson Welles'** troupe on *Mercury Theatre on the Air* and performed on the famous "War of the Worlds" broadcast. Collins also appeared on *Cavalcade of America* and *Grand Central Station* in the late 1930s and early 1940s. His motion picture debut was in Welles' *Citizen Kane*, and scores of other film roles followed. On television, he played Dr. Merriweather on *The Halls of Ivy* (1954) and Lt. Arthur Tragg on *Perry Mason* (1957–1965).

COLLYER, CLAYTON "BUD" (1908–1969). From a theatrical family, Collyer earned a law degree but turned to acting when parts on radio paid more than practicing law. He starred as Superman on *The Adventures of Superman* from 1940 to 1951, well suited for the role because he could speak in one voice as Kent and then lower his voice at least an octave as Superman. He also played Pat Ryan on *Terry and the Pirates*, and announced on many popular programs, including *The Cavalcade of America*, *The Guiding Light*, and *Road of Life*. Collyer became even more famous on television as the host of several popular quiz programs, including *Beat the Clock* and *To Tell the Truth*. In 1968, at the end of his long career, he provided the voice of Batman on a TV cartoon series, *The Batman/Superman Hour*. At one time, Collyer served as president of the American Federation of Television and Radio Artists.

COLMAN, RONALD (1891–1958). A distinguished British actor, Colman was born in Surrey, England, and turned to acting after being wounded in World War I. He came to the United States to act on the stage in 1920, and made his first American silent film, *The White Sister*, in 1922. He made dozens of movies, usually cast in romantic roles, and won an Academy Award as best actor in 1947 for *A Double Life*. On radio he was a frequent guest on *The Jack Benny Program* and later starred in a situation comedy, *The Halls of Ivy* with his wife, British actress Benita Hume.

COLONEL STOOPNAGLE SHOW (THE). See *STOOPNAGLE AND BUDD*.

COLUMBIA BROADCASTING SYSTEM (CBS). CBS can trace its origins to the creation, in 1927, of the **United Independent Broadcasters (UIB)** network. UIB went on the air in October of that year but struggled financially and soon looked for additional investors. The Columbia Phonographic Manufacturing Company rescued the company in 1928, and the network was renamed Columbia Phonographic Broadcasting System.

Even with increased backing, the network continued to lose money, and Columbia Phonographic soon sold its half-interest to **William S. Paley**, son of a Philadelphia cigar manufacturer, and the corporate name was changed to the Columbia Broadcasting System.

The **National Broadcasting Company (NBC)** affiliates had the latest RCA equipment, and were often the best-established stations, but Paley believed that programming was the most important part of broadcast radio, and CBS quickly established itself as the home of many popular musical and comedy stars, among them **Bing Crosby**, **Burns and Allen**, and **Kate Smith**. Some later left for NBC, which was far richer and could pay more, but Paley had an eye for talent and was able to keep the CBS stable of stars well-stocked.

Paley also broadened the offerings of CBS by establishing an independent news division and, in 1935, brought in **Edward R. Murrow** as Director of European Talks. Murrow assembled a brilliant team of reporters, including Erik Sevareid, Charles Collingswood, and Howard K. Smith, and it was their reports, along with Murrow's on-the-spot reports of the London blitz, which contributed to CBS News' image for timely and informed coverage.

All through the 1930s and 1940s, CBS programs were often the highest-rated. A much-publicized "talent raid" on NBC in the late 1940s brought many headliners, including **Jack Benny** and **Edgar Bergen**, to CBS, increasing its dominance in program popularity. CBS was also a leader in creating original network programming. Beginning in the mid-1940s, the network began creating and producing its own programs; in time it controlled all programming, so that ad agencies and sponsors no longer had any direct control over what went out over the CBS network.

As late as 1950, CBS owned only one television station, but as television became more popular, CBS began to develop their TV network and their radio network became progressively smaller and less important. Radio stars began to drift to the new medium, leaving only the smaller-budgeted programs until they, too, were discontinued and CBS became a television network with a small radio component.

COLUMBIA WORKSHOP (THE). Beginning in 1936, when the state of drama on radio was still a fairly crude product, *The Columbia Workshop* presented the works of unknown writers and pioneered new techniques in production and sound effects. It was a 30-minute drama anthology heard from 1936 to 1947, and was primarily a director's showcase, with very few restrictions on what might be presented. Several short series by **Norman Corwin** were presented as a part of *The Columbia Workshop*, including *Twenty-Six by Corwin* in 1941, *An American in England* in 1942, and *Columbia Presents Corwin* in 1944. *The CBS Radio Workshop*, heard from 1956 to 1967, was very similar.

COMEDY PROGRAMS. Comedy programs heard on old-time radio were of two general types: **situation comedy**, which is discussed separately, and programs that presented comedy of other types, including monologues and skits of various sorts.

Many of the comedians appearing on early radio were veterans of vaudeville, and they often simply moved their vaudeville act to radio, including the visual components of their stage performances. **Ed Wynn**, for example, always wore his costume and full makeup when appearing as *The Fire Chief*. Even those who transformed themselves into true radio comics often continued visual references that had been a part of their theater act: Eddie Cantor was often referred to as "banjo eyes," and frequent comment was made about the size of **Jimmy Durante**'s nose, although the radio audience obviously could not perceive these features directly. **Red Skelton** was essentially a visual comic, but his characterizations were very successful on radio, and **Edgar Bergen** was a ventriloquist who astonished everyone by being a tremendous hit with an audience that could not see him or his dummies.

Although not all vaudeville comedians were successful in the new medium, *The Eddie Cantor Show* was at one time the highest-rated program in radio, and several other long-term hit programs were headed by vaudeville veterans, including *The Jack Benny Program* and *The Fred Allen Show*. Other vaudeville veterans enjoyed early success in radio, but faded relatively quickly because their characterizations or their material became outdated; one could perform the same act for a long time in vaudeville because each performance had a new audience, but radio success required the constant provision of new material. *The Joe Penner Show* was very popular for several years but faded before Penner's premature death in 1941 at the age of 36.

Most of the comedy programs headed by vaudeville-bred comedians followed what was essentially a vaudeville format: monologues or comedic skits interspersed with musical interludes. *The Edgar Bergen–Charlie McCarthy Show*, *The Bob Hope Show*, *The Red Skelton Show*, *The Abbott and Costello Show*, and many others were essentially a collection of more or less unrelated skits each week, often incorporating celebrity guests who would participate in an interview-like episode and then assume a role in the comedy skits. *The Jack Benny Program*, often voted the most popular old-time radio comedy program by modern listeners, began in this way, but evolved over time until it was almost a situation comedy, often presenting an episode that pretended to pertain to preparation for the upcoming weekly program. *See also* SITUATION COMEDIES.

COMMAND PERFORMANCE. A **variety program** produced during World War II and for a few years after (1942–1949), *Command Performance* was intended for direct shortwave transmission to American troops overseas. Although the biggest names in the entertainment industry appeared, all talent was donated, including the production facilities and staff. Troops were allowed to request ("command") what they would like to hear. After the first year, the program was moved from New York to Los Angeles to make it easier to fill the requests for the appearance of motion picture stars. People in the United States ordinarily could not hear the program, which was not broadcast over any regular networks, although everything was recorded and many episodes of the program are now available. One of the best-remembered of the show's highlights was *Dick Tracy in B-Flat*, a spoof of the popular comic strip produced in 1945 with an all-star cast that included **Bing Crosby**, **Jimmy Durante**, **Bob Hope**, and many others. CBS produced a spin-off series called *Return Performance* in 1945–1946.

COMO, PERRY (1913–2001). After starting life as a barber, Como came to national attention in the late 1930s after he became the featured vocalist with the Ted Weems Orchestra. He began his career on radio with *Beat the Band* in 1940–1941 and then on the *Perry Como Show* from 1943–1944. He starred as the singing emcee of *The Chesterfield Supper Club* in 1944 and continued to host the program until 1949. Como was known for his casual style, wearing cardigan sweaters that were later dubbed "Perry Como sweaters" by his fans. His record contract with RCA resulted in more than a score of gold records over the course of his long singing career. When *The Chesterfield Supper Club* moved to television in the late 1940s, Como continued to be the featured vocalist, supported by the Mitchell Ayres Orchestra and the Fontane Sisters.

CONCERT MUSIC. Old-time radio presented a surprising amount of what might be thought of as "serious" music; symphony orchestras, operas, and famous classical soloists. This was partly because such music was readily available in most large cities, but there was also a genuine interest among network music directors in presenting "good" music. Virtually every major orchestra appeared on radio, and several networks maintained symphony orchestras of their own. Many concert music programs began very early and some remained on the air for very long periods; *The Cities Service Concerts* were heard from 1927 to 1956, *The Telephone Hour* was on the air for 18 years, and *Andre Kostelanetz* for 16 years. *The Metropolitan Opera* began broadcasts in 1931 and still is on the air.

CONRAD, FRANK (1874–1941). In 1890, Conrad left school to work in the Westinghouse plant in Pittsburgh, where an aptitude for mechanics soon advanced him to the plant's testing department. His first important invention—a meter to measure the consumption of electric power—became a universal home installation. After conducting experimental work for the government during World War I, he returned to his amateur radio station in Wilkinsburg, Pennsylvania, five miles outside of Pittsburgh. On 17 October 1919, bored with the usual equipment-oriented chat heard on amateur radio, he placed his microphone before the speaker of his phonograph and played phonograph records over the air. The experiment was a huge success and led to regular broadcasts of recorded music. By the next summer, the broadcasts had become very popular in the Pittsburgh area. An executive at Westinghouse saw the possibilities that such programming might increase the demand for radios built by Westinghouse, and the company applied for a license to establish a commercial station at the Westinghouse factory. This station (**KDKA**) broadcast the Harding-Cox election bulletins on 2 November 1920 and pioneered many of the very earliest efforts in broadcasting, including the broadcast of live sporting events. Conrad was appointed general engineer of the Westinghouse Company in 1904 and assistant chief engineer in 1921. He received an honorary Doctor of Science degree from the University of Pittsburgh in 1928 and many other honors and awards, including the Edison Medal from the American Institute of Electrical Engineers in 1931.

CONRAD, WILLIAM (1920–1994). Although best remembered as a television and movie actor, Conrad was a star on radio for many years. He began his radio career in Beverly Hills at age 17; and during World War II served first as a fighter pilot and later with the **Armed Forces Radio Service**. Possessed of a deep baritone voice, Conrad was heard frequently on many dramatic anthology programs, including *Escape*, *Suspense*, *The Whistler*, and *Lux Radio Theatre*, but he is best remembered as Marshal Matt Dillon on the radio version of **Gunsmoke**. His film debut in 1946 was as a villain in *The Killers* and he later starred in several television series, including *Cannon* and *Jake and the Fat Man*. In the 1960s, he both produced and directed movies.

CONREID, HANS (1917–1982). Although he played Shakespearean roles while in college, Conreid is best remembered today for the several comic characters he created on radio and television. On radio, he was featured on many programs, sometimes appearing on several concurrently, including *Maisie*, *Burns and Allen*, *The Judy Canova Show*, *Life With Luigi*, and *My Friend Irma*. On television, he was a regular or semi-regular on many popular TV shows, such as *The Danny Thomas Show* (1958–1964), *The Tony Randall Show* (1977–1978), and *American Dream* (1981). On *The Bullwinkle Show*, a children's cartoon program, he was the voice of the villainous Snidley Whiplash. Conreid also appeared on TV talk and quiz shows; in 1964, he emceed the **quiz program** *Made in America*.

CONWAY, TOM (1904–1967). Born Thomas Sanders, Conway was the brother of actor George Sanders. The suave Conway replaced his equally suave brother as "The Falcon" in a series of movies about the amateur sleuth and ladies' man made in the 1940s. On radio, Conway portrayed two other famous detectives, replacing Basil Rathbone as **Sherlock Holmes** in 1946 and replacing Vincent Price as *The Saint* in 1951. Later, on television, he starred as *Mark Saber*.

COOPER, WYLLIS (1899–1955). In 1935, Cooper was the creator–writer–producer of *Lights Out*, billed as "the ultimate in horror," principally because of its effective use of sound effects. At the time, Cooper was a young staff member in Chicago's NBC studios. In 1936, he left *Lights Out* in the capable hands of **Arch Oboler**, and became a Hollywood scriptwriter, returning to radio in the late 1940s as the creator–writer–director of another memorable program, the fantasy drama *Quiet, Please*. In the early 1950s, Cooper was writer–director of *Whitehall 1212*, a program that presented "baffling cases" of Scotland Yard. Always a prolific writer, Cooper once recalled that when he was continuity editor for NBC in Chicago, he wrote two half-hour shows and did 15 soap opera scripts a week.

CORRELL, CHARLES (1890–1972). Correll played the character of Andy Brown on the immensely popular *Amos 'n' Andy* radio program for 34 years. Earlier, he and his partner **Freeman Gosden** (who played Amos) appeared as *Sam 'n' Henry* on station WGN in Chicago. In 1928, they were offered more money by WMAQ, but when they moved to that station, they were required to find a new name for their act. They chose *Amos 'n' Andy*, and, in November 1929, went coast to coast on NBC, sponsored by Pepsodent toothpaste. Correll and Gosden ended their radio careers with *The Amos 'n' Andy Music Hall*, which aired from 1954 to 1960, a daily show that featured brief skits and recorded songs. Before *Amos 'n' Andy* moved to television in 1951, Correll and Gosden sold all legal rights to their characters for $2.5 million.

CORWIN, NORMAN (1910–). Corwin began his career as a journalist, later becoming a local radio commentator in Boston. He moved to New York in 1936 and became very successful as a writer–director–producer. He was responsible for several of the "prestige" dramas presented by CBS during the next decade, two of which bore his name: *Twenty-Six by Corwin* (1941) and *Columbia Presents Corwin* (1944–1945). Other CBS programs on which he was a major contributor were *So This is Radio*, *So This is War*, and *An American in England*. All of these programs were broadcast under the umbrella of *The Columbia Workshop*, a 30-minute drama anthology. His most famous work is *On a Note of Triumph*, a celebration of the end of World War II in Europe, first broadcast on V-E Day, 8 May 1945. Martin Gabel narrated the radio show, which featured vignettes and voices from every front. The show was accorded almost universal acclaim, and was repeated five days later. Three months later, he wrote *14 August*, a V-J Day documentary narrated by **Orson Welles**. After he left CBS, Corwin remained active, writing and directing two plays produced on Broadway, *The Rivalry* in 1959 and *The World of Carl Sandburg* in 1960. He also wrote several books, including *Trivializing America* (1983). More recently, National Public Radio commissioned six new plays from him and aired them in 2001 under the title *More by Corwin*. Corwin was inducted into the Radio Hall of Fame in 1993.

COSTELLO, LOU (1906–1959). Born Louis Cristillo, Costello was the fall guy of the popular Abbott & Costello comedy team. He and

Bud Abbott first worked together at a vaudeville theater in 1929, and formed a permanent partnership in 1936. They first appeared on radio on *The Kate Smith Hour* in 1938 and then on *The Chase and Sanborn Hour* in the early 1940s before starring in their own show, *The Abbott & Costello Show* (1942–1949). Costello suffered an attack of rheumatic fever in 1943 and was unable to work for nearly a year. On the day he returned to the radio show, his infant son drowned in the pool at his home and many acquaintances said that he never recovered from the tragedy. Abbott and Costello made more than 30 movies between 1940 and 1956, and moved their radio program to television 1951, finally breaking up their partnership in 1957. Costello died of a heart attack in 1959, three days before his 53rd birthday.

COTSWORTH, STAATS (1908–1979). In 1946, Cotsworth was described as "the busiest actor in radio" and was reported to have made more than 7,500 broadcasts during a 12-year period. In addition to his radio work, he was a Shakespearean actor, a painter, and a photographer. Cotsworth appeared on some of radio's most popular programs, including *Lorenzo Jones*, *Cavalcade of America*, *Stella Dallas*, *Mr. and Mrs. North*, and *When a Girl Marries*. He was best known to most radio listeners, however, as the original Casey in the popular CBS crime drama *Casey, Crime Photographer*.

COUNT OF MONTE CRISTO (THE). A 30-minute **adventure program** heard from 1946 to 1951, *The Count of Monte Cristo* was based on a figure from a novel by Alexandre Dumas. Edmund Dantes was a young Frenchman who had been imprisoned on a false charge of treason. He escaped, retrieved a fabulous treasure that had been revealed to him in prison by a fellow prisoner, and established himself as a nobleman. He devoted his time and fortune to fighting injustice, aided by his faithful manservant, Rene. Carleton Young was heard as Dantes and **Parley Baer** as Rene.

COUNTERSPY. This 30-minute espionage **adventure program** featuring David Harding, a U.S. counterespionage agent, is sometimes listed as *David Harding, Counterspy*. When the program first appeared in 1942, David and his assistant, Peters, were fighting against both the German Gestapo and Japan's Black Dragon. After the war, they struggled against other threats to the nation's security. The program was very popular and very durable, remaining on the air until 1957. Don MacLaughlin played Harding, with Mandel Kramer as Peters.

CRIME PROGRAMS. Crime programs were some of the most popular programs on old-time radio. One of the earliest of these, *The Eno Crime Club*, began as a 15-minute daily program in 1931, dramatizing stories that appeared in a popular series of crime novels of the day. The program later changed to a 30-minute program featuring the continuing adventures of a central crime fighter, and this format became the standard for most of the popular crime programs on radio.

The Shadow appeared in 1937 and was loosely based on a character first found in the pulp magazines that were popular during the 1930s and 1940s. It was popular for many years, and did involve a crime-fighting central character, but was not typical of radio crime programs, containing some features that resembled a **juvenile adventure program**, including fantastic plots and elements of mysticism. Most crime programs involved more conventional crime fighters, often private detectives.

The Golden Age of Radio coincided with the popularity of the hard-boiled private detective in American fiction and many of these were adapted to radio. Tough-guy Philip Marlowe, created by Raymond Chandler, appeared in *The Adventures of Philip Marlowe*, and *Michael Shayne*, the hero of a long series of detective novels by Brett Halliday, also had his own program. The heroes of both these programs were similar to those portrayed in the novels on which they were based, although the original creators did not write for the radio programs.

In other programs, the radio characters developed somewhat beyond those in the original source. *The Adventures of the Thin Man* featured a husband-and-wife crime-solving team, Nick and Nora Charles, first seen in a Dashiell Hammett novel, but best known from a movie adaptation of the novel starring William Powell and Myrna Loy. The stars of the original version of the radio show, **Les Damon** and **Claudia Morgan**, sounded so much like the stars of the movie that many listeners could not tell them apart; but the stories were all new, written for radio.

Another program starring a crime-solving couple, *Mr. and Mrs. North*, was based on the novels of Richard and Frances Lockridge. It was one of the most popular crime programs of the day, and was said at one time to have had 20 million listeners. *The Saint*, based on the novels of Leslie Charteris and the movies that starred George Sanders, was also light in tone. In the best-known version, starring Vincent Price, the dialogue was essentially a series of one-liners by the suave Simon Templar, who, like Nick Charles, was a sophisticate who patronized the arts and ate at fine restaurants.

The Adventures of Sam Spade was based on another character originated by Dashiell Hammett, but the personality of the Sam Spade on radio was very different from the unsmiling Spade portrayed by Humphrey Bogart in the movie *The Maltese Falcon*. As played by **Howard Duff**, the radio version of Sam Spade was a street-smart, wise-cracking tough guy who had a light-hearted, unspoken romance with his secretary and a good-natured adversarial relationship with the police. In *Richard Diamond, Private Detective*, the star was an ex-cop who maintained a sarcastic but friendly relationship with the police. *Rogue's Gallery* featured a private detective named Richard Rogue, who chased girls and smart-mouthed almost everyone until he was knocked unconscious by someone, which happened almost every week.

Several police programs either dramatized real cases or were based on some aspects of a real case. The earliest of these was *Gang Busters*, which began in 1935 and is remembered today primarily for the noisiness of its opening, which consisted of policeman's whistles, sirens, machine-gun fire, broken glass, and all manner of noise so loud that it gave rise to the slang term "coming on like Gang Busters." *Mr. District Attorney* began in 1939 and was extremely topical, sometimes presenting dramatizations of real-world events that had occurred only weeks before. The programs themselves were similar to the private detective programs, with the investigation led by the District Attorney (who was never referred to by name) but with any actual dirty work done by his assistant, Harrington. *Mr. District Attorney* won many awards and was extremely popular, nearly always appearing among the top-ten programs.

Popular though these programs were, the most popular and authentic crime program ever to appear on radio was *Dragnet*, which first appeared in 1949. The program presented cases in a meticulous, very detailed manner, describing police procedure and incorporating police terminology. Cases of every type were presented, from murder to shoplifting, including such previously forbidden topics as sex crimes and violence against children. The program made use of dramatic music and authentic sound effects, but the dialogue was very low-key. It was immensely successful for seven years on radio and then moved to television.

CROSBY, BING (1903–1977). Crosby, whose real first name was Harry, was a star in radio, television, motion pictures, and music. He began his radio career on *Meet the Artist* in the early 1930s, and ended it with *The Ford Road Show* in the late 1950s. In between, he appeared on several other programs, including *Fifteen Minutes with Crosby*, *Music That Satisfies*, the *Woodbury Radio Program*, **The Kraft Music Hall** (which he hosted for a decade), and *This Is Bing Crosby*. Crosby's ABC program, technically named **Philco Radio Time**, was the first major network program in prime time to be transcribed. On television, *The Bing Crosby Show* was broadcast during 1964–1965; and he was frequently the host of *The Hollywood Palace* from 1964 to 1970. His recordings sold in the millions, and his version of "White Christmas" is still an all-time best seller. He began his film career in 1930 with *King of Jazz* and appeared in scores of movies from the 1930s through the 1960s, receiving an Academy Award as best actor for *Going My Way* (1944). He also received a **Peabody Award** in 1969. Bing was the father of actors Gary and Mary Crosby, and the brother of bandleader **Bob Crosby**. His autobiography, *Call Me Lucky*, was published in 1953 and an authorized biography by Charles Thompson, titled simply *Bing*, appeared in 1976.

CROSBY, BOB (1913–1993). Bing Crosby's younger brother always suffered from the comparison with his more famous sibling, but he made a name for himself as a band leader. Bob Crosby and his Bobcats made best-selling records during the late 1930s and early 1940s and the radio program bearing his name, *The Bob Crosby Show*, was heard 1943–1944, 1946–1947, and 1949–1950. On television, he hosted a daily daytime show on CBS from 1953 to 1957 and he had his own NBC prime-time program in 1958, a summer replacement for *The Perry Como Show*. Crosby also made occasional guest appearances in movies starring his brother.

CROSS, MILTON J. (1897–1975). One of the first generation of great radio announcers, Cross initially appeared on pre-network radio as both a singer and an announcer. Later on NBC, he inaugurated the long-running *Metropolitan Opera* broadcasts (1931 to present) and helped make The Met a national institution. He continued as "The Voice of the Met" until 1973. He was also a commentator on the talent show, *Metropolitan Opera Auditions of the Air*, from 1939 to 1942, and the announcer on **The Chamber Music Society of Lower Basin Street**. In 1929, the American Academy of Arts and Letters gave him the highest honors they could confer on a radio announcer.

CROSSLEY RATINGS. *See* RATING SYSTEMS.

CRUMIT, FRANK (1889–1943). After appearing in vaudeville for many years, Crumit made his radio debut in 1925, singing tunes while accompanying himself on a ukulele. He and his wife, soprano Julia Sanderson, appeared on radio from 1929 to 1943, billed as "The Singing Sweethearts." They headlined a number of musical programs, including *Blackstone Plantation*, *Norge Musical Kitchen*, and *It's Florida's Treat*. They also hosted *The Crumit and Sanderson Quiz* and the first two years of *The Battle of the Sexes*. Crumit and his wife were among the first established entertainers to headline a **quiz program**. After her husband's death, Sanderson performed alone on a Mutual series, *Let's Be Charming*, during 1943–1944.

CULLEN, BILL (1920–1990). Cullen is said to have been associated with more game shows than any other entertainer in radio or television history. He began his radio career as a disc jockey at age 19, became an announcer on CBS in 1944, and later became the host of that network's *Winner Take All* and several other programs. On television, he was seen as host or panelist on more than a dozen **quiz programs** including *Name That Tune*, *To Tell the Truth*, *The Price Is Right*, and *I've Got a Secret*. At one time in the mid-1960s, he could be seen on all three major TV networks.

CURTIN, JOSEPH (1910–1979). Curtin was a graduate of the Yale School of Drama, and performed on the stage in the early 1930s. He came to radio in 1934, and was the originator of the character Jerry

North on the popular radio mystery drama, *Mr. and Mrs. North*. Before that, he had been a regular on such daytime **soap operas** as *Backstage Wife*, *Young Widder Brown*, *Second Husband*, and *Stella Dallas*. When Golden Age of Radio came to an end, Curtin joined a family insurance agency in Massachusetts. Those who knew him personally said he bore a striking physical resemblance to **Bob Hope**.

– D –

DALEY, CASS (1915–1975). Born Katherine Dailey, Cass Daley was a comedienne who started her professional career as a band vocalist. She early displayed a talent for comedy and starred in clubs and vaudeville before breaking into motion pictures in the early 1940s, where she appeared in several light musicals for Paramount. She came to radio in the mid-1940s as Frank Morgan's niece on *Maxwell House Coffee Time*. She then starred on *The Fitch Bandwagon*, which was also known as *The Cass Daley Bandwagon* and *The Cass Daley Show*. Daley retired from show business in the early 1950s to raise a family. She later tried a comeback, appearing in the movie *Norwood* in 1970, but before her career could gain much momentum, she died as a result of an accidental fall over a glass coffee table in her apartment.

DAMON, LES (1908–1962). A former Old Vic Theatre player, Lester Damon spent most of his professional career working in radio and television on **soap operas** and detective programs. The radio soap operas included *Portia Faces Life*, *The Right to Happiness*, *Woman in White*, *Young Dr. Malone*, and *Girl Alone*. The detective programs included lead roles on *The Adventures of the Thin Man* and *The Falcon*. On *The Thin Man*, he successfully imitated the voice of William Powell, the movie star who played the popular Dashiell Hammett character in a series of films about the retired detective and his wealthy wife. On television, Damon originated the role of Jim Lowell on *As the World Turns*, and was one of the actors to play Dr. Bruce Banning on CBS' long-running *The Guiding Light*.

DAMROSCH, WALTER (1862–1950). A major figure in American serious music, Damrosch conducted a symphony orchestra on the very first radio broadcast on NBC on 15 November 1926. He is best remembered today for the music education series, *The Music Appreciation Hour*, which he hosted. On this program, Damrosch conducted the orchestra in the playing of a piece of music after having explained the piece in detail. The program aired for 60 minutes each Friday morning, divided into segments for grammar school and high school students, and was a part of the curriculum in many schools. He also appeared with his orchestra on *The Symphonic Hour*, a 60-minute Sunday afternoon **concert music** program. At the age of 75, he wrote an opera, *The Man without a Country*. It was produced by The Met, and starred Helen Traubel in her debut role. Damrosch Park in Lincoln Center was named in honor of him and his family.

DANGEROUS ASSIGNMENT. This 30-minute **adventure program** appeared on NBC from 1949 to 1953 and then in syndication for another year. The network program starred Brian Donlevy, a major motion picture star of the time, as Steve Mitchell, a globe-trotting troubleshooter who would be sent to a different exotic locale each week. It was narrated in the first person by Donlevy. Lloyd Burrell played Steve Mitchell in the syndicated version.

DANNY KAYE SHOW (THE). Kaye was primarily a movie comedian, who starred in this 30-minute **comedy program** heard during 1945–1946. The program was written by **Goodman Ace**, among others, and featured a series of unrelated comic skits interspersed with musical interludes by one of the several bands that appeared during the run, including **Harry James**. The program had a cast of talented supporting actors, including **Jim Backus**, **Eve Arden**, and **Kenny Delmar**.

DATE WITH JUDY, (A). A 30-minute **situation comedy** that was broadcast during 1941–1950 featuring a "lovable teenage girl," *A Date with Judy* was much like other programs of the same type, highlighting comical problems with family and friends because of teenage enthusiasm or ineptness. In Judy's case, many of the plots revolved around arranging dates. Judy was originally played by 14-year-old Ann Gillis, who was replaced by Dellie Ellis the next year, and by Louise Erickson the year after that. The rest of the cast also changed considerably over the course of the run.

DAVE GARROWAY SHOW (THE). Although best known as the long-time host of the *Today* show on television, **Dave Garroway** hosted a series of similar variety programs on radio, beginning in 1949 and continuing until 1955, overlapping the time when he appeared on television. The shows appeared in a variety of time formats, ranging from 15-minutes to two hours, and under a variety of names, including *Reserved for Dave Garroway*, *Dial Dave Garroway*, and *Fridays with Dave Garroway*.

DAVID HARDING, COUNTERSPY. See COUNTERSPY.

DAVID HARUM. One of the many 15-minute daytime **soap operas** produced by **Frank and Anne Hummert**, *David Harum* appeared from 1936 to 1951, making several network changes and sometimes appearing concurrently on more than one network. David was a small-town banker and kindly philosopher who lived with his sister, Aunt Polly, and was everybody's friend. Harum's hobby was horses, and a contest to re-name his horse (which was named *Xanthippe*) drew more than 400,000 responses. The program was one of the first to feature premiums and they were extremely popular: an offer to send listeners a packet of seeds for 10 cents and a label from the sponsor's product drew 275,000 responses, which delighted sponsors and convinced many stations to carry the program.

DAVIS, ELMER (1890–1958). Davis was a news commentator who obtained a classical education at Franklin College in Indiana and was a Rhodes Scholar at Oxford. He was foreign correspondent and editorial writer for the *New York Times* from 1914 to 1924, then a freelance journalist and fiction writer. His first network show, *Elmer Davis and the News*, was on CBS from 1939 to 1942. At one time during this period, his audience was estimated at 12.5 million. He quit this job in 1942 to become director of the newly created **Office of War Information (OWI)**, which coordinated all government news and propaganda. When the war ended in 1945 and the OWI was dismantled, Davis returned to broadcasting. Until 1953, when high blood pressure forced him to retire, he delivered a 15-minute broadcast of news and analysis from Washington three times a week over ABC. In 1954, he had a Sunday television program of news commentary over ABC, but ill health again forced him to retire. He once described himself as a liberal, but said that he had no political affiliation, "as becomes a voteless resident of Washington."

DAVIS, JOAN (1907–1961). Joan Davis, whose real name was Madonna Josephine Davis, began her professional career on the stage as a child. She married comedian Si Wills in 1931 and teamed up with him in the vaudeville comedy act of Wills and Davis. She got her start on radio in 1941 when she appeared on *The Rudy Vallee Show*. She became a regular the following year and when Vallee joined the Coast Guard in 1943, she took over the show, which was renamed *The Sealtest Village Store*. Two years later, she left the show to star in her own program. At one point in her radio career, she was voted the top radio comedienne in a newspaper poll. In television, she co-starred with **Jim Backus** in the popular domestic situation comedy *I Married Joan*, owned by her own production company.

DAY IN THE LIFE OF DENNIS DAY (A). Sometimes listed as *The Dennis Day Show*, this 30-minute situation comedy starring the tenor and comedian featured on *The Jack Benny Program* was heard from 1946 to 1951. In the best-known version of his own program, Dennis Day played a singing soda jerk of the same name as his character on the Benny show, and of the same general type: a naive innocent who made a lot of wisecracks. Most of the plots centered around his problems with his girlfriend and her parents. Toward the end of the run, the program changed to a variety format. Day continued to perform on the Benny program throughout the run of his own show.

DAY, DENNIS (1917–1988). Born Owen Patrick McNulty, Day was an Irish Tenor who was the vocalist for **Jack Benny** for nearly three decades, first on radio and then on television. He became Benny's vocalist when **Kenny Baker** left Benny for **Fred Allen** in the late 1930s. Day sent a recording to Benny's wife, **Mary Livingstone**, was granted an audition, and won a two-week tryout on the program. In addition to *The Jack Benny Program*, Day appeared on *Ray Bloch's Varieties*, starred in his own program, *A Day in the Life of Dennis Day*, and appeared as a guest star on other programs. During the 1940s and 1950s, he also appeared in motion pictures, with and without Benny. Day and his wife raised 10 children.

DEATH VALLEY DAYS. A 30-minute drama anthology program heard from 1930 to 1944, *Death Valley Days* dramatized pioneer life in the western United States. The program early developed the introduction for which it was well known: a fading bugle call, over which announcer Dresser Dahlstead introduced the "Old Ranger," who then narrated the story to come. The first and best known of the Old Rangers was Jack MacBryde, although the role was later played by a number of others. In 1944, the program name and format changed to *Death Valley Sheriff*, introduced by the same bugle call, but featuring sheriff Mark Chase, a modern sheriff using automobiles rather than horses. The name of the program changed again the next year to *The Sheriff* and continued under that name until leaving the air in 1951.

DE FOREST, LEE (1873–1961). Lee De Forest was an American inventor, credited with the development of the audion, a type of vacuum tube and one of the breakthrough products in early radio. Graduating from Yale in 1899 with a Ph.D., De Forest patented his new type of tube in 1907. He admitted that he did not know how it worked, and was involved in a long series of lawsuits as technical developments by others were needed to make it practical. He was later involved in another very acrimonious and long-running lawsuit with **Edwin Armstrong** over the development of the regenerative circuit. In 1922, De Forest improved on the work of some German inventors and developed the Phonofilm process, which synchronized sound directly onto motion picture film.

Active in business as well as in the laboratory, De Forest built his own radio station and was responsible for several of the early demonstrations of radio broadcasting. His capitalization was insufficient to allow him to continue when network broadcasting arrived, however, and he sold his holdings to the **Radio Corporation of America (RCA)** in 1931.

DEHNER, JOHN (1915–1992). Dehner, who was born John Forkum on Staten Island, was a multi-talented person who began his acting career as a stage actor. He was also, at various times, an animator for Walt Disney, a disc jockey, a pianist, and General George Patton's publicist during World War II. He is best known to the public today for his many roles in motion pictures and on television. He appeared in his first movie in 1945, and had regular roles on 11 television series, beginning in 1960. Before turning to television, however, he also played an important role in the latter days of dramatic radio. He played the father, Elmer Truitt, on *The Truitts*; J. B. Kendall on *Frontier Gentleman*; and starred as Paladin, the professional gunman, on the radio version of *Have Gun, Will Travel.*

DEKOVEN, ROGER (1907–1988). DeKoven was an actor who specialized in roles on radio's afternoon soap operas. He was Professor Jason McKinley Allen on *Against the Storm*, the only daytime soap opera to win a **Peabody Award**. He also appeared on *Life Can Be Beautiful*, *Myrt and Marge*, *The O'Neills*, and *Stella Dallas*. He acted on *Gang Busters* and *The Mysterious Traveler*, and narrated *Famous Jury Trials*. A graduate of the Theatre Guild School, he was also active on Broadway.

DELEATH, VAUGHN (1894–1943). Although largely forgotten today, Vaughn DeLeath, whose real name was Leonore Vondeleith, was one of the earliest stars of broadcast radio and is believed by some authorities to have been the first woman to speak into a microphone for broadcast. In December 1919, she sang "Swanee River" without musical accompaniment over **Lee De Forest**'s experimental radio station. For the next 12 years, she was associated with radio either as an announcer, performer, or executive, and was at one time known as "The First Lady of Radio" and "The Original Radio Girl." Able to accompany herself on ukulele, banjo, guitar, or piano, she would sometimes perform for hours, an ability much valued in the early days of radio, when program material was scarce. She left entertainment entirely after 1931 and little is known of the last 10 years of her life, before her death in 1943.

DELMAR, KENNY (1910–1984). Delmar began his professional career touring the country with his mother and aunt's vaudeville act. By his late twenties, he was both acting and announcing, and was later one of the actors who played Commissioner Weston on *The Shadow*, as well as being a regular member of **Orson Welles'** *Mercury Theatre on the Air* (and performing on the famous "War of the Worlds" broadcast in 1938). He was best known as one of the residents of **Allen's Alley** on *The Fred Allen Show*, where he played the part of the bombastic Southerner, Senator Beauregard Claghorn.

As Claghorn, he was famous for his catchphrase "That's a joke, son!" He was also Allen's announcer. Delmar appeared in a few movies, and starred on television in 1949 as the harried teacher of a group of precocious children on *The School House.*

DeVOL, FRANK (1911–1999). DeVol's father was bandleader for the local vaudeville theater in Canton, Ohio, and Frank began playing in his father's band at the age of 14. He played the saxophone for several orchestras, including those of Horace Heidt and Alvino Rey, before appearing in programs on the **Don Lee Network**. **Rudy Vallee** hired him as a conductor in 1944 and DeVol later provided the music on the programs of other radio stars, including **Ginny Simms**, **Jack Carson**, and Dinah Shore. DeVol was also an executive with Columbia Records, and wrote and conducted music for several major motion pictures, including *Cat Ballou* (1965) and *Guess Who's Coming to Dinner* (1967), receiving five Oscar nominations for his scores. On television, he was the orchestra leader on several programs from 1954 to 1962 and received five Emmys for his TV themes and scores. He also acted on TV's *I'm Dickens—He's Fenster* and played bandleader Happy Kyne on *Fernwood 2-Night.* After the death of his first wife in the 1980s, DeVol married singer Helen O'Connell. The couple performed together on cruise ships until O'Connell's death in 1997.

DICK TRACY. A **juvenile adventure program** based on the popular comic strip by Chester Gould, *Dick Tracy* appeared in several different formats over a 14-year period. A 15-minute daily version appeared from 1935 to 1939, another 15-minute daily version ran from 1943 to 1948, and a 30-minute weekly version ran concurrently with the daily version during 1945–1946. All versions were peopled by the various characters appearing in the comic strip and the 1943–1948 version was opened by a burst of static, followed by Tracy's terse commands as he gave orders by wrist radio, an invention that figured prominently in the comic strip. There was considerable cast turnover, with at least three different actors playing the title role, including Ned Wever, Matt Crowley, and Barry Thomson. The Dick Tracy Club was very popular and the program offered many premiums, some of which are quite valuable today.

DICK TRACY IN B-FLAT. *See COMMAND PERFORMANCE.*

DIMENSION X. A high-quality 30-minute science fiction **drama anthology** heard on NBC in various time slots from April of 1950 to September of 1951, *Dimension X* was one of the first network programs to be produced on tape. The program utilized the finest radio actors and other radio personnel to dramatize stories by the greatest science fiction authors of the time, and the result was a series of programs that compare favorably with the best drama ever produced on radio. Some of the scripts were later re-enacted on a similar program, *X Minus One*, which aired from 1955 to 1958.

DINAH SHORE SHOW (THE). Dinah Shore was a popular vocalist who made her first appearance on radio on the **Ben Bernie Show** in 1939, and thereafter hosted several 15-minute programs. She became the regular singer on **The Eddie Cantor Show** in 1940, and her popularity increased until she was given her own 30-minute program, *Birdseye Open House*, in 1943. The name of her programs changed with sponsor changes, to *The Ford Show* in 1946 and *Call for Music* in 1948; but all were commonly referred to as *The Dinah Shore Show*. After leaving radio for television, her television program was simulcast on radio from 1953 to 1955.

DOBKIN, LARRY (1919–2002). Lawrence Dobkin began acting while still in high school, and later attended the Yale School of Drama. He starred in *The Adventures of Ellery Queen*, and *The Adventures of Nero Wolfe*, appeared in supporting roles on *The Man from Homicide* and *The Saint* and was the announcer/narrator on *Rocky Jordan*. On television, he played the director on *Mr. Adams and Eve*, a comedy starring **Howard Duff** and Ida Lupino as film stars. On TV and in the movies, Dobkin often wore wigs, having lost his hair to makeup poisoning early in his career.

DR. CHRISTIAN. An unusual 30-minute light drama heard from 1937 to 1954, *Dr. Christian* was originally based on a 1936 motion picture, *The Country Doctor*, starring **Jean Hersholt** as the physician who delivered the Dionne Quintuplets. Dr. Christian was a small-town physician, a kindly matchmaker, and a wise and gentle friend. His nurse, Judy, began each program by answering the telephone "Dr. Christian's Office" and the show was sometimes listed by that name. In 1942, the program began a contest to solicit scripts from listeners and the response was overwhelming; as many as 10,000 scripts were received in some years. The program was renamed *The Vaseline Program* and it was eventually written entirely by listeners. Hersholt played the title role for the entire run; Judy was played by several actresses, but usually by **Lurene Tuttle** (1937–1943) or Rosemary DeCamp (1943–1954).

DR. I.Q. One of the first of the great radio **quiz programs**, *Dr. I.Q.* was a very fast-paced 30-minute weekly program that traveled the country, broadcasting from motion-picture theaters in various cities, staying in each locale only a few weeks. Six assistants roamed the theater, selecting contestants from among the audience who were asked a question by Dr. I.Q., winners being awarded small prizes in silver dollars. The contestant had only 10 seconds to answer and typically 35 to 40 contestants would appear in a 30-minute show. The program was on the air from 1939 to 1950. For much of that time, Lew Valentine was the quizmaster, although Jimmy McClain held the role during 1942–1946, while Valentine served in the Army during World War II.

DONALD, PETER (1918–1979). A British-born dialect specialist, Donald started in radio as a child; by age 12, he was a regular cast member on a network **children's program**, *The Lady Next Door*. Donald is known to today's radio enthusiasts primarily as the host of the panel comedy program *Can You Top This?* and as **Allen's Alley** resident Ajax Cassidy (who was "not long for this world") on *The Fred Allen Show*. In 1949, he also starred in his own three-times-a-week daytime show, *Talk Your Way Out of It*, on ABC. In addition to his comedy work, Donald appeared on several radio dramas. He moved to television in the 1950s, appearing as a host, panelist, and/or emcee on a variety of network quiz programs.

DON LEE NETWORK (THE). Don Lee was a Cadillac dealer in California who was the owner of radio stations KHJ in Los Angeles and KFRC in San Francisco. In 1928, he set up a wire-line connection between his two stations and three West coast stations belonging to the McClatchy newspaper syndicate, to establish the first Don Lee Network. The next year, he entered an agreement with the **Columbia Broadcasting System (CBS)** and the Don Lee stations became the

West Coast outlet for CBS, as the Don Lee–Columbia Network. The network expanded considerably and was quite successful but there was friction with CBS because the Don Lee stations wanted more programming autonomy than CBS was willing to grant. In 1936, the former McClatchy stations broke away to affiliate with the **National Broadcasting Company (NBC)** and the Don Lee Network joined the **Mutual Broadcasting System**. The Mutual–Don Lee Broadcasting System was inaugurated on 30 December 1936 and the arrangement continued after the Don Lee Network became a stockholder in the Mutual Broadcasting System in 1940. In 1951, the Don Lee Network was sold to General Teleradio, which later merged into RKO Pictures to form RKO General.

DON WINSLOW OF THE NAVY. A 15-minute daily **juvenile adventure program** based on the comic strip by Frank Martinek, *Don Winslow of the Navy* was heard during 1937–1939 and was then off the air until 1942, when it appeared for a brief final run. Don Winslow was a naval commander, assigned to Naval Intelligence, along with his friend, Lt. Red Pennington. Motion picture serials were also based on the same character. Bob Guilbert was the original Don Winslow, but in the 1942 series, the role was played by **Raymond Edward Johnson**.

DOUBLE OR NOTHING. A 30-minute weekly **quiz program** heard from 1940 to 1947, *Double or Nothing* became a daily daytime program and ran from 1947 to 1954. Although changing slightly over the years, the essence of the format was a series of questions, each of which was worth twice as much as the preceding question. The contestant could stop at any point and take what had been won, or continue to the next question, risking losing all for a chance to win twice as much. The actual prizes were small compared to other quiz programs; the attraction of the show was the ad-libbing of the various hosts, and the humorous answers sometimes given by contestants. There were several different hosts, although the first was Walter Compton, and the longest-running was **Walter O'Keefe**, who hosted the program during its entire daytime run.

DOWNEY, MORTON (1901–1985). Downey was an Irish tenor who began his professional singing career in the early 1920s. As a youth he sang at amusement parks, in clubs and restaurants, and at political rallys until discovered by **Paul Whiteman**. Known as "The Irish Thrush," Downey in 1931 was described by *Variety* as the most popular new voice on radio. He became the Camel Minstrel Boy in 1931, and his signature song was "Wabash Moon." He appeared on many radio programs, and starred in *The Morton Downey Show* and in *Songs by Morton Downey*. He appeared on music and variety series on television in the late 1940s and early 1950s, until retiring from singing in the mid-1950s. One of his sons, Morton Downey, Jr., became a popular and controversial talk show host and disc jockey.

DOYLE, LEN (1893–1959). Leonard Doyle was a Broadway actor, director, and producer who attended the American Academy of Dramatic Arts and acted in stock in Pennsylvania before making his debut on the stage at age seventeen. He was best known in radio for his role as "ace detective" Harrington on *Mr. District Attorney*, a popular **crime program** heard from 1939 to 1953. Doyle played Harrington for 13 years, 11 on radio and then two on television in the mid-1950s.

DRAGNET. The greatest of all the **crime programs** ever to appear on radio, *Dragnet* was a 30-minute weekly program that was heard from 1949 to 1957, with the last part of the run being repeats of earlier programs. The intention of the program was to present criminal investigations in as realistic a setting as possible and the plots were taken from police files. Dialogue contained a great deal of authentic police lingo, and police procedure was followed as closely as possible. Sergeant Joe Friday was played by **Jack Webb**, who created and directed the show. His partner Ben Romero was played by radio veteran **Barton Yarborough** until his death in 1951; Ben Alexander became Friday's partner, Frank Smith, the next year. The program moved to television in 1951, with almost no change in format or personnel.

DRAGON, CARMEN (1914–1987). Dragon, a protégé of **Meredith Willson**, initially went to Hollywood as an arranger and won an Oscar for his scoring of the 1944 musical *Cover Girl*. He arranged and conducted music for radio's *The Passing Parade*, *Maxwell House Coffee Time*, *The Old Gold Program*, and *The Baby Snooks Show*, among others. His longest stint on radio was on *The Railroad Hour* where he and his orchestra provided the music from 1949-1954. His son Daryl was the "Captain" in the popular musical act, "The Captain and Tennille."

DRAGONETTE, JESSICA (1904–1980). Jessica Dragonette was a soprano who was a great favorite of early radio listeners, beginning with guest appearances on *General Motors Family Party* in 1926. She is credited with popularizing operetta and semiclassical music on radio, and in 1935 was voted Radio's Favorite Woman Star. She starred on *The Philco Hour* from 1927 to 1929, and sang 75 different roles during the two and a half years. She was later heard on *Cities Service Concerts*, the *Palmolive Beauty Box Theater*, and *Saturday Night Serenade*. Dragonette was decorated by Pope Pius XII, made an honorary colonel in the air force in recognition of her war work, and published her autobiography, *Faith is a Song,* in 1967.

DRAMA ANTHOLOGY PROGRAMS. In addition to the light entertainment fare provided by the crime and adventure dramas, there were attempts on radio to produce higher-quality drama, and some were quite successful, utilizing the best writers and performers from radio, stage, and motion pictures.

The Lux Radio Theater began in 1934, with adaptations of both motion pictures and Broadway plays. After originating from New York for the first two years, the program moved to Hollywood, where Cecil B. DeMille became the host; the biggest names in Hollywood starred in radio adaptations of their movies.

There were also some excellent drama anthology programs that were not related to motion pictures, such as *Cavalcade of America*, which dramatized events in the life histories of famous Americans, and *Theatre Guild on the Air*, which presented radio adaptations of stage productions. *Hallmark Playhouse* presented dramatizations of lesser-known but critically acclaimed novels, and *The First Nighter* presented light three-act plays in a context that pretended the listener was attending a small off-Broadway theater. Several programs presented original dramas by repertory companies, and the best-known single radio program of all time, "War of the Worlds," was produced by one of these, *Mercury Theatre on the Air.*

Some of the most popular drama anthologies were dedicated to suspense or crime stories. One of the best known, *Suspense*, ran for 20 years, from 1942 until the very end of old-time radio. It was a high-budget production with top performers, directors, and writers, and another famous individual program, "Sorry, Wrong Number," was an episode of this series. *Escape* was a program similar to *Suspense*, as was *Lights Out*, although the latter tended more toward horror stories and was noted for particularly grisly sound effects.

None of the drama anthologies had continuing characters or plots; often the only element common between programs was the introduction, which was sometimes very distinctive. *Inner Sanctum Mysteries* is remembered primarily for the creaking door that opened to the narrator who told morbid jokes at the beginning of the program; the programs themselves were less memorable. *The Whistler* introduced a spooky narrator with echoing footsteps and a whistled melody that grew gradually louder until it blended into an orchestral background. The melody was strange (and extremely difficult) but neither footsteps, melody, nor narrator played any direct part in the stories that followed.

DUFF, HOWARD (1913–1990). Duff's network radio career began in the 1940s on **soap operas**, including *Dear John* in 1941. He left radio work for military service during World War II, and was attached to the **Armed Forces Radio Service** as a correspondent. After the war, his radio career soared when his rich voice won him the starring role of Sam Spade on *The Adventures of Sam Spade*. He left the show when it moved to NBC in 1950, and took the part of Mike McCoy on *The McCoy*, a similar detective role. His film debut was in *Brute Force* in 1947, and he went on to play mostly tough-guy movie roles throughout the 1950s. He also had a successful television career, appearing on many dramatic anthology programs and starring in several series, beginning in 1957 with *Mr. Adams and Eve* (with his wife, actress Ida Lupino). Duff's last regular TV role was during 1984–1985 as Paul Galveston on the prime time soap opera *Knots Landing*.

DUFFY'S TAVERN. A 30-minute **situation comedy** appearing from 1941 to 1952, *Duffy's Tavern* began with the ringing of a telephone at the tavern and Archie's famous opening line: "Hello, Duffy's Tavern, where the elite meet to eat. Archie the manager speaking.

Duffy ain't here." Duffy was never there, only Archie and a collection of characters, including Duffy's daughter, who populated the bar. Duffy called every week, although listeners only heard Archie's side of the conversation. Archie was played by **Ed Gardner**, who had conceived the program, and Miss Duffy was originally played by his wife, Shirley Booth. After Booth left the show in 1943, Miss Duffy was played by several actresses, beginning with **Florence Halop**.

DUNNINGER, JOSEPH (1892–1975). Billed as the "Master Mind of Mental Mystery," Dunninger started as a magic act in vaudeville, and later appeared in theaters and clubs. In the 1920s, he was a close friend of magician Harry Houdini, and was even asked to perform before presidents. His program, *Dunninger, the Mentalist*, appeared on ABC in 1943 and became quite popular. The program was also known as *Dunninger, The Master Mind* and *The Dunninger Show*. Dunninger claimed he could read minds 97 percent of the time, and throughout his long career had a standing offer of $10,000 to anyone who could prove he used accomplices in his act. Although there were always rumors of trickery, no one ever collected the reward. He co-hosted (with ventriloquist Paul Winchell) television's *The Bigelow Show* during 1948–1949 and hosted his own TV program on ABC, *The Dunninger Show*, during the summers of 1955 and 1956.

DURANTE, JIMMY (1893–1980). Before James Francis Durante became one of the most famous and best-loved entertainers of the 20th century, he was a hot piano player and band leader who made several records in the early days of jazz. In vaudeville, he teamed with Lou Clayton and Eddie Jackson to form a comedy team called "Clayton, Jackson, and Durante." Durante was known as "schnozzola" because of his large nose, which was often the topic of jokes, both in vaudeville and later on radio and television. He had a long career in radio, beginning in 1935 when he starred as the press agent for a circus in *Jumbo*. He later co-starred with **Garry Moore** on *The Camel Caravan*, sponsored by Camel cigarettes, with the show known on alternate weeks as the *Garry Moore–Jimmy Durante Show* and the *Jimmy Durante–Garry Moore Show*. In 1945, Rexall became the sponsor, and the show was called both *The Rexall Drug Program* and *The Jimmy Durante Show*. From 1950 to 1970, Durante hosted several television programs, receiving an Emmy Award as Best

Television Comedian in 1952. He made his film debut in 1930, and appeared in his last movie, *It's a Mad Mad Mad Mad Mad World*, in 1963. Durante suffered a stroke in 1972 and retired from the entertainment business.

– E –

EAST AND DUMKE. Although primarily a 15-minute program of songs, chatter, and humorous advice to homemakers, Ed East and Ralph Dumke also featured satirical skits of the sort later done by **Bob and Ray**. Appearing from 1930 to 1938, the program was also known as *Sisters of the Skillet* and *The Quality Twins*. East and Dumke were both large men, who had been featured in vaudeville as "The Mirthquakers." After the team broke up in 1938, East teamed with his wife, Polly Smith, for *Ed East and Polly* during 1943–1944, a 30-minute afternoon audience participation show similar in format to *House Party*. East and his wife also originated and hosted a similar program, *Ladies Be Seated*, in 1944.

EASY ACES. A comedic dialogue between **Goodman Ace** and his real-life wife, Jane, *Easy Aces* was written by Ace, who later became one of the most successful writers in radio and television. The program purported to present the daily life of the Aces and their friends. Jane played the part of a Midwestern bubblehead and was famous for malapropisms ("We are all cremated equal"). A 15-minute program from 1932 to 1943, the program changed to a 30-minute weekly show during 1943–1945 and was heard for two more years in syndication, as old shows were recycled. In 1948, the Aces appeared in a **situation comedy** called *Mr. Ace and Jane*.

EDDIE CANTOR SHOW (THE). Eddie Cantor, whose real name was Edward Iskowitz, was the first of the major vaudeville stars to transition to radio, hosting his own comedy–variety program in 1931. He was a comedian famous for his bulging eyes, which were a trademark, much like the nose of **Jimmy Durante**. Over the next 18 years, he hosted *The Chase and Sanborn Hour*, *The Camel Caravan*, and *Time to Smile*; most of these programs also known as *The Eddie Cantor Show* when he was the host. In addition to showcasing new talent, including the first network appearance of **Gracie Allen**, Cantor's show had a number of regular performers who later became very well known, including Dinah Shore and **Bert Gordon**, who played a comic character called The Mad Russian. Cantor's was the first major radio program to use live audiences because he thought laughter would reach out to the audiences at home. His marriage to Ida Tobias lasted 48 years, and he mentioned her and their daughters frequently on his program. His **comedy program** left the air in 1949, but he later hosted a disc jockey program from 1951 to 1954. He made many movies, and was given a special Academy Award in 1956 for his contributions to the film industry. *The Eddie Cantor Story*, released in 1953, was a film biography starring Keefe Brasselle in the title role.

EDDY DUCHIN SHOW (THE). Eddy Duchin was a popular pianist and orchestra leader remembered for his elegant style and his courageous fight against leukemia. He was very influential in the development of the "sweet" bands of the 1930s and 1940s; Carmen Cavallero acknowledged his influence. Duchin's first program was heard in 1933, and he was on the air more or less continuously until entering the Navy during World War II. He returned in 1947 with a program called *A Date with Duchin*, but died four years later. His son Peter became a successful pianist and orchestra leader.

EDGAR BERGEN–CHARLIE MCCARTHY SHOW (THE). Ventriloquist **Edgar Bergen** and his wisecracking dummy, Charlie McCarthy, first appeared on Rudy Vallee's *Royal Gelatin Hour* in 1936. As a result of their success on the show, they became the headliners on NBC's *The Chase and Sanborn Hour* in 1937, where they remained until 1948. They moved to CBS in 1949 and remained on the air until 1956, under various sponsors. Over the years, *The Edgar Bergen–Charlie McCarthy Show* featured top line comedians, musicians, and actors, including W. C. Fields, Nelson Eddy, and Dorothy Lamour; **Don Ameche** and **Frances Langford** originated their famous skit, *The Bickersons*, on the program. Bergen added another dummy to his act in 1940, the dopey Mortimer Snerd; in 1944, he added a third, the man-crazy Effie Klinker. Bandleader Ray Noble was an important part of the program, contributing wisecracks in a dry English accent.

EDWARDS, RALPH (1913–2005). Edwards worked as an announcer on the West Coast until the mid-1930s, then hitchhiked to New York to break into the big time. By 1936, he had jobs at both NBC and CBS and was announcing nearly 50 shows each week. He came up with the idea of an audience participation contest, based on "penalty" stunts, and this program, *Truth or Consequences*, made its debut on CBS on 23 March 1940. The show was an instant hit, and after a long run on radio, Edwards took the program to television in 1950. His second hit program, *This Is Your Life*, was created for radio in 1948 and moved to TV in 1952. Edwards also produced several other game shows over the course of his long career in the entertainment business.

EINSTEIN, HARRY. *See MEET ME AT PARKY'S.*

ELLIOT, WIN (1915–1998). Elliot, whose real name was Irwin Elliot Shalek, studied radio writing and announcing at the University of Michigan. His network-hosting career began with *Musical Mysteries* on NBC in 1944, and the same year he also began the CBS audience-participation show *Fish Pond*. After service in the Merchant Marines, he was on *County Fair* on CBS (1946–1950) and *Quick as a Flash* on Mutual (1948–1951). Later, he worked on the quizzes *Winner Take All* and *Break the Bank*. On the sports front, Elliot announced for *The Gillette Cavalcade of Sports* for a dozen years. On television, he announced on *Fireside Theatre*, emceed two quiz programs (*Tic Tac Dough* and his own creation, *Win with a Winner*) and was a commentator on the bowling series *Make That Spare* (1961–1962). Elliot was also heard regularly on radio sports roundup shows into the 1980s.

ELLIOTT, BOB (1923–). Elliott and his partner **Ray Goulding** comprised the comedy team of **Bob and Ray**. They appeared on network radio from 1951 to 1960 and were heard on public radio as late as 1987. Elliott worked as an usher at Radio City Music Hall and as a page at NBC and his first on-air assignment was on a weekly show at WINS described as "a page boy's impressions of radio." After his military service, he met newscaster Goulding at WHDH in Boston and they discovered they were kindred souls as far as comedy was concerned; the result was *Matinee with Bob and Ray*. They performed their special brand of offbeat satirical humor for the next 40-odd years on various networks and in various formats. They received a **Peabody Award** as the foremost satirists on radio in 1951, and again in 1957 for radio entertainment.

ELSA MAXWELL'S PARTY LINE. Elsa Maxwell was reputed to be the world's greatest party giver. Her program was not about parties, however, it was a gossipy 15-minute program heard from 1942 to 1947, on which she told stories about famous people she had met. She was very heavy, and at one time undertook a diet on the air, weighing herself using a special scale operated by announcer **Graham McNamee**. Ms. Maxwell's program was sponsored by Ry-Krisp, a kind of cracker that was promoted as an aid in dieting.

ELSTNER, ANNE (1899–1981). Elstner began her radio career in 1923 by recreating a scene from a Broadway play on radio. In 1930, she obtained a permanent part in *Moonshine and Honeysuckle*, a 30-minute weekly serial drama based on the lives of mountain people in the little Southern town of Lonesome Hollow. She was later a part of the cast of several programs, but she is most famous for the title role in the **soap opera** *Stella Dallas*. Elstner played Stella for the entire duration of the program, from 1938 to 1955. She was one of the group of highly skilled professionals who performed in many of the daytime serial dramas originating in New York and, in spite of her close identification with *Stella Dallas*, she once claimed to be appearing on as many as 10 shows every day. In retirement, Elster operated a restaurant in New Jersey.

ENO CRIME CLUB (THE). Named for the sponsor, Eno Effervescent Salts, the Eno Crime Club first appeared in February of 1931 and was one of the earliest of the radio detective dramas. Originally a 15-minute daily program based on the Crime Club novels (a series of monthly crime novels), the format changed to 30-minutes twice-weekly in 1932, with each story complete in two parts. In the 1933–1936 version, the name was changed to *Eno Crime Clues*, and featured the adventures of Spencer Dean, called "The Manhunter." Dean was played by Edward Roose and later by Clyde North. His partner Dan Cassidy was played by Jack MacBryde. The program was written by Stewart Sterling. *See also* CRIME PROGRAMS.

ERSKINE JOHNSON'S HOLLYWOOD. Erskine Johnson was a Hollywood entertainment columnist who hosted a series of short programs of entertainment gossip from 1942 to 1950. The programs appeared on several different networks and had different names on each network, including *Hollywood Spotlight* and *Tonight in Hollywood*, as well as *Erskine Johnson's Hollywood*. One of the features of the latter program was a "confession" portion on which celebrities revealed harmless secrets about their private lives, such as their food preferences or their hobbies.

ESCAPE. A high-quality 30-minute dramatic adventure anthology, *Escape* was heard in many different time slots on CBS from 1947 to 1954. The early programs were dramatizations of classic fiction, but original scripts were later incorporated. The program featured some of the finest actors and writers in radio and many of the programs were so well received that they were later repeated on the CBS sister program, ***Suspense***. *See also* DRAMA ANTHOLOGY PROGRAMS.

ETHEL AND ALBERT. A 15-minute daily comedic program heard from 1944 to 1950, *Ethel and Albert* was the story of a young couple living in the small town of Sandy Harbor. The program consisted primarily of dialogue between the couple; the first voice other than Ethel and Albert heard on the program was that of Baby Susy, a daughter born to them in 1946. Richard Widmark was the first Albert, but left after six months. Alan Bunce played the role for the remainder of the run, as well as for three seasons on television. Ethel was played by Peg Lynch, who was also the creator and writer of the program. Baby Susy was played by Madeleine Pierce.

EVANS, DALE (1912–2001). Born Frances Octavia Smith in Uvalde, Texas, Evans was a singer of popular music before she co-starred with her future husband, Roy Rogers, in the movie *The Cowboy and the Senorita* (1944). Other movies together followed, and she and Rogers married in 1947. On radio, Evans was on ***The Roy Rogers Show*** from 1948 to 1955. She had previously been the featured vocalist on ***The Chase and Sanborn Hour***. On television, Evans played herself on *The Roy Rogers Show* from 1951 to 1957, and then co-starred with her husband on *The Roy Rogers and Dale Evans Show* in 1962. A songwriter as well as a singer, in 1947, she wrote "Happy Trails to You," the theme song she and her husband sang at the end of their program. During her later years, she was active in charitable organizations, receiving several public service awards.

EVEREADY HOUR (THE). *The Eveready Hour* was the first major **variety program** to appear on network radio. It was first broadcast over WEAF New York in 1923, before there were any networks, and then was heard on NBC from 1926 to 1930. It was a true variety program, featuring drama, news, music, and comedy. The stars of the program made nationwide tours, appearing on local stations not served by the networks. Top headliners of the Broadway stage made guest appearances, including **Eddie Cantor** and Will Rogers.

– F –

FADIMAN, CLIFTON (1904–1999). Clifton Paul "Kip" Fadiman was a 1925 graduate of Columbia University, worked as an editor at Simon and Schuster from 1929–1935 and as a book reviewer for *The New Yorker* from 1933–1943. His radio career began in 1931 as a book reviewer on the *Book Report*. In 1938, he became moderator of the popular **quiz program**, *Information, Please*, where he remained until the program went off the air in 1951. During the 1940s, *Information, Please* was hailed as one of the best programs on the air. The program and Fadiman both moved to television in 1952, but the TV show lasted only one season. Fadiman later emceed several other quiz and variety programs on TV, including *The Quiz Kids* in 1956. In the mid-1950s, he was the host on *Conversation*, an NBC Sunday evening talk program.

FALCON (THE). *The Falcon* was a 30-minute detective drama based on a character created by Michael Arlen in a short story in 1940. In the literary version, the main character's name was Gay Stanhope Falcon; the radio program was heard from 1943 to 1954 and changed both the plot and the name of the lead character. It originally featured James Meighan as Michael Waring, a private detective and insurance investigator who referred to himself as The Falcon in his dealings with the underworld. Later in the series, during the period when **Les**

Damon was playing the title role, The Falcon became an American intelligence agent, working on espionage cases in foreign countries. A series of movies based on the same character began in 1941 with George Sanders in the title role, again changing the name of the lead character. There was also a brief syndicated television series of the same name, but with further changes to the character and the plot.

FAMILY THEATER (THE). A 30-minute **drama anthology** created and hosted by a Catholic priest, Father Patrick Peyton, *The Family Theater* promoted prayer as a vehicle for world peace and personal satisfaction. The program appeared from 1947 to 1956 and was essentially a high-quality drama anthology; the stories were not specifically religious or dogmatic, although they often were uplifting. The program was unsponsored, with the Mutual network donating the time. A major Hollywood star appeared each week; Bing Crosby was on the first show and Loretta Young appeared more than 30 times during the show's long run.

FAMOUS JURY TRIALS. A **drama anthology** program presenting dramatized versions of actual trials, *Famous Jury Trials* was heard from 1936 to 1949. The show was ahead of its time in the development of the technique of supposedly transporting the listener back in time to be present at the trial as it transpired, with a reporter–narrator offering comments and bridging between sections of the trial. Maurice Franklin played the part of the judge.

FAT MAN (THE). A 30-minute weekly detective drama heard from 1946 to 1951, *The Fat Man* was based on a character created by Dashiell Hammett, although the radio version did not at all resemble the original Hammett character. The radio Fat Man was Brad Runyon, a private detective who weighed 237 pounds. Each episode began with Runyon stepping on a scale and having his weight announced aloud. The lead role was played by **J. Scott Smart**, an actor who in real life weighed 270 pounds.

FATHER COUGHLIN. Charles Edward Coughlin was a Catholic priest and the pastor of the Shrine of the Little Flower in Royal Oak, Michigan. He hosted a radio program heard locally in Detroit, Chicago, and Cincinnati, before moving to CBS in 1930. Dropped by the network the next year, Coughlin bought time on local stations and formed his own radio chain, gradually increasing his coverage until he was heard almost everywhere in the nation. He became known as both "The Fighting Priest" and "The Radio Priest" and, at one time during the 1930s, had a radio audience of 40 million listeners. He paid for the air time from contributions sent in by listeners. His speeches were radical and inflammatory; he was pro-Hitler and anti-Semitic, as was his magazine, *Social Justice*; but a poll in 1934 showed that, after the president, he was considered the most important public figure in the United States. The popularity of the program declined in the early 1940s, and under church pressure, Father Coughlin left the air in 1942.

FATHER KNOWS BEST. A 30-minute **situation comedy** about the lives of an average American family, *Father Knows Best* is best remembered as a very successful television program; but it was heard on radio from 1949 to 1953, before migrating to television in 1954. Jim Anderson, an insurance agent in an average American town, was played by Robert Young, who also played the part when the program moved to television.

FAYE, ALICE (1912–1998). Born Alice Jeanne Leppert in New York, Faye was spotted in the chorus line of a 1931 Broadway production by **Rudy Vallee**, who signed her to tour with his band as a singer. Her first film role was in 1934 in *George White's Scandals*, and she subsequently became a major movie star. She was married (1936–1940) to singer Tony Martin, whom she met when both appeared in the movie *Sing, Baby, Sing* in 1938. After their divorce, a friend and movie co-star, comedian Jack Oakie, introduced her to bandleader **Phil Harris** and she and Harris were married in 1941. In 1946, with two young daughters to raise, she gave up her movie career to star on radio with her husband. Their program, a **situation comedy** about their home life in Hollywood, was titled *The Phil Harris–Alice Faye Show* and ran on NBC from 1948 to 1954. Ms. Faye once said in a television interview that she wanted to move their show to TV after its radio run but that Harris was against it, arguing that there were too many similar programs already on television.

FBI IN PEACE AND WAR (THE). A 30-minute **crime program** heard from 1944 to 1958, *The FBI in Peace and War* was inspired by the Frederick L. Collins book of the same name, although the scripts for the program were written primarily by Louis Pelletier and Jack Finke. The Federal Bureau of Investigation (FBI) was represented by Field Agent Sheppard, played by Martin Blaine. The program was not sanctioned by the FBI and did not claim to be presenting actual cases from the files of the Bureau. Each episode ended with the disclaimer that later became virtually standard on other programs: "any similarity to persons living or dead is purely coincidental." One of the best-remembered features of the early years of the program are the commercials for Lava Soap, with a deep male voice spelling out the name of the sponsor to the accompaniment of a bass drum.

FELTON, VERNA (1890–1966). Verna Felton began her radio career with appearances on *Death Valley Days* in the 1930s and then played important continuing roles on many of the top programs of the 1940s and early 1950s. She was a regular on such programs as *The Sealtest Village Store*, *The Rudy Vallee Show*, *The Red Skelton Show*, and *The Jack Benny Program*. On television in the 1950s and early 1960s, she played continuing characters on *The RCA Victor Show*, *December Bride*, and *Pete and Gladys*. In the movies, she usually played next-door neighbors and/or busybodies. As a voice actress, she was Wilma's mother on television's *The Flintstones*; she also had a 25-year career providing voices for Disney's animated movies, starting with *Dumbo* in 1941.

FENNELLY, PARKER (1891–1988). Known principally for his portrayal of elderly characters, Fennelly began on radio in the late 1920s on *Soconyland Sketches*, where he often played the character Hiram Neville. On *The Fred Allen Show*, he had his most memorable role, that of Titus Moody, the "Howdy, Bub" resident of **Allen's Alley**. Fennelly also appeared on many other radio shows over the years, including *Grand Central Station*, *The Aldrich Family*, and *Cavalcade of America*. On television, he played Mr. Purdy, the custodian, on CBS's *Headmaster*, starring Andy Griffith. Fennelly was also the longtime TV spokesman for Pepperidge Farm.

FENNEMAN, GEORGE (1919–1997). The good-natured radio and television foil of **Groucho Marx** on *You Bet Your Life* was born in Peking, China, where his father was an accountant for an import–export company. When he was nine months old, his parents moved to San Francisco, where he grew up, and after graduation from San Francisco State College, he was hired as an announcer by a local San Francisco radio station. He later moved to Los Angeles and while announcing at KGO was hired as the announcer for Groucho's new game show. He remained with the program from 1947 to 1960 on radio and from 1950 to 1962 on television. Fenneman also was the announcer on the radio and TV versions of *Dragnet*. On television he hosted *Anybody Can Play* and *Your Funny, Funny Films* and was the announcer on *Tell It to Groucho* in 1962 and *Donny and Marie* from 1976 to 1979. He also did many radio and TV commercials over the years and was the television spokesman for Home Savings of America for 17 years.

FESSENDEN, REGINALD (1866–1932). Fessenden was a Canadian inventor who is credited with the major technological breakthrough of superimposing voice or music information on a high-frequency carrier. His persistent work along these lines led to what many experts regard as the first radio broadcast, from Brant Rock, Massachusetts, on Christmas Eve in 1906. On the broadcast, Fessenden played his violin while his wife sang Christmas carols. The "high-frequency alternator" used was actually developed by others in the late 1880s, but Fessenden is credited with being the first person to apply it to radio communication.

FIBBER MCGEE AND MOLLY. One of the most popular and long-running programs of all time, *Fibber McGee and Molly* was a 30-minute **situation comedy** heard from 1935 to 1956, with some short vignettes later heard on the weekend program *Monitor* until 1959. Fibber and Molly were Jim Jordan and his wife Marian, who had begun their careers in vaudeville and on the radio in the Chicago area. In 1929, they began to use the material of a young writer named **Don Quinn**, and with him created a program called *Smackout* that first appeared on NBC in 1931, with Jordan and his wife each playing dozens of roles. In 1935, *Smackout* morphed into *Fibber McGee and Molly*, with many of the same characters. The program originally featured a couple who traveled over the country but after a few weeks Fibber won a house in a raffle and 79 Wistful Vista became the site of the program and one of the most famous addresses in America. The program each week was essentially a series of visitors to the

McGee home, many of whom became famous in their own right and several of whom spun off to their own shows, including *The Great Gildersleeve* and *Beulah*. McGee's junk-filled closet was as famous as many of the characters, with the contents crashing down on anyone unwary enough to open the door. The program was also known as *The Johnson's Wax Program*.

FIDLER, JIMMY (1900–1988). Fidler was a radio gossip commentator who headlined a 15-minute program that appeared on several different networks from 1933 to 1951. He was often forced to change networks because he was very plain spoken and would not edit his comments about powerful figures in the film industry. On his show, he "dished the dirt" about members of the Hollywood community to an estimated 20 million listeners. At one time, his program was known as *Hollywood on the Air* and went out over 500 stations each week. He also rated movies, awarding four bells to those he considered excellent, one bell to those he considered terrible. Fidler, a former silent movie actor under the name of James Marion, also wrote a gossip column that appeared in more than 300 newspapers in the early 1950s.

FIRE CHIEF (THE). Also known as *The Texaco Fire Chief*, and as *Ed Wynn, The Fire Chief*, this 30-minute **comedy program** was heard from 1932 to 1935 and starred **Ed Wynn**, a famous vaudeville comic who had also starred in several Broadway productions. The "Fire Chief" title refers to an advertising symbol used by Texaco Gasoline, the sponsor of the program. Wynn was really more a clown than a comic, and he performed in costume and full makeup, trading comments with **Graham McNamee**, who was the announcer and co-star.

FIRESIDE CHATS. The fireside chats were informal radio reports given by President Franklin D. Roosevelt, on which he discussed happenings in the government and in the world. He had a relaxed style that was a great comfort to listeners who were worried about the important issues that he discussed. The broadcasts took place from 1933 to 1944, essentially the entire term of his presidency, and were hugely popular; he was once voted the most popular personality on radio. The president was usually announced by **Robert Trout**, and the broadcasts were heard on all networks.

FIRST NIGHTER (THE). A 30-minute **drama anthology** that presented light drama in three acts, *The First Nighter* was heard from 1930 to 1953. In the introduction, the host, "Mr. First Nighter," strolled to "the little theater off Times Square" to the accompaniment of traffic and crowd noises. He was seated in the fourth row, center, where he read aloud the program for the night as an introduction to the play. Mr. First Nighter was played by several people over the long run, including Charles Hughes, Macdonald Carey, and **Marvin Miller**. **Don Ameche** was the male lead of the repertory company until 1936, **Les Tremayne** from 1936 to 1943, and **Olan Soule** thereafter.

FITCH BANDWAGON (THE). *The Fitch Bandwagon*, named for the sponsor, Fitch Shampoo, began in 1938 as a showcase for visiting orchestras and guest stars. In 1944, the program format shifted, with Dick Powell as the singing host and Andy Devine as a regular cast member. The next year, **Cass Daley** became a feature of the program, presenting several related comedy skits each week, separated by performances by guest orchestras. In 1946, her place was taken by **Phil Harris** and **Alice Faye** and the program became essentially a **situation comedy**, with brief musical interludes. The program was last heard in 1948, after which Harris and Faye left to star in their own program, *The Phil Harris–Alice Faye Show.*

FITZGERALDS (THE). A breakfast-time discussion program hosted by a husband-and-wife team, *The Fitzgeralds* was first heard locally in New York for several years before appearing on ABC in 1945. Both Ed and Pegeen Fitzgerald were New York radio personalities, hosting talk programs of various kinds, and these were merged into a single morning program, completely unscripted, at which they discussed current events, happenings in New York, or anything else that took their fancy. Their stay on the network was only until 1947, but they remained on local New York radio until 1982. Their program was instrumental in establishing the husband-and-wife breakfast format that was very popular throughout the nation for several years. *See also* TALK AND INFORMATION PROGRAMS.

FLEISCHMANN YEAST HOUR (THE). *See RUDY VALLEE SHOW (THE).*

FLEMING, SIR JOHN AMBROSE (1849–1945). An English electrical engineer and physicist, Fleming was a consultant to the Marconi Wireless Telegraph Company and later to the Edison Electric Light Company. In 1904, he invented and patented a two-electrode radio rectifier, which he called the oscillation valve, subsequently often referred to as the "Fleming Valve." Used to detect wireless signals, this invention is often considered to have been the beginning of electronics. In 1906, **Lee De Forest** added a control grid to the valve to create a vacuum tube called the audion, leading Fleming to accuse him of plagiarism. Fleming's research contributed to several scientific fields, and he was knighted in 1929.

FLYNN, BERNARDINE (1904–1977). After majoring in speech in college, where she acted in plays with fellow student **Don Ameche**, Flynn had several minor roles on Broadway before winning an audition at NBC. She became one of the stars of *Vic and Sade*, a comedic dialogue program so popular that it developed a cult following and remained on the air for more than 14 years. She also had roles on several radio **soap operas**, including *The Affairs of Anthony* and *The Right to Happiness*. From 1943 to 1945, she was a newscaster on CBS's *News for Women*. On television, she played Lona Drewer Carey on the NBC serial *Hawkins Falls*.

FLYNN, BESS (1884–1976). Irna Phillips, who wrote and starred in the early **soap opera** *Painted Dreams*, left WGN in 1932 because the station refused to sell the program to the network. Bess Flynn took her place and both wrote and starred in the program, as well as directing and producing it. She also wrote and acted in several other soap operas, including *Bachelor's Children* and *We, the Abbotts*, and had a major role on *The Gumps*. Her son, Charles Flynn, was also a radio actor and in addition to appearing on *The Gumps* with his mother, played the title role on *Jack Armstrong, the All-American Boy* for more than 10 years. In 1939, Bess Flynn published a small illustrated booklet about the award-winning *Bachelor's Children*.

FOLEY, RED (1910–1968). Red Foley, born Clyde Julian Foley, was one of the biggest singing stars in country music in the postwar years, selling more than 25 million records. He had many hits in both the country and popular fields and his recording of *Peace in the Valley* was the first gospel record to sell one million copies. On radio, he appeared in the early 1930s in Chicago on the *WLS Barn Dance*, and then stayed with the program when it joined the NBC Blue Network as *The National Barn Dance*. In 1946, he replaced Roy Acuff as the singing emcee of *The Grand Ole Opry*, staying in this position until 1953. He also had his own radio program, *The Red Foley Show*, beginning in 1950 on ABC.

FORD SUNDAY EVENING HOUR (THE). A 60-minute Sunday evening program of **concert music** first heard from 1934 to 1942, *The Ford Sunday Evening Hour* was called *The Ford Summer Hour* when it appeared during the summers from 1938 to 1941. It featured guest soloists and conductors each week, with music provided by an orchestra composed largely of members of the Detroit Symphony. The program left the air in 1942 due to wartime cutbacks at the Ford Motor Company, but returned for a final year in 1945.

FORD THEATER (THE). A 60-minute **drama anthology**, *The Ford Theater* first appeared in 1947, featuring top radio professionals in works from literature and the theater. Although well-received by critics, ratings were low and the program was reorganized the next year. In the revised format, Fletcher Markle directed Hollywood stars performing in radio adaptations of famous films and plays. Ratings were similarly low for this version of the program, and it left the air in 1949.

FORD, WHITEY (1901–1986). Whitey Ford, whose real name was Benjamin Francis Ford, was a comedian and banjo player who first appeared on radio with his own band in 1925 at KTHS Hot Springs. Later, he was the emcee for **Gene Autry** at WLS, where he acquired the stage nickname "The Duke of Paducah." He originated Mutual's *Renfro Barn Dance*, and appeared on *Plantation Party*, but is best known for his many appearances on *The Grand Ole Opry* during the 1940s. On the Opry, he was the emcee of the network part of the show, participated in comedy sketches, played his banjo, sang, and became well known for his catchphrase: "I'm going to the wagon, boys, these shoes are killing me."

FORECAST. An unusual program appearing on CBS only during the summers of 1940 and 1941, *Forecast* was an on-the-air audition of programs that were being considered by CBS for inclusion in the network schedule. Listener reaction was solicited and considered in making the decision. Among the programs first heard on *Forecast* were **Duffy's Tavern** and **Suspense**.

FORT LARAMIE. Heard only from January to October in 1956, *Fort Laramie* was a 30-minute adult western created by Norman Macdonnell, who also produced and directed *Gunsmoke*, and both programs had the same gritty, realistic approach, using many of the same soundmen, writers, and supporting actors. Every effort was made to be historically accurate with respect to place names, military procedures and terms, and Indian practices, and to give a picture of the everyday life of a frontier soldier. Raymond Burr starred as Captain Lee Quince, and most episodes featured **Vic Perrin**, Harry Bartell, and Jack Moyles in supporting roles. All 40 episodes were taped and are currently available.

FOUR STAR PLAYHOUSE. *Four Star Playhouse* was a 30-minute **drama anthology** featuring four major film stars, each of whom was featured in turn in the weekly presentations. The stories were adapted from a popular magazine and the four stars were Fred Mac-Murray, Loretta Young, Rosalind Russell, and Robert Cummings. The program was not a success, and was heard only during 1949. A television version with different stars was more successful, running from 1952 to 1956.

FRANCIS, ARLENE (1908–2001). Born Arline Francis Kazanjian in Boston, Arlene Francis is known today principally for her appearances on television. She began her professional acting career in the late 1920s as a stage actress and then had a modest career in movies, but she became a star when she appeared on numerous radio shows in the 1930s and 1940s, hosting several of them. She was on *The Hour of Charm*, *The March of Time*, *Big Sister*, *Portia Faces Life*, *Light of the World*, and many others, but is best remembered as a panelist on *What's My Line?* When this panel program moved to television in 1950, she moved with it and appeared on the show for the next 25 years. She returned to radio in 1957 as moderator of NBC's *Family Living*. From 1961 to 1990, she hosted a daily radio interview program on WOR New York. Her autobiography, *Arlene Francis: A Memoir*, was published in 1978.

FRANK MORGAN SHOW (THE). Frank Morgan, remembered for his movie portrayal of the Wizard in *The Wizard of Oz*, was a comedian whose stock in trade was telling fantastic stories. He and **Fanny Brice** were regulars on ***Maxwell House Coffee Time*** from 1940 to 1944 and shared equal time and billing. When Brice left to headline ***The Baby Snooks Show***, Morgan continued alone and the program was renamed, but it was heard only during 1944–1945.

FRANK SINATRA SHOW (THE). Sinatra was the headliner on several shows extending from 1944 to 1955, some of them under his own name, some under the name of the sponsor, but all of them consisting primarily of music. In addition to appearing on *Songs by Sinatra*, *Light Up Time*, *Meet Frank Sinatra*, and *To Be Perfectly Frank*, he was twice the star of ***Your Hit Parade*** (1943–1945, 1947–1949). Axel Stordahl worked with him on almost all of his programs, sometimes as orchestra leader, sometimes as arranger.

FRED ALLEN SHOW (THE). Believed by many of his contemporaries to be the finest comedian in America, **Fred Allen** and his wife, **Portland Hoffa**, were the stars of a **comedy program** that appeared under many names, beginning in 1932 with *The Linit Bath Club Revue*, followed the next year by *The Salad Bowl Revue*, then by *The Sal Hepatica Revue*, also called *The Hour of Smiles* and *Town Hall Tonight*. The name was changed to *The Fred Allen Show* in 1939, but when Texaco became the sponsor the next year, it was changed again to *The Texaco Star Theater*. His programs are best remembered for **Allen's Alley**, a portion of the show where he interviewed a succession of comedic characters, several of whom became very well known, including Mrs. Nussbaum, played by **Minerva Pious**, and Senator Claghorn, played by **Kenny Delmar**. The program left the air in 1949, partly because it had to compete with an extremely popular **quiz program**, *Stop the Music*, that ABC aired in the same time slot, and partly because ratings had dropped sharply in the last year.

FRED WARING SHOW (THE). Fred Waring was the leader of The Pennsylvanians, a large orchestra and chorus, sometimes using more than 50 musicians and singers. He appeared on a long series of programs beginning in 1933 and extending to 1957. From 1939 to 1944, when he was sponsored by Chesterfield Cigarettes, his program was sometimes called *Chesterfield Time*, and occasionally *Pleasure Time*. From 1945 to 1949, he hosted a daytime program under his own name on NBC that was said to be the most expensive daytime program ever produced. He subsequently conducted several other programs, remaining active in radio until 1957.

FREES, PAUL (1920–1986). Born Solomon Hersh Frees in Chicago, Frees was known during his long career as both "the man of a thousand voices" and "America's most versatile actor." He was a regular performer and/or host on such shows as *Escape*, *Suspense*, *Nightbeat*, and *Wild Bill Hickok*. A superb voice actor, Frees provided the television voice of John Beresford Tipton on *The Millionaire* and also the cartoon character voices of Inspector Fenwick on *The Dudley Do-Right Show*, Boris Badenov on *The Rocky and Bullwinkle Show*, and Professor Ludwig von Drake on *The Wonderful World of Disney*. In films, he was the narrator of *The Shaggy Dog*, *War of the Worlds*, and other classics. He also did hundreds of commercials and voiceovers. A book about Frees and his career, *Welcome Foolish Mortals: The Life and Voices of Paul Frees*, was published in 2004.

FROMAN, JANE (1907–1980). Jane Froman was a singer who appeared on several radio programs during the 1930s and 1940s, including *The Intimate Review* (with **Bob Hope**, in his first radio series) and *The Jane Froman Show*. On a flight with a troupe of other U.S.O. performers during World War II, her plane crashed off the coast of Lisbon, Portugal. Most of the plane's occupants were killed, and Froman survived only because the plane's co-pilot kept her from drowning. After many operations on her legs, which were crushed in the crash, she returned to perform for World War II servicemen while sitting in a wheelchair. In 1952, a movie was made of her life, *With a Song in My Heart*, starring Susan Hayward, with Froman providing the singing voice. After the movie came out, Froman's records began to sell extremely well and she became the hostess of a CBS television variety show, *Jane Froman's U.S.A. Canteen*, from 1952 to 1955.

FRONT PAGE FARRELL. One of the many **soap operas** produced by **Frank and Anne Hummert**, *Front Page Farrell* was unusual in that it was also a **crime program** of sorts. David Farrell, a crusading young reporter, and his wife Sally worked together to solve crimes, primarily murders. Most investigations were a week long, with the crime being discovered on Monday and solved on the Friday episode. The program was heard from 1941 to 1954, with Richard Widmark as the first Farrell, and the role later played by **Staats Cotsworth** and Carleton Young.

FRONTIER GENTLEMAN. A late-appearing **western program** that was heard only in 1958, *Frontier Gentleman* was the story of J. B. Kendall, an Englishman who worked for the *London Times* and whose assignment was to write stories about the West of the 1870s. Also a gunman, he took an active part in many of the stories he reported and met many famous people in the course of his adventures, including Calamity Jane and Jesse James. Kendall was played by **John Dehner**, and the cast included some of the best talents in radio, including **Virginia Gregg**, **Vic Perrin**, and Jeanette Nolan.

FROST, ALICE (1910–1998). After small parts in Broadway plays in the early 1930s, Alice Frost originated the role of Ruth Evans on *Big Sister* (1936–1942), and then played the same part on the spin-off series, *Bright Horizon*. She also had parts on many other **soap operas**, including *David Harum*, *The Second Mrs. Burton*, and *Lorenzo Jones*; but she is best remembered for her portrayal of Pamela North on *Mr. and Mrs. North*. For nearly 10 years, she helped her radio husband Jerry, played by **Joseph Curtin**, solve crimes on this popular NBC weekly thriller. Although she was very successful on radio, she was always more interested in the stage and was once quoted as saying: "People in the theater sort of stuck their nose up at radio, but it was a good place to make a little money while you were waiting for a job." She also appeared on the television comedy *Mama* from 1949 to 1957.

FU MANCHU. A **juvenile adventure** series based on the stories by Sax Rohmer, *Fu Manchu* featured a Chinese physician who launched a campaign of revenge against western civilization and the white race after his wife was killed accidentally by a British officer during the Boxer Rebellion. He specialized in the use of unusual murder plots, often involving snakes, spiders, bacteria, and poisons. He was pursued by Nayland Smith of Scotland Yard and Smith's associate, Dr. James Petrie. Originally heard as a part of *The Collier Hour* from

1929 to 1931, it became a 30-minute weekly program on CBS from 1931 to 1933. A 15-minute syndicated version called *The Shadow of Fu Manchu* was broadcast during 1939–1940. In the original version, Fu Manchu was played by John Daly, Nayland Smith by Charles Warburton, and Dr. Petrie by Bob White. On the syndicated version, Nayland Smith was played by **Hanley Stafford** and Dr. Petrie by **Gale Gordon**.

– G –

GALLOP, FRANK (1900–1988). A former brokerage firm employee, Gallop began working on radio in the mid-1930s. The deep-voiced announcer stayed with the medium until the mid-1950s, at which time he moved to television. On radio, he worked on dozens of programs, including *Hilltop House*, *Gang Busters*, *Stella Dallas*, *Quick as a Flash*, and *Monitor*. On *The Milton Berle Show*, he was both announcer and comedy foil for Berle; on television, he performed the same roles on *The Perry Como Show* from 1955 to 1961.

GANG BUSTERS. A 30-minute police drama created by **Phillips H. Lord**, *Gang Busters* appeared from 1935 to 1957 and was the first of the police dramas to claim authenticity, dramatizing actual cases and interviewing lawmen who had been connected with the cases. Known for the loud and dramatic introduction featuring whistles, gunshots, and sirens (that gave rise to the term "coming on like *Gang Busters*"), the program originally concentrated on nationally known criminals, but was later broadened to include interesting crimes of all sorts. At the end of each program, detailed descriptions of wanted men were broadcast; over the years, hundreds of criminals were apprehended as a result of these descriptions. Lord was the first narrator, but later narrators included Colonel H. Norman Schwarzkopf (father of the Gulf War commander), who had been Superintendent of the New Jersey State Police, and Lewis J. Valentine, a retired Commissioner of the New York City Police.

GARDNER, ED (1901–1963). New York-born Gardner created the role of Archie, the manager of *Duffy's Tavern*, and all the other denizens of the seedy Third Avenue eatery. As a young man, Gardner worked as a salesman, but changed to creating and directing radio programs after marrying actress Shirley Booth. He produced *The Baker's Broadcast* in the 1930s, and was producer–director of *The Rudy Vallee* **Show** in the early 1940s. It was working on the program *This is New York*, that inspired him to create the characters who later populated *Duffy's Tavern*. While demonstrating the kind of character he wanted for the lead role, he decided to play the part himself. His creation ran on the networks from 1941 to 1952, inspired a movie in 1945, and then moved to television in 1954.

GARGAN, WILLIAM (1905–1979). Gargan, who had actually worked as an investigator, turned to acting in 1924, often playing the part of a private detective. After working on Broadway and in the movies (once playing the character of Ellery Queen), he starred on several popular radio series, including *Barrie Craig: Confidential Investigator* and *Martin Kane, Private Eye*. This latter program was so successful on radio that it was moved to television in 1949, where it became one of the first popular TV detective series. Gargan's acting career ended in 1960 when he developed cancer of the larynx, but he subsequently became a spokesman for the American Cancer Society and lectured (using an artificial voice box) against smoking. His autobiography, *Why Me?*, was published in 1969.

GARROWAY, DAVE (1913–1982). Garroway, the son of an electrical engineer, began his professional career in 1937 as a page boy for NBC, and then broke into Chicago radio as a sports reporter, sometimes assisting Bill Stern. On radio, he worked on *Musical Americana* and *The World's Great Novels* before starring in several programs that bore his name: *The Dave Garroway Show* (1947–1951), *Reserved for Garroway* (1949–1950), and *Dial Dave Garroway* (1950–1953). On television, he hosted *Garroway at Large* (1949–1951), *The Dave Garroway Show* (1953–1954), *Today* (1952–1961), and *CBS Newcomers* (1971). He was also a host on one of the segments of *Monitor* during its long run on radio. Despondent over declining health and embittered at the way his career had turned out, he committed suicide in 1982.

GARRY MOORE SHOW (THE). Although the program under his own name appeared only during 1949–1950, Garry Moore was active on radio for many years before that, first appearing on *Club Matinee* in 1939 with **Ransom Sherman**. It was on that show where he changed his name from Thomas Garrison Morfit to Garry Moore, as a result of a contest conducted among listeners. He was the co-host of *The Camel Caravan* with **Jimmy Durante** and from 1943 to 1945 that the program was known as *The Garry Moore–Jimmy Durante Show* on alternate weeks. *The Garry Moore Show* of 1949–1950 was a daytime variety program that later moved to television.

GAY NINETIES REVIEW (THE). A 30-minute program that featured the songs and comedy of America at the end of the 19th century, *The Gay Nineties Review* was heard from 1939 to 1944. It was hosted by Joe Howard, who was 73 when the series began and had been a singer, dancer, and songwriter during the Gay Nineties. Beatrice Kay was the lead singer until 1943, when Lillian Leonard took her place. Kay headlined a virtually identical spin-off program, *Gaslight Gaieties*, in 1944–1945.

GENE AND GLENN. Gene and Glenn were Gene Carroll and Glenn Rowell, a comedy duo who were first featured on *The Quaker Early Birds Program* from 1930 to 1932, where they chatted and did skits and Carroll did the voices of both Jake and Lena, the handyman and the landlord of a boardinghouse. They later hosted their own program in 1934 and again from 1938 to 1941. Carroll later played the part of Lena the maid on *Fibber McGee and Molly* when Beulah, the previous maid, moved to a spin-off program.

GENE AUTRY'S MELODY RANCH. A long-running program of music and western adventure heard from 1940 to 1956, this program supposedly took place at Gene Autry's real-life Melody Ranch in California. Each episode featured a short adventure involving outlaws or rustlers with many of the characters played by actors who had appeared with Autry in his movies. Western music was supplied by Autry and a stable of high-quality western musicians, including Johnny Bond and Alvino Rey.

GENERAL MILLS HOUR (THE). *The General Mills Hour* was an umbrella term used to refer to a group of four **soap operas** that appeared consecutively on NBC, all sponsored by General Mills. The programs were *The Guiding Light*, *Woman in White*, *Today's Children* (all written by **Irna Phillips**), and the biblically oriented *The Light of the World*. The four together comprised the 2:00–3:00 P.M. hour on NBC's weekday schedule.

GEORGE JESSEL SHOW (THE). Jessel was a famous vaudeville comedian and toastmaster who appeared on several **comedy programs**, beginning with his own show in 1934, which was renamed *The George Jessel Variety Hour* during the summer of that year. He was then heard on *Thirty Minutes in Hollywood* in 1937–1938, co-starring with his wife, Norma Talmadge. He joined *For Men Only* as emcee in 1939, and the name of the program was changed to *George Jessel's Celebrity Program* in the fall of that year. After a long absence from the air, he returned to host *George Jessel Salutes* in 1953.

GERSON, BETTY LOU (1914–1999). Betty Lou Gerson played many roles on early radio, including Helen on *Road of Life*, Laura on *Ma Perkins*, Karen Adams on *Woman in White*, and Charlotte Wilson on *The Guiding Light*. She also appeared on many other popular programs, including *The First Nighter*, *The Adventures of Sam Spade*, *Box 13*, *Broadway Is My Beat*, *Grand Hotel* (paired with **Jim Ameche**), *The Whistler*, and *Richard Diamond, Private Detective*. For a time she also had the lead role on *The Story of Mary Marlin*. In 1961, she was the voice of Cruella DeVil in the animated Disney movie *101 Dalmatians*.

GIBBONS, FLOYD (1889–1939). Gibbons was a reporter for the *Chicago Tribune* who in 1929 appeared on a weekly 30-minute NBC program called *The Headline Hunter*. On this show, he told colorful tales of his previous adventures in addition to conducting remote broadcasts. He saw himself primarily as an explorer, and his next radio program was a 1930–1931 NBC-Blue series *World Adventures with Floyd Gibbons*. He also appeared in quasi-news portions of various entertainment programs and was never averse to personal publicity, affecting an eye patch and often wearing bush jackets or other explorer-like outfits. Gibbons was an extremely active correspondent in Ethiopia when the Italians invaded that country in 1935, and his involvement in such events set a precedent for radio journalists who followed him. He was known for his very rapid delivery, and was once clocked at 217 words per minute; but as radio journalism became more mature, his style became less acceptable and he left broadcasting in the late 1930s.

GIBSON, WALTER B. (1897–1985). A writer, the amazingly prolific Gibson served in the army during World War I and later became a reporter on a Philadelphia newspaper. In the next 10 years, he ghosted articles and books for leading professional magicians, including Houdini, Thurston, and Blackstone. Over the course of his writing career, Gibson wrote more than 100 books on magic, games, and other subjects. He is best remembered as the creator of *The Shadow*; he wrote 282 pulp magazine novels about The Shadow under his pen name of Maxwell Grant. During the time he was writing The Shadow stories, a newspaper article reported that he had written more than 1,000,000 words a year for 10 straight years. When The Shadow character was moved to radio in the 1930s, Gibson and the scriptwriter, Edward Hale Bierstadt, worked on the first scripts together, although Gibson did not receive author credit on any of them. He also wrote scripts for other radio programs such as *The Adventures of Frank Merriwell* and *Nick Carter, Master Detective*. A book of his work, *Man of Magic and Mystery: A Guide to the Work of Walter B. Gibson*, was published by Scarecrow Press in 1988.

GILMAN, PAGE (1918–). Gilman began his acting career as a teenager under the name of Billy Page, but for nearly 28 years (1932–1959), he played the role of Jack Barbour, the youngest child of Henry and Fanny Barbour on *One Man's Family*, the immensely popular and long-running serial drama created by **Carlton E. Morse**. Morse also cast him in parts on his other radio programs, including *I Love a Mystery*. Gilman was the son of NBC vice president Don Gilman, and also worked as a national ad manager for a newspaper in Watsonville, California. His newspaper work overlapped his radio career for several years.

GINNY SIMMS SHOW (THE). Ginny Simms was a popular vocalist with the **Kay Kyser** orchestra and in 1942 was featured on *Johnny Presents*, a program named for the bellhop featured in Philip Morris Cigarette commercials. The program was renamed *Johnny Presents Ginny Simms* in 1943. In 1945, she changed networks and sponsors, and her program appeared under her own name on CBS until 1947. Simms returned to radio as the featured singer on *Botany Song Shop* in 1950–1951.

GIRL ALONE. A 15-minute daily **soap opera** heard from 1936 to 1941, *Girl Alone* was the story of a wealthy woman's search for a man who would love her for herself rather than for her money or social position. The plot was very complex, and the cast very large; it included several actors who later became well known, including John Hodiak, **Raymond Edward Johnson**, and **Willard Waterman**. The lead role was played by **Betty Winkler**.

GLAMOUR MANOR. *Glamour Manor* was an unusual 30-minute program usually appearing daily at noon. On Monday, Wednesday, and Friday, it was a **situation comedy** featuring Cliff Arquette as the manager of the Glamour Manor Hotel. On Tuesday and Thursday, Arquette and **Lurene Tuttle**, who was also a cast member on the Monday, Wednesday, and Friday shows, conducted an interview program with members of the studio audience. The program was heard from 1944 to 1947, with **Kenny Baker** assuming the lead role in 1946.

GODFREY, ARTHUR (1903–1983). The folksy, low-key Godfrey was one of the most popular performers on radio during the medium's Golden Age. He was a success on WFBR Baltimore before moving to Washington and NBC in the early 1930s. Personal remarks on the air got him fired in 1934, but he became successful as a disc jockey on *Sun Dial*, and then as an announcer on *Professor Quiz*. "The Old Redhead" then starred on both *Arthur Godfrey Time* from 1945 to 1972 and *Arthur Godfrey's Talent Scouts* from 1946 to 1958. When he moved to television in the late 1940s, he also became a TV star: one season in the early 1950s, he starred on two evening programs while simultaneously hosting a top-rated show in the daytime. Poor health forced him to leave television in 1959, but he returned briefly in 1960 as co-host of *Candid Camera*. After his TV career ended, Godfrey ventured into films, played on Broadway, and made recordings. Late in life, he promoted aviation and spoke out on environmental issues.

GOFF, NORRIS. *See LUM AND ABNER.*

GOLDBERGS (THE). First called *The Rise of the Goldbergs*, *The Goldbergs* was a 15-minute daily serial drama that ran from 1929 to 1950, documenting the daily lives of a Jewish family living in the Bronx. Written by **Gertrude Berg**, who also starred as Molly Goldberg, it was both a **situation comedy** and a **soap opera**, but it stayed close to real-life situations and to events that could be believed. Performed in Jewish dialect, the program changed to a 30-minute weekly format in 1949–1950, when it ran concurrently with the television version of the show.

GOOD NEWS. Originally a 60-minute program created to replace ***Showboat***, which had left the air in 1937, this program was titled by the year for the first three years of its existence: *Good News of 1938*, *Good News of 1939*, and *Good News of 1940*. Each week, a new MGM film was previewed with a major cinema star serving as host. In 1940, the program was reduced to 30 minutes and in the fall of that year was renamed ***Maxwell House Coffee Time***, with a change in format, Frank Morgan and **Fanny Brice** each appearing in 15-minute comedy segments.

GOODRICH SILVERTOWN ORCHESTRA (THE). An early program that is notable chiefly because it was one of the first programs to appear on network radio, *The Goodrich Silvertown Orchestra* joined NBC in the fall of 1926. It appeared until 1928 under various titles, including *The Silvertown Orchestra*, *The Goodrich Zippers*, *The Silvertown Zippers*, and *The Silvertown Cord Orchestra*. Silvertown was the name of a type of tire produced by the Goodrich Tire Company, sponsor of the program. One of the features of the program was a "Silver Masked Tenor" who did indeed wear a silver mask while performing and whose identity was closely guarded. He was later revealed to be a singer named Joseph M. White. A 15-minute transcribed version of the program appeared in syndication in 1935–1936.

GOODWILL COURT (THE). *The Goodwill Court* was a 60-minute Sunday evening program, hosted by A. L. Alexander, that offered free legal advice to anyone who was willing to describe his or her problem to the NBC microphone. Advice was offered by two New York judges, and the program staff answered all mail, giving advice even to those who did not appear. The show was a huge success, but the New York Supreme Court soon barred all judges and lawyers from appearing, and the program left the air after only a three-month appearance on the network in 1936. Alexander returned with a program called *A. L. Alexander's Mediation Board* in 1943, on which advice was offered by sociologists and educators.

GOODWILL HOUR (THE). Heard in formats ranging from 15-minutes to 60-minutes, *The Goodwill Hour* was a human-interest and advice program on which people presented their problems and were given advice by John J. Anthony, whose real name was Lester Kroll. Although claiming to have several degrees, Kroll had in fact not graduated from high school, and his advice was usually very conventional, much like that offered by various newspaper advice columnists. The program first appeared in 1937 and capitalized on the popularity of the earlier *Goodwill Court*, which had been forced to leave the air the previous year. It was heard from 1937 to 1946 and then appeared again from 1951 to 1953.

GOODWIN, BILL (1910–1958). Goodwin began his professional career at a small station in Sacramento, California and on the **Don Lee Network** in Hollywood, before going to work for CBS in 1934. His main network radio appearances were as announcer on *The Bob Hope Show*, *Blondie*, and *Burns and Allen*. During 1947–1948, he starred on his own CBS variety show, *The Bill Goodwin Show* (also known as *Leave It to Bill*) and also played leads on a few dramatic radio programs. On television, the genial Goodwin played himself on *The George Burns and Gracie Allen Show*, was the host of the question-and-answer daytime game show *It Pays to Be Married*, the host of the prime-time game show *Penny to a Million*, and the narrator on the cartoon program *The Gerald McBoing-Boing Show*. During 1951–1952, he hosted his own half-hour NBC variety program. Goodwin entered films in the early 1940s, playing primarily character roles in more than a score of pictures during the 1940s and 1950s.

GORDON, BERT (1900–1974). Gordon was a comedian who created a comedic character called "The Mad Russian," heard for years on *The Eddie Cantor Program*. Before *The Eddie Cantor Program*, he appeared on *Time to Smile* for a number of years and later played Yasha on ***Duffy's Tavern***. Gordon began his professional career as a comedian in vaudeville and was in George White's *Scandals* in 1921. As The Mad Russian, he always introduced himself with the catchphrase, "How do you DO!"

GORDON, GALE (1906–1995). Educated in England, Gordon landed a part on Broadway as a teenager, and then worked in stock companies and motion pictures before becoming Mary Pickford's romantic lead in her first radio program and the first actor to play *Flash Gordon*, both in the mid-1930s. He later played the lead on *The Casebook of Gregory Hood*, and appeared on such other dramatic programs as ***Big Town***, ***Tarzan***, and ***The Whistler***. He was best known on radio for playing strong supporting characters on **comedy programs**: he was both Mayor LaTrivia and weatherman Foggy Williams on ***Fibber McGee and Molly***, Mr. Scott on ***The Phil Harris–Alice Faye Show***, and Madison High principal Osgood Conklin on ***Our Miss Brooks***. When Gordon entered television, he again played Osgood Conklin on *Our Miss Brooks*. He also played prominent supporting roles on all the Lucille Ball TV series.

GOSDEN, FREEMAN. *See AMOS 'N' ANDY.*

GOTHARD, DAVID (1911–1977). After graduating from high school in Los Angeles, Gothard acted in local theater groups until in 1932, intrigued by radio, he hitchhiked to Chicago and got a job as an announcer there. Subsequently, he appeared on many popular radio programs including ***Hilltop House***, ***The O'Neills***, ***Woman in White***, and ***The Adventures of the Thin Man***. He also had dramatic roles on ***Big Sister***, ***The Light of the World***, ***The Right to Happiness***, and ***The Romance of Helen Trent***. For this last program he is most remembered today; Gothard played the role of Helen Trent's suitor for 19 years of the show's 29-year run, in both the Chicago and New York casts.

GOULDING, RAY. *See BOB AND RAY SHOW.*

GRACIE FIELDS SHOW (THE). Gracie Fields was an English singer and comedienne whose first appearance was on an unusual five-minute nightly show on which she told one story and sang one song. First heard in 1942, the program was expanded to 15 minutes the next year and renamed *The Gracie Fields Victory Show*. It was expanded to 30 minutes in 1944, when it became a weekly show with the Lou Briney orchestra. The program left the air in 1945, but returned for a final season during 1952–1953.

GRAND CENTRAL STATION. The introduction to *Grand Central Station* always centered on the arrival of a train at Grand Central Station in New York City. As the passengers disembarked, the narrator and the radio listeners followed one of them and a 30-minute **drama anthology** began. There was no further connection with the station or the railroad; the stories were about the lives of the characters after they left the station. The program was heard from 1937 to 1953 and the dramas were light, often comedies. The best-known narrator was Jack Arthur, although he was later succeeded by **Alexander Scourby**.

GRAND HOTEL. A 30-minute anthology program of light dramas, *Grand Hotel* opened each week with the hotel operator connecting calls to various rooms. One of these calls would be expanded to introduce the story of the week. First heard on the network in 1933, the program aired until 1945, although it was off the air for several short periods. The switchboard operator was **Betty Winkler** and many talented radio performers appeared in the dramas, including **Don Ameche**, **Anne Seymour**, and **Betty Lou Gerson**.

GRAND OLE OPRY (THE). Arguably the most famous of the country music programs, *The Grand Ole Opry* was primarily a stage performance, only a portion of which was broadcast. It was heard regionally on WSM Nashville for 14 years before NBC aired a 30-minute segment in 1939. It was then heard on the network continuously until 1957, with time slots varying from 30 minutes to four hours in length; and it is still on the air today on a regional basis. Originally called *The WSM Barn Dance*, it was conceived and hosted by George D. Hay, who was billed as "The Solemn Old Judge" on the show, although he was only 30 when the program began. Demand for tickets soon caused the program to be moved from the studio to several different venues until the present Grand Ole Opry House was built for it in 1974. Many of the original performers were either local favorites or vaudeville veterans, but the program gradually became a venue for country music recording artists. Roy Acuff was a long-time staple of the program. **Red Foley** hosted the show for many years and virtually every important country artist of the 1940s, 1950s, and 1960s made an appearance.

GRAND SLAM. An unusual 15-minute daily musical **quiz program**, *Grand Slam* was hosted by Irene Beasley, who sang five-part questions that had been submitted by listeners. Heard from 1946 to 1953, it was an outgrowth of an earlier program, *Irene Beasley Sings*. Scoring was loosely based on that of bridge, with each part of the question referred to as a "trick." Answering all five parts correctly was called a "Grand Slam," a term used in bridge to indicate a hand in which one side takes all the tricks. Winners received a $100 savings bond.

GRAUER, BEN (1908–1977). A one-time child actor who first appeared in silent films, Benjamin Franklin Grauer joined NBC in 1930 as a special-events reporter and remained with the network as an announcer/narrator/host for more than 40 years. He worked on many popular network programs, including *Believe It or Not, Information, Please, Pot O' Gold*, and *Your Hit Parade*. The National Academy of Vocal Arts once proclaimed his voice to be "the most authoritative in the world"; in 1944, he won the H. F. David Award as the best NBC announcer. Grauer moved to television in the late 1940s, and over the next 25 years appeared as a newscaster, moderator, or narrator on several programs. In 1950, he hosted his own talk program, *The Ben Grauer Show*. He became famous for covering the Times Square New Year's Eve ball drop. He retired in 1973.

GREAT GILDERSLEEVE (THE). A long-running **situation comedy** heard from 1941 to 1957, *The Great Gildersleeve* featured Throckmorton P. Gildersleeve, the Water Commissioner in the fictitious town of Summerfield. The Gildersleeve character was first heard as one of the regular characters on *Fibber McGee and Molly*, where he was a manufacturer of girdles for women and was played by **Harold Peary**, and Peary continued in the role when the new program was created in 1941. On the Gildersleeve program, Gildersleeve was raising his nephew Leroy, played by **Walter Tetley**, and his niece, Marjorie. During the course of the run, the program developed a stable of comedic characters nearly as well known as those on *Fibber McGee and Molly*. **Willard Waterman** assumed the role of Gildersleeve in 1950 and remained with the program until it left the air. A television version, also starring Waterman, was seen during 1955–1956.

GREATEST STORY EVER TOLD (THE). Heard from 1947 to 1956, *The Greatest Story Ever Told* was a 30-minute **drama anthology** series, loosely based on the book by Fulton Oursler, and featuring dramatizations of events in the life of Jesus. The program gave no on-air credits, although Jesus was played by Warren Parker throughout. There were no commercials, only an announcement at the end of each program that it had been brought to you by the Goodyear Tire and Rubber Company.

GREEN HORNET (THE). Heard on the network from 1938 to 1952, *The Green Hornet* was the second of the three great **juvenile adventure programs** created by **George W. Trendle** and **Fran Striker** (along with *The Lone Ranger* and *Sergeant Preston of the Yukon*). It was the story of a young publisher, Britt Reid, who battled criminals of all types in his secret identity as *The Green Hornet*. His true identity was known only to Kato, his valet and the expert driver of the Black Beauty, a superfast car whose exhaust note resembled the buzzing of a giant bee and was the signature noise of the program. Britt Reid was distantly related to the **Lone Ranger**: Britt's father was Dan Reid, the Lone Ranger's young nephew. The original Hornet was played by Al Hodge, who held the role until 1943 when he left for military service; the role was later played by several other actors.

GREGG, VIRGINIA (1916–1986). Originally a musician, Virginia Gregg began her professional career in California playing the bass viola in the Pasadena Symphony and then, in the late 1930s, was part of the Singing Strings for CBS and Mutual. She later became an actress and appeared in many programs on radio, including *The Adventures of Ellery Queen*; *One Man's Family*; *Have Gun, Will Travel*; and *Richard Diamond, Private Detective*. She also had many appearances on dramatic programs such as *Screen Director's Play-*

house and *Escape* and was active on television and in the movies, usually playing supporting roles.

GRIMES, JACK (1926–). From an early age, Grimes was one of the busiest actors in the golden age of radio. He was both the first **Jimmy Olsen** on *The Adventures of Superman* and the first Archie on *The Adventures of Archie Andrews*. A graduate of the Professional Children's School, he appeared on many other programs, usually playing the role of an outgoing boy. He was a regular on *Let's Pretend* for many years and had continuing parts on *Second Husband*, *The Life of Riley*, and *Lorenzo Jones* as well as starring in episodes of both *Dimension X* and *X Minus One*. At one time in the early 1940s, it was reported that he played almost half of the male child roles in New York radio. Grimes also performed on Broadway at an early age and later appeared on more than 200 television programs. On TV, he was Homer on *The Aldrich Family* and Cadet T. J. Thistle on *Tom Corbett, Space Cadet* in the early 1950s; the voice of both Sparky and Chim Chim on the animated *Speed Racer* in the late 1960s; and Baxter in *On The Rocks*, a comedy about prison life, in the mid-1970s.

GUIDING LIGHT (THE). A 15-minute **soap opera** that became the longest-running serial drama in broadcast history, *The Guiding Light* appeared on radio from 1937 to 1956 and continued on television for 50 years after that. Created by **Irna Phillips**, it was originally the story of John Ruthledge, a minister in a small town; but the story and the main characters changed over the course of the long run, with the Bauer family the focus for many years. The characters were played by dozens of different performers, although Arthur Peterson was the first Ruthledge.

GUNSMOKE. A 30-minute **western program** featuring Matt Dillon, marshal of Dodge City, Kansas, *Gunsmoke* first appeared in 1952 and remained on the air until 1961. At that time it moved to television with a new cast. *Gunsmoke* was one of the first westerns to attempt any significant amount of authenticity with respect to the hard conditions of the day, and the plots and characters were more realistic than on most radio westerns. Matt Dillon was played by **William Conrad** and his deputy, Chester Proudfoot, by **Parley Baer**.

– H –

HALL, WENDELL (1896–1969). Hall, a tall and lanky crooner billed as "The Red-Headed Music Maker," was considered by many to be radio's first big star. He began his career in vaudeville in 1917, singing and playing the xylophone, later changing to the ukulele. On *The Eveready Hour* on 24 June 1924 he and his fiancée became the first couple to marry in a ceremony broadcast over radio. Hall was a featured vocalist on several musical **band remotes** in the late 1920s, including those of **Guy Lombardo.** He hosted *The Majestic Theater of the Air* (also known as *The Majestic Hour*) and *The Sign of the Shell*, and then appeared on *The Pineapple Picador* in 1931. Hall's contract on *The Sign of the Shell* was said to have made him the highest priced artist working out of the NBC Chicago studios. During 1936–1937, he was part of an unusual Sunday evening program, *The Gillette Community Sing*, on which the studio audience was directed in community singing, with Hall and **Milton Berle** leading one audience in New York, while Billy Jones and Ernie Hare led another in Philadelphia. Hall also appeared on his own program, *The Wendell Hall Fitch Program* (also known as *The Red-Headed Music Maker*) from 1933 to 1936. He wrote "It Ain't Gonna Rain No More" and once used it as his theme song.

HALLMARK PLAYHOUSE (THE). A 30-minute **drama anthology** featuring dramatizations of stories from literature, *The Hallmark Playhouse* was hosted by author James Hilton, with the lead roles in the plays often played by Hollywood stars. The program was heard from 1948 to 1953. It then became *The Hallmark Hall Of Fame* and was broadcast from 1953 to 1955. The revised program featured stories of famous historical figures, and was hosted by Lionel Barrymore.

HALLS OF IVY (THE). A 30-minute **situation comedy** created by **Don Quinn**, who also wrote *Fibber McGee and Molly*, *The Halls Of Ivy* was based on the events of the life of a president of a small college. The program starred **Ronald Colman** as President William Todhunter Hall and his real-life wife Benita, who played President Hall's wife, Vicky. The show was heard from 1950 to 1952, and a later version was seen on television.

HALOP, FLORENCE (1923–1986). Florence Halop began her radio career in the late 1920s, while still a young child, with appearances on *Coast-to-Coast on a Bus*. She took over the role of Miss Duffy on *Duffy's Tavern* in 1943, and was cast as Hotbreath Houlihan on *The Jimmy Durante Show* during 1948–1950. She also appeared in supporting roles on *The Henry Morgan Show* and the *Jack Paar Show* during the mid-1940s. Halop switched to television in the early 1950s when her best-known role was as bailiff Florence Kleiner on *Night Court*. Her younger brother, Billy Halop, also a child performer, starred in the "Dead End Kids" movies of the late 1930s. In the mid-1930s, he and Florence both appeared on radio's *Let's Pretend* and *Bobby Benson and the B-Bar-B Riders*.

HAPPINESS BOYS (THE). The Happiness Boys were Billy Jones and Ernie Hare, two stage performers who sang duets and told jokes on local radio in New York long before there were any networks, being heard as early as 1921. They claimed to be the first entertainers to have been paid for an appearance on radio. They went on the NBC network in 1926, sponsored by Happiness Candies, and they often changed their title to correspond with changes in sponsors. They were called *The Interwoven Pair* when they were sponsored by Interwoven Sox, *The Best Foods Boys* when sponsored by Hellmann's Mayonnaise, and *The Tastyyeast Breadwinners* or *The Tastyyeast Jesters* when sponsored by Tastyyeast Bakers. They were heard on the network until 1938 and continued to appear on local New York radio until Hare died in 1939. Jones continued performing on the radio until his death the next year.

HARDY FAMILY (THE). A 30-minute **situation comedy** based on the series of Andy Hardy motion pictures, *The Hardy Family* starred Mickey Rooney as Andy, Lewis Stone as his father, and Fay Holden as his mother. Heard first in syndication and later on Mutual, the program appeared from 1949 to 1953 and the plots were similar to those of the *Andy Hardy* movies: chaos surrounding Andy and his teenage friends.

HARE, ERNIE. *See THE HAPPINESS BOYS.*

HARRIS, PHIL (1904–1995). A singer, bandleader, and actor, Harris appeared on several Golden Age radio programs including *Let's*

Listen to Harris, **The Fitch Bandwagon**, **Kay Kyser's Kollege of Musical Knowledge**, **The Jack Benny Program**, and **The Phil Harris–Alice Faye Show**. Harris began his professional career as a drummer and bandleader in the early 1930s, and became a popular attraction at Hollywood's Coconut Grove. He became a national star when he joined **The Jack Benny Program** in 1936 as Benny's bandleader and comic foil. Harris married actress **Alice Faye** in 1941, and they starred in their own radio **situation comedy** from 1948 to 1954. Both of them sang on their show, with Harris usually performing one of the novelty numbers he had recorded. Beginning in 1933, he acted in musical comedy films and appeared in an occasional musical on television. In later life, he also played a few dramatic roles in films and provided voices for animated features.

HARRY RICHMAN SHOW (THE). Harry Richman was a vaudeville entertainer, primarily a singer, who hosted a **music program** heard during 1934–1935. He later hosted *Club Richman* (also called *The Dodge Program*) in 1936–1937 and in 1937–1938 was the host of a program sponsored by the state of Florida called *It's Florida's Treat*. Richman was a songwriter as well as a singer and wrote several popular songs, including "Walking My Baby Back Home."

HASTINGS, BOB (1925–). As a child actor and singer, Hastings appeared on many of the early **children's programs** on radio, including *Let's Pretend* and *Coast-to-Coast on a Bus*, as well as singing on **The National Barn Dance**. He later played the title role on **The Adventures of Archie Andrews** for ten years, was heard as Jerry on the serial version of **The Sea Hound**, and played various teenagers on **The Aldrich Family**. Hastings moved to television in the early 1960s and had continuing roles on three popular TV comedies: *The Phil Silvers Show*, *McHale's Navy*, and *All in the Family*. He is the older brother of Don Hastings, who also appeared on radio before becoming the teenaged Video Ranger, the main assistant of the Captain, on TV's *Captain Video and His Video Rangers*.

HATCH, WILBUR (1902–1969). Hatch was first a pianist at KYW Chicago in 1922 before becoming director of music at the **Columbia Broadcasting System (CBS)** in 1930. During his long association with CBS, he and his orchestra were featured on many of their programs, including *Broadway Matinee*, *Calling All Cars*, *Fletcher Wiley*, *Gateway to Hollywood*, *Man about Hollywood*, **My Favorite Husband**, **Our Miss Brooks**, and **Screen Guild Theatre**. A composer of background music on many programs, he created the famous mood music for **The Whistler**. He was also the music conductor on television's *I Love Lucy*.

HAVE GUN, WILL TRAVEL. One of the last radio dramas to appear, *Have Gun, Will Travel* was heard from 1958 to 1960, and was one of the very few radio programs to originate on television. The radio version was very similar to the television production, even using the same theme music. Just as on television, the leading character, Paladin, was a gunman for hire who lived in a San Francisco hotel between jobs. The role was played by **John Dehner**, who did not attempt to imitate the television role, but the scripts and production were so similar that the programs sounded very much alike.

HAWAII CALLS. Almost forgotten now, *Hawaii Calls* was a long-running **music program** broadcast directly from Waikiki Beach in Hawaii before a live audience. It was heard on various regional and national networks from 1935 until the 1990s, with most of the national appearance on the Mutual network between 1945 and 1956. Created by Webley Edwards, who also produced and directed, the program sometimes played to as many as 2,000 people in the live audience.

HAWK LARABEE. A 30-minute **western program** heard from 1946 to 1948, this program was originally titled *Hawk Durango* and featured **Elliott Lewis** as Hawk Durango and **Barton Yarborough** as his side-kick, Brazos John. After one season, the title was changed to *Hawk Larabee*, with Yarborough in the title role and Barney Phillips as his sidekick, Somber Jones. Later that year, Lewis returned as Hawk, and Yarborough again took the role of sidekick. The program was one of the first to use singing bridges between segments.

HEAR IT NOW. Heard only from late 1950 until mid-1951, *Hear It Now* was a 60-minute documentary program produced and written by **Edward R. Murrow** and Fred W. Friendly. The pair had previously produced a successful series of record albums titled *I Can Hear It*

Now, that replayed broadcasts of famous events. The intent of the program was to present the news events of the week in the voices of the newscasters on the spot and the newsmakers themselves, both by transcription and by live broadcast. Although successful (the winner of a **Peabody Award** in 1950), the program moved to television in 1951 as the news documentary, *See It Now*.

HEART'S DESIRE. A 30-minute human-interest program, *Heart's Desire* asked listeners to write to the program describing things that they would like to have and their reason for desiring them. The program staff chose the letters thought best and they were read to the studio audience. The audience, in turn, selected the letters to be read on the air; and the writer of each winning letter was granted his or her wish. Hosted by Ben Alexander, the program was heard from 1946 to 1948. Alexander once estimated that well over half of the requests were from people who wanted things for others.

HEATTER, GABRIEL. Heatter was a news commentator known for his optimistic and knowledgeable view of current events. A newspaperman by trade, he began his radio career in 1932 on WOR New York. His network program began in 1935 and in 1936 he was the reporter who covered the trial of Bruno Hauptmann, the kidnapper of the Lindbergh baby. He was exceedingly popular during the World War II years and was noted for his catchphrase: "Ah, there's good news tonight." *See also* NEWS PROGRAMS.

HEINZ MAGAZINE OF THE AIR (THE). An unusual 30-minute daytime program heard from 1936 to 1938, *The Heinz Magazine of the Air* consisted of 15 minutes of interviews, music, and chat, and a 15-minute soap opera, *Trouble House*, written by **Elaine Carrington**. The program was well received during its first year but there were several later changes, including the replacement of *Trouble House* with another serial, *Carol Kennedy's Romance*.

HENRY MORGAN SHOW (THE). Henry Morgan was a comedian noted for his tendency to make fun of sponsors and his irreverence with commercials. As a result, he was in more or less constant trouble with sponsors and stations, but he was popular with listeners and his programs were heard in both 15-minute and 30-minute formats from

1940 to 1951. He later appeared for many years as a panelist on the television program *I've Got a Secret.*

HERE'S TO ROMANCE. A 30-minute program heard from 1943 to 1945, *Here's to Romance* originally featured singer Buddy Clark, with vocalist Martha Tilton and the Ray Bloch Orchestra. Clark was later replaced by Dick Haymes and in 1944 the program added dramatic skits that featured guest stars. The next year, **Robert Ripley** was added with a "Believe It or Not" segment, and this version of the program is sometimes listed as *Romance, Rhythm, and Ripley.*

HERLIHY, ED (1909–1999). Edward Joseph Herlihy was a well-known announcer from 1935 until the early 1970s, announcing for such programs as *The Adventures of the Thin Man*, *The Big Show*, *Dick Tracy*, *The Falcon*, *The Henry Morgan Show*, *Information, Please*, *Just Plain Bill*, *Life Can Be Beautiful*, *Truth or Consequences*, *Vic and Sade*, and *The Kraft Music Hall*; he was the spokesman for Kraft foods for more than 40 years. For 15 years, he presided over the cast of *The Horn & Hardart Children's Hour* that was broadcast on both radio and television. On television, he also announced on *Kraft Television Theatre*, *The Perry Como Show*, *The Tonight Show*, and *The Kraft Music Hall*. In the movies, Herlihy was the voice of Universal newsreels for many years.

HERMITS CAVE (THE). Although broadcast primarily on local or regional outlets, this 30-minute horror anthology was syndicated and widely heard, particularly from 1940 to 1943. Like many other programs of the same type, it was distinguished primarily by its introduction, which in this case featured a "Hermit" who told horror stories in his cave, accompanied by howling winds. The Hermit was played originally by Mel Johnson, and later by **John Dehner.**

HERRMANN, BERNARD (1911–1975). Herrmann studied music composition at New York University, and later founded and led the New York Chamber Orchestra. He composed, arranged, and conducted musical scores for hundreds of radio programs including *CBS Radio Workshop* and *Suspense*. In association with **Orson Welles**, he wrote the music for the "War of the Worlds" broadcast by *Mercury*

Theatre on the Air, and then accompanied Welles to Hollywood to work on *Citizen Kane*, the first of more than five dozen films for which he wrote the scores. During the late 1950s and early 1960s, he worked on several Alfred Hitchcock films. Herrmann won an Academy Award in 1941 for his scoring of *All That Money Can Buy*.

HERROLD, CHARLES (1876–1948). Herrold is sometimes credited with being the inventor of broadcasting. His station in San Jose, California, began its broadcasting activities in 1909, before stations were required to have call letters; it simply identified itself by using the name of its founder, Charles David Herrold, who was the principal of the Herrold College of Engineering and Wireless. The direct descendent of Herrold's small 15-watt spark transmitter is KCBS San Francisco, a 50,000 watt station of CBS.

HERSHFIELD, HARRY (1885–1974). A cartoonist and humorist, Hershfield began his radio career in 1940 as a panelist on the hit **comedy program** *Can You Top This?* and appeared on the television version of the program when it was televised during the 1950–1951 season. Hershfield was also on *Stop Me if You've Heard This One*, where he was a member of a three-person panel that attempted to finish jokes begun by the host. After his radio career, Hershfield was a popular toastmaster and after-dinner speaker at hundreds of functions each year.

HERSHOLT, JEAN (1886–1956). Born in Copenhagen, the son of a famous Danish actor and actress, Hersholt appeared on the stage in Europe before coming to the United States in 1914. He made his film debut the following year, and in the 1920s became a leading character actor in silent films. On the radio, Hersholt played the leading role on *Dr. Christian* for the entire run of the popular program, from 1937 to 1954. The program moved to television in 1956, but Hersholt was not a part of it. Off screen in Hollywood, he was known for his humanitarian activities and was awarded two special Oscars (1939, 1949) for service to the industry. In 1956, the year of his death from cancer, the Academy of Motion Picture Arts and Sciences, of which he had been president, instituted the Jean Hersholt Humanitarian Award, a special Oscar that is awarded each year to a film personality for humanitarian achievements.

HIGBY, MARY JANE (1909–1986). As a young girl, Higby acted in silent films directed by her father. As an adult radio actress, she worked on both coasts, appearing in such dramatic programs as *Grand Central Station*, *Hollywood Hotel*, *Lux Radio Theatre*, and *Nick Carter, Master Detective*. She also had roles on several daytime **soap operas**, but is best known for having played the lead on *When A Girl Marries* from 1939 to 1956. Her memoir of her life as a radio actress, *Tune in Tomorrow*, was published in 1968.

HILDEGARDE'S RALEIGH ROOM. Hildegarde Loretta Sell was a singer from Milwaukee, Wisconsin, who could sing convincingly in French, Russian, Italian, and German, as well as in English, and she was promoted as "The Incomparable Hildegarde." Her show was a **music program** heard from 1944 to 1947, originally called *The Raleigh Room* because it was sponsored by Raleigh cigarettes. She replaced **Red Skelton** when he left for military service in 1944, but her program was continued when he returned. In 1946, the sponsorship was assumed by Campbell's soups and the name of the program was changed to *The Campbell Room*. Her nationality was not mentioned on the program, but it was hinted that she was internationally known.

HILL, EDWIN C. (1884–1957). Hill had been a star reporter for the *New York Sun* but left in 1923 to become a director of Fox newsreels, returning to journalism in 1927 before making his radio debut in 1931. As a reporter, he was said to have interviewed more than a thousand men and women while covering major news stories. His radio program was usually called *The Human Side of the News*, which was also the title of his syndicated column for King Features. The program was very popular, if somewhat sentimental, and was heard until 1952, first on CBS and then on NBC. As the years went by, he and his program grew more political and more politically conservative. At one time in his career, Hill broadcast weekly for NBC and simultaneously had five programs a week on ABC. He was compared favorably to **Lowell Thomas**.

HILLTOP HOUSE. A 15-minute daily **soap opera**, *Hilltop House* first appeared in 1937 with Bess Johnson appearing under her own name as a caseworker at an orphanage called Hilltop House. In 1941, the program was cancelled and Johnson moved to another network to star in a soap opera created for her, *The Story of Bess Johnson*. From 1948 to 1957, another version of *Hilltop House* was broadcast, with **Jan Miner** playing the lead role of the orphanage supervisor.

HOAGY CARMICHAEL SHOW (THE). Hoagy Carmichael, the composer of many popular songs, was first heard in 1944–1945 as host of a 30-minute program called *Tonight at Hoagy's*, which featured many famous musicians and singers in a jam-session atmosphere. The next year, the program name was changed to *Something New* and featured new or previously unknown musical performers. From 1946 to 1948 *The Hoagy Carmichael Show* was a 15-minute program featuring songs performed by Carmichael himself.

HOBBY LOBBY. A 30-minute human-interest program that afforded people with unusual hobbies an opportunity to describe and discuss them, *Hobby Lobby* was hosted by Dave Elman, himself a collector and hobbyist. The program solicited submissions from listeners and Elman chose the most interesting to appear on the program. It was heard, with several interruptions, from 1937 to 1949.

HOFFA, PORTLAND. *See THE FRED ALLEN SHOW.*

HOLLYWOOD HOTEL. A 60-minute **variety program** heard from 1934 to 1938, *Hollywood Hotel* was one of the first major network programs to be broadcast from the West Coast. Hosted by **Louella Parsons**, the program presented Hollywood gossip, musical numbers, and dramatizations of current movies. Major Hollywood stars appeared without compensation until union objections stopped the practice and ended the program.

HOLLYWOOD PLAYERS (THE). Sometimes listed as *The Cresta Blanca Hollywood Players*, this was a 30-minute **drama anthology** heard during 1946–1947. Several major film stars, including Claudette Colbert, Bette Davis, Joan Fontaine, John Garfield, and Gregory Peck formed a repertory company and each week presented a radio dramatization of a hit movie, novel, or stage production.

HOLLYWOOD PREMIERE. A 30-minute **drama anthology** appearing in 1941, *Hollywood Premiere* presented brief dramatizations of recent motion pictures and interviews with the stars of the picture that had been dramatized. The performers appeared without payment in return for publicity for their picture. Hosted by **Louella Parsons**, the program was in many ways similar to the earlier *Hollywood Hotel* and met similar objections from both the screen actors and radio actors unions.

HOLLYWOOD STAR PLAYHOUSE. A 30-minute **drama anthology** heard from 1950 to 1953, *Hollywood Star Playhouse* featured major screen stars in original suspense dramas. Directed by Jack Johnstone and hosted first by Herbert Rawlinson and later by Orval Anderson, the program was well received and one of the episodes, *The Six Shooter*, starring James Stewart, later became a network series.

HOLLYWOOD STAR PREVIEW. A 30-minute **drama anthology** heard from 1947 to 1952, *Hollywood Star Preview* was a vehicle for introducing new Hollywood performers to a wide audience. On each episode, a Hollywood film star introduced a promising newcomer, who then performed in a 20-minute dramatic skit. The star and the newcomer then chatted, plugging their latest films and discussing how they had met. The name of the program was changed to *Hollywood Star Theater* in 1948 and later to *Tums Hollywood Theater*.

HONEST HAROLD. A 30-minute **situation comedy** heard in 1950–1951, *Honest Harold* starred Harold Peary as Honest Harold Kemp, a radio entertainer who lived in the small town of Melrose Springs with his mother and nephew. Peary had just left his starring role on *The Great Gildersleeve*, and although *Honest Harold* was supposed to be very different, both the lead character and the program itself were very like *The Great Gildersleeve*.

HOOPER RATINGS. *See* RATING SYSTEMS.

HOP HARRIGAN. A **juvenile adventure program** heard from 1942 to 1948, *Hop Harrigan* featured a daredevil flyer who was first seen in comic books. Aided by his mechanic and buddy, Tank Tinker, Hop was heavily involved in World War II, serving in both the European and Pacific theaters. Written by Bob Burtt and Wilfred Moore, who also created and wrote *Captain Midnight*, the program was in many ways similar to *Captain Midnight*, with clubs to join and appeals to patriotism. A feature of the program was the "Aviation Question Box," during which announcer Glenn Riggs answered questions about flying sent in by listeners. Each program began with Hop calling on his radio, "CX-4 to control tower" and ended with another radio call, "Okay, this is Hop Harrigan, taking off! See you tomorrow. Same time, same station."

HOPALONG CASSIDY. A 30-minute **juvenile adventure program** heard from 1950 to 1952, *Hopalong Cassidy* was based on the western novels of Clarence Mumford. Played by **William Boyd**, who also played Hoppy in the movies, the character was much more civilized than the rough-cut character portrayed in the novels. Originally produced in syndication, the radio program was already appearing in many markets when the television version began in 1949, and it was soon picked up by CBS to capitalize on the popularity of the character on television and in motion pictures.

HOPE, BOB (1903–2003). Leslie Townes Hope was a success in vaudeville, musical theater, movies, and television, as well as radio. Born in England, he moved with his family to Cleveland, Ohio, when he was four and became a U.S. citizen in 1920. He started performing as a teenager in vaudeville with an act of "song, patter, and eccentric dancing." He reached Broadway in the late 1920s, where he appeared in several musical comedies. On radio, he appeared on *Atlantic Family* in the mid-1930s and on *Rippling Rhythm Revue* in 1937, and then starred on ***The Bob Hope Show*** from 1938 to 1955. When television came along, he jumped into the new medium, making his debut on Easter Sunday, 1950. He subsequently starred on two TV variety shows and then hosted *Bob Hope Presents the Chrysler Theatre* from 1963 to 1967. Hope began making movies in 1938 and starred in them for the next 30 years, winning special Academy Awards in 1940, 1944, and 1952. Some of his most popular films were the seven highly successful "Road" pictures he made with **Bing Crosby** and Dorothy Lamour. It has been said that, over his career, Hope won more awards than any other entertainer of the 20th century. Many of these were for his charitable and public service work, including entertaining servicemen all over the world. An autobiography, *The Road to Hollywood*, was published in 1977.

HOPPER, HEDDA (1890–1966). Hopper was an ex-actress who became one of Hollywood's most well-known and influential gossip columnists, known particularly for her collection of outrageous hats. She hosted a long series of radio programs in several different formats over the years, all of which included gossip and celebrity interviews. There were several different names for her shows, among them *Hedda Hopper's Hollywood* and *This Is Hollywood*. William Hopper, her son by vaudeville superstar De Wolf Hopper, played detective Paul Drake on the television version of *Perry Mason*. *See also* PARSONS, LOUELLA.

HORACE HEIDT SHOW (THE). Heidt was a popular orchestra leader who headlined many **music programs** from 1932 to 1953, including *Anniversary Night with Horace Heidt*, *Pot O' Gold*, and *The Tums Treasure Chest*. Although he achieved his first major success on *Pot O' Gold*, his best-known program was *The Youth Opportunity Program*, which was in some ways like *Major Bowes' Original Amateur Hour*: Heidt's orchestra and troupe moved to a different town each week, auditioning local musical talent and presenting the best performers on his weekly radio program in a talent contest with both cash and professional opportunity as prizes.

HOUR OF CHARM (THE). A long-running 30-minute **music program** featuring an all-girl orchestra, *The Hour of Charm* was heard from 1934 to 1948. Directed by Phil Spitalny, the orchestra was usually composed of 20 to 25 musicians and played a mixture of popular and symphonic music. Several of the featured players became very well known, particularly Evelyn Kaye Klein, who was billed as "Evelyn and Her Magic Violin." She and Spitalny were married in 1946.

HOUSE OF MYSTERY (THE). A dramatic mystery anthology program for children, *The House of Mystery* was heard from 1945 to 1949, first appearing as a 15-minute daily program but changing to a 30-minute Saturday morning program in the fall of 1945. It was hosted by "The Mystery Man," Roger Elliott, who told mysterious tales to an audience of children who made "oohs and aaahs" and were allowed to ask questions after the story was over. The intent of the program was to debunk stories of ghosts and phantoms and to prove that they existed only in one's imagination. *See also* CHILDREN'S PROGRAMS.

HOUSE PARTY. Sometimes listed as *Art Linkletter's House Party*, this 30-minute daily program was heard from 1945 to 1957. It was hosted by **Art Linkletter**, was largely unscripted, and depended on Linkletter's ability to ad-lib and to conduct the games, interviews, household and beauty hints, and other features of the program. It was produced by John Guedel, who also produced ***People Are Funny***. The best-known segment of the program was Linkletter's unrehearsed interviews with schoolchildren, which produced unpredictable and sometimes embarrassing results. *See also* AUDIENCE-PARTICIPATION PROGRAMS.

HOUSEBOAT HANNAH. A 15-minute daily **soap opera** created by **Frank and Anne Hummert**, *Houseboat Hannah* was heard on regional networks from 1936 to 1938 and then moved to NBC until 1941. It was the story of Hannah O'Leary, whose husband had lost his arm in an accident in a canning factory and whose family had subsequently been forced to live in poverty on a houseboat in San Francisco Bay. Hannah was played by Henrietta Tedro and then by Doris Rich; her husband Dan was played by Norman Gottschalk.

HOWARD, TOM (1886–1955). Howard was a comedian who once said that his first job on radio consisted of reading some jokes into a microphone each week and then going home. Howard appeared on several variety programs during the 1930s and then starred on *It Pays to Be Ignorant* from 1942 to 1951. Appearing with him on this popular program that satirized panel quizzes was his former vaudeville partner **George Shelton**. He and Shelton had performed their act on radio many times in the 1930s, often on *The Rudy Vallee Show*. Howard and *It Pays to Be Ignorant* enjoyed a run on television from 1949 to 1951.

HOWDY DOODY. A 60-minute Saturday morning program for children that was essentially an audio version of the television program, *Howdy Doody* was the story of a circus troupe led by Buffalo Bob that tried to perform in Doodyville, opposed by Phineas T. Bluster, who did not want people to have fun. Buffalo Bob and a little puppet boy named Howdy Doody were both played by Bob Smith. Phineas T. Bluster was played by Dayton Allen, and Indian princess Summerfall-winterspring by Judy Tyler. *See also* CHILDREN'S PROGRAMS.

HULL, WARREN (1903–1974). Hull dropped out of college to study voice at the Eastman School of the University of Rochester, and made his professional debut in the chorus of an operetta, later starring in several musical comedies. In the late 1930s and early 1940s, he played leads in low-budget movies, including several serials in which he portrayed such popular culture heroes as The Green Hornet, The Spider, and Mandrake the Magician. He started on radio in 1923, and continued in broadcasting while performing on stage and in the movies. He was the announcer or host on such programs as *Good News of 1939*, *Vox Pop*, *Spin to Win*, and *Strike It Rich*. On *Strike It Rich*, he achieved stardom, and he remained its emcee when a television version was created in 1951. On TV, he appeared as host or emcee of a half-dozen other programs, including *The Warren Hull Show*, a talk program that was broadcast during the 1950s.

HUMMERT, FRANK (1882–1966) and ANNE (1905–1996). This husband-and-wife writing team was responsible for more than 60 radio programs broadcast during the golden age of radio. Beginning in 1931 with *The Stolen Husband*, they turned out successful programs for 20 years until the last one, *Hearthstone of the Death Squad*, premiered in 1951. In between, they were responsible for such long-running and popular serial dramas as *Just Plain Bill*, *The Romance of Helen Trent*, *Ma Perkins*, *Backstage Wife*, *Lorenzo Jones*, *Young Widder Brown*, and *Stella Dallas*. At one time, they had 36 programs airing concurrently. The Hummerts created the concepts and plot lines for their programs and employed a half-dozen editors, a score of writers, and dozens of clerical workers to finish the work. The programs were written using assembly-line methods, with the Hummerts setting inflexible guidelines that had to be followed by all who worked for them. Their production company, *Air Features Incorporated*, was often referred to as a **soap opera** factory.

HURT, MARLIN (1904–1946). Hurt was a singer and actor who had originally been Dick in the popular singing trio of Tom, Dick, and Harry on Chicago radio. The trio appeared on *Plantation Party*, *Show*

Boat, and other musical-variety programs and Hurt sometimes used a falsetto voice in playing women on *Show Boat*. When a member of the singing trio died, Hurt became a solo act, doing a radio show on which he played saxophone and did dialects. On *Fibber McGee and Molly*, Hurt created Beulah, the lovable African American maid who became so popular that CBS gave Hurt his own show in 1945. On *The Marlin Hurt and Beulah Show*, he played not only Beulah, but also himself and Beulah's boyfriend, Bill Jackson. Hurt died suddenly of a heart attack at the end of the show's first full season.

– I –

I LOVE A MYSTERY. One of the most popular of all old-time radio programs among today's listeners, *I Love a Mystery* was an adventure serial written by **Carlton E. Morse**, who also wrote *One Man's Family*. It was heard from 1939 to 1944 and was then broadcast again from 1949 to 1952, using the original scripts but a new cast. Beginning as a 15-minute daily program, it was also heard in a 30-minute format from 1940 to 1942. The show featured the adventures of three partners in the A-1 Detective Agency: Jack Packard, who was the leader, Texan Doc Long, and Englishman Reggie Yorke. Although headquartered in Hollywood, the trio's adventures took place in exotic foreign settings and were sometimes very violent, with several murders sometimes occurring during a single episode. In the original version, Jack was played by **Michael Raffetto**, Doc by **Barton Yarborough**, and Reggie by Walter Paterson, three actors who also had featured roles on *One Man's Family*. In the 1949 broadcasts, these three characters were played by Russell Thorson, Jim Boles, and Tony Randall, respectively.

I LOVE ADVENTURE. A 30-minute weekly **adventure program** heard only in 1948, this continuation of the adventures of the heroes of *I Love a Mystery* was also written by **Carlton E. Morse.** The show appeared after the original version of *I Love a Mystery* had left the air and before the appearance of the remake in 1949. The A-1 Detective Agency had been disbanded when the three partners went to war in World War II and they were now re-united in a struggle against various international criminals and enemies of peace. As in the original series, Jack Packard was played by **Michael Raffetto** and Doc Long by **Barton Yarborough**; but Reggie Yorke was played by Tom Collins.

I WAS A COMMUNIST FOR THE FBI. A 30-minute espionage drama, *I Was a Communist for the FBI* was produced in syndication by ZIV and was never actually a network program. It was widely heard, however, and at one time appeared on more than 600 stations. The show was based on the real-life story of Matt Cvetic, a double agent who infiltrated the Communist Party and reported to the Federal Bureau of Investigation (FBI). Produced without the cooperation of the FBI, the program starred Dana Andrews as Cvetic.

IDELSON, BILLY (1920–). Billy Idelson is best remembered by old-time radio enthusiasts as the young man who played the role of Rush, the adopted son on *Vic and Sade*. He played this role for 10 years and was also heard as Hank Murray, one of the Barbour's grandsons, on *One Man's Family* for eight years. Idelson started out on radio as Skeezix on the radio version of the comic strip *Gasoline Alley*, and also played in *The Truitts*, *Those Websters*, and *Woman in My House*. After radio, he moved to television, where he both acted and produced, playing Bud Abbott on *Mixed Doubles* and Clifford Barbour on the TV version of *One Man's Family*, thus accomplishing the feat of playing his own uncle (from the radio series). As a producer, Idelson was responsible for such popular television programs as *The Bob Newhart Show* and *Love, American Style*.

INFORMATION, PLEASE. Heard from 1938 to 1948, *Information, Please* was a 30-minute panel **quiz program** on which questions from listeners were submitted to a panel of experts, with the listener receiving a small prize if the experts could not answer his question correctly. The actual questions were relatively unimportant; they simply served as starting points for intellectual discussion and clever commentary by the panel. Created, produced, and directed by Dan Golenpaul, the program was moderated by **Clifton Fadiman** and although the panel changed over the course of the run, the best-known version consisted of Franklin P. Adams and John Kieran, with one or two guest panelists. Actor-musician Oscar Levant appeared frequently as a panel member.

INNER SANCTUM MYSTERIES. A 30-minute horror anthology program heard from 1941 to 1952, *Inner Sanctum Mysteries* had one of the most famous openings in the history of radio. After an initial greeting, a door squeaked slowly open and the listener was greeted by the host, who made a gruesome joke and then introduced the story. Although the title came from the Simon and Schuster line of mystery stories, the programs presented were not so much mysteries as spook stories of one kind or another, many of them very fanciful or improbable. After the end of the story, the host returned to make another gruesome joke about the plot and the door squeaked shut to end the program. The first and best-known host was **Raymond Edward Johnson**, who was replaced in 1945 by Paul McGrath and still later by **House Jameson**.

IRENE RICH DRAMAS. An unusual 15-minute weekly **drama anthology** program that appeared from 1933 to 1944, *Irene Rich Dramas* appeared under several different titles, depending on the story being presented at the time. Irene Rich was a silent film star who left the film industry in a contract dispute and became the star of this radio anthology. Some of the dramas presented had storylines that were quite extended, lasting for several months; one titled "Dear John" was heard for years.

IT PAYS TO BE IGNORANT. Heard from 1942 to 1951, although off the air occasionally, *It Pays to Be Ignorant* was a 30-minute satire of the intellectual panel programs that were popular at the time. Ridiculous questions were presented to the panel and the answers degenerated into a collection of puns, one-liners, insults, and other irrelevant comments. The program was written by Bob and Ruth Howell, and moderated by **Tom Howard**, Ruth's father and an old vaudevillian. The panelists were Harry McNaughton, Lulu McConnell, and **George Shelton**, who had been Howard's partner in vaudeville.

– J –

JACK ARMSTRONG, THE ALL-AMERICAN BOY. A long-running **juvenile adventure program** heard from 1933 to 1950, *Jack Arm-*

strong was produced by the **Frank and Ann Hummert** agency and was originally written by **Robert Hardy Andrews**, although many other writers were employed later. Jack was a Frank Merriwell-like character who was a student and super-athlete at Hudson High, in Hudson, U.S.A. Jack sought adventure all over the world with his friends, Billy and Betty Fairfield, and their uncle, Jim Fairfield. The program had the same sponsor for the entire run and made Wheaties into a household word and a commercial bonanza by offering dozens of different premiums that could be obtained only by sending in a boxtop. Six different actors played Jack over the course of the long run; the best known were **Jim Ameche** and Charles Flynn. A 15-minute daily serial for the first many years, the program changed to a 30-minute format in 1947, with a complete adventure in each episode. In 1950, Jack grew up and became an agent of the Scientific Bureau of Investigation and the show became *Armstrong of the SBI.*

JACK BENNY PROGRAM (THE). Heard from 1932 to 1955, *The Jack Benny Program* was one of the longest-running and most successful programs in the history of radio. Benny was a vaudeville comedian whose early programs were primarily musical, with comedy skits interspersed between musical numbers. Over time, the comedy came to be primary and the later program was organized as a **situation comedy**. The show often began with an opening period of repartee among cast members and continued with a comic skit featuring many of the supporting characters who became household names: **Dennis Day**, **Phil Harris**, Rochester, the gravel-voiced valet, played by Eddie Anderson; and **Mary Livingstone**, Benny's girlfriend on the show, who was his wife in real life. **Mel Blanc** and Frank Nelson played many different comic characters. **Don Wilson** was the announcer. The program often was referred to by the sponsor's name: *The Jell-O Program* (1934–1942) and *The Lucky Strike Program* (1944–1955). The program also had a very successful run on television, and was seen until the mid-1960s.

JACK BERCH AND HIS BOYS. This long-running 15-minute music and talk program was also called *The Jack Berch Show* and was heard from 1935 to 1954; sometimes daily, sometimes twice or three times weekly. Berch, who was a baritone vocalist and a whistler, was assisted by a variety of musicians over the course of the long run, including the Mark Warnow Orchestra, The Three Suns, and organist John Gart.

JACK CARSON SHOW (THE). Carson was a comedian who was best known for his work in motion pictures, but he also had a successful career in radio. After hosting ***The Camel Caravan*** and *The Signal Carnival*, he headlined his own **comedy program** from 1943 to 1947. Carson took over as host of the *New Sealtest Village Store* in 1947, but his own program returned in 1948–1949 and again in 1954–1955.

JACK HALEY SHOW (THE). Haley, a comedian who is best remembered as the Tin Man in *The Wizard Of Oz*, hosted a 30-minute **comedy program** from 1937 to 1939. When sponsored by Log Cabin Syrup in 1937–1938, the program was called *The Log Cabin Jamboree*. The next season, when sponsored by Wonder Bread on CBS, the program was sometimes called *The Wonder Show*, although there was also a drama anthology by that name. Haley later returned to radio on ***The Sealtest Village Store.***

JACK KIRKWOOD SHOW (THE). Kirkwood was a comedian who hosted several programs of different names between 1943 and 1953. All of them were **comedy programs** that featured comedic skits and vaudeville-like dialogue. His first program was a daily morning show named *Mirth and Madness*, that featured his wife, Lillian Leigh, and **Ransom Sherman**. In 1944, the show moved to CBS in a 15-minute nightly format and was renamed *The Jack Kirkwood Show*. It went off the air in 1946, but during 1948–1949, the Kirkwoods starred in a satirical husband-and-wife series named *At Home with the Kirkwoods*; and in 1949–1950 they were featured in a variety program named *The Kirkwood Corner Store*. The Jack Kirkwood Show was heard again as a 30-minute nightly program on Mutual from 1950 to 1953, with Wally Brown and Steve Dunne.

JACK OAKIE'S COLLEGE. A **comedy program** heard from 1936 to 1938, *Jack Oakie's College* featured Oakie as the president of a mythical college that served as the setting for the vaudeville-like skits and jokes that comprised the majority of the show. First heard as a 60-minute program, the format was changed to 30 minutes in

1937 and the program became a portion of *The Camel Caravan*, with *Benny Goodman's Swing School* providing the other 30 minutes.

JACK PEARL SHOW (THE). Jack Pearl was a vaudeville comedian who brought his character of Baron Munchausen to radio in 1932, and the show was sometimes listed as *Baron Munchausen*. The Baron told ridiculous stories in a heavy German dialect, and Cliff Hall, who had been Pearl's partner in vaudeville, acted as his straight man, Charlie (which led to a catchphrase of the day, "Vas you dere, Sharlie?"). Originally a 60-minute program, the show was initially very successful, but soon lost its popularity and in 1934 was reduced to a 30-minute format. The next year, Pearl appeared in *Peter Pfeiffer*, a **situation comedy** featuring a German tavern keeper, and during 1936–1937, he headlined *The Raleigh-Kool Program*. Pearl left the air in 1937 and was not heard again until a brief appearance in 1948 in *Jack and Cliff* and another in 1951 as a summer replacement show for *Fibber McGee and Molly*.

JACK SMITH SHOW (THE). Smith was a tenor billed as "The Singer with a Smile in His Voice," more or less contrary to the crooning style that was popular during the time. He hosted a series of 15-minute daily programs of light music from 1943 to 1951, often named for the sponsor. He is sometimes confused with an earlier singer of the same name, a baritone known as Whispering Jack Smith, who hosted a popular **music program** in the 1930s.

JAMES, HARRY (1916–1983). A bandleader and trumpet virtuoso, James played in his father's circus band and at age twelve led a band for the Christy Brothers Circus. In the mid-1930s, he was hired by Ben Pollack and in 1937 joined the brass section of Benny Goodman's orchestra, becoming a jazz soloist. In 1939, he organized his own band, The Music Makers. On radio, he was featured on several programs including *Chesterfield Time*, *The Danny Kaye Show*, *The Fitch Bandwagon*, *Spotlight Bands*, *Everything for the Boys*, and *Call for Music*. From 1942 to 1945, he and his band starred on their own program, *Harry James and His Music Makers*. In the 1940s, he and his band had several hit records for Columbia Records, including the company's first million seller, "I've Heard That Song Before." Beginning in 1937, James made a score of movies, usually playing his trumpet and acting in supporting roles. He was musical director of 1950's *Young Man with a Horn* and played the trumpet numbers supposedly done in the film by Kirk Douglas, the star. James was married to Betty Grable, a movie star and the leading World War II pin-up girl, from 1943 to 1965.

JAMESON, HOUSE (1902–1971). Jameson began his professional career acting on Broadway and ended up performing on television, but for many years in between he was a steady player on several popular old-time radio programs. He played the title role on ***Renfrew of the Mounted*** from 1936 to 1940, and was on ***Young Widder Brown*** from 1938 to 1942. He is best remembered, however, for his performance on ***The Aldrich Family***. For the entire run of the program on radio, from 1939 to 1953, Jameson played Sam Aldrich, the father on the popular program about family life in middle America. When the program moved to TV in the early 1950s, Jameson moved with it, still playing the role he had made famous on radio.

JANE FROMAN SHOW (THE). See FROMAN, JANE.

JIMMY DURANTE SHOW (THE). **Jimmy Durante** was a singer, piano player, and comedian who appeared as a guest on many programs before he and Garry Moore combined to take over *The Camel Cavavan* in 1943. Moore was more than 20 years younger than Durante, but they worked well together and the contrast in their ages and styles enlivened the program. Their show was titled differently on alternate weeks, each of them having a turn at first billing. Moore left in an amicable parting in 1947 and Durante continued as the star of the program, now called *The Jimmy Durante Show*. Durante closed each program with the phrase "Goodnight, Mrs. Calabash, wherever you are," which became a famous catchphrase; the phrase's exact meaning has always been unclear, although several explanations have been offered.

JOAN DAVIS SHOW (THE). **Joan Davis** was a comedienne who first appeared on *The Rudy Vallee Show* when it was sponsored by Sealtest. When Vallee entered the Coast Guard in 1943, she took over the starring role and the program was renamed *The Sealtest Village Store*. In 1945, the sponsor changed and the program became *Joanie's*

Tea Room. In 1947, the name was changed to *Joan Davis Time*, sometimes called *The Joan Davis Show*, and in 1949–1950 the name was changed again to *Leave It to Joan*. All of her programs were situation comedies with Davis playing a dizzy female character.

JOE PENNER SHOW (THE). A vaudeville comedian who was noted for his catchphrase, "Wanna buy a duck?," Joe Penner became the star of a 30-minute **comedy program** called *The Baker's Broadcast* in 1933 and was voted radio's outstanding comedian in 1934. He left the program in 1935 but returned in 1936 as the star of a **situation comedy** called *The Park Avenue Penners*. The name of the program was changed to *The Tip Top Show* in 1939 when the sponsorship was assumed by Tip Top bread. The program left the air in 1940. In 1941, Penner died of a heart attack while touring in a play at the age of 36.

JOHNNY PRESENTS. *Johnny Presents* was the umbrella title used for a series of 30-minute **music programs** sponsored by Philip Morris cigarettes from 1934 to 1946. The "Johnny" referred to the company trademark, a uniformed bellboy who appeared both in print advertisements and on the radio, walking though a hotel lobby and crying "Calll forrrr Phillipp Morrraaiiss" in the manner of bellhops of the day, who, before public address systems were common, paged hotel customers by calling their name throughout the lobby. As with *The Camel Caravan*, the composition of the program changed from year to year, but always featured well-known orchestras and singers. When **Ginny Simms** became the star in 1942, the name was changed to *Johnny Presents Ginny Simms*.

JOHN'S OTHER WIFE. A 15-minute NBC **soap opera** written by Bill Sweets and produced by **Frank and Anne Hummert**, *John's Other Wife* was heard from 1936 to 1942. The plot revolved around the concerns of an insecure wife, who suspected her husband, John Perry, a department store owner, of being in love with another woman. The other woman usually was his secretary, Annette Rogers, although suspicion sometimes also fell on his assistant, Martha Curtis. John was played by many actors during the program run, including **Hanley Stafford**, **Richard Kollmar**, and **Joseph Curtin**. His wife Elizabeth was played by Adele Ronson and Erin O'Brien-Moore; Annette, his secretary was played by Franc Hale. Martha, John's beautiful assistant, was played by Phyllis Welch and Rita Johnson. The program name was often lampooned by radio comedians.

JOHNSON FAMILY (THE). A 15-minute daily program heard from 1937 to 1950, *The Johnson Family* was a combination **soap opera** and **situation comedy** that portrayed life in a village of African Americans. Jimmy Scribner, who was white, wrote the program, produced it, played all the parts, provided the sound effects, and even played the music on a banjo. Beginning with eight characters, he was eventually using at least 22 different voices. All of the characters were based on people Scribner had known as a youth.

JOHNSON, RAYMOND EDWARD (1911–2001). Remembered primarily today as the sinister host of *Inner Sanctum Mysteries*, Johnson was also a featured performer on several daytime serial dramas, including *Today's Children*, *Girl Alone*, *Valiant Lady*, *Tennessee Jed*, and *Joyce Jordan, M.D.* He also appeared on *The Guiding Light* and *Stella Dallas* and was featured on *There Was a Woman*. Johnson played the lead on the juvenile serials *Don Winslow of the Navy* and *Mandrake the Magician* and appeared on other popular golden age programs, such as *The Aldrich Family*, *Mr. District Attorney*, and *Arch Oboler's Plays*.

JOHNSTONE, WILLIAM (1908–1996). One of radio's most dependable and versatile supporting actors, Bill Johnstone appeared on many programs during the medium's golden age, including *The Casebook of Gregory Hood*, *The Lineup*, *Valiant Lady*, and *Joyce Jordan, M.D.* Johnstone played the lead on *The Shadow* from 1938 to 1943 and made numerous appearances on popular **drama anthology programs**, such as *The Cavalcade of American*, *Irene Rich Dramas*, *The Lux Radio Theater*, *The Mysterious Traveler*, *Suspense*, and *The March of Time*. On television, he appeared for many years on *As the World Turns* (as Judge Lowell).

JONES, BILLY. *See THE HAPPINESS BOYS.*

JONES, SPIKE (1911–1965). Lindley Armstrong (Spike) Jones played drums while still in grammar school, and then was a drummer with both **Victor Young** and **John Scott Trotter** before organizing the City Slickers, a goofy orchestra that played on cowbells, foghorns, and kitchen utensils, as well as on regular instruments. During the 1940s, the City Slickers had several novelty record hits and one of their recordings, "Der Fuehrer's Face," sold more than 1.5 million copies. It achieved a sort of immortality when Walt Disney made a cartoon that featured the song. On radio, Jones and his band appeared as a summer replacement for *The Edgar Bergen–Charlie McCarthy Show* in 1945, starred on *Spike's at the Mike* during 1946, and finally co-starred with singer Dorothy Shay on *Spotlight Revue*—with the name changed to *The Spike Jones Show* when Shay left in 1949. Jones and his band later toured with his Musical Depreciation Revue that featured Jones' wife, singer Helen Graco, and comic Winstead "Doodles" Weaver. From the mid-1950s until the early 1960s, Jones hosted or starred on several television programs.

JORDAN, JIM (1896–1988) and MARIAN (1898–1961). The Jordans began in vaudeville, first appearing on radio at station WIBO in Chicago in 1924 as the singing "O'Henry Twins." In 1931, they started their own **situation comedy**, *Smackout*, which eventually brought them to network radio. On this program, Jim Jordan played a grocer who was always "smack out" of everything. The Jordans also appeared together (as Mickey Donovan and Gertie Glump) on *Kaltenmeyer's Kindergarten* in the mid-1930s. They developed their signature radio characters of Fibber McGee and his wife, Molly, and played them from 1935 until 1956 on their own program, *Fibber McGee and Molly*. Following Marian's death in 1961, Jim Jordan retired from show business although he continued to make guest appearances throughout the 1970s. On 21 December 1983 a bronze star bearing "Fibber McGee & Molly" was unveiled on the Walk of Fame in Hollywood.

JOSTYN, JAY (1905–1977). Jostyn began his professional radio career in New York in the mid-1930s, and although he was featured on several daytime serials, including *Second Husband* and *Our Gal Sunday*, he is best remembered for playing the title role on *Mr. District Attorney* from 1939 to 1951. He also narrated on the poetry-music show *Moon River*, starred on the **situation comedy** *The Parker Family*, and was featured on several dramas, such as *Foreign Assign-*

ment, Famous Jury Trials, and *The Mystery Man*. During 1951–1952, he starred as *Mr. District Attorney* on television.

JOYCE JORDAN, M.D. A 15-minute **soap opera** heard primarily from 1938 to 1948, this program was originally titled *Joyce Jordan, Girl Interne*. After becoming *Joyce Jordan, M.D.* in 1942, the theme remained the same: the difficulties encountered by a woman torn between her attempt to achieve success in a man's world and her desire for marriage and a family. Joyce practiced medicine in the small town of Preston, and later became a brilliant surgeon. The program changed gradually until she was more a hostess than a performer, narrating tales of her patient's experiences. The first version of the program ended in 1948, but it was later revived for a year in 1951 and had another brief run in 1955. Joyce was played by seven different actresses during the run.

JUDY AND JANE. One of the earliest of the soap operas, and unusual in that it was fundamentally humorous, *Judy and Jane* was a 15-minute daily program heard from 1932 to 1936 on CBS and NBC and then in transcription on regional networks for many years thereafter. The story of the amusing struggles of two young women to find romance and financial security during the Depression, it was produced by **Frank and Anne Hummert**, and originally written by **Robert Hardy Andrews**, although it was later written by Jim Whipple.

JUDY CANOVA SHOW (THE). A 30-minute **situation comedy** heard from 1943 to 1953, *The Judy Canova Show* centered on the life of a country bumpkin who had moved to the big city to live with her aunt. Canova was a talented singer who had been trained in opera and each program featured her singing in country dialect as well as in her natural voice. The supporting cast was excellent and included **Hans Conried**, **Verna Felton**, **Sheldon Leonard**, and **Mel Blanc**. Blanc's portrayal of Pedro the Mexican handyman always began with the entry line "Pardon me for talking in your face, Senorita," which became a nationally known catchphrase.

JULIAN, JOSEPH (1911–1982). Julian was a frequent narrator and actor in the prestigious CBS dramas of **Norman Corwin**. In the 1940s, he also appeared on many popular programs, including *Young*

Doctor Malone, **Front Page Farrell**, **The Goldbergs**, **Nero Wolfe**, **Superman**, **The Greatest Story Ever Told**, and **Lorenzo Jones**. Julian promoted the idea that performers should memorize a radio role rather than reading it from a script and in a series of articles published in *Variety* and the *New York Times* claimed that most actors on radio were not fulfilled by their work and did not take themselves seriously. During the Red Scare of the 1950s in the United States, he was one of those blacklisted in *Red Channels*; but he filed suit and eventually was exonerated.

JUMBO. Although heard only in 1935–1936, *Jumbo* was the most extravagant radio program of the day. Broadcast from the stage of the Hippodrome Theater in New York, where the stage production of the same name was appearing, it was the story of John Considine, a circus owner who was in competition with another circus, owned by Matt Mulligan. His problems were complicated by the fact that his daughter and Mulligan's son were in love. **Jimmy Durante** was featured prominently as the press agent for Considine. Sponsored by Texaco gasoline and intended as a replacement for **Ed Wynn, the Fire Chief**, it is sometimes listed as *The Jumbo Fire Chief Show*. The program had a large cast, a large orchestra and chorus, and a huge budget; but ratings were never high and it was discontinued after less than one full season. John Considine was played by Arthur Sinclair, and Mulligan by W. J. McCarthy.

JUNIOR MISS. A 30-minute **situation comedy** based on the character created by Sally Benson, *Junior Miss* centered on the teenage problems of 15-year-old Judy Graves. First heard in 1942 with Shirley Temple starring as Judy, the program left the air after only a few months. It returned in 1948 with an entirely new cast, including Barbara Whiting as Judy and **Gale Gordon** in a supporting role. The program was discontinued in 1950 but had another brief run from 1952 to 1954.

JUST PLAIN BILL. One of the earliest **soap operas**, *Just Plain Bill* was also one of the most successful, remaining on the air from 1932 until 1955. Written by **Robert Hardy Andrews** and produced by **Frank and Anne Hummert**, it was the story of Bill Donovan, a widower and the barber in the small town of Hartville. A folksy philosopher of the type later seen on many other soap operas, Bill was played by Arthur Hughes for the entire run. Musical bridges and interludes were played on the guitar or harmonica, unlike most soap operas, which relied heavily on organ music for the same purposes.

JUVENILE ADVENTURE PROGRAMS. Most of the programs intended for older children appeared during the late afternoon, when it was assumed that they would be home from school, and most were serial dramas, with cliff-hanger endings for each episode. The first of these afternoon children's serials to appear on network radio was *Little Orphan Annie*, based on the comic strip character who was very popular at the time. The program was particularly noted for offering many premiums, a pattern later followed by many other programs aimed at juvenile audiences. Another early serial, *The Air Adventures of Jimmie Allen*, was written and produced by **Robert M. Burtt** and **William G. Moore**, the same team that later wrote *Captain Midnight*. There were very few sound effects and the program consisted almost entirely of dialogue read by the characters, but it was a smash hit from 1933 to 1936.

Jack Armstrong, The All-American Boy began at about the same time as *The Air Adventures of Jimmie Allen*, and also featured an adolescent hero who had adventures all over the world. It was produced by the **Hummert** agency and was written by **Robert Hardy Andrews**, who also wrote daytime serials for adults. *Tom Mix* began the same year as Jimmie Allen and Jack Armstrong, but did not have a juvenile hero. It was a western adventure series originally based on the real-life exploits of Tom Mix; it later evolved into a program with entirely fictitious plots.

The Adventures of Superman first appeared in 1938, the same year that the Man of Steel first appeared in a comic book. Originally syndicated, it soon became a network program and had a very long run, eventually moving to television, although with different performers than those on the radio version. *Hop Harrigan*, another program based on a comic book character, appeared in 1942. Although his adventures were more realistic, Hop was a sort of juvenile *Captain Midnight*, which is perhaps not greatly surprising, because Robert M. Burtt and William G. Moore, who were also the writers of *Jimmie Allen* and *Captain Midnight*, were part of the writing team for *Hop Harrigan*.

The same individuals were thus responsible for the production of several programs, a practice that became more common as broadcast radio developed and a pool of skilled writers and producers emerged. *The Lone Ranger*, *The Green Hornet*, and *Sergeant Preston of the Yukon*, for example, are among the best-remembered programs of radio's golden age and they were all produced by **George W. Trendle** (who owned station WXYZ in Detroit), were written by many of the same writers, and starred many of the same performers.

All of the Trendle programs featured adult heroes, and children seldom appeared, although the Lone Ranger did have a teen-age nephew who was a part of some of the later shows. *The Cisco Kid* also had only adult characters, and even made some passing reference to romance, with Cisco often stealing a kiss from a beautiful senorita at the end of each program. *Sky King* also had an adult hero, although two juvenile protagonists were a part of every adventure, accompanying their Uncle Sky who piloted his plane to adventure in various exotic locations.

Premiums could be obtained from many of these programs by sending a small amount of money, sometimes as little as 10 cents, with a box top or other proof-of-purchase from the sponsor's product. Often there was a club that the listener could join, with membership certificates and/or badges and a secret code that would allow the listener to decode messages heard on the program. *See also* CHILDREN'S PROGRAMS.

JUVENILE JURY. Heard from 1946 to 1953, *Juvenile Jury* was a 30-minute program on which a panel of children discussed the answers to questions sent in by listeners. Created and hosted by Jack Barry, the program was unrehearsed and there was no script; the questions were chosen by Barry and usually pertained to children's subjects, but also included serious concerns such as discipline and morality.

– K –

KABIBBLE, ISH. *See* MERWYN A. BOGUE.

KALTENBORN, H. V. (1878–1965). Hans von Kaltenborn was a journalist on the *Brooklyn Eagle* when he debuted on radio in 1922.

In 1924, he became a weekly commentator and in 1930, at age 52, he turned to full-time radio newscasting on CBS. On his *Current Events* program, he covered many political events, including national elections. He then went to NBC and covered similar assignments on his weekly *Kaltenborn Edits the News*, which aired from 1930 to 1955. Harvard-educated, well-traveled, and speaking fluent German and French, Kaltenborn interviewed many world leaders in their native languages. In 1936, he covered the Spanish Civil War at his own expense and made a famous broadcast by shortwave from within a battle. During the 20 days of the Munich crisis in 1938, he made 102 broadcasts. Kaltenborn helped organize the Association of Radio News Analysts as well as the Radio Pioneers. He was considered by many experts to have been both the best-known and the most widely respected news commentator of the 1930s and 1940s. At least one authority called him "the personification of the American radio commentator." From 1948 to 1950, he was on NBC's *Who Said That?*, a 30-minute program on which a panel of experts answered questions based on a current news event. He wrote several books during his lifetime, including the autobiographical *Fifty Fabulous Years*, published in 1950. *See also* NEWS PROGRAMS.

KALTENMEYER'S KINDERGARTEN. A 30-minute comedy program heard from 1933 to 1940, *Kaltenmeyer's Kindergarten* was set in "The Nonsense School of the Air," with Bruce Kamman as Professor August Kaltenmeyer, D.U.N. (Doctor of Utter Nonsense). **Jim and Marian Jordan** were members of the cast, as were **Harold Peary** and Isabel Randolph; all four of them left in 1936 to appear on *Fibber McGee and Molly*. In 1940, the title of the program was changed to *Kindergarten Kapers*, with the lead character's name changed to Ulysses S. Applegate (U.S.A.), because of anti-German sentiment in the nation leading up to World War II.

KATE SMITH HOUR (THE). Kate Smith was a vocalist who was one of the biggest stars of radio, headlining a long series of **music programs** in 15-minute, 30-minute, and 60-minute formats from 1930 to 1958. Her programs appeared under many titles, although unlike many other stars, almost all of the programs on which she appeared had titles that included her name: *Kate Smith Sings*, *The Kate Smith Matinee*, *The Kate Smith New Car Review*, *The Kate Smith Hour*, *The*

Kate Smith A&P Bandwagon, etc. She also hosted a long-running daytime talk program, *Kate Smith Speaks*, on which she and her manager Ted Collins chatted about current events, as well as talk shows titled *Kate Smith's Column* and *Speaking Her Mind*. A large woman, she had a powerful voice and was noted for having introduced Irving Berlin's "God Bless America" in 1938. She had exclusive rights to the song for several years and made it one of the most famous songs in America. She was also featured in a television version of *The Kate Smith Hour* (seen 1950–1954) and two later television series, *The Kate Smith Evening Hour* and *The Kate Smith Show*. She was inducted into the Radio Hall of Fame in 1999.

KAY KYSER'S KOLLEGE OF MUSICAL KNOWLEDGE. An unusual **music program** heard from 1938 to 1949, featuring a quiz portion, as well as comedy and music, *The Kollege of Musical Knowledge* featured the **Kay Kyser** Orchestra and vocalists **Ginny Simms**, **Harry Babbitt**, Sully Mason, and Georgia Carroll (Kyser's wife). Trumpet player and comedian **Merwyn A. Bogue** developed a comic character, Ish Kabibble, who sang novelty songs and became the most popular performer on the show. The quiz portion of the show was not at all difficult, although the cash prizes were substantial. Kyser always dressed in academic cap and gown and gave broad hints regarding the answers to the questions. He opened every show with his catchphrase, "Evening folks, how y'all?" The program moved to television in 1949.

KDKA. KDKA Pittsburgh, started broadcasting on 2 November 1920 and claims to have been the world's first commercial radio station, as well as the first radio station broadcasting on a regular schedule. The original purpose of the station was to stimulate sales of a radio receiver produced by Westinghouse.

Inspired by the results obtained by **Frank Conrad**, a Westinghouse engineer who had been broadcasting music from the experimental station that he operated from his home, Westinghouse decided to construct a station on the roof of a Westinghouse building located in East Pittsburgh in order to broadcast the results of the 1920 presidential election. Application was made for a commercial license and construction of the station was begun only a month prior to the election. The call letters were assigned by the government from a roster maintained to provide identification for ships and marine shore stations, the only regular radio services then in operation under federal license.

The broadcast of the election results was immensely successful and KDKA continued in operation, playing popular music and providing news bulletins. In 1921, the station broadcast a major league baseball game and one of the matches from the Davis Cup, and, in 1922, hosted Will Rogers on his first radio appearance. The station is still in operation today, as a news–talk station, with the same call letters.

KELK, JACKIE (1922–2002). Best known for his role as Homer Brown, the adolescent friend of Henry Aldrich on *The Aldrich Family*, Kelk was a Professional Children's School graduate, and began his acting career on Broadway at the age of nine. On radio, he was heard on *The Chase and Sanborn Hour*, *Coast-to-Coast on a Bus*, *Let's Pretend*, *Dick Tracy*, *Terry and the Pirates*, *The Aldrich Family*, and *The Adventures of Superman*. When *The Aldrich Family* moved to television in 1949, Kelk moved with it, again playing Homer Brown.

KELLY, JOE (1901–1959). Kelly began his radio career in a comedy singing act, "The Two Lunatics of the Air," that was broadcast from Battle Creek, Michigan. From there, he went to WLS, where he worked as an announcer, which led to his being chosen to emcee *The National Barn Dance* in 1934 (where he remained until 1946). In 1940, he was named moderator of *The Quiz Kids*, the program on which he achieved his greatest fame. Kelly had quit school at an early age to sing in a touring company, but his easygoing manner allowed him to relate well with the precocious youngsters, and he stayed with the popular program until it left the air in 1951. He was also the first moderator of the television version of the program. From 1947 to 1949, Kelly hosted another radio program, *RFD America*, an unusual quiz show that featured contests between farmers from different states.

KENT, ATWATER (1873–1949). Kent was a prolific inventor and engineer; at his death, he held 93 patents on automotive ignition systems and electronics. He attended Worcester Polytechnic Institute, majoring in mechanical engineering, and although he did not graduate, he returned in 1926 to accept an honorary doctorate from the school. In the late 1890s, he opened the Atwater Kent Manufacturing Works, making batteries and other items. In 1906, he developed the Uni-Sparker ignition system for automobiles, which became an industry standard; and, in 1919, the company began building headsets for the nascent radio industry. Manufacture of radio components followed in 1922 and the first complete radio set was shipped in November of that year. From 1926 to 1929, the company was the largest manufacturer of radios in the country; in 1929, they were producing a million Atwater Kent radio receivers a year. When the market changed, he decided not to produce the cheaper radios that were in demand, closing his company in 1936.

KILGALLEN, DOROTHY (1913–1965). Kilgallen had both a syndicated newspaper column and a radio program called *The Voice of Broadway* and her work in these media attracted New York radio executives, who put her and her husband **Richard Kollmar** into an early morning talk show, *Breakfast with Dorothy and Dick*. Beginning in 1945, this daily early morning husband-and-wife show enjoyed a long run, not ending until 1963. Kilgallen also appeared on other radio programs, including *Leave It to the Girls* and *Battle of the Sexes*; and from 1947 to 1949, she starred on her own program, *The Dorothy Kilgallen Show*. When television's *What's My Line?* began in 1950, she was one of the game show's regular panelists and continued on the program for the next 17 years. She also was a panelist on the radio version of the program during 1952–1953. Kilgallen died on 9 November 1965, officially of a heart attack; but some investigators thought her death occurred under suspicious circumstances.

KINSELLA, WALTER (1900–1975). A former model and athlete, Kinsella began his acting career in the theater in the mid-1920s. On radio, he appeared on *Dick Tracy*, *Abie's Irish Rose*, *Stella Dallas*, *Mr. and Mrs. North*, *Mr. District Attorney*, and *Martin Kane, Private Eye*. When *Martin Kane* moved to television in 1949, Kinsella went with it, both playing a retired police lieutenant and doing the program's commercials.

KITTY FOYLE. A 15-minute daily **soap opera** heard from 1942 to 1944, *Kitty Foyle* originated as a segment of *Stories America Loves*, an anthology program that dramatized popular romance novels. The story of Kitty was first heard in June of 1942 and proved so popular that in October of that year, the anthology format was abandoned and the show was continued as *Kitty Foyle*. Kitty was a working-class girl who was in love with wealthy Wynn Strafford, and the program used first-person narrative and frequent flashbacks to detail the difficulties involved in their romance. Kitty was played by Julie Stevens. Mel Allen, later to become a hall-of-fame sportscaster, was the announcer.

KITTY KEENE, INCORPORATED. A 15-minute daily **soap opera** heard from 1937 to 1941, *Kitty Keene, Incorporated* was a **Frank and Anne Hummert** production that detailed the experiences of a female private detective who ran her own detective agency. The program's storyline largely involved Kitty's family problems, rather than the activities of the detective agency. Kitty herself was a somewhat mysterious character, with relatively little being known about her, other than that she had previously been a showgirl. Several actresses played Kitty during the show's brief run, including Beverly Younger, Gail Henshaw, and **Fran Carlon**.

KNICKERBOCKER PLAYHOUSE. Heard from 1939 to 1942, *Knickerbocker Playhouse* was originally a 30-minute **drama anthology** hosted by **Elliott Lewis** with big-name Hollywood guest stars. In 1940, the format changed to include a host named "Mr. Knickerbocker" who said a few words about the upcoming production before a buzzer sounded and a stagehand announced that the curtain was going up. The plays presented changed to light dramas and one of these, **Abie's Irish Rose**, was so successful that it became a weekly program and replaced the *Knickerbocker Playhouse*.

KOLLMAR, RICHARD (1910–1971). Both an actor and a producer, Kollmar appeared on many radio programs, including the lead role on **Boston Blackie** from 1945 to 1950. He married columnist **Dorothy Kilgallen** in 1940, and they subsequently formed a husband-and-wife team on an early morning conversation program, **Breakfast with Dorothy and Dick**, for nearly 20 years. They were billed as "one of America's most charming couples." Kollmar also appeared on several daytime serial dramas, including **Big Sister**, **John's Other Wife**,

Life Can Be Beautiful, and *When a Girl Marries*. When the **Palm-olive Beauty Box Theater** presented 30-minute versions of operettas, Kollmar performed the speaking portions for the male singers; and he was one of the host-narrators on *The Radio Reader's Digest*.

KOSTELANETZ, ANDRE (1901–1980). Kostelanetz was an orchestra conductor who made his radio debut early in 1928 on the Atlantic Broadcasting Company. In 1930, he was hired by the **Columbia Broadcasting System (CBS)** to conduct its symphony orchestra and his long series of **concert music** programs began in 1932 when he appeared on his own Sunday night program. From 1934 to 1938, he hosted a series of 30-minute programs sponsored by Chesterfield cigarettes. In 1939–1940, he and his orchestra were part of *Tune-Up Time* (with singer Tony Martin), and from 1940 to 1944 they were featured on *The Pause That Refreshes* for Coca-Cola. He hosted *The Music of André Kostelanetz* for Chrysler in 1945–1946 before returning to *The Pause That Refreshes* for a final year in 1947–1948. Kostelanetz married soprano Lily Pons in 1938, and they toured widely during World War II, entertaining servicemen. He became the guest conductor of the New York Philharmonic in 1952 and remained in that position until his death in 1980. His memoirs, *Echoes*, were published in 1981.

KRAFT MUSIC HALL (THE). *The Kraft Music Hall* was the umbrella title for a long-running series of **music programs** sponsored by Kraft foods. Heard from 1933 to 1949, the program was originally hosted by music critic **Deems Taylor** and featured **Paul Whiteman** and his orchestra, but Al Jolson became the star later during the first year. After Jolson left the program in 1934, **Bing Crosby** became the headliner in 1935 and stayed until 1946; both of these versions of the program were often listed under the name of the star performer. After Crosby left, the show was hosted by Eddie Foy and Edward Everett Horton until Al Jolson returned from 1947 to 1949. There were also summer versions of the program, hosted by Nelson Eddy, from 1947 to 1949.

KUPPERMAN, JOEL J. (1936–). Joel Kupperman was the most famous member of *The Quiz Kids*, radio's **quiz program** featuring precocious children. He was a math wizard with an IQ estimated at over 200. On the program, he once answered a complicated math problem submitted by a university professor, and was told he had answered incorrectly; but when his answer was checked later, it was discovered that he was correct and the professor wrong. His popularity led to appearances on other radio programs and a role as a Quiz Kid in the 1944 movie, *Chip Off the Old Block*. He left *The Quiz Kids* in 1952 and has had a very successful career as a professor of philosophy at the University of Connecticut. He has published several books and won many awards in his chosen field.

KYSER, KAY (1906–1985). Kyser was a bandleader who formed his first band at the University of North Carolina when he was a student there in the mid-1920s. The band toured the country and in 1934 broke attendance records at the Blackhawk Restaurant in Chicago. Lew Wasserman of Music Corporation of America (MCA) saw them perform and hired Kyser to do a **quiz program** with musical questions, posing Kyser as "professor" and fans as "students." The resulting *Kay Kyser's Kampus Klass* developed into his *Kollege of Musical Knowledge*, which was heard from 1938 to 1949. During World War II, Kyser and his band made more than 1,000 appearances at functions where war bonds were sold. He retired from show business in the 1950s, and later became head of film and broadcasting for the Christian Science Church.

– L –

LAKE, ARTHUR (1905–1987). Born Arthur Silverlake, Lake was the son of a circus acrobat and an actress who had a vaudeville act in which he appeared as a young child. He appeared in movies in child roles from age 12, and then adolescent leads and light romantic roles, but in 1938 landed the part of Dagwood Bumstead in the *Blondie* series of light films based on the Chic Young comic strip. Subsequently, 28 movies were in the series, all of them starring Lake as Dagwood. The radio version, with Lake and many of the same performers from the films, appeared soon after the first *Blondie* movie and was heard from 1939 to 1950; he also starred in the television version of the program.

LAND OF THE LOST. A 30-minute **children's program** heard from 1943 to 1948, *Land of the Lost* was written, produced, and narrated by Isabel Manning Hewson. The stories purported to be her adventures as a child. Betty Jane Taylor played the part of the young Isabel, with Ray Ives playing Billy, her brother. The Land of the Lost was an enchanted kingdom at the bottom of the sea to which everything lost in the world found its way. Billy and young Isabel were guided by Red Lantern, a talking fish, played by Junius Mathews and others, including William Keene and Art Carney.

LANDT TRIO (THE). Consisting of three brothers, The Landt Trio was formed in Scranton, Pennsylvania, along with self-taught piano player Howard White, and they were booked as The Landt Trio and White. They moved to New York and were an immediate hit, performing in vaudeville and on numerous radio shows, as well as being given their own program *On the 8:15*, in December of 1928. They were then heard regularly on several networks until Howard White died suddenly in 1937. The trio later continued from 1941 to 1946 with another accompanist but were never again as successful. Although extremely popular in their day, they are not well remembered today because they did very little recording.

LANGFORD, FRANCES (1914–2005). Frances Langford was a popular singer during the 1930s and 1940s and appeared on several radio programs during this period, including *Hollywood Hotel*, *Texaco Star Theater*, and *Drene Time*. On *Drene Time*, she and **Don Ameche** created *The Bickersons*, a comedy skit that later evolved into a show of its own. Langford joined *The Bob Hope Show* in 1941 and remained with **Bob Hope** for more than 40 years, joining him on numerous tours to entertain servicemen both at home and abroad. Langford was married to movie actor Jon Hall from 1938 to 1955 and later married outboard motor manufacturer Ralph Evinrude and retired to Florida, where the couple owned a resort–restaurant.

LANSON, SNOOKY (1914–1990). Lanson, whose given name was Roy, began his singing career on a Nashville radio station in 1934 and adopted his childhood nickname as his professional name. He went on to sing with the Ted Weems and Ray Noble orchestras before being featured on the *Snooky Lanson Show*, a 15-minute Saturday afternoon program heard in 1946. He replaced Frank Sinatra as the lead male singer on *Your Hit Parade* in 1950, also appearing on the television simulcast. After the TV series ended, Lanson hosted other TV programs, did guest appearances, and sang in nightclubs. He later hosted a syndicated disc jockey program.

LASSIE. Lassie was a 15-minute **juvenile adventure program** heard from 1947 to 1950, featuring a collie that had been the star of a popular film, *Lassie Come Home*. The original Lassie, a male collie, could respond to cues for whining, barking, and panting, given him by his trainer, Rudd Weatherwax. Animal imitator Earl Keen did the sounds of other dogs on the show as well as filling in when Lassie missed a cue. The programs were mostly narration, with a little dialogue, but they were produced in front of a live audience of children and the children were entranced by both Lassie and Keen. The program was sponsored by Red Heart dog food for the entire run.

LAUCK, CHESTER A. (1902–1980). Chester Lauck and Norris Goff were the famous comedy team of *Lum and Abner*. Lauck and Goff were both from Mena, Arkansas, and they first performed as the rustic team on an amateur talent show in their hometown, broadcast over the Hot Springs radio station. In addition to performing the role of Columbus (Lum) Edwards on the program, Lauck also played Grandpappy Spears, Snake Hogan, and Cedric Weehunt. After the team retired from show business, Lauck became the public relations director of an oil company in Houston.

LAVENDER AND OLD LACE. Although thought of primarily as producers of **soap operas**, **Frank and Anne Hummert** also produced other types of programs, including several musical shows. *Lavender and Old Lace* was a 30-minute musical program heard from 1934 to 1936, featuring many of the same musicians heard on other Hummert **music programs**, including the Abe Lyman orchestra, and vocalists Fritzi Scheff, Lucy Monroe, and **Frank Munn**. The music was traditional "sweet" music, primarily waltzes and ballads.

LAWRENCE WELK SHOW (THE). Welk was the leader of an extremely popular dance orchestra, and is better known for his long-running television program, but he hosted several radio programs from 1949 to 1957, including *High Life Review*, *The Treasury Hour*, *Music on Deck*, and *The Lawrence Welk Show*, the latter an **Armed**

Forces Radio Service program, of which many episodes are available. Although born in North Dakota, Welk did not learn to speak English until he was 21, leaving him with a distinctive accent that became a trademark of his programs, along with the bubbles that accompanied his "champagne music."

LEAVE IT TO THE GIRLS. A 30-minute panel program heard from 1945 to 1949, *Leave It to the Girls* was originally a serious discussion program with professional women discussing problems submitted by listeners. During the course of the run, the program became more comedic, with a panel composed of female celebrities and topics that were often humorous or ridiculous. In addition to the panel, a male celebrity was included who could interrupt the discussion by blowing a whistle, indicating that there was a male point of view that he wished to present. Created and produced by Martha Rountree, the program was hosted by Paula Stone.

LEONARD, SHELDON (1907–1997). Born Sheldon Leonard Bershad, Leonard acted on Broadway, in movies and television, and on radio. He appeared on such hit radio shows as *The Martin and Lewis Show*, *The Judy Canova Show*, *Broadway Is My Beat*, *The Jack Benny Program*, and many others. He also appeared on several daytime **soap operas**, including *Big Sister* and *David Harum*. When dramatic radio ended, Leonard acted in several television programs and after he stopped acting became a very successful TV writer, director, and producer, producing such hugely popular television series as *The Danny Thomas Show*, *The Andy Griffith Show*, *The Dick Van Dyke Show*, and *I Spy*. His autobiography, *And the Show Goes On*, was published in 1995.

LEONIDAS WITHERALL. A 30-minute detective drama heard in 1944–1945, *Leonidas Witherall* was based on the character in the novels written by Alice Tilton. Witherall was a teacher at a New England school for boys who also wrote a detective series for radio. He was also an amateur detective and many of his personal exploits were quite like those of the hero of his radio series. His most distinguishing characteristic was that he bore such a strong physical resemblance to William Shakespeare that some people referred to him by that name. Witherall was played by Walter Hampden; his housekeeper, Mrs. Mollet, was played by Ethel Remey.

LET'S PRETEND. A 30-minute Saturday morning program for children heard from 1934 to 1954, *Let's Pretend* was written and directed by **Nila Mack** for nearly the entire duration of the program. It was an outgrowth of an earlier program, *The Adventures of Helen and Mary*, and was similar in content: a fantasy for children featuring talking animals, enchanted forests, witches, dragons, and all manner of mythical creatures. Although many original plays were presented, classical tales were favored, sometimes substantially modified by Mack. Most of the cast members were children and some remained with the program for many years; others moved on to successful careers in radio, television, and motion pictures as they grew up. Uncle Bill Adams was the host for the entire run. Mack died in 1953 and Jean Hight became the director, but the program lasted only one more year.

LEWIS, CATHY (1918–1968). Cathy Lewis began her professional performing career as a teenaged singer with big bands of the 1930s. She then acted in films, on stage, on television, and in several popular radio programs. The most important of the radio shows were ***The Great Gildersleeve***, ***Michael Shayne***, and ***My Friend Irma***. From 1943 to 1958, she was married to **Elliott Lewis**, and together they co-starred on the CBS drama anthology series *On Stage*.

LEWIS, ELLIOTT (1917–1990). Excelling in every phase of the medium, Lewis wrote, produced, and directed radio as well as being a featured performer on both dramatic and comedy radio programs, including ***The Casebook of Gregory Hood***, ***Meet Me at Parky's***, ***The Phil Harris–Alice Faye Show***, ***The Voyage of the Scarlet Queen***, ***Knickerbocker Playhouse***, ***Big Town***, and many others. During World War II, he served with the **Armed Forces Radio Service**. After his radio career, he worked as a producer in television.

LEWIS, FULTON JR. (1903–1966). A conservative news commentator, Lewis was born a fifth-generation Washingtonian and was a member of Washington's Association of Oldest Inhabitants, which even presidents of the United States could not join. His radio program, *The Top of the News*, was first heard on Mutual in 1937. At one time, he was heard on 370 different stations nationwide, and had more than 530 different sponsors on the various network affiliates.

His career was devoted to rooting out and exposing corruption or mismanagement in government. His label as an arch conservative was partly a reflection of the fact that most governments during his time were liberal Democratic administrations, and his anti-government attacks were seen as an expression of a political position. Lewis founded and was the first president of the Radio Correspondents Association, the accrediting agency for admission to the press galleries of Congress. He did some commentaries on television, but they were not as successful as his radio work.

LIBERTY BROADCASTING SYSTEM. The Liberty Broadcasting System was the creation of **Gordon McLendon**, one of the great innovators of early radio. In need of programming for his Dallas radio station KLIF, he began in 1947 to re-create baseball games from the ticker-tape play-by-play information furnished by the wire services. The broadcasts were very creative, with sound effects and colorful commentary, and were so popular that other stations affiliated with KLIF in order to carry them. In 1948, these affiliates were incorporated into the Liberty Broadcasting System. The network had more than 450 affiliates by 1951 and secured the rights to broadcast games live from major league ballparks. The rights were withdrawn the next year; however, in 1952, the network was forced to declare bankruptcy and left the air.

LIFE BEGINS AT 80. A 30-minute panel discussion program heard during 1948–1949 and then again during 1952–1953, *Life Begins At 80* featured a panel composed entirely of octogenarians. Hosted and created by **Jack Barry**, who also created *Juvenile Jury*, the program had to be taped to allow editing because some of the panel members made exceedingly frank comments.

LIFE CAN BE BEAUTIFUL. A 15-minute daytime **soap opera** heard from 1938 to 1954, *Life Can Be Beautiful* had the unusual distinction of appearing on two networks simultaneously from 1939 to 1941. Often referred to as "Elsie Beebe," a term resulting from the pronunciation of the acronym based on the initials of the program (LCBB), it was the story of Carol Conrad, called "Chichi," who was the ward of Papa David Solomon, the kindly proprietor of a bookstore. After several years, Chichi married Stephen Hamilton, a crippled law student. Stephen died quite soon in the storyline, however. For the rest of the run, Chichi's major male interest was Toby Nelson, who loved her, but whom she saw only as a friend. Chichi was played by Alice Reinhart until 1946, when the role was assumed by Teri Keane. Ralph Locke played Papa David for the entire run. The program was written by Don Becker and Carl Bixby, who were sometimes referred to collectively as "Beckby."

LIFE OF RILEY (THE). There were two versions of this program, the best remembered being a 30-minute **situation comedy** heard from 1944 to 1951, based on the home life of Chester A. Riley, a blue-collar aircraft worker played by William Bendix. Riley was enthusiastic and good-hearted, but his plans almost never worked out and the advice he received from Gillis, his best friend at the aircraft factory, did not help. Another friend, Digger O'Dell, the Friendly Undertaker, appeared on each program and always exited by announcing that he had to be "shoveling off." Riley was noted for the catchphrase "What a revoltin' development this is." Gillis and Digger were both played by **John Brown**. The earlier version of the program was heard for only a few months in 1941 and starred Lionel Stander as J. Riley Farnsworth. There were also two different versions of the program on television, the first in 1949–1950 with Jackie Gleason in the lead role and the second from 1953 to 1958, with Bendix again appearing as Riley.

LIFE WITH LUIGI. A 30-minute **situation comedy** heard from 1948 to 1953, *Life with Luigi* always began with Italian immigrant Luigi Basko reading a letter to his mother in Italy. The reading faded out to accordion music and the story of the week began. Luigi ran an antique store in Chicago, next door to Pasquale's Spaghetti Palace; many of the plots revolved around Pasquale's attempts to get Luigi to marry his 250-pound daughter, Rosa. Luigi was played by **J. Carrol Naish** and Pasquale by **Alan Reed**. After the weekly plot had finished, accordion music signaled the return to Luigi's reading of the letter to his mother, which ended the program.

LIGHT OF THE WORLD (THE). An unusual 15-minute daily serial drama created by Don Becker, *Light of the World* was produced by **Frank and Anne Hummert** and based on stories from the Bible.

Heard from 1940 to 1950, the program took considerable liberties with the stories, modernizing some, adding dialogue and sometimes inserting characters. The format was quite like a soap opera, with daily episodes that had cliff-hanger endings. The program was hosted by a narrator, called "The Speaker," originally played by **Bret Morrison**, and later by **David Gothard** and Arnold Moss.

LIGHTS OUT. A 30-minute weekly horror anthology heard from 1935 to 1947, *Lights Out* was created by **Wyllis Cooper**, who left in 1936, to be replaced by **Arch Oboler**. The program left the air in 1939, returning for another year in 1942–1943. It reappeared as a summer replacement program in 1945, 1946, and 1947. The 1945 program was called *Fantasies from Lights Out*; the 1947 program was again directed by Wyllis Cooper, with Boris Karloff as the star.

LINEUP (THE). A 30-minute police drama heard from 1950 to 1953, *The Lineup* starred **Bill Johnstone** as Lt. Ben Guthrie. A realism-oriented show, similar in some ways to *Dragnet*, each program began with a police lineup, thus introducing the case that would be investigated. Much of the action took place in police headquarters. In an effort to create a realistic police environment, there were few heroics on the program.

LINKLETTER, ART (1912–). Linkletter, whose real name was Gordon Arthur Kelly, was abandoned at an early age and was adopted by the Linkletter family. He was the host of two of radio's longest running audience-participation programs, *People Are Funny* (1942–1960) and *Art Linkletter's House Party* (1945–1963). When versions of both programs were developed for television in the early 1950s, Linkletter hosted them also. He also emceed other TV shows, including *Life with Linkletter*, a variety show; and *The Art Linkletter Show*, a quiz program. He occasionally acted in dramas, several on the *General Electric Theater*. In the 1970s, after his programs were off the air, he devoted his time to writing, lecturing, and his extensive business interests. His eldest son, Jack Linkletter, also hosted several daytime game and variety TV programs from the 1950s into the 1970s.

LITTLE ORPHAN ANNIE. One of the earliest of the 15-minute **juvenile adventure programs** that became so popular on radio, *Little*

Orphan Annie was based on the popular comic strip of the same name. The program stories were more or less related to the comic strip at first, but gradually drew away from the print version, with many characters appearing on the radio version who were not seen in the comic strip. Annie herself had nearly disappeared from the stories by the time the program went off the air.

Heard from 1931 to 1942, the program was famous for the number of premiums that were given away, the best known being the Ovaltine shake-up mug, with which a listener could prepare Ovaltine (the sponsoring product) by simply adding milk and shaking. Premiums often identified the show as *Radio Orphan Annie*. Many actors appeared over the long run, but Annie was first played by Shirley Bell. Her pal Joe Corntassel was first played by Allan Baruck and later by a very young Mel Torme.

LIVINGSTON, MARY (1908–1983). Jack Benny's real-life wife, Mary appeared with him as his wisecracking girlfriend both in vaudeville and on *The Jack Benny Program*. Her real name was Sadye Marks; she first met Benny when she was 13, marrying him when she was 18. A standing joke on their program was that she had met him when she was selling hosiery at the May Company in Los Angeles. She moved to television with the program in 1950 but developed such a bad case of stage fright that she was written out of many of the shows and finally retired in 1958.

LOMBARDO, GUY (1902–1977). Lombardo was the leader of a popular dance orchestra, the Royal Canadians, for many years. His orchestra was heard on radio from the late 1920s, beginning with the *Robert Burns Panatella Program* on CBS. During 1944–1945, he hosted *Musical Autographs*, and his 1949 to 1956 program was called *Lombardoland USA*. His orchestra also included his brothers Lebert, Carmen, and Victor; his sister Rosemarie and brother-in-law, Kenny Gardner, were vocalists. For nearly 50 years, Lombardo and the Royal Canadians closed the old year and opened the new on network radio (and then on television). His orchestra's theme song was *Auld Lang Syne* and its slogan was "The sweetest music this side of heaven."

LONE JOURNEY. A 15-minute **soap opera** that made several appearances on radio, first from 1940 to 1943, again in 1946–1947, and finally in 1951–1952, *Lone Journey* was written by Sandra and Peter Michael and produced by **Frank and Anne Hummert**. It was the story of architect Wolfe Bennett and his wife Nita, who had left Chicago to live on a ranch in Montana, and the problems they encountered in adjusting to the new life. Sandra Michael lived in Montana and knew the environment. *Lone Journey* was thought by critics to be of better literary quality than most other soap operas.

LONE RANGER (THE). A 30-minute **juvenile adventure program** heard from 1933 to 1955, *The Lone Ranger* was conceived by **George W. Trendle**, owner of station WXYZ Detroit, and written by **Fran Striker**. One of the greatest success stories in the history of radio, it was the story of a masked man and his Indian companion who roamed the early western United States, combating crime and injustice of every kind. Almost everything about the program became famous: the music, the silver bullets used by The Lone Ranger, his great horse Silver, his partner Tonto, and Tonto's horse Scout. Many of the phrases spoken by the two protagonists became catchphrases known to nearly everyone in the nation. Earle Graser was the first Lone Ranger, but was killed in an automobile accident in 1941 and the role was assumed by announcer **Brace Beemer**, who kept it until 1955. Tonto was played by John Todd for the entire run. Dozens of premiums were offered, and some of them are now quite valuable.

LONE WOLF (THE). A 30-minute detective drama heard only in 1948–1949, *The Lone Wolf* was based on the novels of Louis Vance and a long series of movies featuring the same character. Private investigator Michael Lanyard was a sort of charming rogue who was a reformed jewel thief, called The Lone Wolf because he always worked alone. **Gerald Mohr** was the original Lone Wolf; the role was later played by Walter Coy. There was a later television program of the same name.

LOPEZ, VINCENT (1894–1975). Lopez was an orchestra leader who was born in Brooklyn and began as a pianist in a Brooklyn tavern before leading a small orchestra at a Chinese restaurant on Broadway, and then moving into vaudeville and into radio. Over the years, his sidemen included such noted musicians as Xavier Cugat, Glenn Miller, and Artie Shaw; and he is credited with discovering singer

Betty Hutton. Lopez was first heard on radio in 1921; in 1926, NBC featured his orchestra on its inaugural program. He and his orchestra appeared on a long series of **music programs** of various titles and formats on all major networks, often appearing on two networks simultaneously. For many years on Mutual there was a 15-minute daily noontime broadcast from the Taft Hotel in New York called *Luncheon with Lopez*. Other programs on which he and his orchestra appeared included *The Valvoline Program*, *Pleasure Parade*, *Shake the Maracas*, *The Speed Show*, and *The Treasury Show*.

LORA LAWTON. A 15-minute daily **soap opera** produced by **Frank and Anne Hummert** and heard from 1943 to 1950, *Lora Lawton* was the story of a poor girl who married a rich shipping owner, Peter Carver, and encountered the usual attempts by other women to steal him away. Lora and Peter were originally played by Joan Tompkins and **James Meighan**, later by **Jan Miner** and Ned Wever. The program was a particularly prolific source of premiums, many of which were incorporated into the plot lines.

LORD, PHILLIPS H. (1902–1975). Lord was an actor, writer, and producer who originated and played the part of Seth Parker in 1929 and almost literally became the character. In 1933–1934, Lord bought a large schooner, named it the *Seth Parker*, and set sail with numerous friends and cast members, producing a new program with on-location reports from Lord each week. The program was billed as *The Cruise of the Seth Parker*, but in early 1935 the ship was destroyed in a storm at sea. Passengers and crew were rescued, but the incident was denounced by the press as a publicity stunt and the program left the air as a result. Lord also created *We, the People*, a human-interest program that aired from 1936 to 1939. He then turned to creating and producing **crime programs**, such as *Gang Busters*, *Mr. District Attorney*, and *Counterspy*.

LORENZO JONES. A 15-minute daily **soap opera** heard from 1937 to 1955 and produced by **Frank and Anne Hummert**, *Lorenzo Jones* featured a lovable but impractical mechanic who was always involved in schemes that did not work out, somewhat like **Fibber McGee**. When the ratings began to drop during the last three years of the run, Lorenzo developed amnesia and wandered away to New

York City to become involved in various adventures while his wife Belle searched for him. When the network announced plans to cancel the program, Lorenzo recovered his memory and returned to Belle and his friends for the final episodes. Lorenzo was played by Karl Swenson throughout the entire run; Belle was played by Betty Garde and **Lucille Wall**.

LOUELLA PARSONS SHOW (THE). **Louella Parsons** was a Hollywood gossip columnist who hosted a series of 15-minute programs over the period of 1931–1951. The best known of these appeared from 1944 to 1951 on Sunday night, immediately after **Walter Winchell**. Although the two programs were both basically gossip programs, Winchell was primarily concerned with items from New York while Parsons concentrated on happenings in Hollywood. Both she and Winchell were sponsored by Jergens Lotion, but their personal relationship was frosty.

LOVEJOY, FRANK (1912–1962). Lovejoy, who often acted with his wife, **Joan Banks**, got his start on radio in the 1930s at WLW Cincinnati. He later appeared on several daytime serials and starred on many popular **crime programs** including *Mr. and Mrs. North*, *This Is Your FBI*, and *Nightbeat*. On television in the 1950s, he starred on both *Man against Crime* and *Meet McGraw*. He also appeared in many motion pictures during the 1940s and 1950s.

LUDDY, BARBARA (1907–1979). Known especially for her voice work in animated films, Luddy started as a child performer in vaudeville and as a teenager toured with a stock company in Australia. Her radio career was centered in Chicago, where she was the leading lady on the long-running **drama anthology program**, *The First Nighter* (1936–1953). Beginning in the mid-1950s, she was a voice actress in such Disney classics as *The Lady and the Tramp*, *Sleeping Beauty*, *Winnie the Pooh*, and *Robin Hood*.

LUM AND ABNER. One of the great **comedy programs** of all time, *Lum and Abner* consisted primarily of a dialogue between Columbus (Lum) Edwards and Abner Peabody, rustic co-owners of The Jot-Em-Down Store in the fictitious town of Pine Ridge, Arkansas. Heard from 1931 to 1953, the program was so popular that the town of

Waters, Arkansas, changed its name to Pine Ridge in 1936. The title roles were played by **Chester Lauck** and **Norris Goff**, both from the small town of Mena, Arkansas. Lauck and Goff also played a variety of other characters who appeared on the show and, although other cast members were added later, continued to play multiple roles for the entire run.

LUX RADIO THEATER (THE). A 60-minute **drama anthology** heard from 1934 to 1955, *The Lux Radio Theater* was first produced in New York but moved to Hollywood in 1936, where Cecil B. DeMille became the host. After the move, the biggest names in Hollywood were the stars of the episodes, often appearing in radio adaptations of their own films. The program was very expensive, involving more than 50 people to produce each episode, sometimes with more than 20 speaking parts. DeMille left in 1945 and—after a brief period during which various film celebrities hosted the program—Walter Keighley took over until 1952, at which time Irving Cummings assumed the role.

LYNCH, PEG (1916–). Shortly after she graduated from college, Lynch was employed on the radio station in Albert Lea, Minnesota, where she wrote programs and commercials as well as acted. She later moved to Charlottesville, Virginia, and created a series called *Ethel and Albert*, in which she played the lead female character. In 1944, she moved to NBC with a 15-minute version of the program, and in 1952 it became a 30-minute show. When the program moved to television in 1953, she moved with it and continued to write the scripts and to play the role of Ethel until 1956. Lynch also wrote and starred in a similar program, *The Couple Next Door*, from 1957 to 1959; and from 1963 to 1965, she was on a reprised version of this program on NBC's *Monitor*. During her six-decade career, Lunch estimated that she had written more than 10,000 scripts for radio and television.

– M –

MA PERKINS. A 15-minute daily **soap opera** produced by **Frank and Anne Hummert**, *Ma Perkins* was one of the longest-running programs on old-time radio, appearing from 1933 to 1960. Ma Perkins was a widow who lived in a small town and operated her late husband's lumberyard. Assisted by Shuffle Sober, her longtime partner—and later by grandsons and various spouses of her two daughters—Ma was a wise mother-figure to everyone on the program. **Virginia Payne** played the lead role for the entire run, never missing one of the 7,065 episodes that were aired. Charles Egleston lasted nearly as long in the role of Shuffle Sober, although the role was also played by Edwin Wolfe from 1958 to 1960. Ma's son John was killed during World War II, the only major soap opera figure to be lost to the war.

MACDONNELL, NORMAN (1916–1979). A writer, producer, and director, Macdonnell was responsible for some of the best-remembered dramatic programs on radio. He was the force behind *Escape* for much of its run, and was the producer/director of the long-running adult western *Gunsmoke*, as well as *Fort Laramie* and *The Adventures of Philip Marlowe*. Macdonnell was one of the several distinguished directors who worked on *Suspense*, and he directed *Yours Truly, Johnny Dollar* in 1949 and *Honest Harold* in the early 1950s, as well as producing and directing the CBS version of *Romance* that aired in 1950. When *Gunsmoke* moved to television in 1955, Macdonnell moved with it and produced the show until 1964.

MACK, NILA (1891–1953). Mack's early professional career began in vaudeville and in traveling repertory companies. When her husband, Roy Briant, joined Paramount Pictures as a writer, she became a member of Nazimova's dance company, appeared in films, wrote scenarios for screen short features, and acted on Broadway and on radio. When her husband died in 1927, Mack returned to Kansas to nurse her ill mother and became the program director of a local station, the beginning of her career in radio programming. In 1930, CBS asked her to return and take over *The Adventures of Helen and Mary*, a **children's program**. This program was renamed *Let's Pretend*, and Mack produced it for the next 23 years. She also produced other radio programs and wrote children's books and children's stories for magazines. She won numerous awards for *Let's Pretend* and for her other accomplishments. During her time working in radio, she was known as the "Fairy Godmother of Radio."

MACK, TED (1904–1976). Born Edward Maguiness, Mack was a longtime associate of Major Edward Bowes, host of *Major Bowes' Original Amateur Hour*. The program was off the air for two years following the death of Bowes in 1946; but was revived by Mack as the *Original Amateur Hour*. He hosted the show on radio from 1948 to 1952 and on television from 1948 to 1970. He also hosted his own TV variety show in 1951, *The Ted Mack Family Hour*.

MAGIC KEY (THE). Sometimes listed as *The Magic Key of RCA*, *The Magic Key* was a high-budget 60-minute **variety program** heard from 1935 to 1939. Hosted by **Milton Cross**, with music by the NBC Symphony Orchestra, the program often featured concert music but also presented popular music, jazz, drama, political commentary, and remote broadcasts from all over the world. Sponsored by RCA, the purpose of the program was to showcase radio itself, demonstrating the versatility and power of the medium.

MAISIE. A 30-minute **situation comedy** based on the series of motion pictures of the same name, *Maisie* was first heard on CBS from 1945 to 1947. A syndicated version was offered by MGM in 1949 and was heard on various networks until 1952. The plot lines were slightly different on the two versions, but the title role was much the same (played by **Ann Sothern**, who had also played the role in the film series). In both radio versions, Maisie was a working-class girl from Brooklyn whose various plans usually worked out poorly.

MAJOR BOWES' CAPITOL FAMILY HOUR. A long-running **variety program** first heard in 1925, before the advent of network radio, *The Capitol Family Hour* was an outgrowth of an earlier program called *Roxy and His Gang*. Edward Bowes, who assumed the title "Major" for his show business activities, teamed with showman Samuel "Roxy" Rothafel to produce the original program. When Rothafel left in 1926, Bowes took over the program and hosted it until it left the air in 1941. Known by several other names, including *The Family Hour*, and *The Major Bowes Family Hour*, the program was largely devoted to serious music, with a smattering of talk and comedy; opera singer Belle Silverman, who later changed her name to Beverly Sills, appeared frequently in the late 1930s.

MAJOR BOWES' ORIGINAL AMATEUR HOUR. The greatest of the amateur talent programs to appear on radio, the *Major Bowes' Original Amateur Hour* was an amateur talent program heard on the networks from 1935 to 1945. Immensely popular, the program auditioned between 500 and 700 amateur performers each week, with 20 selected to appear on that week's show. Listeners in New York City, and another city chosen each week, were allowed to cast ballots by telephone or by mail, and winners were announced the following week. Winners were often invited to perform again and multiple winners might be chosen for the year's championship program. Although only a few performers achieved professional stardom, anyone appearing on the program might be asked to join one of the several road companies that toured the country. Two years after Major Bowes' death in 1946, the program was revived by **Ted Mack**, a long-time associate of Bowes, and was called both *The Original Amateur Hour* and *Ted Mack's Original Amateur Hour*. This later program appeared on radio until 1952 but is better known as a television program, where it was seen until 1970.

MALONE, TED (1908–1989). Ted Malone, whose real name was Alden Russell, was working as an announcer at a Kansas City radio station in 1929 when he was asked to fill 15 minutes of air time by reading poetry. Embarrassed to do so, he asked to use another name for the task. The announcer dubbed him Ted Malone, which became his professional name after fan mail began to arrive. The readings were popular locally and grew into a program of readings called **Between the Bookends**, which appeared on network radio for more than 20 years. Malone later hosted several other programs, including *Pilgrimage of Poetry*, *American Pilgrimage*, and a **quiz program** called *Yankee Doodle Quiz*. In 1942, he published an anthology of poetry that later expanded to several volumes and is still in print.

MAN BEHIND THE GUN (THE). A high-quality **drama anthology** heard from 1942 to 1944, *The Man Behind the Gun* was dedicated to the fighting men of the United States and other countries involved in World War II. The stories dramatized were based on fact, but the characters were fictitious, often composites of several real-life individuals. The program was directed by William Robson and the actors were some of the best of the New York radio performers. The program was awarded a **Peabody Award** in 1943 as radio's outstanding dramatic program.

MAN CALLED X (THE). A 30-minute adult **adventure program** heard from 1944 to 1952, *The Man Called X* starred **Herbert Marshall** as Ken Thurstone, an American intelligence agent. Thurstone traveled to exotic settings all over the world, where he became involved in mysteries of various kinds, often involving mysterious women. His slightly larcenous sidekick, Pagan Zeldschmidt, was played by Leon Belasco.

MANDRAKE THE MAGICIAN. A 15-minute **juvenile adventure program** heard from 1940 to 1942, *Mandrake the Magician* was based on the popular comic strip of the same name. Mandrake was an American who had been taught the secrets of ancient magic by a Tibetan mystic. He lived in a "house of mystery" with his gigantic servant, Lothar, who was an African prince. He and Lothar battled evil all over the world, sometimes aided by the beautiful Princess Narda, who, like Lothar, was of royal blood. Mandrake was played by **Raymond Edward Johnson**, Lothar by Juano Hernandez, and Narda by Francesca Lenni.

MANHATTAN MERRY-GO-ROUND. A program of popular music that resembled *Your Hit Parade* in the material presented, *Manhattan Merry Go-Round* was heard from 1932 to 1949. Produced by **Frank and Anne Hummert**, it pretended to be a tour of Manhattan night clubs, with the latest popular songs sung by a series of regular vocalists. The songs were chosen on the basis of sheet music and record sales and an attempt was made to have the selections be as current as possible. There were some attempts to add comedy to the program, but it remained basically a showcase for popular music.

MARCH OF TIME (THE). One of radio's earliest news programs, *The March of Time* was first heard in 1931, initially focusing on domestic stories, but expanded to international coverage as world events developed. The program was organized much like a news magazine or newsreel, with bulletins, melodramatic reportage, sound effects, and interviews with world figures. The interviews were at first dramatized, but the dramatizations were later replaced with actual on-the-spot interviews. In 1942, the program became a straight news program, using shortwave reports from correspondents around the world. The narrator, referred to as "The Voice Of Time," was played by Westbrook Van Voorhis from 1933 until the program left the air in 1945. For much of the long run, the program was sponsored by *Time* magazine.

MARCONI, GUGLIELMO (1874–1937). Marconi began experimenting with radio waves in 1894 and eventually was able to detect signals over a distance of several kilometers. He tried to interest the Italian Ministry of Posts and Telegraphs in his work, but was unsuccessful. In 1896, however, an Irish cousin arranged an introduction to the Engineer-in-Chief of the British Post Office. After demonstrations in London, Marconi obtained an English patent in 1897 and established the Wireless Telegraph and Signal Company, which opened the world's first radio factory in Chelmsford, England (1898). Experiments and demonstrations continued, and by 1902 Marconi's apparatus was reliably receiving signals from 700 miles away during the day and more than twice that distance at night. A good businessman as well as an inventor, Marconi built stations in both England and the United States and was the director of a thriving enterprise in both radio production and transmission. He was a member of the Fascist Party in Italy and, in his later years, made Fascist speeches in many countries.

MARK TRAIL. A **juvenile adventure program** heard in both 30-minute and 15-minute formats from 1950 to 1952, *Mark Trail* was based on the popular comic strip of the same name by Ed Dodd. Mark was a wildlife photographer and a writer whose assignments often led him to discover environmental criminals of various sorts. The character was loosely based on the career of Charles N. Elliot, a U.S. Forest Ranger who later became editor of *Outdoor Life* magazine. Mark lived in a national forest with his St. Bernard, Andy, Veterinarian Doc Davis, Doc's daughter, Cherry, and her young son, Rusty. Trail, who was played by Matt Crowley (and later by **Staats Cotsworth**), offered camping tips and promoted conservation.

MARRIAGE (THE). A 30-minute light drama heard weekly during 1953–1954, *The Marriage* was primarily a vehicle for Hume Cronyn and Jessica Tandy, who played Ben and Liz Marriot. Ben was a New York City attorney, and Liz had been active in business before their marriage. Many of the plots revolved around her attempts to adjust to life as a non-working housewife, although she was far from an average housewife, being interested in theater and the arts.

MARSHALL, HERBERT (1890–1966). Born in London, Marshall made his stage debut in 1911 in Brighton, and began appearing on the London stage soon after. He lost a leg during World War I, but was able to conceal the fact while acting and became a leading man on both sides of the Atlantic. His mellifluous voice and precise English made him very effective on radio, and he appeared on many of the **drama anthology programs** of radio's golden age, hosting two of them: *Hollywood Startime* and *Your Radio Theatre*. The radio work for which he is best remembered today is *The Man Called X*, an **adventure program** on which he starred from 1944 to 1952.

MARTIN AND LEWIS SHOW (THE). Although better known as motion picture comics, Dean Martin and Jerry Lewis were popular nightclub entertainers and their program was developed by NBC in response to the talent raids that had led several prominent NBC stars to move to CBS. Heard from 1949 to 1953, with a brief interruption during 1950–1951, the program was loosely organized as a **situation comedy**, but was never as successful as the network had hoped, because much of Martin and Lewis's comedy was visual.

MARTIN KANE, PRIVATE EYE. A 30-minute detective drama heard on radio from 1949 to 1952, *Martin Kane, Private Eye* was broadcast concurrently on television. Kane always found reason to pass through Happy McMann's tobacco shop, where it was convenient to plug the sponsor, U.S. Tobacco. Kane was different from many radio detectives in that he was quiet and had a good relationship with the police. Underneath, however, he was a tough guy and nobody's fool. The lead was originally played on both radio and television by **William Gargan**, who had been an investigator detective in real life, but he was later replaced by Lloyd Nolan and then by Lee Tracy. There was a later syndicated program called *The New Adventures of Martin Kane*, but it never appeared on a national network.

MARX, GROUCHO (1890–1977). Groucho, whose real name was Julius, and his brothers are best known for their motion pictures of the 1930s, but Groucho also had a successful career on radio and later on television. He and brother Leonard (Chico) starred on radio in the *Flywheel, Shyster and Flywheel* **comedy program** in the early 1930s. All of the Marx brothers appeared at times on *The Marx Brothers Show* during 1937–1938, although Groucho and Chico were the stars, playing Hollywood agents. Groucho and Chico also were regulars on *The Circle*, a 1939 NBC talk program that was hosted by **Ronald Colman** and featured several show business personalities. Groucho hosted *Blue Ribbon Town*, a 30-minute variety during 1943–1944, but finally found his radio niche with *You Bet Your Life*, a **quiz program** that ran from 1947 to 1960 on radio and also had a long run on television (1950–1961). The program, with **George Fenneman** as his announcer and sidekick, was primarily a vehicle for quizmaster Groucho's wit and zanyness rather than for the questions asked of contestants and their answers. Groucho wrote several books of memoirs during his lifetime, including *The Secret Word Is Groucho* (1976).

MARY AND BOB. A very early romantic drama, *Mary and Bob* was heard from 1928 to 1931 as a weekly 60-minute program and then in both 45-minute and 30-minute formats until 1932. Off the air until 1938, it then had another brief run until 1939. It was basically a love story, featuring a married couple who toured the country and related their various experiences. Sponsored by *True Story* magazine, it was sometimes listed as *Mary and Bob's True Stories* or *The True Story Hour with Mary and Bob*. Nora Stirling and William Brenton were the first Mary and Bob, although the roles were later played by other performers.

MARY MARGARET MCBRIDE PROGRAM (THE). Mary Margaret McBride was an interview host and writer, whose program was heard nationally from 1937 to 1954. Sometimes referred to as the female **Arthur Godfrey**, her appeal was similar in its informality, although her program was quite different and consisted almost entirely of interviews with celebrities. She interviewed more than 1,200 people during an 18-year run, always without notes and without a script. She sometimes had more than a dozen sponsors, but would not accept sponsors whose products she had not tried herself. In addition, she often insisted on proof of advertising claims. She hosted an interview program on television in 1948, and penned two volumes of memoirs: *A Long Way from Missouri* (1959) and *Out of the Air* (1960). *See also* TALK AND INFORMATION PROGRAMS.

MAXWELL HOUSE COFFEE TIME. See GOOD NEWS.

MAXWELL, MARILYN (1921–1972). A singer, dancer, and actress whose real name was Marvel Marilyn Maxwell, Marilyn Maxwell joined Buddy Rogers' orchestra as a vocalist in 1938 and in the early 1940s appeared with Ted Weems on radio's musical **quiz program**, *Beat the Band*. She also appeared on *The Kraft Music Hall*, *The Abbott & Costello Show*, and *The Bob Hope Show*. She began appearing in motion pictures in 1942 and made films into the 1960s. Her film co-stars included Broderick Crawford, Jerry Lewis, and Mickey Rooney, and her radio co-stars included **Bud Abbott**, **Lou Costello**, and **Bob Hope**. On television, she starred as the owner of the diner on the drama *Bus Stop*.

MAYOR OF THE TOWN. A 30-minute **situation comedy** heard from 1942 to 1949, *Mayor of the Town* starred Lionel Barrymore as mayor of the town of Springfield. **Agnes Moorehead** played Marily, his housekeeper, and Conrad Binyon was his nephew, whose mother had died and whose father was away. The plots resembled those of *The Great Gildersleeve*, with the grumbling but kindly mayor interacting with a number of interesting town characters.

MCDANIEL, HATTIE (1895–1952). Although she was one of the first African American women to sing on radio, and a featured performer on several programs, including *The Eddie Cantor Show* and *Showboat*, Hattie McDaniel is best known as a film actress, winning an Academy Award in 1939 for her supporting role in *Gone with the Wind*. She became the first African American actress to star on a prime-time network program when she was hired to play the lead role on the popular **situation comedy** *Beulah* in 1947. She continued in the role until 1952, when she was forced to leave the program because of illness. McDaniel appeared in more than 300 pictures during her film career, often playing the part of a maid, just as she did in *Beulah*. She showed no resentment at the racial typecasting, once commenting, "I'd rather make $700 a week playing a maid than $7 a day being a maid."

MACLAUGHLIN, DON (1906–1986). An English major at the University of Iowa, MacLaughlin taught school after graduation until leaving in 1933 for New York and an acting career. On radio, he played the lead roles on *Tennessee Jed* and *Counterspy* as well as being a regular performer on several soap operas. Although MacLaughlin later appeared on Broadway and in the movies, he is best remembered today for his television role as Chris Hughes on *As the World Turns*, a part he played from 1956 to 1986.

MCLENDON, GORDON (1921–1986). McLendon was one of the most innovative people in the history of radio broadcasting. After service in the United States Navy during World War II, he attended Harvard Law School for a year before buying station KNET Palestine, Texas, in 1946. The following year he moved to Dallas, Texas, and launched station KLIF. Unable to afford live baseball broadcasts, he adopted the on-air persona of "The Old Scotchman" and broadcast recreations of major league games with the help of wire service reports and the creative use of sound effects. He created the **Liberty Broadcasting System** based on a network of stations that contracted to carry these broadcasts, but was forced out of business by legal complications. KLIF later became the city's top-rated radio station when McLendon changed it to one of America's first "Top-40" stations. In 1959, McLendon created the "beautiful music" format for KABL San Francisco; in the early 1960s, he started the first all-news radio station at WNUS Chicago. He bought other radio stations over the years, both AM and FM, ran unsuccessfully for public office in the 1960s, and also became a motion-picture producer. McLendon was involved in philanthropic activities most of his life and in the 1960s was named a communications advisor to the Peace Corps. He was inducted posthumously into the Radio Hall of Fame of the National Association of Broadcasters in 1987.

MCNAMEE, GRAHAM (1889–1942). Graham McNamee first appeared on radio as a singer, making his singing debut in New York in 1920 and singing on tour for several years. In 1923, he auditioned at WEAF, New York, and was hired to both sing and announce. He turned to sports broadcasting that year and covered both prize fights and the World Series. He subsequently abandoned his singing career and became known as both a sportscaster and announcer. His longest and most notable assignment was the 1924 Democratic Convention in Madison Square Garden, during which he worked 15 hours a day for 15 days. He also appeared on several network radio programs, including *The Fleischmann Yeast Hour*, *Party Line*, and *The Treasury Hour*, and was one of the first to make the announcer a personality on a program. *You're on the Air* (1928), his book on broadcasting, was one of the first published on the subject. *See also* SPORTS BROADCASTS.

MCNEILL, DON (1907–1996). Don McNeill hosted *The Breakfast Club* for 34 years, from 1933 to 1968. It was one of radio's longest-running programs and ABC's most valuable daytime series. McNeill was a journalism graduate and wrote radio columns in the *Milwaukee Journal* and the *Louisville Times* before beginning in radio in 1932 as host of a Chicago program called *Pepper Pot*. He changed the name of the program to *The Breakfast Club*, and it became a highly successful morning show with audience participation and guests. McNeill hosted the 60-minute program for some 7,500 broadcasts. It was also seen on television in the 1950s, both in nighttime (1950) and daytime (1954) versions, but was not successful. *See also* AUDIENCE-PARTICIPATION PROGRAMS.

MCVEY, TYLER (1912–2003). McVey was a character actor who was extremely busy during the period of old-time radio, once estimating that he had appeared on more than 1,000 radio broadcasts. He began his acting career in his hometown of Bay City, Michigan, and then joined an acting company that put on shows in New England. At a young age, McVey became a producer and director, but was not very successful and eventually moved to Los Angeles for acting work. His appeared on such popular programs as *The Jack Benny Program*, *Gene Autry's Melody Ranch*, *Dr. Christian*, *The Red Skelton Show*, *The Great Gildersleeve*, *Wild Bill Hickok*, and *Lux Radio Theatre*. On television, he acted on hundreds of live and taped shows; he also appeared in several movies, including *The Day the Earth Stood Still*, *Seven Days in May*, *The Caine Mutiny*, and

Hello, Dolly. McVey served on the board of the American Federation of Television and Radio Artists for more than 30 years and at one time was its president.

MEET CORLISS ARCHER. Similar in many ways to *A Date with Judy*, which was then running on another network, *Meet Corliss Archer* presented the sort of good-hearted chaos that was at the time often represented as a picture of teenage life. Corliss was a teenage bubblehead created by F. Hugh Herbert in several magazine stories. The program was a 30-minute **situation comedy** heard from 1943 to 1956, with some interruptions in continuity. Several performers played Corliss and her boyfriend Dexter Franklin during the long run; but **Janet Waldo** played the title role for ten years, and Sam Edwards is the best-remembered Dexter.

MEET ME AT PARKY'S. A 30-minute **situation comedy** heard from 1945 to 1948, *Meet Me at Parky's* was based on the experiences of Nick Parkyakarkus, the proprietor of a Greek restaurant. Parky was a comic character role created by Harry Einstein, who had portrayed the character on several other programs, most notably **The Eddie Cantor Show**. Einstein wrote most of the program as well as playing the lead character; he was assisted by several well-known radio performers, including Joan Barton and **Sheldon Leonard**. Einstein had back surgery in 1947, which left him partially paralyzed; he died of a heart attack at a roast for Lucille Ball and Desi Arnaz in 1958. Two of his sons also went into show business: Bob, whose stage name is Super Dave Osborne; and Albert, whose stage name is Albert Brooks.

MEET MILLIE. A 30-minute **situation comedy** heard from 1951 to 1954, *Meet Millie* was based on the misadventures of a Brooklyn shopgirl who was having a sort of romance with her boss's son—an arrangement encouraged by her mother and discouraged by her boss. Audrey Totter was the first Millie, but left in 1952 when the program migrated to television, where it appeared concurrently with the radio version.

MEET THE PRESS. A press conference on-the-air heard on radio from 1945 to 1986, *Meet the Press* featured Lawrence Spivak, editor of *American Mercury* magazine interviewing prominent newsmakers. The program was originally created by Martha Rountree, who had previously created *Leave It to the Girls*. Prominent journalists joined Spivak on the interview panel and provocative questions were a regular part of most programs. The program migrated to early television in 1947 and from 1952 until the radio program ended, the TV and radio versions were simulcast.

MEIGHAN, JAMES (1906–1970). Meighan began his acting career with a stock company, then appeared on Broadway before working on radio. Although best known for playing matinee idol Larry Noble on *Backstage Wife*, he also played *The Falcon* from 1945 to 1947 and had continuing parts on such programs as *Death Valley Days*, *Just Plain Bill*, *Lora Lawton*, and *Flash Gordon*.

MEL BLANC SHOW (THE). Heard only during 1946–1947, this 30-minute **situation comedy** starred **Mel Blanc**, who did countless character impersonations on other radio programs, as well as being the voice of many movie cartoon characters. On his own program, Blanc played himself in his natural voice and was the bumbling owner of a fix-it shop that never was able to fix anything. The best-remembered feature of the program was the password at Mel's lodge, The Loyal Order of Benevolent Zebras, "ugga-ugga-boo, ugga-boo-boo-ugga," which became a popular catchphrase of the day.

MERCURY THEATRE ON THE AIR. A 60-minute **drama anthology program** that was responsible for the production of the most famous single radio program ever broadcast, "War of the Worlds," The *Mercury Theatre on the Air* was the radio version of a Broadway repertory company formed in 1937 by John Houseman and **Orson Welles**. Their stage productions were very successful and, in 1938, they were offered a contract by CBS. Although ratings were low, their radio offerings were much praised by critics and the success of "War of the Worlds" led Campbell's soups to undertake sponsorship of the program. The program name was changed to *The Campbell Playhouse* and the character of the program also changed, becoming a more conventional drama anthology, featuring famous stars in the lead roles.

MICHAEL SHAYNE. A 30-minute detective adventure program based on the character created by Brett Halliday, *Michael Shayne* was first heard on the network during 1946–1947 and then in syndication as *The New Adventures of Michael Shayne* from 1948 to 1950. After a brief interruption, the program was again heard during 1952–1953. Several actors played the part of Shayne during the various versions of the program, including Wally Maher, **Jeff Chandler**, and Robert Sterling.

MILLER, MARVIN (1913–1985). Miller began working on radio while a student at Washington University. By 1940, he was working in Chicago as an announcer on 40 radio programs a week. When he moved to Los Angeles, he added acting to his radio work. He hosted *Behind the Story* and played all the characters on the program himself. He also co-hosted *Stop That Villain*, hosted **The First Nighter**, and was featured on **The Romance of Helen Trent** and **Space Patrol**. On **One Man's Family**, he played more than 20 different characters. Miller became famous from 1955 to 1960 when he starred on television as Michael Anthony, the personal secretary who gave away a million dollars each week on the hit series, *The Millionaire*. Miller also worked on several other TV programs, portraying a wide range of nationalities, including Oriental characters. He turned to voice work in the 1960s, doing Saturday morning cartoons and narration for TV movies.

MILTON BERLE SHOW (THE). Best known for his success on television, **Milton Berle** was a vaudeville comedian who hosted a long series of radio programs from 1936 to 1949. There were many different titles for his shows, including *Stop Me If You've Heard This One*, *Let Yourself Go*, and *Kiss and Make Up* before he began headlining *The Milton Berle Show* in 1947 and **The Texaco Star Theater** the next year. Basically a visual comic, Berle was much better suited to television and was an immediate hit when he appeared on the TV version of *The Texaco Star Theater* in 1948.

MINER, JAN (1917–2004). Born in Boston, Miner began acting professionally at age 16. She entered radio via a station in Hartford, Connecticut, and in 1946 landed the starring role on a soap opera, *Lora Lawton*. She also appeared on **Hilltop House**, **Boston Blackie**, **Perry Mason**, and **Casey, Crime Photographer**, as well as playing the female lead on episodes of several **drama anthology programs**, including **Dimension X**. During the 1950s, she was voted the favorite dramatic actress on radio. She moved to television in the early 1950s, where she was a repertory player on *Robert Montgomery Presents* and played Ann Williams on *Crime Photographer*, the TV version of radio's popular *Casey, Crime Photographer*. Miner is remembered by many TV viewers for her portrayal of Madge the manicurist in the Palmolive liquid detergent commercials.

MITCHELL, SHIRLEY (1919–). Shirley Mitchell began her radio acting career on a local station in Toledo and then moved to Chicago in 1942, where *The First Nighter* was her first network program. On radio, she is remembered primarily as Leila Ransom, the Southern widow on *The Great Gildersleeve*; but she also had continuing parts on several other programs, including *The Rudy Vallee Show*, *Fibber McGee and Molly*, *Joanie's Tea Room*, and *The Life of Riley*. On television, she again played Leila Ransom on the television version of *The Great Gildersleeve* and also had featured roles on *Bachelor Father*, *Pete and Gladys*, and *Please Don't Eat the Daisies*. She relocated to Los Angeles in the early 1950s and acted in TV and films into the late 1980s.

MR. AND MRS. NORTH. A mystery program heard from 1942 to 1955, *Mr. and Mrs. North* was based on the characters created by Richard and Frances Lockridge in a series of mystery novels. Jerry and Pam North were a married couple who just happened to stumble over a corpse every week. They depended on their good friend Lt. Bill Weigand of homicide for any actual police work. Originally conceived as a comedy, the program remained light in tone, with clever interplay between the characters being as prominent as the detective work. **Joseph Curtin** and **Alice Frost** appeared as Jerry and Pam in the early version, with **Frank Lovejoy** as Bill Weigand. All three roles were later played by other performers during the show's long run. There was a broadway play of the same name, as well as a 1942 movie and a television series that was seen from 1952 to 1954.

MR. CHAMELEON. A 30-minute detective drama produced by **Frank and Anne Hummert** and heard from 1948 to 1953, *Mr. Chameleon* featured a detective who utilized many disguises and operated out of "central police headquarters." He was referred to as "the man of many faces" and appeared in disguise at least once in every program.

Karl Swenson played the title role; his assistant, Detective Dave Arnold, was played by Frank Butler.

MR. DISTRICT ATTORNEY. A detective drama heard from 1939 to 1953, usually in a 30-minute weekly format, *Mr. District Attorney* was for many years the most popular crime program on radio. Inspired by the career of Thomas E. Dewey, a New York District Attorney who made headlines in the late 1930s with his racket-busting investigations, it was directed and written by Ed Byron, a crime buff and former law student who had a library of more than 5,000 books on crime, read five newspapers daily, and personally visited some of the most disreputable, crime-ridden haunts in the city. The program was extremely topical, often presenting cases very similar to those that had recently made headlines. The DA was never referred to by name, but was called "chief" or "boss" by Harrington, his chief investigator and Miss Miller, his secretary. Several actors played the title role, but **Jay Jostyn** held the role the longest. Miss Miller was played by **Vicki Vola** and **Len Doyle** is the best-remembered Harrington. David Bryan played the lead role in a syndicated version of the program produced by ZIV in 1952.

MR. KEEN, TRACER OF LOST PERSONS. A detective drama produced by **Frank and Anne Hummert**, *Mr. Keen* was first heard as a 15-minute serial drama from 1937 to 1943 and then became a 30-minute weekly program for most of the rest of the long run, which lasted until 1955. Originally Mr. Keen was a private detective who traced missing persons, but when the program changed to a 30-minute weekly format, he became an investigator of murders, assisted by his assistant, Clancy. Neither Keen nor Clancy had any official police position, although they acted very much like policemen and often seemed to have police powers. Bennett Kilpack played Mr. Keen for most of the run, with Jim Kelly as Mike Clancy.

MR. PRESIDENT. An unusual 30-minute **drama anthology** heard during 1947–1953, *Mr. President* portrayed little-known events from the lives of American presidents. Edward Arnold took the role of a different president each week. The name of the president being portrayed was never revealed until the completion of the episode. The presidential secretary was played by **Betty Lou Gerson**.

MOHR, GERALD (1914–1968). While still in college, Mohr was persuaded to try radio by announcer **Andre Baruch**, who overheard him talking and thought he had a future in the medium. Mohr began as an announcer at CBS, and at age 20 he covered the Morro Castle ship disaster off the New Jersey coast. Work with **Orson Welles** led to appearances on several popular radio programs including *Lux Radio Theatre*, *Suspense*, and *The Whistler*. Subsequently, he played the leads on *The Lone Wolf* and *The Adventures of Philip Marlowe*. On television in the mid-1950s, he starred as Christopher Storm on *Foreign Intrigue*. In Hollywood, Mohr appeared in movies from the early 1940s until the late 1960s.

MOLLE MYSTERY THEATER (THE). Beginning as a 30-minute **drama anthology** in 1943, this program featured dramatizations of mystery stories by both classic and modern writers. In 1948, production was assumed by **Frank and Anne Hummert**, the title was changed to *Mystery Theater*, and it became a series featuring the exploits of Inspector Hearthstone of the Death Squad, which spun off to become a program of that name in 1951. *Mystery Theater* continued as the story of Inspector Mark Sabre; this version, heard until 1954, is sometimes listed as *Mark Sabre* or as *Mystery Time*.

MONITOR. A weekend magazine program created by NBC in 1955, *Monitor* presented interviews, commentators, musical variety, and comedy from a long list of performers that eventually came to include hundreds. *Monitor* originally ran for 40 hours each weekend, from 8:00 A.M. Saturday to midnight Sunday. The hours and format changed over the years, including attempts to expand the format to weekday programming, but by 1961 the program was being heard for 16 hours each weekend, and that format continued with minor changes until it left the air in 1975. *Monitor* eventually broadcast more than 20,000 hours of programming, far more than any other program in the history of radio.

MOONSHINE AND HONEYSUCKLE. A 30-minute Sunday afternoon serial drama often cited as a precursor to the daytime **soap operas**, *Moonshine and Honeysuckle* was heard from 1930 to 1933. It was the story of life in the little community of Lonesome Hollow and featured a great deal of homespun rural humor, much in the manner of *Lum and Abner*. **Anne Elstner**, who later played *Stella Dallas* on the daytime soap opera, began her radio career on this program, playing the part of Cracker Gaddis.

MOORE, GARRY (1915–1993). Born Thomas Garrison Morfit, Moore's first network job was in 1939 as a writer and comedian on *Club Matinee*. On that show, it was decided to conduct a contest among listeners to give him a name that was easier to pronounce. A Pittsburgh woman won $50 for suggesting Garry Moore, the name that Moore used for the rest of his professional life. He hosted or emceed many programs, including *The Fitch Summer Bandwagon*, *Beat the Band*, *The Camel Caravan*, and *Take It or Leave It*. He headlined a show with **Jimmy Durante**, from 1943 to 1948 and then began his own program in 1949. Moore moved to television in 1950, when he starred in *The Garry Moore Show* (1950–1951, 1958–1964, 1966–1967), moderated *I've Got a Secret* (1952–1964), and emceed *To Tell the Truth* (1969–1976).

MOOREHEAD, AGNES (1906–1974). Before winning important dramatic parts, Moorehead earned a doctorate in literature, taught high school, and studied at the American Academy of Dramatic Arts. She helped **Orson Welles** found the Mercury Theatre and appeared on many of the broadcasts of *Mercury Theatre on the Air*. She also was featured on *The Shadow* (as Margo Lane), *Mayor of the Town*, and *Cavalcade of America*. On the popular dramatic show, *Suspense*, she played the role of the bedridden wife about to be murdered in the classic "Sorry, Wrong Number" story on 25 May 1943 and reprised the role seven times over the years. Moorehead also starred on Broadway, in motion pictures, and on television.

MORGAN, CLAUDIA (1911–1974). Although she also acted successfully on the stage, Morgan is known today primarily for her work on radio. She appeared on *Against the Storm*, *David Harum*, *The Right to Happiness*, and on numerous **drama anthology programs**, but she is remembered most for playing Nora Charles on *The Adventures of the Thin Man* during the 1940s. Morgan sounded so much like Myrna Loy, who created the character in the movies, that many who listened to the radio program thought Loy was playing the part.

MORGAN, HENRY (1915–1994). Morgan was born Henry Lerner von Ost Jr. He was first heard locally on WOR New York with a program called *Meet Mr. Morgan*. This show evolved into a network show on Mutual called *Here's Morgan*, a 15-minute program of patter and comedy skits of various kinds (with a liberal sprinkling of insults for all institutions, including radio executives). After a break while he was in the military during World War II, he returned to network radio on ABC in 1946 with *The Henry Morgan Show*. The program was dropped in 1947, but Morgan returned in 1949–1950 with a similar show, this one co-starring Arnold Stang and **Kenny Delmar** with announcer **Ben Grauer**. Morgan moved to television in the early 1950s and appeared on such programs as *I've Got a Secret*, *Draw to Win*, and *That Was the Week That Was*.

MORRISON, BRET (1912–1978). Morrison is remembered today as the last actor to play Lamont Cranston, *The Shadow*. He first played the role in 1943–1944, then played it again from 1945 to 1954. He also played on many other radio programs during the medium's golden age, hosting *The First Nighter* and *Listening Post*, and appearing as "The Speaker" on *Light of the World*. Morrison worked on several **soap operas**, including *Stella Dallas*, *Road of Life*, *The Romance of Helen Trent*, and *The Guiding Light*. During the 1970s, he appeared on *The CBS Radio Mystery Theater*, one of the shows that attempted to bring back network radio drama.

MORSE, CARLTON E. (1901–1993). One of the leading scriptwriters of radio dramas, Morse began his career at NBC in 1929 and was the creator of two of the best-remembered programs of old-time radio: *One Man's Family* and *I Love a Mystery*. From 1922 to 1929, he wrote for several newspapers, beginning with the *Sacramento Union*, and ending with the *San Francisco Bulletin*. When the latter was absorbed by another paper, Morse lost his job and brought several scripts he had written to NBC in San Francisco. Hired as a scriptwriter, Morse worked on several programs before he began writing scripts for *One Man's Family* in 1932. In 1939, he began *I Love a Mystery* and later created several other programs, including *Adventures by Morse*, and *I Love Adventure*. Morse received many honors during his lifetime, including a star on Hollywood's Walk of Fame.

MORTON DOWNEY SHOW (THE). Morton Downey was an Irish tenor who hosted a long series of 15-minute and 30-minute **music programs** from 1930 to 1951. In 1932, he was selected as the nation's best male vocalist by a newspaper poll; by 1936, he was one of radio's top stars. There were many different names for his various programs, including *The Camel Quarter-Hour*, *Morton Downey's Studio Party*, and *Songs by Morton Downey*. He was, for many years, the host of *The Coke Club*.

MUNN, FRANK (1894–1953). A tenor who was known at one time as "The Golden Voice of Radio," Munn began his radio career in the 1920s and was a major star for years although he made very few guest appearances due to being self-conscious about his appearance. He was short and stocky and wanted to be judged only by his voice, which was perfect for early radio and early recording microphones, where a powerful voice was required. He made hundreds of recordings; among his many hits were "When Irish Eyes Are Smiling" and "Something to Remember You By." He began his network radio career on *The Palmolive Hour*, and then starred on *American Album of Familiar Music*, *American Melody Hour*, *For America We Sing*, *Lavender and Old Lace*, *Sweetest Love Songs Ever Sung*, and *Waltz Time*. The majority of these programs were produced by **Frank and Anne Hummert**. At one point, Munn sang on three different weekly programs concurrently. He retired from show business at age 51, and never sang again professionally.

MURDER AND MR. MALONE. John J. Malone was an attorney and part-time detective who was the protagonist in a long series of novels and short stories by Craig Rice. The radio series based on the same character was a 30-minute **crime program** heard from 1947 to 1951. There were several name changes during the run, and the program is sometimes listed as *The Amazing Mr. Malone*. Malone was played by **Frank Lovejoy** in the original version, later by Gene Raymond and **George Petrie**. The television version in 1951–1952 starred Lee Tracy.

MURRAY, KEN (1903–1988). Murray was a comedian who starred on *The Ken Murray Show* in 1933, and on *Laugh with Ken*, heard in 1936. He also hosted ***Hollywood Hotel***, ***The Texaco Star Theater***, and several other programs. On television, he hosted *The Ken Murray Show* and was a regular on *The Judy Garland Show*. Murray was an amateur movie enthusiast and became Hollywood's unofficial historian, taking many home movies of celebrities. He edited these movies, added commentary, and then presented the finished product in theaters and on television. In 1947, he received an Academy Award for his production of a feature film, *Bill and Coo*, that had trained birds as its stars. His autobiography, *Life on a Pogo Stick*, was published in 1960.

MURROW, EDWARD R. (1908–1965). In the early 1940s, when radio had become a fixture in most American homes, the radio correspondents who went overseas to broadcast the war news back home often became household names. Murrow was prominent among these. In London at the start of the European war, he assembled a staff that included Charles Collingwood, Eric Severeid, William L. Shirer, and Howard K. Smith. Each was selected because of his knowledge of European politics. Murrow's reporting often involved great personal risk, including broadcasting from London rooftops during the 1940 German Blitz. His signature line, "This is London," brought World War II into America's living rooms. After the war, he returned home and, in addition to headlining *Edward R. Murrow and the News* from 1946 to 1959, became a vice president of CBS News. He became famous on television with his *See It Now*, *Person to Person*, and *Small World* programs. In 1961, he left CBS to enter government service as director of the U.S. Information Agency, where one of his duties was supervision of Voice of America. Murrow received many awards during his lifetime, and in 1988 was inducted into the Radio Hall of Fame. *See also* NEWS PROGRAMS.

MUSIC APPRECIATION HOUR (THE). A 60-minute musical education program for children, *The Music Appreciation Hour* was heard from 1928 to 1942. The program was hosted by **Walter Damrosch**, who explained a classical selection in detail and then conducted the orchestra in its playing. The program was part of the curriculum in many schools and at one time was heard by as many as seven million school children weekly.

MUSIC PROGRAMS. Musical programs provided the majority of programming during early radio; in the very early years of the networks, they accounted for over 70 percent of daily broadcast hours. Although the percentage of programs devoted to music declined over the years, music still accounted for over 40 percent of all network programming as late as 1946.

The music presented on network radio frequently included classical or semiclassical music. This was partly a reflection of the musical tastes of the time, but also an indication of the desire of many network program directors to present "good" music. Symphony orchestras were a feature of the very earliest network programming, and many of them broadcast weekly for over 30 years. Classical music was important enough to the networks for NBC to have its own excellent symphony orchestra. The Metropolitan Opera first appeared on radio in 1931 and remained on the air throughout the entire period of old-time radio.

Live programs of music by dance orchestras, often called **band remotes**, were heard on every network and were sometimes almost the entirety of overnight broadcasting, usually heard in 30-minute segments from ballrooms, hotels, night clubs, and anywhere else a dance orchestra might be appearing. Hundreds of these programs are available but many of them were undocumented beyond the name of the orchestra and the remote location.

Even when created in the studio, early musical programs were often poorly documented, partly because documentation was a low priority in studios that ran on tight schedules. No one gave any thought to creating an archive or to memorializing the parade of musicians who peopled every studio. As a result, almost all that is known of many early musical programs is the name as it appeared in newspapers or program logs.

As radio matured, almost every well-known musician or singer had his or her own program, often technically named for the sponsor, but usually known by the name of the featured performer. *The Bing Crosby Show*, for instance, was actually named *The Kraft Music Hall* for 10 years and was then named *Philco Radio Time* when the sponsor changed. *The Perry Como Show* was actually named *The Chesterfield Supper Club* for much of its long run. Most of these performer-centric programs consisted of musical numbers alternated with comedy episodes or skits of one sort or another, often including well-known guest stars. *See also* CONCERT MUSIC.

MUTUAL BROADCASTING SYSTEM (MBS). The Mutual Broadcasting System did not begin until 1934, and was organized very differently from the other major networks. It did not own any stations, had no studios, employed no engineers, and did not produce any programs other than an occasional special news broadcast. It was a working agreement between independently owned stations, with all stations maintaining a good deal of autonomy. Programs were produced by member stations or by sponsors and were then sold to other stations in the network. The network was originally owned in equal parts by WGN Chicago, WOR New York, WLW Cincinnati, and WXYZ Detroit. Arrangements were made to interconnect the four stations by telephone line and contracts were secured with advertisers with the understanding that their advertisements would be broadcast on all four stations.

Mutual did not require that member stations be associated exclusively with the Mutual network; and, by 1939, the network had grown to 107 stations, of which 25 were also associated with NBC and 5 with CBS. By the end of 1940, 160 stations were in the Mutual network. Both WXYZ and WGN subsequently sold their shares in the network and Mutual later went through a long series of changes in corporate ownership, until use of the Mutual name was discontinued in 1999.

MY FAVORITE HUSBAND. A 30-minute **situation comedy** heard from 1948 to 1951, *My Favorite Husband* starred Lucille Ball and Richard Denning as George and Liz Cooper, a married couple who "live together and like it." George's best friend, Rudolph Atterbury, was played by **Gale Gordon** and Rudolph's wife, who was Liz's best friend Iris, was played by Bea Benaderet. Lucy's role was rather like the one she played on her later television program. In fact, many episodes of the radio program were used as patterns for later *I Love Lucy* episodes; and sometimes the exact same lines were used.

MY FRIEND IRMA. A 30-minute **situation comedy** heard from 1947 to 1954, *My Friend Irma* starred **Marie Wilson** as Irma Peterson, a secretary who was the prototypical "dumb blonde." The stories were narrated by her long-suffering roommate, Jane Stacy, who was played by **Cathy Lewis**. Irma's boyfriend, Al, was a Brooklyn hustler played by **John Brown** and Professor

Kropotkin, who lived downstairs from the two girls, was played by **Hans Conreid**. The program was the basis for a movie of the same name in 1949, in which Dean Martin and Jerry Lewis made their film debut.

MY LITTLE MARGIE. A 30-minute **situation comedy** heard from 1952 to 1955, *My Little Margie* ran concurrently on both radio and television. It was one of the few radio programs to appear after its television counterpart. Gale Storm played the role of Margie Albright, who lived with her father in a New York apartment building. Margie was always scheming with old Mrs. Odetts, who lived next door, to keep her widower father from becoming involved with other women, as well as to circumvent any control he tried to exercise over her. Mrs. Odetts was played by **Verna Felton** and Gil Stratton Jr. played Freddie, Margie's boyfriend.

MYRT AND MARGE. An early 15-minute **soap opera**, *Myrt and Marge* was first heard evenings from 1931 to 1937 and then moved to daytime radio, where it was heard until 1942. The broadcast history is complicated; the program appeared on two networks concurrently for some time and there was a syndicated version that appeared some years after the original run ended. It was the story of two sisters in show business. The older sister, Myrt, was a veteran performer who tried to protect her younger sister, sometimes causing conflicts between them. It was written by Myrtle Vail, who also played Myrt, and Marge was originally played by her daughter, Donna Fick. Fick died in childbirth in 1941 and the role was assumed by Helen Mack and later by several other performers.

MYSTERIOUS TRAVELER (THE). A 30-minute **drama anthology** heard from 1943 to 1952, *The Mysterious Traveler* featured Maurice Tarplin as the host and "Mysterious Traveler." The Traveler was both spooky and humorous, like the hosts of several other horror anthology shows. He arrived at the beginning of each program on a train and invited the listener to join him on a trip into the strange and terrifying. The plots were wide-ranging, including science fiction, crime, and tales of the supernatural. The Traveler also closed each program, often with a macabre joke, and invited the listener to return again the next week.

– N –

NAGEL, CONRAD (1896–1970). Nagel began his professional acting career in 1914, playing juvenile leads with a stock company, and in his long career acted in nearly all entertainment media. On radio, he hosted *The Silver Theatre* until 1942, was the first host-narrator on *The Radio Reader's Digest*, and both hosted and starred in *Proudly We Hail*, a **drama anthology** series sponsored by the U. S. Army and Air Force. Nagel moved to television in 1949, where he hosted the television version of *Silver Theatre*, and also emceed *Celebrity Time*, an ABC-TV variety program. A co-founder and former president of the Academy of Motion Picture Arts and Sciences, he was involved in the creation of the Academy Awards.

NAISH, J. CARROLL (1897–1973). Joseph Patrick Carrol Naish dropped out of high school at age 16 to serve in the armed forces during World War I. After the war, he roamed around Europe doing various odd jobs and learning several foreign languages. He returned to Hollywood in 1930, and began a long movie career that lasted until the 1960s and resulted in two Academy Award nominations. He was very skilled with dialects and played a wide variety of ethnic roles on the screen, but the radio part that brought him fame was the title role on the comedy *Life with Luigi*. The program ran on CBS from 1948 to 1952, and Naish also played Luigi on a short-lived television version in 1952–1953.

NATIONAL AMATEUR NIGHT. The first of the amateur talent programs to appear on network radio, *National Amateur Night* was a 30-minute Sunday evening program hosted by Ray Perkins and heard from 1934 to 1936. Although similar in format to the much more popular *Major Bowes' Original Amateur Hour*, the performers who appeared were much less talented. The poorest were cut off by a whistle blown by Perkins or by a chord played by the orchestra. A panel of judges determined the winner, who received a medal and a contract to appear on radio.

NATIONAL BARN DANCE (THE). A country **music program**, *The National Barn Dance*, like *The Grand Ole Opry*, was a stage performance, only a part of which was broadcast. The two programs were heard on Saturday nights in consecutive time slots, and had very similar ratings for many years. *The National Barn Dance* was heard regionally in the Chicago area beginning in 1924, on the national networks from 1933 to 1950, and then again on a regional basis until 1968, although live performances ended in 1957. Hosted by **Joe Kelly**, who also hosted *The Quiz Kids*, *The National Barn Dance* was staged in the Eighth Street Theater in Chicago after demand for tickets outgrew the capacity of the radio studio where it had originally been performed. The program had a more Midwestern tone than did the Southern-oriented *Opry* and was also less oriented to recording artists, although several recording stars appeared on the program during its long run.

NATIONAL BROADCASTING COMPANY (NBC). NBC was the first of the national networks to go on the air, beginning broadcasting on 15 November 1926 with a network of 24 stations. The **Radio Corporation of America (RCA)** had been operating a small network of broadcasting stations headed by WJZ, New York, and in 1926 purchased station WEAF, New York, along with an affiliated network from American Telephone and Telegraph (AT&T). NBC was created to manage the broadcasting activities of the two networks. For a time, the networks operated side-by-side but in 1927 NBC formally separated them, creating the NBC Red Network, headed by station WEAF, and the NBC Blue Network, headed by WJZ. Most of the entertainment and music programming was carried by the Red Network, as well as most of the news and cultural programs, and most of the unsponsored or "sustaining" programs were carried on the Blue Network, although there were exceptions on both networks. According to legend, the color-naming of the networks related to the color of the pins that NBC executives used to mark the presence of the various network stations on a map. The famous NBC three-note chimes (G-E-C) were developed in 1931 as a signal to the various stations that they were switching between feeds from the two NBC networks.

From the time of its creation in 1934, the Federal Communications Commission had been concerned that RCA's ownership of two networks might have a monopolistic effect on broadcasting, restricting free trade. In 1939, they forced RCA to divest itself of one of its two networks and after losing an appeal in the courts, RCA sold the Blue Network in 1943 to Edward J. Noble, who re-named the network **The American Broadcasting Company (ABC)**. After the sale, the NBC Red Network was referred to as simply NBC. During the golden days of radio, NBC was a dominant force, home to many of the most popular programs and best-known stars. As the popularity of broadcast radio began to wane, NBC gradually became more and more involved in television, often moving radio programs to the new medium. The last major programming effort of the radio portion of the company was *Monitor*, a weekend mixture of news, music, and short features that endured from 1955 to 1975, after which NBC radio became little more than brief hourly news summaries.

NATIONAL FARM AND HOME HOUR (THE). A long-running program of news, music, and country humor directed at the American farmer, *The National Farm and Home Hour* was heard at noon, six days a week, from 1929 to 1958. Originally a 60-minute program, it was later heard in both 45-minute and 30-minute formats and the name was changed to *The Farm and Home Hour* from 1941 to 1945; but the program remained the same, offering news, tips from experts, entertainment, and live coverage of happenings in agricultural settings. Hosted by Everett Mitchell, the program was produced in collaboration with the Department of Agriculture and often with the help of various farm organizations, including the American Farm Bureau and the Farmers Union.

NAVY HOUR (THE). Beginning in 1930, the U.S. Navy sponsored a long series of **music programs** by the Navy band. Sometimes called *The U.S. Navy Band* and sometimes *The Navy Hour*, these 30-minute programs were usually heard on Saturday morning. In 1945, the Navy produced *The Navy Hour* on a more formal basis; at first it featured the talents of celebrities who had joined the Navy during World War II, but it continued as a program of band music until 1968.

NBC BLUE NETWORK. *See* NATIONAL BROADCASTING COMPANY.

NBC RED NETWORK. *See* NATIONAL BROADCASTING COMPANY.

NBC UNIVERSITY THEATER (THE). A quality **drama anthology program** associated with correspondence courses from several universities, *The NBC University Theater* was heard from 1948 to 1951, usually in a 60-minute format. Although the quality of the programs was excellent, ratings were low. In 1949, the name of the program was changed to *The NBC Theater* in hopes that removing the word "university" from the title would broaden the listener base. At the time, NBC already had a drama anthology by that name, but it was re-named ***Screen Director's Playhouse***. There is sometimes confusion with old-time radio sources in the listing of the two programs.

NED JORDAN, SECRET AGENT. A 30-minute **adventure program** heard from 1940 to 1942, *Ned Jordan* featured a federal agent who worked undercover, posing as a detective for the railroad and using this position to gather information on foreign agents. The program was produced by **George W. Trendle**, who produced *The Lone Ranger* and other famous adventure programs, and was heard locally on WXYZ Detroit, Trendle's station, before joining the Mutual network. Ned was played by Jack McCarthy and FBI agent Proctor was played by Dick Osgood.

NEWS PROGRAMS. By 1939, more than 25 percent of Americans depended on radio for most of their news; three years later, that had increased to 73 percent. In addition, most listeners felt that radio news was more objective than news reported in newspapers. By 1946, only 35 percent of Americans said that newspapers were for them a major source of news.

The reasons for this were several, as with any sweeping social change, but a major reason was the inherent superiority of radio for the timely provision of news. Radio could not only produce almost immediate event coverage, it could also compete with the editorial aspects of print journalism, providing immediate interpretation and informed comment on breaking news. Commentary was an important part of radio journalism; radio commentators, like newspaper editors, felt free to shape the news as they saw fit in this editorial context. Radio commentators became genuine stars, of a magnitude at least equal to that of the television news anchors of today, although their function was quite different.

In addition to the inherent advantages of the medium, the events leading to World War II and the war itself were major reasons that broadcast journalism became so dominant so quickly. When events moved rapidly, immediate reports became more valuable. When the issues involved were more complex, the insights offered by commentators were more welcome. World War II was the heyday of the radio commentator and there were a number of commentators of various political persuasions who became prominent during that period, including **H. V. Kaltenborn**, **H. R. Baukhage**, **Fulton Lewis Jr.**, **Lowell Thomas**, and **Gabriel Heatter**, among others.

By the end of the war, all of the networks had developed large news departments, dedicated not only to the collection of news, but to analysis. In the absence of war news and war concerns, commentators began to devote more attention to social issues, and a tradition of social activism and exposure of government misbehavior developed among radio newsmen, led by **Drew Pearson**, who was sort of a government gossip columnist, with informants everywhere. **Edward R. Murrow**, who had become famous for his on-the-spot reporting of the Battle of Britain, became a vice-president of CBS News in 1946 and expanded the governmental oversight function in broadcasting by producing documentary programs based on investigative reporting of the type now familiar to everyone.

News programs, along with every other kind of programming, began a steady migration to television during the early 1950s. For a time, leading news personages appeared on both media, but television replaced radio as a primary news source with a speed equal to the speed with which radio had replaced newspapers only 25 years earlier, and radio news was eventually relegated primarily to the production of hourly bulletins, much as it had been at the inception of network radio.

NICK CARTER, MASTER DETECTIVE. A 30-minute **crime program** heard from 1943 to 1955, this program featured Lon Clark as Nick Carter, a private detective who had been featured in magazines of the late 1800s. The setting for the radio program was modern, however, and the Nick Carter portrayed on radio was quite different from the literary version. Much like many other radio detectives, Nick always seemed to get the best of the police. Nick's secretary, Patsy, was a part of every story, as was Scrubby Wilson, a reporter, and police Sergeant Mathieson. Patsy was played by Helen Choate until 1946, then by Charlotte Manson; Scrubby was played by John Kane and Sergeant Mathieson by Ed Latimer.

NIELSEN RATINGS (THE). *See* RATING SYSTEMS.

NIGHTBEAT. A 30-minute **adventure program** heard from 1950 to 1952, *Nightbeat* featured **Frank Lovejoy** as Randy Stone, a reporter who covered the "nightbeat" for a Chicago newspaper. The stories were primarily human interest rather than traditional crime dramas, although crime was sometimes involved. Each program ended with Stone typing out his story and then calling "copy boy!" Many famous Hollywood radio actors appeared on the show, including **William Conrad**, **Lurene Tuttle**, and **Joan Banks**.

NILES, KEN (1906–1988). Niles began working in broadcasting in the late 1920s at KJR Seattle, and his 1928 program, *Theatre of the Mind*, was one of the first to present original dramas on the West Coast. He announced for many network programs during radio's golden age, including *Big Town*, *Blue Ribbon Time*, *The Camel Caravan*, *Hollywood Hotel*, *Kay Kyser's Kollege of Musical Knowledge*, and *Take It or Leave It*. His brother, Wendell Niles (1904–1994), was also a network radio and television announcer.

– O –

OBOLER, ARCH (1909–1987). A writer, director, and producer, Oboler is remembered today primarily for his association with *Lights Out*, which he joined in 1936, replacing **Wyllis Cooper**. Oboler wrote and directed over 100 episodes of *Lights Out* from 1936 to 1938. During World War II, he worked on several patriotic radio programs, including *Everything for the Boys*, *Four for the Fifth*, *Free World Theater*, and *Treasury Star Parade*. From the mid-1940s until the late 1960s, Oboler also worked in the motion picture industry, writing screenplays and directing films, including the first 3-D movie, *Bwana Devil*, in 1952.

OFFICE OF WAR INFORMATION (OWI). The OWI was a U.S. Government agency created in 1942 to consolidate government information services during World War II and to limit the careless leaking of sensitive information that could be used by spies and saboteurs. **Elmer Davis**, a CBS newsman, was named director. In addition to clearing commercial broadcast scripts, the OWI produced several radio series, including *This Is Our Enemy*, and established the **Armed Forces Radio Service**, which was responsible for the production of hundreds of transcriptions of network radio programs for shipment to servicemen overseas. In 1942, the OWI established the Voice of America, which is still today the official broadcasting service of the United States. The OWI was abolished in 1945.

OFFICIAL DETECTIVE. A **crime program** heard from 1947 to 1957, *Official Detective* was heard first as a 15-minute program, but changed to a 30-minute format in late 1947. Produced in cooperation with *Official Detective Stories* magazine, it featured Craig McDonnell as Lt. Dan Britt and Tommy Evans as Sgt. Al Bowen in the original version; the roles were later played by other performers. The crimes portrayed were not always murders, and an effort was made to present police work in a realistic light.

O'KEEFE, WALTER (1900–1983). O'Keefe was a man of many accomplishments: comedian, quizmaster, emcee, newspaper columnist, and musician. He attended Notre Dame, later performed in vaudeville as a monologist, and in 1937 wrote a humor column that appeared in daily newspaper syndication. On network radio, O'Keefe appeared on *The Camel Caravan*, *Town Hall Tonight*, and *Double or Nothing*, which he hosted for six years. He moved to television in the early 1950s, interviewing celebrities on *Mayor of Hollywood* and then hosting the quiz program *Two for the Money*.

OLD GOLD PROGRAM (THE). The *Old Gold Program* was an umbrella title for a long series of programs sponsored by Old Gold cigarettes that appeared from 1933 to 1948, sometimes under other titles, including *The Old Gold Show* and *The Old Gold Comedy Theater*. Dick Powell was the star of the 1933 version, and Artie Shaw and Robert Benchley co-starred in the 1938 program, which is sometimes listed as *The Robert Benchley Show* or as *Melody and Madness*. The 1945 *Frank Sinatra Show* was part of this series; in 1947, the program was also listed as *The Frank Morgan Show*.

OLMSTED, NELSON (1914–1982). Nelson Olmsted was a popular radio actor who hosted a long series of 15-minute programs of various titles from 1939 to 1951. On all these shows, he read and dramatized short stories. Some of the program titles were *Stories by Olmsted, Story for Tonight, Nelson Olmsted Playhouse*, and *The World's Greatest Short Stories*. He was also the narrator of *Sleep No More*, a 15-minute horror program. After his radio career, Olmsted was featured on several television programs and appeared in scores of movies.

ON STAGE. A 30-minute **drama anthology** produced and directed by **Elliott Lewis**, *On Stage* was heard during 1953–1954 and was sometimes listed as *Cathy and Elliott Lewis on Stage*. The intent was to produce a series of programs centered on male–female situations, with a strong part for each, and both Lewis and his actress wife appeared in many of the productions. The Lewis' were supported by some of the finest radio performers in Los Angeles, including **William Conrad**, **John Dehner**, and Peggy Webber.

ONE MAN'S FAMILY. A long-running evening **soap opera** that was structured like a novel, with installments referred to as "books" and "chapters," *One Man's Family* was of superior literary quality, winning a **Peabody Award** and other national awards for excellence. Written by **Carlton E. Morse**, the program was realistic rather than melodramatic, with none of the stock formulas often seen in soap operas. Beginning on the network as a 30-minute weekly program in 1933, it remained so until changing to a 15-minute format in 1950. It left the air in 1959, having broadcast 3,274 separate episodes concerning the story of the Barbour family of San Francisco. Henry and Fanny Barbour had five children and the program followed the aging and growth of all, eventually encompassing several generations of Barbour descendents. Henry Barbour was played by **J. Anthony Smythe** for the entire run; Fanny was played by Minetta Ellen from 1933 to 1955, at which time Mary Adams assumed the role.

O'NEILLS (THE). A 15-minute **soap opera** heard from 1934 to 1943 in several different time slots and on several different networks, *The O'Neills* sometimes appeared on more than one network at a time.

It was the story of an elderly widow with two married children and two adopted children whom she cared for after their parents died. Mother O'Neill was a sage, common-sense philosopher, a fountain of good advice, as was her best friend, Morris Levy. Mother O'Neill was played by Kate McComb for the entire run; Morris was played by Jack Rubin.

ORTEGA, SANTOS (1906–1976). Although best known today for having appeared on television's *As the World Turns* for more than 20 years, Ortega had a rich background in radio **soap opera** as well, having played on no fewer than 14 different series. He was a radio performer of almost unbelievable output; in addition to his work in soap operas, he appeared on at least 41 other series, including many detective programs. He was the original Inspector Queen on *The Adventures of Ellery Queen*, as well as being the first actor to play the title role on *The Adventures of Nero Wolfe*, and the second actor to portray *Perry Mason*. He was also featured on *Dimension X*, and its successor *X Minus One*.

OUR GAL SUNDAY. A 15-minute daily **soap opera** produced by **Frank and Anne Hummert** and heard from 1937 to 1959, *Our Gal Sunday* was the story of an orphan girl who had been named *Sunday*, because she had been found on that day. She was raised by two old prospectors and later married a handsome and rich young English nobleman, Lord Henry Brinthrope. The major problems encountered by the couple revolved around the fact that both were very attractive and that Lord Henry, in particular, was often pursued by scheming women of various sorts. The program had the unusual distinction of occupying the same time slot for the entire long run.

OUR MISS BROOKS. A 30-minute **situation comedy** heard from 1948 to 1957, *Our Miss Brooks* starred **Eve Arden** as Connie Brooks, a high school English teacher. Her supporting cast was excellent: **Gale Gordon** as the high school principal, **Jeff Chandler** as biology teacher Philip Boynton, and Richard Crenna as Walter Denton, a bumbling student who was in love with the principal's daughter. The program moved to television in 1952, running concurrently with the radio version until 1956.

– P –

PACKARD SHOW (THE). The first version of this show, appearing in 1934, was a 30-minute program of **concert music** featuring baritone Lawrence Tibbett. In 1936 the program changed networks and became a 60-minute **variety program** called *The Packard Hour*, starring Fred Astaire and Charlie Butterworth. Astaire did not return the next year and the 1937–1938 version of the program was renamed *Mardi Gras*, starring singer **Lanny Ross** and comedian **Walter O'Keefe**. All versions were sponsored by the Packard Motor Company.

PAINTED DREAMS. Considered by many to be radio's first daytime **soap opera**, *Painted Dreams* was first heard locally over WGN Chicago in 1930. It was written by **Irna Phillips**, who also played the lead character, Mother Moynihan. Much of the story consisted of dialogue between Mother Moynihan and another character, often played by **Ireene Wicker**, rather than action sequences. Phillips left WGN in 1932 when the station turned down an offer to place the program on a national network. She subsequently produced a very similar program, ***Today's Children***, heard for many years on the NBC network. *Painted Dreams* continued to be heard locally on WGN for many years and had several short network runs from 1933 to 1940.

PALEY, WILLIAM S. (1901–1990). Paley was the chief executive who built the **Columbia Broadcasting System (CBS)** into a dominant radio and television network. In early 1927, a group called the **United Independent Broadcasters (UIB)** attempted to establish a radio network, but failed to sell enough air time to advertisers. In the fall of that year, the network was sold to William S. Paley and his father, the owner of a cigar company. Paley renamed the network the Columbia Broadcasting System (CBS), guided the network as its president and chairman for over 50 years, and was still in a figurehead position as chairman at his death in 1990. Paley changed broadcasting's business model by providing network programming to affiliate stations at nominal cost, thereby ensuring the widest possible distribution; thus being able to charge more for advertising time. Affiliates were required to carry programming offered by the network for part of the broadcast day, receiving a portion of the network's take from advertising revenue. Paley was also responsible for the network procedure of producing programs in their own studios, thus reducing the influence of sponsors and advertising agencies on artistic content. After World War II, CBS expanded into television and Paley became the best-known executive in network television.

PALMOLIVE BEAUTY BOX THEATER. From 1934 to 1936, the *Palmolive Beauty Box Theater* was a 60-minute program featuring Broadway musicals and operettas, but the format changed the following year and the program became a 30-minute **music program** starring **Jessica Dragonette**, who had for many years been the star of the *Cities Service Concerts*. This version of the program, sometimes listed as *Beauty Box Theater*, was heard only during 1937.

PARKER, FRANK (1903–1999). Parker was a popular radio tenor who was the singer on the early version of *The Jack Benny Program* and later appeared on the programs of other major radio stars, such as **Burns and Allen** and **Eddie Cantor**. Born Frank Ciccio in New York City, Parker was photogenic and appeared in movies, as well as having several radio programs of his own. He was a regular on the **Arthur Godfrey** radio and television programs from 1950 to 1956. In 1957, he was a panelist on the TV quiz program *Masquerade Party*.

PARKS, BERT (1914–1992). Born Bert Jacobson, Parks started in radio in Atlanta while still a teenager. His first network job on radio was as a singer and straight man on *The Eddie Cantor Show* and he was an announcer for many years; but most of his radio success was as the enthusiastic and energetic emcee on several very popular **quiz programs**, including *Break the Bank*, *Stop the Music*, and *Double or Nothing*. These programs moved to television in the late 1940s and early 1950s, and Parks moved with them, as well as starring on another dozen TV programs over the years. He achieved his greatest fame because of his appearances on the annual Miss America Beauty Pageant, which he hosted from 1955 to 1980, and on which he sang "There She Is, Miss America" at the end of each program.

PARKYAKARKUS. Parkyakarkus was the name of a character created by dialect comedian Harry Einstein. He developed the character, a Greek immigrant, on *The Eddie Cantor Show* and later on the *Al Jolson Show*. Einstein, in the role of Parkyakarkus, starred in his own **situation comedy**, *Meet Me at Parky's*, from 1945 to 1948 in spite of a back condition that left him partially paralyzed for many years.

PARSONS, LOUELLA (1881–1972). Louella Parsons was a Hollywood gossip columnist during the period when Hollywood was dominated by large studios. Born Louella Rose Oettinger, her column for the *Los Angeles Examiner* appeared in more than 600 newspapers the world over, with an estimated 25 million readers. Beginning in 1928, she hosted a weekly radio program featuring movie star interviews. In 1934, she began hosting *Hollywood Hotel*, a 60-minute program featuring stars in scenes from their upcoming movies. Her own 15-minute gossip show, *The Louella Parsons Show*, ran for many years and, for a time in the 1940s, was broadcast immediately following **Walter Winchell**. Parsons herself appeared in many cameo spots in films. She has two stars in the Hollywood Walk of Fame, one for motion pictures and one for radio. *See also* HOPPER, HEDDA.

PASSING PARADE (THE). Heard in many different time slots and on several different networks from 1938 to 1949, *The Passing Parade* was an unusual program of strange stories and peculiar happenings. The episodes were narrated without sound effects by John Nesbitt, who also wrote and produced the program. In some ways similar to those heard on *Believe It or Not*, the stories were usually fantastic or unbelievable, but were carefully researched. Also, like *Believe It or Not*, *The Passing Parade* sometimes appeared as a segment on omnibus programs.

PAT NOVAK FOR HIRE. One of the several early detective dramas starring **Jack Webb**, *Pat Novak for Hire* originally was written by Richard Breen and produced in San Francisco, appearing only on the ABC West Coast network during 1946–1947. Although the subject matter was crime, the dialogue had a light touch, with many one-liners offered by Novak. When Webb left in 1947, his place was taken by Ben Morris, but without Webb, the show was not a success. The program reappeared on the national network in 1949 with Webb in the lead role, but he left when his new show, *Dragnet*, began later that year.

PAUSE THAT REFRESHES (THE). The slogan of the Coca-Cola company for many years, *The Pause That Refreshes* was the title given to several **music programs** sponsored by Coca-Cola from 1934 to 1949. Sometimes listed as *The Pause That Refreshes on the Air*, the 1934–1935 version featured a huge orchestra under the direction of **Frank Black**. The **Andre Kostelanetz** orchestra was featured on several of the programs in the 1940s, replaced by Percy Faith with another large orchestra in 1948.

PAYNE, VIRGINIA (1910–1977). Payne starred as "Oxydol's Own Ma Perkins" on the daytime **soap opera** from 1933 until the program left the air in 1960. She acted on other radio soap operas as well, including *The Carters of Elm Street*, *Lonely Women*, and *Today's Children*. She was instrumental in the founding of the American Federation of Radio Artists (AFRA) and became a member of its national board in 1940. During the last decade and a half of her life, Payne acted in the legitimate theater; she made her musical debut in 1964 with Carol Burnett in *Fade Out–Fade In*.

PEABODY AWARDS (THE). The Peabody Awards are annual international awards given for excellence in radio and television broadcasting. First awarded in 1941, they are administered by the Henry W. Grady College of Journalism and Mass Communication at the University of Georgia. Selections are made by the Peabody Board following review by screening committees of faculty, staff, and students. The awards are named after George Foster Peabody, a wealthy investment banker who donated the funds to initiate the awards. The Peabody Awards were originally only for radio, but in 1948 television awards were introduced, and additional categories for material distributed over the Internet have since been added. Materials created for motion picture release are not eligible.

PEARL, JACK (1894–1982). Born Jake Perlman, Pearl began as a comedian in Broadway shows, with his first stage appearance in Gus Edwards' *School Days*. When a German comic became ill, Pearl took his place, adopting a German accent. This led to the development of the Baron von Munchausen character that Pearl played in several network radio programs during the 1930s and 1940s, including *The Jack Pearl Show*, *The Baron and the Bee*, *Cresta Blanca Carnival*, and *Jack and Cliff.* Cliff Hall, who had worked with Pearl in vaudeville, played his straight man on radio as well.

PEARSON, DREW (1897–1969). A journalist best known for his muckraking column in the *Washington Post* called "Washington Merry-Go-Round," Pearson was a frequent critic of government and one of the few journalists to publicly oppose McCarthyism in the 1950s. Born Andrew Russell Pearson, Pearson graduated Phi Beta Kappa from Swarthmore and first worked on the *Baltimore Sun* before moving to the *Washington Post* in 1941. He had network radio programs from 1935 to 1953, one of which was also called **Washington Merry-Go-Round**. Pearson was very controversial but also very influential, and he had confidential sources everywhere in the government. In the early 1950s, Pearson was a news commentator on television, and he appeared as himself in the 1951 movie *The Day the Earth Stood Still.*

PEARY, HAROLD (1908–1985). Hal Peary began his radio career as a 13-year-old singer billed as "The *Oakland Tribune*'s Boy Caruso." By 1928, he was a regular on San Francisco radio, featured on an NBC program called *The Spanish Serenader*. Peary appeared in dozens of radio programs from the 1930s to the 1950s, and had continuing roles in several, but it is for the character of Throckmorton P. Gildersleeve that he is most remembered. He played this good-hearted windbag on **Fibber McGee and Molly** and then was one of the first radio characters to be spun off to his own series as **The Great Gildersleeve**. He played the character of Gildersleeve with great success from 1941 to 1950, at which time he left the program to star in *Honest Harold* on another network. In the 1950s, he worked in television; one of his roles was that of Mayor La Trivia on the TV version of *Fibber McGee and Molly.* As late as the 1970s, he was still working in television, doing commercials and voices for Saturday morning cartoons.

PENNER, JOE (1904–1941). Born Josef Pinter in Hungary, Penner came to the United States as a child and performed in vaudeville and burlesque, where he first used his "Wanna buy a duck?" catchphrase. **Rudy Vallee** introduced him to radio audiences, and **Mel Blanc** had one of his first roles on network radio as the voice of Penner's duck

Goo Goo. Penner starred on *The Joe Penner Show*, a **comedy program** also known as *The Baker's Broadcast*, and was voted radio's outstanding comedian in 1934. He left the show in 1935 but returned the next year to star in a **situation comedy** called *The Park Avenue Penners*, which was less successful. His popularity led to leads in musical movies during the late 1930s and early 1940s, including *The Boys from Syracuse* in 1940. Penner died at age 36 of a heart attack while touring in a play.

PEOPLE ARE FUNNY. An **audience-participation program** heard from 1942 to 1960, *People Are Funny* was hosted by Art Baker for the first year but then by **Art Linkletter** for the remainder of the long run and it was the program that brought Linkletter to national prominence. Each contestant was asked an absurd question that could not be answered and when the inevitable failure occurred, he or she was asked to perform ridiculous stunts as a penalty for having failed to answer correctly. They were rewarded with gifts and cash for doing so, but the real purpose of the program was to show that most people are good sports and can be both fun and funny. It was created by John Guedel, who also created Linkletter's later hit program, *House Party*.

PEPPER YOUNG'S FAMILY. A 15-minute daily **soap opera** heard from 1932 to 1959, *Pepper Young's Family* was written by **Elaine Carrington**. The program was first heard as *Red Adams*, the story of a high school athlete and his family. The name was changed to *Red Davis* in 1933 when sponsorship was assumed by Beech-Nut gum, because Adams was the name of a competing gum company. In 1936, the name of the family was changed to Young and the program was called *Forever Young*. The central figure was still a high school athlete, Larry Young, whose nickname was Pepper. Later the same year, the name was changed to *Pepper Young's Family* and remained so for the next 23 years as the serial followed the story of Pepper's life. Several different actors played the lead role, beginning with Burgess Meredith, who played Red Adams and Red Davis in the two early versions of the program, followed by Curtis Arnall, Lawson Zerbe, and **Mason Adams**, all of whom played Pepper. Elizabeth Wragge played Pepper's little sister for the entire run, although the name of the character changed during one of the format changes.

PERRIN, VIC (1915–1989). A versatile actor, Victor Perrin appeared on dozens of radio shows and had continuing roles on such programs as *The Clyde Beatty Show*, *The Zane Grey Theater*, **Fort Laramie**, and **One Man's Family**. He began working in television in the early 1950s, acted on scores of shows with continuing roles on several, including *Dragnet*, *Gunsmoke*, *Star Trek*, and *Mission: Impossible*. He was also the "control voice" on the original series of *The Outer Limits*.

PERRY COMO SHOW (THE). Although better known as the host of his own television program, Perry Como was an immensely popular singer who headlined several **music programs** on radio from 1943 to 1955, including *The Chesterfield Supper Club*, which he hosted with Jo Stafford from 1944 to 1949. His 1954–1955 radio program was simulcast on television.

PERRY MASON. A 15-minute daily **crime program** heard from 1943 to 1955, *Perry Mason* featured the character created by Erle Stanley Gardner in his long series of crime novels. The radio program was quite different from either the novels or the later successful television version, although Gardner himself wrote some of the early scripts. On the radio, Mason was more like a detective than a lawyer, sometimes exchanging gunfire with criminals or otherwise participating in their apprehension. During the run, there were many different performers in the lead roles, including Bartlett Robinson as the first Perry Mason, followed by **Santos Ortega**, Donald Briggs, and John Larkin.

PET MILK SHOW (THE). *See SATURDAY NIGHT SERENADE.*

PETRIE, GEORGE O. (1912–1997). Petrie began working on radio in 1937 and appeared on several network daytime **soap operas** and evening dramas, as well as starring in adventure and police programs. He had the lead role on **The Casebook of Gregory Hood**, *Charlie Wild, Private Detective*, and **The Falcon**, and played District Attorney Markham on **Philo Vance**. After radio, he worked in the movies and on television, appearing in films such as *Gypsy* in 1962 and *Baby Boom* in 1987; on TV he appeared on *The Honeymooners*, *General Hospital*, and *Mad about You*, as well as on *Dallas*, where he played the role of Harve Smithfield from 1979 to 1991.

PETRILLO, CAESAR (1892–1984). Chicagoan James Caesar Petrillo was president of the American Federation of Musicians (AFM) from 1940 to 1958. During his presidency, he called several strikes against radio, television, and recording companies in order to strengthen the AFM. After he resigned the national presidency, he served as president of the AFM's Chicago branch. Although not a radio performer himself, his name was well known to many listeners because radio comedians often made jokes that mentioned him.

PHIL BAKER SHOW (THE). Phil Baker was a comedian and accordionist who had previously been a vaudeville partner of band leader **Ben Bernie**. He headlined a series of comedy–variety programs from 1933 to 1939, which were usually referred to by his name, but like so many other variety programs of the time, also had other names. The first of these was *The Armour Jester* in 1933, followed by *The Gulf Headliner* in 1935, and *Honolulu Bound* in 1939. Baker returned to radio in 1941 as the host of the quiz program *Take It or Leave It.*

PHIL COOK SHOW (THE). Phil Cook was the host of many different 15-minute morning programs from 1930 to 1952, all of them featuring imaginary characters played by Cook. He also played the ukulele, sang, and provided good-natured commentary on current events. The earliest version of his show was called *The Quaker Oats Man* and there were several other program names later, including *The Silver Dust Serenade*, *Phil Cook's Almanac*, and *Cook's Kitchen*.

PHIL HARRIS–ALICE FAYE SHOW (THE). First heard on *The Fitch Bandwagon* from 1946 to 1948, this 30-minute **situation comedy** was heard from 1948 to 1954, featuring the fictitious home life of bandleader Phil Harris and movie star Alice Faye, his wife in real life. Harris was the bandleader and an important comedy character on *The Jack Benny Program* and his own show was basically a continuation of his role on the Benny show: a wise-cracking, hard-drinking bandleader who murdered the English language. Frankie Remley—the guitar player who was often referred to on the Benny program but never heard—was a major character on the Harris–Faye show and was played by **Elliott Lewis**. **Walter Tetley** played Julius Abbruzio, the annoying delivery boy; and **Gale Gordon** appeared as

Mr. Scott, an officer of the Rexall Drug Company, the sponsor of the program until 1950.

PHILCO RADIO TIME. *See THE BING CROSBY SHOW.*

PHILIP MORRIS PLAYHOUSE (THE). A 30-minute **drama anthology** sponsored by Philip Morris cigarettes, *The Philip Morris Playhouse* had three separate runs. The first version was an outgrowth of the drama portion of a variety program called *Johnny Presents* and was heard from 1939 to 1944. The program reappeared in 1948–1949 with major Hollywood performers starring in tales of suspense and murder. This version was produced and directed by William Spier, who had previously produced *Suspense*, and in some ways was similar to that program. A third version, heard from 1951 to 1953, was named *The Phillip Morris Playhouse on Broadway* and primarily presented adaptations of Broadway plays.

PHILLIPS, IRNA (1901–1973). Irna Phillips created and wrote many of the early American daytime serials. She studied drama at the University of Illinois and did postgraduate study at the University of Wisconsin. She wanted to be an actress but first worked as a teacher of drama and theater history. While doing so, she acted in several radio productions at WGN Chicago. She eventually left teaching to create and write radio serial dramas, starting with *Painted Dreams* in 1930. This 15-minute daytime serial drama is considered by many authorities to be the first **soap opera**. She also created and/or wrote many other popular radio and television serial dramas, including *The Guiding Light*, *Road of Life*, *The Right to Happiness*, *Days of Our Lives*, and *As the World Turns*.

PHILO VANCE. Philo Vance was a fictitious detective created by S. S. Van Dyne in a series of novels and was the subject of several motion pictures as well as two different 30-minute radio series. The first was heard only in 1945, with Jose Ferrer as the intellectual detective who was also an art collector and a friend of the District Attorney. A syndicated version, starring Jackson Beck as Vance and **George O. Petrie** as District Attorney Markham, was heard from 1948 to 1950.

PIOUS, MINERVA (1903–1979). Born in Odessa, Ukraine, Pious spent the majority of her life and career in New York. She worked extensively in radio, usually in **comedy programs**. She is best remembered for her role as Mrs. Pansy Nussbaum on *The Fred Allen Show*. She joined Allen in 1933, playing a variety of dialect roles on his program, but soon developed her specialty as a Jewish mother in topical spoofs. This character evolved into Mrs. Nussbaum, a resident of **Allen's Alley**, which she played from 1942 until the program went off the air in 1949. She also played Mrs. Nussbaum in guest appearances on other radio programs. After her radio career, she worked in other media. She was a featured voice in the 1964 animated children's movie *Pinocchio in Outer Space*.

PICK AND PAT. Pick and Pat were comedians Pick Malone and Pat Padgett. Veterans of vaudeville, they were best known for a minstrel-like blackface routine in which they played the characters Molasses and January. Like **Bob and Ray**, they often worked without scripts, simply building a routine from a situational dialogue. They starred in a radio minstrel program from 1934 to 1939, also called *Pick and Pat and Their Minstrels*, and were again heard in 1944–1945 with a **variety program** that included the Vincent Lopez orchestra.

PICKENS, JANE (1908–1992). Jane was the most famous member of the Pickens Sisters trio that was popular during the 1930s. On radio, she and her sisters Patti and Helen appeared on several programs (including *The Pickens Sisters*) from 1932 to 1935. When the trio broke up in 1937, Jane continued as a solo act. She starred on *The Jane Pickens Show* that began in 1948 and continued on the air until 1957. The 1951 to 1954 version of her program was known as *Pickens' Party*.

POPEYE THE SAILOR. A 15-minute **children's program** heard from 1935 to 1938, *Popeye the Sailor* was based on the comic strip by E. C. Segar and was very similar to the popular motion picture cartoons based on the same character. The radio program featured the same orchestra as the motion picture cartoons, Victor Irwin's Cartoonland Band. Popeye was originally played by Detmar Poppen. The major difference between the movie and radio versions was that on radio Popeye did not become powerful by consuming Spinach, but by eating a helping of the sponsor's product, Wheatena. The famous Popeye jingle was re-written to accommodate this change.

PORTIA FACES LIFE. A 15-minute daily **soap opera** written by Mona Kent and heard from 1940 to 1951, *Portia Faces Life* was the story of Portia Blake, a young attorney who was widowed and raising her son alone. Because of listener response, the program gradually began to concentrate more on domestic matters, and Portia eventually married a journalist named Walter Manning, who had many of the weaknesses and problems common in male soap opera characters. Although the program had elements of courtroom drama, the plots became more elaborate and complex over time. When the program ended, Portia had been sentenced to prison for a crime she did not commit. **Lucille Wall** played Portia for the entire run except for a period of six months in 1948 when she was ill.

POT O' GOLD. The first radio program to award large cash prizes, *Pot O' Gold* had two separate appearances, the first from 1939 to 1941, hosted by **Ben Grauer** with music by the Horace Heidt orchestra. It was a simple giveaway format, phone calls being made to people chosen from a huge library of telephone books. The selection was made by spinning the Wheel of Fortune three times: the first spin determined the phone book to be used, the second spin the page number and the third spin the line number on that page. The Heidt orchestra played between spins and the suspense was drawn out until near the end of the program, when Ben Grauer would dial the selected number. If the phone was answered, a $1000 prize was awarded. If not answered, the person who had been called was awarded $100 and $900 was added to the jackpot for the next week. The program was discontinued after two years because popularity declined in the face of several controversies over bad connections and other details of the calls being placed. The program reappeared briefly in 1946–1947 with Happy Felton as host.

PREMIUMS. During radio's golden age, many programs offered premiums to their listeners. These radio premiums were often parts of the storylines and played important roles in the programs' continuities. **Soap operas** and programs for children and juveniles were particularly prolific with respect to premiums, usually offered for a proof of purchase from the product of the show's sponsor and a few cents for "postage and handling." Among the soap operas, ***David Harum*** and ***Lora Lawton***, produced by **Frank and Anne Hummert** under the supervision of marketing expert Duane Jones, were particularly enthusiastic about premiums; but nearly all soap operas occasionally offered premiums of some kind. Flower seeds, recipes, and costume jewelry were especially popular because they were easy to package and ship; but photo albums, books, glassware and a variety of other items were also offered. Among the **juvenile adventure programs**, the most premium offers were made by *Tom Mix*, *The Lone Ranger*, *Little Orphan Annie*, and *Jack Armstrong*, but most other programs also offered premiums of one sort or another. Usually these premiums were small toys, badges, pins, adjustable rings, mugs, club memberships, cast pictures, certificates, and maps costing next to nothing. Today, some of these "free" offers of the past sell for considerable sums of money.

PRENTISS, ED (1909–1992). Born Paul Edward Prentiss, Prentiss appeared on *Painted Dreams* and was the host of several other **soap operas**; but he is best remembered as *Captain Midnight*, whom he played during 1938–1939 and from 1940 to 1949. He was also Johnny Lujack's sidekick on ABC's *The Adventures of Johnny Lujack* during 1949, a narrator on *The Silver Eagle*, and an announcer *on Jack Armstrong, the All-American Boy*. After his work on radio, Prentiss moved to television, where he was the host of two early series, and later acted on scores of popular dramas such as *Bonanza*, *Perry Mason*, *Laramie*, and *Dragnet*. Prentiss also appeared on some TV soap operas, including *The Guiding Light* and *Days of Our Lives*.

PRETTY KITTY KELLY. A 15-minute daily **soap opera** heard from 1937 to 1940, *Pretty Kitty Kelly* was the story of an Irish girl who arrived in New York with amnesia, having only a vague recollection of an Irish orphanage. Over the course of time, she became involved with Michael Conway, a policeman who became a lawyer and accompanied her on most of her adventures, which were many. It was later discovered that she was, in fact, a long-lost Irish countess, and her romance with Michael was thus thrown into question because of her much higher social status. The incidents on the program were often both dramatic and violent, and included murder and kidnapping. Kitty was played by Arline Blackburn.

PROFESSOR QUIZ. One of the earliest radio **quiz programs**, *Professor Quiz* was a 30-minute program heard from 1936 to 1941 and again from 1946 to 1948. Listeners were invited to submit questions and those whose questions were selected were paid $25. Prizes for contestants were similarly modest: the winner was awarded $25, with $15 going to the runner-up. The host of the program was Craig Earl, whose identity was concealed for some time, and the program was sometimes called *Professor Quiz and His Brainbusters*. Two different sponsors produced booklets of questions and information about the program. The first, by Kelvinator, titled *The Original Professor Quiz and His Quizzical Questions*, was produced in 1937. The second, titled *The Original Professor Quiz Brain Teasers*, was produced in 1939 and was given away with the purchase of a 50-cent jar of Noxema. There was also a board game called *Quizzical Questions by Professor Quiz*, produced in 1939.

PRUDENTIAL FAMILY HOUR (THE). A **concert music** program heard from 1941 to 1948, *The Prudential Family Hour* originally featured Metropolitan Opera soprano Gladys Swarthout, who was later replaced by several other talented sopranos. The program also presented a short dramatic sketch of a different composer each week and a popular song sung by Smiling Jack Smith. The program was originally hosted by **Deems Taylor**, who was later replaced by Jose Ferrer. The program began in a 45-minute format, but was reduced to 30 minutes in 1945. In 1948, the program was re-named *The Prudential Family Hour of Stars* and it became a 30-minute **drama anthology** performed by a repertory company of Hollywood performers, including Gregory Peck, Bette Davis, Humphrey Bogart, Barbara Stanwyck, Robert Taylor, and Ginger Rogers. *The Prudential Hour of Stars* left the air in 1950.

– Q –

QUALITY TWINS (THE). *See THE HAPPINESS BOYS.*

QUEEN FOR A DAY. A 30-minute daytime **audience-participation program** heard from 1945 to 1957, *Queen for a Day* originated in New York with Dud Williamson as host but soon moved to Hollywood, where **Jack Bailey** became the host for the remainder of the run. Each day, several women were chosen from the studio audience and interviewed concerning their fondest wishes. The winner was chosen by audience applause and was granted her wish as well as being showered with a variety of gifts. A television version of the program began in 1956 and ran until 1964, with a format almost identical to the radio program.

QUICK AS A FLASH. A **quiz program** heard from 1944 to 1951, *Quick as a Flash* had an unusual and complex format in which sequential clues were given to the answers to questions. The clues were elaborate and were sometimes presented as dramatizations or as musical numbers. Several contestants were chosen from the studio audience and each had his or her own response button, with which the presentation of clues could be halted and an answer attempted. If correct, a prize was awarded and the questioning moved on to another category. If incorrect, the contestant was dropped from that competition and the clues continued where they had been interrupted. There were several hosts during the run, including Ken Roberts, **Win Elliot**, and **Bill Cullen**.

QUIET, PLEASE. A 30-minute thriller anthology heard from 1947 to 1949, *Quiet Please* was written and directed by **Wyllis Cooper**, who had created another thriller anthology, ***Lights Out***, some years before. The stories were narrated by **Ernest Chappell**, who also played the lead role each week. At the end of each program, he teased the program for the following week by means of the kind of ominous/humorous comment that was common among hosts of thriller anthologies.

QUINN, BILL (1912–1994). William Quinn was a graduate of the Professional Children's School in New York, and made his debut on Broadway at age six as Billy Quinn. He was a regular performer on several radio programs, including ***Just Plain Bill***, ***The Molle Mystery Theatre***, and ***The Big Story***, and played the lead on ***Front Page Farrell***. Moving to television in the 1950s, he appeared in scores of programs and had continuing roles on *The Rifleman*, *Please Don't Eat the Daisies*, and *All in the Family*. Quinn was the father-in-law of actor–comedian Bob Newhart.

QUINN, DON (1900–1967). Quinn started out as a commercial cartoonist and gag writer, but became famous as the scriptwriter for Jim and Marian Jordan, radio's *Fibber McGee and Molly*. He wrote the *Smackout* program for them in the early 1930s and was a full partner with the Jordans. Quinn was the principal writer for *Fibber McGee and Molly* from 1935 to 1950, when he left the show to create *The Halls of Ivy* radio series. He won a **Peabody Award** for this series, which later moved to television.

QUIZ PROGRAMS. Quiz programs did not appear on the networks until the late 1930s, but quickly became very popular. Although some programs awarded very substantial prizes, others offered not much more than token awards, and popularity was not necessarily related to the size of the prizes. *Professor Quiz* is cited by some authorities as the first network radio quiz and the largest prize on the program was $25. The extremely popular *Dr. IQ* featured program assistants with portable microphones who circulated through the studio audience looking for participants. Each selected participant was asked one question and winners were awarded small prizes in silver dollars, paid on the spot. *Quick as a Flash* was also very popular, although the size of rewards was small; the program relied on clever questions and interesting presentations of the clues to hold listener interest. *Take It or Leave It* paid a maximum of $64 and *Double or Nothing*, which survived for more than 14 years, paid quite small amounts of money; the major attraction of the program was clever repartee between host and contestant.

Other programs paid more, sometimes a great deal more, but most of the high-jackpot shows were not true quiz programs. As early as 1939, the same year that *Dr. IQ* first appeared on the network, *Pot O' Gold* dialed telephone numbers randomly chosen from telephone books and paid $1,000 to anyone who answered the phone. *Stop the Music* appeared in 1948 and required only that the person who answered the phone know what song the orchestra had been playing while the telephone number was being dialed; prizes averaged over $20,000 in cash and gifts.

QUIZ KIDS (THE). Created by Louis G. Cowan, *The Quiz Kids* was a 30-minute panel program heard from 1940 to 1953, on which precocious children answered questions sent in by listeners. The program had a panel of five children, and the three who answered the most questions appeared again the next week, along with two new members. In general, the children appearing on the panel were between six and 16, although younger children appeared occasionally. **Joe Kelly**, the host, was an ex-vaudevillian who freely admitted that he didn't even understand many of the questions submitted, much less the answers; but he was personable and pleasant and gave the program a friendly, down-to-earth air that might have been difficult for a more intellectual moderator to achieve. The best known of the many child prodigies to appear on the program was **Joel Kupperman**.

– R –

RADIO CITY PLAYHOUSE (THE). A 30-minute **drama anthology program** heard from 1948 to 1950, *The Radio City Playhouse* was conceived as a showcase for what NBC termed "good drama." The program's premier episode, *Long Distance*, in which **Jan Miner** played the part of a woman trying to phone in new evidence in order to gain a stay in her husband's execution, was favorably compared to *Sorry, Wrong Number*, the famous episode that appeared on *Suspense*. Many of the scripts were written by the program's director, Harry W. Junkin, who began each episode with a personal introduction. John Larkin and Jan Miner had the lead roles in many of the stories, supported by a cast of New York–based radio actors.

RADIO CORPORATION OF AMERICA (RCA). In the early 20th century, the dominant company in commercial radio in the United States was American Marconi, the majority of whose stockholders were British. During World War I, all production of radio equipment was for the military, and the assets of American Marconi were seized by the United States Navy. After the war, when private ownership was restored, many American politicians were uncomfortable with foreign ownership of radio-related companies. As a response to government pressure, RCA was formed in 1919 as a publicly held company owned by General Electric, American Telephone & Telegraph (AT&T), and a company called Wireless Specialty Apparatus Company for the purpose of purchasing the assets of American Marconi and placing them in the hands of American owners. The original three companies were later joined by Westinghouse.

With **David Sarnoff** as director, RCA also assumed responsibility for most of the radio-related activities of its major stockholders, as well as acquiring the radio-related patents of several other large companies. In 1929, RCA purchased the Victor Talking Machine Company and became RCA Victor. As RCA grew, the government eventually became concerned that it might constitute a restraint to competition and filed suit to require the component companies to divest themselves of their interests. RCA was an independent company from 1932 forward.

Although RCA was originally concerned primarily with the sale of radio receivers, Sarnoff was alert to the possibilities of broadcast radio and RCA began sponsoring broadcasts in the early 1920s, primarily on four stations owned by Westinghouse, eventually creating a small network called the **Radio Group Network**. When AT&T decided to leave the broadcasting field, RCA purchased the AT&T network and merged it with its own network, forming a subsidiary corporation to manage them both: the **National Broadcasting Company (NBC)**. For many years, RCA, through its subsidiary, operated two NBC networks, NBC Red and NBC Blue, but the government intervened again because of concern over restraint of competition. In 1943, RCA was forced to sell NBC Blue, which became the **American Broadcasting Company (ABC)**.

In addition to its radio activities, RCA was an innovator in both the record industry and in television. After David Sarnoff died in 1970, the company developed financial problems. It was eventually sold to General Electric in 1986 and subsequently broken up; the RCA logo is now used by two separate companies: Thomson SA, which manufactures electronic equipment, and Sony BMG Music Entertainment, which owns the RCA Victor and RCA record labels.

RADIO GROUP NETWORK (THE). In the early 1920s, radio station WEAF New York was owned by American Telephone and Telegraph (AT&T) and served as a laboratory for developing technologies for transmitting voice- and music-grade audio over short and long distances. AT&T began to experiment with "simultaneous broadcasting" in 1922 and gradually began to add stations and to create the first vestigial broadcasting network. By 1924, they had produced a transcontinental broadcast by including KPO San Francisco in the network. In the fall of that year, a presidential address was broadcast over a 23-station network. By the end of 1925, AT&T was operating a network of 26 stations.

RCA responded by forming the Radio Group Network, centered on WJZ Newark, one of the four original Westinghouse stations. Because AT&T would not allow them to use their telephone lines to connect the stations, the Radio Group had to use telegraph lines, which were not well suited to the task, and they encountered many technical problems getting the network established. While they were still dealing with these technological issues, however, AT&T decided to withdraw from the broadcasting business, to sell the AT&T network to RCA, and to revert to leasing telephone lines, which was their primary business. RCA formed the **National Broadcasting Company (NBC)** for the purpose of purchasing and operating the two networks and the former AT&T network was designated the NBC Red Network; the former Radio Group Network was renamed the NBC Blue Network.

RADIO GUILD (THE). An early **drama anthology** heard from 1929 to 1940, *The Radio Guild* was directed by Vernon Radcliffe and was noted for experimental theater, producing plays by new and unknown writers as well as versions of classic dramas. A 60-minute program for most of the long run, the format was changed to 30 minutes in 1939.

RADIO HALL OF FAME (THE). There was a program of this name heard during 1943–1946, an elaborate 60-minute **variety program**, sometimes listed as *The Philco Radio Hall of Fame*. The program was produced by *Variety* magazine and the performers were chosen by the *Variety* staff as a sort of weekly award for excellence in broadcasting. In the final year, the format was reduced to 30 minutes.

There is also an organization of this name, a non-profit division of the Museum of Broadcast Communications in Chicago, Illinois. It recognizes those who contributed significantly to the medium; nominations are made by a steering committee that is appointed by the president of the museum. As of 2005, there were 130 inductees.

RADIO READER'S DIGEST (THE). A 30-minute **drama anthology** heard from 1942 to 1948, this program is sometimes listed as *Reader's Digest Radio Edition* or *The Hallmark Program*. It was not sponsored by *Reader's Digest*, but drew its material from the magazine, often dramatizing true stories from past issues. **Conrad Nagel** was the first host, followed by **Richard Kollmar** and **Les Tremayne**. The program became *Hallmark Playhouse* in 1948.

RAFFETTO, MICHAEL (1899–1990). Born Elwyn Creighton Raffetto, Rafetto was the original Paul Barbour on the long-running *One Man's Family* and he also starred as the first Jack Packard on the **Carlton E. Morse** adventure series *I Love a Mystery*. He also wrote and directed radio plays, especially during the times he experienced poor health and was unable to act. From the early 1940s until the late 1950s, he acted in a number of motion pictures, usually in supporting roles; in the early 1960s, he performed in several dramatic series on television.

RAILROAD HOUR (THE). A musical program heard from 1948 to 1954, *The Railroad Hour* presented musical dramas of all kinds, including operettas, Broadway musicals, and dramatizations of the lives of famous musicians. Gordon MacRae was the male lead each week, both singing and acting, but the emphasis was always on the music rather than on the drama. The program was sponsored by the railroad industry and each program began with the arrival of the "show train" and ended with the sounds of the train departing.

RANDOLPH, LILLIAN (1898–1980). Randolph is best known for her portrayal of the maid Birdie Lee Coggins on *The Great Gildersleeve*, a role she played for nearly 18 years. She acted on other radio programs as well, including *The Billie Burke Show* and *Beulah*. On television, she continued playing the role of Birdie on *The Great Gildersleeve*, and was featured on other shows such as *Amos 'n' Andy*, *The Bill Cosby Show*, and *Roots*. From the early 1940s until the late 1970s, she also worked in films. She was the sister of actress Amanda Randolph.

RATHBONE, BASIL (1892–1967). Born Philip St. John Basil Rathbone in Johannesburg, South Africa, Rathbone grew up in England. In school, he excelled in sports and developed a love for the theater. He came to the United States to appear in both the theater and in motion pictures, making numerous films from the 1930s to the 1960s. On radio, he appeared as *Sherlock Holmes* from 1939 to 1946, as well as appearing as the same character in a series of 14 motion pictures. He left the successful radio series to star in *Scotland Yard* (1947), and then in *Tales of Fatima* (1949), both mystery dramas. Rathbone also appeared on many television dramas, and in 1952 hosted *Your Lucky Clue*, a TV mystery quiz show. His autobiography, *In and Out of Character*, was published in 1962.

RATING SYSTEMS. Networks and sponsors were both very interested in the popularity of programs they were producing; beginning in 1930, popularity was measured by various rating systems. The first of these was the Cooperative Analysis of Broadcasting ratings, generally referred to as the Crossley Ratings, named for Archibald Crossley, the man who conducted them. Crossley chose numbers at random from telephone directories and called listeners in about 30 cities, asking them what they had listened to the previous day. In 1935, another system, developed by C. E. Hooper, Inc. became available and the Hooper Ratings were preferred by many stations and networks because they asked listeners what they were listening to at the time of the call, rather than asking them to remember what they had listened to the previous day. The Nielsen Company began its ratings in 1942, using a device called an "audimeter" that was attached to the radio and kept a record of the time the set was on and the stations to which it was tuned. By 1947, Nielsen began to offer serious competition to the Hooper ratings, publicly challenging their accuracy. In 1950, Hooper sold its national radio and television rating service to Nielsen. Nielsen discontinued national radio ratings in 1963, although they remained active in rating television programs.

RED RYDER. A 30-minute **juvenile adventure program** based on the comic strip cowboy created by Fred Harman, *Red Ryder* was heard from 1942 to 1951. Red lived on a ranch in Painted Valley with his partner Buckskin Blodgett and his Indian ward Little Beaver. Riding his horse, Thunder, Red often intervened on the side of justice, although like *The Lone Ranger*, he seldom killed anyone, often just shooting the gun out of the villain's hand. Many **premiums** were offered by the radio program, and more than 40 commercial Red Ryder products were available. The Red Ryder BB gun has been produced by Daisy since 1938 and is still in production today. Several actors played the part of Red on the radio program, beginning with

Reed Hadley and followed by Carlton KaDell and Brooke Temple. Buckskin was played by Horace Murphy. Little Beaver was played by Tommy Cook, Henry Blair, Johnny McGovern, and others. In addition to the radio program, there was a later television program and a series of Red Ryder movies.

RED SKELTON SHOW (THE). The son of a circus clown, Red Skelton had performed in almost every type of entertainment venue before he first appeared on *The Rudy Vallee Show* in 1937. He became a headliner on *Avalon Time* in 1939 and was given his own show in 1941, *The Raleigh Cigarette Program*. Skelton was a visual comic, who essentially did vaudeville routines on the radio, playing several comic characters who became very popular with listeners, including "the mean widdle kid," a bumpkin named Clem Kadiddlehopper, and an inept gunfighter named Deadeye. His radio program ran until 1953, by which time his television program had already been on the air for two years. The television series ran for more than 20 years and Skelton appeared in more than 25 motion pictures, as well. Almost all of his radio programs were written by his wife, Edna Stillwell, who created most of his best-remembered routines.

REED, ALAN (1907–1977). Born Teddy Bergman, Reed enjoyed a long career on Broadway, in motion pictures, on television, and on radio. On radio, he appeared on scores of programs and was featured on *Abie's Irish Rose*, *Big Sister*, *Duffy's Tavern*, *The Eddie Cantor Show*, *The Fred Allen Show*, *Life with Luigi*, *My Friend Irma*, *Myrt and Marge*, and *The Shadow*. On television, he acted on several programs, including the TV versions of *Life with Luigi* and *Duffy's Tavern*. He was also the original voice of Fred Flintstone on *The Flintstones* cartoon show. Bergman adopted the professional name of Alan Reed in 1939.

RENFREW OF THE MOUNTED. A **juvenile adventure program** heard from 1936 to 1940, *Renfrew of the Mounted* was similar in many ways to *Sergeant Preston of the Yukon*. Based on the stories by Laurie York Erskine, Inspector Douglas Renfrew was a serious, dedicated member of the Royal Canadian Mounted Police. The program was introduced by the cry of a wolf, over which announcer **Bert Parks** intoned the title of the show. The wolf howl and all the other animal sound effects on the program were provided by animal imitator Brad Barker. Renfrew was played by **House Jameson**.

RICHARD DIAMOND, PRIVATE DETECTIVE. A 30-minute detective drama heard from 1949 to 1953, *Richard Diamond, Private Detective* starred Dick Powell as a wise-cracking private detective, an ex-cop who had an abrasive but friendly relationship with police lieutenant Walt Levinson. Although concerned with serious crimes, the program was often glib and light-hearted, featuring many one-liners by Diamond, often at the expense of the police. Powell, who was an excellent singer with a previous career in music, sang a song every week, usually while playing the piano at the home of his rich girlfriend, Helen Asher. Lieutenant Levinson was played by Ed Begley and Helen by **Virginia Gregg**. Many of the early programs were written by Blake Edwards. A television version of the program was seen from 1957 to 1960, with David Janssen in the title role.

RIGHT TO HAPPINESS (THE). A 15-minute daily **soap opera** written by **Irna Phillips** and heard from 1939 to 1960, *The Right to Happiness* originally featured Rose Kransky, one of the characters from another Irna Phillips program, *The Guiding Light*, but the focus of the program soon shifted to another character, Carolyn Allen. Carolyn married four times during the course of the long run, the first three times to men who were difficult in every imaginable way. Phillips continued to write the program until 1942, when she sold it to Procter & Gamble, who moved the production of the program from Chicago to New York and had the writing taken over by John M. Young. Eloise Kummer played Carolyn when the program originated from Chicago, **Claudia Morgan** assuming the role when production moved to New York.

RIGGS, GLENN (1907–1975). Glenn Riggs began his radio career on station **KDKA** Pittsburgh as an announcer and the host of a recorded breakfast program, *The Musical Clock*. He joined NBC in 1938 and went to work for the Blue Network, which later became ABC when NBC was forced to divest itself of one of its networks. He was the announcer on many popular radio programs of radio's golden age, including *Hop Harrigan*, *Boston Blackie*, *Philco Radio Time*, and

The Adventures of the Thin Man. He spent nearly 30 years working for ABC radio and television, retiring in 1972.

RIN-TIN-TIN. *Rin-Tin-Tin* was the name of a dog who was discovered by an American soldier in a bombed-out kennel just before the end of World War I. He was named for a puppet that French children gave to American Soldiers for good luck. The soldier who found him, Lee Duncan, trained the dog and brought him to the U.S. after the war. The dog performed in dog shows, eventually found a place in the early movie industry, and was featured in 26 films before dying in 1932. There were two radio programs based on Rin-Tin-Tin. The first was a 15-minute **juvenile adventure program** heard from 1930 to 1934, starring Francis X. Bushman, with the dog sounds being done by the original dog until his death, and then by Rin-Tin-Tin Jr. A 30-minute version of the same program was heard in 1955. In this version, the dog and his boy owner, Rusty, were the only survivors of an Indian massacre and had come to live at Fort Apache with the cavalry. Rusty was played by Lee Aaker.

RIPLEY, ROBERT L. (1893–1949). Robert LeRoy Ripley began his career at age 14 when he sold one of his drawings to *Life Magazine*. Later, while working as a sports cartoonist at the *New York Globe*, he gathered together some athletic oddities, made them into a cartoon, and captioned them "Believe It or Not." This column soon developed into a weekly feature, subsequently becoming so popular that it appeared in newspapers throughout the world and was translated into a score of languages. From 1930 to 1948, Ripley hosted *Believe It or Not*, a radio program that dramatized unusual events from his columns. He also appeared on several other programs, including *The Baker's Broadcast*, *Saturday Party*, *Scramble*, and *Romance, Rhythm, and Ripley*—as well as a long series of one-minute filler programs. In the years he worked on his column, Ripley visited 100 countries, traveling nearly 600,000 miles in his quest for the odd and unusual.

ROAD OF LIFE (THE). A 15-minute **soap opera** written by **Irna Phillips** and heard from 1937 to 1959, *The Road of Life* was one of the first soap operas to take place in a medical setting. It was the story of Dr. Jim Brent, and followed him from his days as an intern at a city hospital to his maturity as a practicing physician specializing in neuropsychiatry. His specialty meant that he was sought out by many characters on the program to discuss their personal problems, and much of the story took place outside of the hospital setting. Five different actors played the part of Jim Brent, with Ken Griffin perhaps the best known. For many years, the program appeared concurrently on both CBS and NBC, until CBS acquired sole possession in 1954. The brief television version was seen only in 1954–1955.

ROBERT Q. LEWIS SHOW (THE). Lewis was a comedian who was best known as the host of television game shows, but he had a long career in radio, appearing on a series of **comedy programs** from 1945 to 1959, sometimes as host, sometimes as star, and at least once as a disc jockey. His shows appeared under several names in addition to his own, including *The Little Show*, *The Show Goes On*, *The ABC's of Music*, and *Robert Q.'s Waxworks*. His middle initial did not stand for a middle name; he simply added it to his name on a whim one time while on the air and decided to keep it. He was also a talented singer and made records for several different major labels, often featuring vintage music.

ROCKING HORSE RHYTHMS. A song and talk show for children heard from 1943 to 1945, *Rocking Horse Rhythms* featured Bobby Hookey, a remarkable child performer who was only five years old at the inception of the show, and who had already appeared on local radio for three years. He told jokes, did interviews, and sang, sometimes while riding a Rocking Horse with a microphone attached to its head. Hookey was said to have a repertoire of 150 songs. The title of the program was changed to *Hookey Hall* in 1944.

ROCKY JORDAN. A 30-minute **adventure program**, *Rocky Jordan* is well known today primarily because it appeared on West Coast regional networks for some years before and after its brief appearance on a national network in 1951, and many recorded episodes of the program are available. Rocky first appeared in a program called *A Man Named Jordan*, as the rough-cut proprietor of Café Tambourine, a seedy establishment in Istanbul, where he was confronted with a crime or a mystery each week. *Rocky Jordan* was essentially the same program, with the café moved to Cairo, and the addition of Captain Sam Sabaaya of the Cairo police as a continuing character. Jack Moyles played Jordan on the regional programs, and George Raft on the network version; Jay Novello played Captain Sabaaya.

ROGUE'S GALLERY. A 30-minute detective drama heard from 1945 to 1951, *Rogue's Gallery* originally starred Dick Powell in his new incarnation as a tough-guy detective, after many years of playing boyish crooners in romantic movies. The program was in many ways similar to the better-known *Richard Diamond, Private Detective*, which also starred Powell and began in 1949. Like Diamond, Rogue was a wise-cracking tough guy who always had a clever one-liner for every situation. The feature that most distinguished the program from other similar shows was an alter-ego character named Eugor (Rogue spelled backward) who appeared to Rogue whenever he was knocked out, which was on just about every program. Eugor made fun of Rogue, but often gave him a clue to the case he was working on that enabled him to awaken with a plan concerning how to proceed. After Powell left the show, Rogue was played by Barry Sullivan, Chester Morris, and Paul Stewart.

ROMANCE OF HELEN TRENT (THE). The longest-running **soap opera** in the history of radio, *The Romance of Helen Trent* was produced by **Frank and Anne Hummert** and was heard from 1933 to 1960, appearing for 7,222 episodes. Helen was a glamorous middle-aged dress designer whose search for romance was the subject of the program and she never laughed, never did anything of which she should be ashamed, never had an inappropriate thought, and never accepted a suitor, of which there were many. Nearly 30 different men sought her hand during the course of the show's run. The most long-lasting of these was Gil Whitney, who loved her for over 20 years but was always unable to marry her for a variety of reasons. There were several villainous suitors, most of them millionaires, and most of them came to a bad end of one sort or another. Helen was played primarily by Virginia Clark and Julie Stevens, although other actresses occasionally filled in. Gil was played by David Gothard, **Marvin Miller**, and William Green. The number of characters appearing over the years was huge, as was the number of performers who portrayed them. There were also at least six different writers, as well as several different directors.

ROSE, DAVID (1910–1990). A musical conductor and composer, Rose was born in London but grew up in Chicago. He worked with **Red Skelton** for nearly 25 years, and also provided the music for *Bold Venture* and *The Ginny Simms Show*. He also hosted his own 30-minute **music program** on CBS in 1950. Rose moved to television as orchestra leader for *The Red Skelton Show* in 1951 and led the orchestra on *The Tony Martin Show*. He also wrote the music for *Little House on the Prairie* and *Bonanza*. He was married to Martha Raye from 1938 to 1941 and to Judy Garland from 1941 to 1945. He won Emmy Awards for his TV work. His best-known compositions are "The Stripper" and "Holiday for Strings."

ROSEMARY. *Rosemary* was a 15-minute daytime **soap opera** heard from 1944 to 1955, written by **Elaine Carrington**, who also wrote *Pepper Young's Family* and *When a Girl Marries*. It was the story of Rosemary Dawson, who supported her mother and younger sister Patti on her salary as a secretary. She married Bill Roberts, a war veteran who had amnesia as a result of his war experiences, and all of them lived together until Bill recovered his memory and remembered that he was already married to another woman and had a child. Rosemary was played by **Bette Winkler** and Bill by George Keane. In real life, Winkler and Keane met each other on the set, fell in love, and were married. They later left the program when George became ill, and their parts were assumed by Virginia Kaye and Robert Readick.

ROSES AND DRUMS. An early dramatic program heard from 1932 to 1936, *Roses and Drums* was originally an anthology drawing its material from all of American history. After 1933, the show became a series of romantic adventure stories featuring a group of continuing characters who were participants in the Civil War. Betty Graham, who was a spy for the South, had two suitors, Randy Claymore, a Confederate officer, and Gordon Wright, a captain in the Union army. Historical figures were interwoven with the fictitious protagonists and the scripts were checked closely for historical accuracy. The actors always performed in costume and the program was one of the first to allow a studio audience. Betty was played by Elizabeth Love and Helen Claire, Randy by John Griggs, and Gordon by Reed Brown Jr.

ROSS, LANNY (1906–1988). A tenor whose real name was Lancelot Patrick Ross, Lanny Ross was first heard on radio in 1928 and became known to the listening audience as "The Troubadour of the Moon" because of a program of that name on which he starred. He appeared in several other **music programs** over the years, including *Showboat*, *The Packard Hour*, *Your Hit Parade*, and *The Lanny Ross Show*, the latter program airing from 1948 to 1952. During 1948–1949, Ross hosted *The Swift Show* on television. After his singing career ended, he became a radio disc jockey. He was inducted into the National Broadcasters Hall of Fame in 1981.

ROXY AND HIS GANG. Samuel "Roxy" Rothafel was a showman of the 1920s and the manager and impresario of many great theaters. Often cited as the first to broadcast from the stage of a theater, he began his *Capital Family Broadcasts* from the Capital Theater in New York in 1922, before the development of the networks. He left the program in 1925 and opened the Roxy Theater, which had a broadcast studio built-in and from where he broadcast *Roxy and His Gang* from 1927 to 1931. It was a lavish variety show, with singers, comedians, a huge chorus, and a complete symphony orchestra. Many of the same performers appeared every week, but Roxy was also interested in new talent and was credited with giving several major performers their first opportunities to perform. After leaving the air in 1931, Roxy busied himself with the development of the Radio City Music Hall until returning with another **variety program** during 1934–1935, billed as *The Roxy Revue*.

ROY ROGERS SHOW (THE). Beginning as a 30-minute **music program** starring Roy Rogers of singing cowboy fame, this program gradually evolved into a **juvenile adventure program** with musical interludes. Heard from 1944 to 1955, the early episodes featured Roy, **Dale Evans**—his co-star in most of his movies and his real-life wife—and Gabby Hayes, who was his grizzled sidekick from the movies. Gabby was later replaced by Pat Brady, who had played a comical camp cook in several of Roy's movies. Brady was a different sort of sidekick, younger and more useful, although still comical; he drove his jeep "Nellie-belle" more often than he rode a horse. Both he and Roy had previously been members of The Sons of the Pioneers, a western singing group that appeared on the radio program until 1948, when they were replaced by Foy Willing and The Riders of the Purple Sage, a similar group. There was also a television version of the program, seen from 1951 to 1957.

RUDY VALLEE SHOW (THE). Rudy Vallee was an orchestra leader who also sang, and who hosted one of the first of the great radio **variety programs**. His several variety shows were heard from 1929 to 1947 and as with other headliners, they were often named for the sponsor, although usually also referred to by his name. He first hosted *The Fleischmann Yeast Hour* from 1929 to 1936, which became *The Royal Gelatin Hour* until 1939. His 1940 to 1943 program was sponsored by Sealtest and was sometimes listed as *Vallee Varieties* or *The Sealtest Hour*. This show was primarily a **comedy program** and included both John Barrymore and **Joan Davis** in the cast. When Vallee left for military service in 1943, this program evolved into *The Sealtest Village Store*, with Davis as the star. Vallee returned in 1944 to star in *Villa Vallee* with Monty Wooley and later hosted a short-lived disc jockey and talk program in 1955. He became very amiable and accessible during his later years, although he had been known as very aggressive during his early years of popularity, sometimes engaging in fist-fights with hecklers or others who offended him. His trademark greeting "Heigh-Ho, everybody" was a carryover from his early days, when his orchestra had appeared at New York's Heigh-Ho club. Vallee's theme song was "My Time Is Your Time."

RUFFNER, TINY (1899–1983). Announcer Edmund "Tiny" Ruffner received his nickname because of his height of six feet, six inches. He began his career as a singer, and first appeared on radio on KFL Los Angeles during 1924, singing operettas. He then had a brief concert career before becoming an announcer for station WEAF New York in 1927. As director for the Benton & Bowles radio department, he became writer-producer for *Show Boat*, on which he was also the announcer. In addition, he hosted several **quiz programs**, such as *The Better Half* and *Your Happy Birthday* (on which he played "the

Birthday Man"). He also played himself on *Captain Diamond's Adventures.*

– S –

SAINT (THE). A 30-minute detective adventure series heard from 1945 to 1951, *The Saint* featured the adventures of Simon Templar, a character appearing in a long series of novels by Leslie Charteris. Templar was a suave and sophisticated man-about-town who patronized the arts and ate in the finest restaurants in addition to serving in a Robin Hood-like way to right wrongs or to help those who for some reason could not obtain help from the law. Although violence was a staple, the show had a tongue-in-cheek quality, with clever comebacks and one-liners a major part of the dialogue. The version heard from 1947 to 1951, starring Vincent Price, is the best known; but Edgar Barrier was the first Templar and the role was also played by Brian Aherne and **Tom Conway**.

SAMMY KAYE SHOW (THE). Kaye was a popular orchestra leader who hosted a long series of musical programs from 1937 to 1956, some under his own name, some under the sponsor's name. Included were *The Sammy Kaye Show, Sammy Kaye's Showroom,* and *Sammy Kaye's Sunday Serenade Room.* In 1944–1945, his program was called *Tangee Varieties* and was co-hosted by ventriloquist Paul Winchell. Although his slogan was "Swing and sway with Sammy Kaye," his was not a swing band, but a "sweet" band, playing primarily sentimental popular songs and novelty tunes. He was very popular and several times had more than one program running concurrently.

SANDERSON, JULIA. *See* CRUMIT, FRANK.

SARNOFF, DAVID (1891–1971). Sarnoff was born near Minsk, Russia, and immigrated to the United States in 1900. He joined the Marconi Wireless Company in 1906 and studied electrical engineering at the Pratt Institute. He was general manager of the **Radio Corporation of America (RCA)** from its founding in 1919 until 1970. During World War II, Sarnoff was General Dwight D. Eisenhower's top communications expert, overseeing the construction of a radio transmitter that was powerful enough to reach all of the allied forces in Europe. He was given the honorary title of brigadier general for his work during the war, and thereafter preferred to be known as General Sarnoff. While he headed RCA, the company developed extensive research facilities to explore new broadcasting technologies because he recognized the potential of television and was determined that his company should pioneer in the medium. Sarnoff retired in 1970 and died the next year. He was inducted into the Radio Hall of Fame in 1989.

SATURDAY NIGHT SERENADE. A 30-minute **music program** heard from 1936 to 1948, the *Saturday Night Serenade* was sponsored by Pet Milk and originally featured Soprano Mary Eastman and Tenor Bill Perry. In 1941, Mary Eastman was replaced by **Jessica Dragonette**, who left in 1946 when the format changed to feature the Gus Haenschen orchestra and the Emil Cote singers. In 1948, the name of the program was changed to *The Pet Milk Show* and Vic Damone and Kay Armen were the featured vocalists. The **Bob Crosby** orchestra furnished the music during 1949–1950.

SCARLET PIMPERNEL (THE). An **adventure program** based on the character in the novel of the same name by Emmuska Orczy, *The Scarlet Pimpernel* was produced in London as a syndicated program and appeared on NBC in 1952–1953. Set during the time of the Terror in France, it starred Marius Goring as Sir Percy Blakeney, a prominent member of the London social scene who, in his disguise as the Scarlet Pimpernel, effected daring rescues of people in France who were in danger from the repressive regime. He was assisted by his companion, Lord Tony Dewhurst, who was the only person who knew of his secret identity. Lord Tony was played by David Jacobs.

SCATTERGOOD BAINES. There were two versions of this program, both based on the character in the books and short stories by Clarence Budington Kelland. The first was a 15-minute daily serial drama that was rather like a **soap opera**, heard from 1937 to 1942. Baines was a hardware store owner in the small town of Coldriver, and was the kind of folksy philosopher who used his kindly influence to get people to do things that were good for them. He was played by Jess Pugh, with John Hearne as Hippocrates Brown, his helper in the hardware store. Off the air for seven years, the program reappeared in 1949 as a 30-minute **situation comedy**, with Wendell Holmes in the title role. Baines was still the proprietor of a hardware store in Coldriver, but the supporting characters were different. His friend Hannibal Gibbey, a bookkeeper at the local feed store, was played by **Parker Fennelly**.

SCOURBY, ALEXANDER (1913–1985). Scourby was a Shakespearean actor on the New York stage in the 1930s, who began working in radio in daytime serial dramas, sometimes using the name Alexander Scott. One season, he had continuing roles in five different **soap opera**s, including *The Right to Happiness*, *Against the Storm*, *The Second Mrs. Burton*, and *Young Widder Brown*. He was heard on *The Eternal Light* for 14 years; and he played Jor-el, Superman's father, on *The Adventures of Superman*. His bass voice was well suited for making recordings; over the years, he recorded many works for the blind. He also acted in television and motion pictures, mainly in the 1950s.

SCREEN DIRECTOR'S PLAYHOUSE (THE). A **drama anthology** presenting radio adaptations of famous movies, this program is sometimes listed by several different names, including *The NBC Theater*, *The Screen Director's Guild*, or *The Hollywood Screen Director's Playhouse*. Heard from 1949 to 1951, it began as a 30-minute program but the format was expanded to 60 minutes the next year. It was similar in both name and format to the better-known *Screen Guild Theater*, differing from it primarily in that the director of each film being dramatized introduced the radio version. In addition, after the dramatization, the director chatted with the stars about the making of the film on which the radio episode was based.

SCREEN GUILD THEATER (THE). Heard from 1939 to 1951, *The Screen Guild Theater* was known by many different names as various sponsors attached their names to it, including *The Gulf Screen Guild Show*, *The Gulf Screen Guild Theater*, *The Lady Esther Screen Guild Theater*, and *The Camel Screen Guild Players*. Major motion picture performers appeared without pay, with the fees that would have gone to them given to the Motion Picture Relief Fund for the purpose of building and maintaining a facility for the housing of aging and indigent film performers. The program began as a variety program, but soon changed to a drama anthology, with 30-minute adaptations of motion pictures. The format changed to 60 minutes in 1950. *See also* SCREEN DIRECTOR'S PLAYHOUSE.

SEA HOUND (THE). *The Sea Hound* was a **juvenile adventure program** sometimes listed as *The Adventures of the Sea Hound*. It was first heard as a 15-minute daily program from 1942 to 1944 with Ken Daigneau as Captain Silver of the ship *Sea Hound* and Bob Hastings as his boy crewman, Jerry. Two later versions were heard in 1948 and in 1951, both 30-minute programs with Barry Thomson as Captain Silver and his oriental assistant Kukai (pronounced Cookie) played by Alan Devitt. There was also a motion picture serial based on the same characters, with Buster Crabbe playing Captain Silver.

SEALTEST VILLAGE STORE (THE). A 30-minute **situation comedy** heard from 1943 to 1948, *The Sealtest Village Store* began as a skit on *The Rudy Vallee Show*. When Vallee left for military service in 1943, the skit was expanded and **Joan Davis**, who had played the role on the Vallee show, became the proprietor of The Village Store. She was anxious to find a steady beau and engaged in a long series of hopeless man-chasing adventures, often involving her helper in the store, played by Jack Haley. Davis moved to her own show in 1945 and the role was assumed by **Eve Arden**, who left in 1948 to star in *Our Miss Brooks*.

SECOND HUSBAND. One of the many soap operas produced by **Frank and Anne Hummert**, *Second Husband* began as a 30-minute weekly serial drama in 1937 but changed to a 15-minute daily format from 1942 to 1946. It was the story of Brenda Cummings, a widow with two children who had begun a promising career in motion pictures. She married wealthy Grant Cummings and, in addition to the difficulties encountered in getting her children to accept her new husband, found Grant himself to be a problem because of his bitter opposition to her career. Helen Menken and later Kathleen Cordell played Brenda; Grant was played by **Joseph Curtin** and Richard Waring.

SECOND MRS. BURTON (THE). A 15-minute **soap opera** heard from 1946 to 1960, *The Second Mrs. Burton* was an outgrowth of an earlier program called *Second Wife* that was heard only on a West Coast network. It was the story of Stan and Terry Burton, who were short of money because Stan had lost his business in a divorce. Although initially an important character, his first wife, Marion, gradually disappeared from the plot and Stan's mother became the "First Mrs. Burton." Mother Burton was prying and intrusive, although generally benign. The plots were not as melodramatic as those on many soap operas, although the direction of the program changed several times because it was written by a series of six different writers during the course of the run. Terry was played by five different actresses, but Stan was played by Dwight Weist for the entire run.

SECRET MISSIONS. A 30-minute espionage drama heard in 1948–1949, *Secret Missions* was based on the book of the same name by Ellis M. Zacharias, who had been the Deputy Chief of the Office of Naval Intelligence. Admiral Zacharias was the host and narrator and the programs were dramatizations of true stories taken from his records. Most of the stories were set in the United States and dramatized efforts to prevent espionage during and just before World War II. The cast was drawn from New York radio performers and included, among others, **Raymond Edward Johnson**, **Alexander Scourby**, and Leon Janning. Scripts were by Howard Merrill; music was composed and conducted by Elliot Jacoby.

SERGEANT PRESTON OF THE YUKON. A 30-minute **juvenile adventure program** originally called *Challenge of the Yukon*, this was one of the three great adventure programs created by **George W. Trendle** and written by **Fran Striker**. Heard from 1947 to 1955, it followed the adventures of Sgt. William Preston of the Northwest Mounted Police and his dog, Yukon King, who was an integral part of every plot, and often the hero. Many of the cast members who appeared on *The Lone Ranger* also acted on Sgt. Preston and many of the stories were adaptations of stories heard previously on *The Lone Ranger*. Paul Sutton was the first Preston, with **Brace Beemer**, who also played The Lone Ranger, playing the role during the last year of the program. Many **premiums** were offered, the best remembered of which was a deed to one square inch of Yukon Land. There was a television series of the same name from 1955 to 1958.

SETH PARKER. An unusual 30-minute program created by **Phillips H. Lord**, *Seth Parker* began as a weekly hymn-sing, supposedly conducted by a group of friends who met each Sunday evening after supper in the home of Seth Parker, an old gentleman who lived in Maine. There was also some singing of sentimental ballads, considerable joshing among the participants, and the folksy philosophizing of Parker, who was played by Lord. The original program was heard from 1929 to 1933 and was sometimes called *Sunday Evening at Seth Parker's*. In 1933, Lord purchased a large schooner, named it the *Seth Parker*, and set sail with friends and cast members to produce a new program called *The Cruise of the Seth Parker*. The program was heard during 1933–1934, but the ship was severely damaged by a storm in early 1935 and Lord returned to New York, where *Seth Parker* was broadcast again in 1935–1936 and in 1938–1939.

SEYMOUR, ANNE (1909–1988). Anne Seymour began appearing on radio on station WLW Cincinnati in 1932, and then moved to Chicago and co-starred with **Don Ameche** on *Grand Hotel*. That work led to *The Story of Mary Marlin*, on which she played the title role for four years. Seymour also was featured on *The Magnificent Montague*, *Whispering Streets* (as the narrator), and *Woman of America*. After radio, she worked in television, including the drama *Empire*. She also appeared as a character actress in a number of motion pictures, beginning with *All the King's Men* in 1949.

SHADOW (THE). One of the most famous programs in radio, *The Shadow* was a 30-minute program heard on late Sunday afternoons from 1937 to 1954. Based on a character in pulp fiction created by Walter B. Gibson, The Shadow was in reality Lamont Cranston, a wealthy man-about-town who dedicated his life to righting wrongs, protecting the innocent, and punishing the guilty. He had acquired "the power to cloud men's minds" from a Yogi in India many years before and could by this means render himself invisible. His assistant, the lovely Margo Lane, was the only person who knew his true identity. The first performer to play The Shadow was **Orson Welles**, and he was succeeded by several others, of whom **Bill Johnstone** and **Bret Morrison** were the best known. **Agnes Moorehead** was the first Margo Lane, although several others later played the role. The program itself was melodramatic and both the introduction ("Who knows what evil lurks in the hearts of men?") and the closing lines ("The tree of crime bears bitter fruit—crime does not pay!") have become a part of American folklore, as has The Shadow's menacing laugh.

SHELL CHATEAU (THE). See THE AL JOLSON SHOW.

SHELTON, GEORGE (1896–1971). A dancer and comedian in vaudeville, Shelton appeared on several radio programs during the 1930s, but is best remembered for his role on *It Pays to Be Ignorant.* He had been the vaudeville partner of the show's moderator, **Tom Howard**, and was perhaps the zaniest of the mock quiz program's nitwit panel members. He was known for yelling his stock line "I used to work in that town" when a particular city was mentioned. Shelton and Howard had earlier appeared together on another CBS program, *Model Minstrels*, in 1939–1940.

SHERIFF (THE). See DEATH VALLEY DAYS.

SHERLOCK HOLMES. Several different radio programs were based on the famous detective created by Arthur Conan Doyle. They were heard from 1930 to 1956, all of them were 30-minute programs, and most followed the same general format: the stories told in retrospect by Dr. Watson, who was interviewed both before and after the program proper. The first of many actors to play Holmes on the radio was William Gillette, the most famous Holmes of his time. The best-remembered performer to play the part was **Basil Rathbone**, who played Holmes from 1939 to 1946, with Nigel Bruce as Dr. Watson. He and Bruce made 16 motion pictures playing the same characters. Rathbone was succeeded on radio by **Tom Conway** in 1946 and later by John Stanley and Ben Wright; John Gielgud later played Holmes in a BBC series. Edith Meiser wrote the early scripts for radio, at first dramatizing the stories written by Conan Doyle and then creating new stories when the originals had all been used. She was later succeeded by a number of talented writers, including Anthony Boucher and Leslie Charteris, but retained some editorial control for many years of the long run.

SHERMAN, RANSOM (1898–1985). Sherman started his radio career in 1923 and in 1931 gained some prominence as a member of "The

Three Doctors" comedy team. He later appeared on **Club Matinee**, *Hap Hazard* (as both writer and star), **The Ransom Sherman Show**, and **Fibber McGee and Molly**. Sherman is known to many radio fans as the man responsible for the contest featured on *Club Matinee* that gave Garrison Morfit his new name of **Garry Moore**. After leaving radio, Sherman acted in a number of motion pictures, including *The Bachelor and the Bobby Soxer* (with Cary Grant) and *Gentleman's Agreement* (with Gregory Peck), both in 1947.

SHOWBOAT. A 60-minute **variety program** sometimes listed as *The Maxwell House Showboat*, *Showboat* was heard from 1932 to 1937 and was one of the most popular programs of that period. Based on the 1927 Broadway musical of the same name, the program was set on a Mississippi River showboat, and began with announcer **Tiny Ruffner** describing the arrival of the boat, complete with crowd noises, a steamboat whistle, calliope music, and the sound of the paddle wheel. Captain Henry of the showboat then took over as host and introduced the acts. **Lanny Ross** became the singing star of the program, with Muriel Wilson the female singer with whom he sang duets as well as conducted a fictitious romance. Captain Henry was originally played by Charles Winninger, who had been the captain of an actual showboat. When Winninger left in 1935, he was replaced briefly by Frank McIntyre and then by Lanny Ross, and the program lost many of its listeners. The program moved to California for a brief period in 1937, with Winninger and a new cast, but left the air soon thereafter. It was revived briefly in 1940–1941 with **Hugh Studebaker** as host.

SILVER EAGLE (THE). A 30-minute **juvenile adventure program** heard weekly from 1951 to 1955, *The Silver Eagle* was produced by James Jewell, who had been the leader of the repertory company that earlier had produced **The Lone Ranger**, **The Green Hornet**, and **Sergeant Preston of the Yukon**. It was in some ways similar to the latter program. It was the story of the adventures of Jim West, a Mountie noted for never giving up on a case. West's trademark was an eagle-feather arrow. He was assisted by Joe Bideaux, a gigantic French-Canadian who spoke with a heavy accent. West was played by **Jim Ameche**; Bideaux was originally played by Jack Lester, later by Michael Romano.

SILVER THEATER (THE). A 30-minute **drama anthology** heard intermittently from 1937 to 1947, *The Silver Theater* was named for the sponsor, the International Silver Company, maker of Rogers Brothers Silverware. **Conrad Nagel** was the original host, later replaced by John Loder in 1942. Major Hollywood stars were featured in original dramas until 1947, when the program appeared as a summer-replacement program with radio stars playing the lead roles.

SIMMS, GINNY (1916–1994). Ginny Simms was a singer who was born in Texas but raised in California. She was very popular in the 1940s, especially with servicemen during World War II. On radio she was a vocalist on *Kay Kyser's Kollege of Musical Knowledge* and *The Bob Burns Show* and then starred in her own **music program**. Her shows aired under a variety of names and different formats from 1941 to 1947, including *The Ginny Simms Show* and *The Pause That Refreshes*. She also appeared on *Your Hit Parade* in 1947. She was then off the air until 1950, at which time she returned in *Botany Song Shop*, a 15-minute program on ABC.

SINCLAIR WIENER MINSTRELS (THE). A 30-minute **music program** with a minstrel show format, *The Minstrels* was heard from 1932 to 1939 and was extremely popular, although it is largely forgotten today. The unusual name refers not to any association with frankfurters, but because the program was originally produced by station WENR in Chicago and sponsored by the Sinclair Oil Company. It was one of the highest-rated programs on radio in the early 1930s, with Gene Arnold as the original "interlocutor" (replaced by Gus Van in 1936). In 1937, the program was re-named *The NBC Minstrels*.

SINGIN' SAM. *Singin' Sam* was the professional name of Harry Frankel, who was for many years associated with Barbasol shave cream and known as *Singin' Sam, The Barbasol Man,* the title of his first network program. He was heard on a long series of 15-minute **music programs** from 1930 to 1947, with several different names, including *Refreshment Time* when he was sponsored by Coca-Cola and *Reminiscin' with Singin' Sam*, a syndicated program that he transcribed from 1945 to 1947. He had a deep baritone voice and specialized in older songs, rather than popular music.

SINGING STORY LADY (THE). **Ireene Wicker**, who was well-known for her work in **soap operas,** was also featured in a long series of programs for children, heard on the networks in both 15-minute and 30-minute formats, and sometimes billed as *The Singing Lady* or *Stories for Children.* The various versions of the program were heard from 1932 to 1945, with several interruptions, and it was still being heard on local radio in New York until well into the 1970s. On the programs, Wicker narrated stories of all kinds, doing many different voices and dialects, as well as singing when the parts required it. She used only a piano for accompaniment, for many years played by Milton Rettenberg. *See also* CHILDREN'S PROGRAMS.

SINGLETON, PENNY (1908–2003). Singleton, whose maiden name was Dorothy McNulty, began her career as a child actress under that name. She later married dentist Peter Singleton and changed her professional name to Penny Singleton, her chosen first name related to her long habit of saving penny coins. She is best remembered for her title role on *Blondie*, a popular series based on Chic Young's comic strip that aired from 1939 to 1950. Singleton also played the role in a series of 28 feature films that appeared between 1938 and 1950. After she left the *Blondie* radio series, she starred briefly in her own series, *The Penny Singleton Show*, a **situation comedy** that was heard only in the summer of 1950. On television, she was the voice of Jane Jetson on *The Jetsons* cartoon series. After her acting career was over, Singleton worked in union affairs; and at one time was president of the American Guild of American Artists.

SITUATION COMEDIES. Situation comedies, or sitcoms, consisted of individual comedic/dramatic episodes containing regular characters who appeared each week. Although there were instances when a storyline continued over more than one week, each episode was usually self-contained, with the events of the episode being resolved by the end of the program. Events occurring in previous episodes were seldom mentioned. Many episodes revolved around some sort of misunderstanding, an embarrassing coincidence, or a mistake in judgment by the leading character, often because he or she was placed in a situation for which he or she was poorly equipped.

What is arguably the most popular radio program of all time, *Amos 'n' Andy*, was essentially a dialogue between two African American characters who were the owners of a one-car taxicab company in Chicago. Over the years, additional characters appeared, many of them played by the same two white vaudeville veterans who had originated the program. *Lum and Abner* was similar in many ways, although the two leading protagonists purported to be rustics who operated a general store in a small town in Arkansas.

More common were programs that depicted family life in some way, often involving a well-meaning but blundering husband who was stabilized by his intelligent, competent, wife. Best known of these was *Fibber McGee and Molly*, but *Blondie*, *The Phil Harris–Alice Faye Show*, and *Life with Riley* were also of this general type and *The Great Gildersleeve* and *Ozzie and Harriet* made only minor adjustments to the formula. *My Friend Irma*, *I Love Lucy*, and *My Favorite Husband* featured bumbling female protagonists, but followed the same principles. *The Burns and Allen Show* revolved around the bizarre situations created by Gracie Allen's ditzy character.

Several programs purported to depict the life of teenagers, usually presenting a picture of more or less constant chaos and crisis. Of these, *The Aldrich Family* was perhaps the best known, although *Archie Andrews*, *A Date with Judy*, and *Meet Corliss Archer* were all popular and all similar, concerned with various teenage misadventures.

There were a few situation comedies that used other formats, such as *The Halls of Ivy*, which depicted the problems encountered by the president of a small college, but most sitcoms were family-oriented in some way and many of them moved to television with very little change in format or personnel. *See also* COMEDY PROGRAMS.

SIX SHOOTER (THE). A 30-minute **western program** heard during 1953–1954, *The Six Shooter* starred James Stewart as Brett Ponsett. Ponsett was a drifter who traveled the western United States on horseback, becoming involved in a series of episodes with the people he met at various locales. He was very easy going, and always looked for a peaceful solution to any situation, but was a dangerous gunman when provoked. Written by Frank Burt and directed by Jack Johnstone, the program was less melodramatic than many other western adventure programs, with stories that involved more character study than action and also contained some quiet humor.

SKELTON, RED (1913–1977). The son of a circus clown, Richard Bernard (Red) Skelton was successful in all phases of show business. At age 10, he quit school and began entertaining in medicine shows, circuses, burlesque, and vaudeville. On radio, he appeared on *The Rudy Vallee Show* before becoming the headliner on *Avalon Time* in 1939, and was then given his own program, *The Red Skelton Show*, which aired from 1941 to 1952. He moved to television in 1951, and his award-winning TV show was seen for the next 20 years. His motion picture debut was in 1938, and he appeared in films until the mid-1960s. Skelton was also a successful composer and painter. He received many media awards during his lifetime and was inducted into the Radio Hall of Fame in 1994.

SKIPPY. A 15-minute **children's program** heard from 1932 to 1935, *Skippy* was written by **Robert Hardy Andrews**, and produced by **Frank and Anne Hummert**, who were best known for their production of numerous soap operas, although they also produced other types of programs. It was based on a popular comic strip by Percy Crosby and featured the adventures of a Tom Sawyer-like little boy who lived in Shanty Town and was in more or less constant mischief. Skippy was played by Franklin Adams Jr. and his best friend Sooky was played by Francis Smith.

SKIPPY HOLLYWOOD THEATER (THE). A 30-minute **drama anthology** named for the sponsor, Skippy Peanut Butter, this program was sometimes listed as *The Skippy Hollywood Playhouse* and was produced in syndication beginning in 1941, although it was only heard on a national network from 1949–1950. In format, it was similar to *The Lux Radio Theater*, with the host interviewing the stars of each episode after the play was completed. It was hosted by C. P. MacGregor, who also produced the program.

SKY BLAZERS. A 30-minute **drama anthology** heard during 1939–1940, *Sky Blazers* dramatized true events from aviation history. It was produced by **Phillips H. Lord**, who also produced *Seth Parker* and *Gang Busters*, and was hosted by Colonel Roscoe Turner, a famous World War I pilot who held many aviation speed records. The events dramatized ranged over the entire history of aviation. After each episode, Colonel Turner interviewed the aviator who had been featured in the dramatization.

SKY KING. *Sky King* was a **juvenile adventure program** heard as a 15-minute daily serial in 1946–1947, becoming a 30-minute program with a complete adventure in each episode from 1947 to 1954. It was based on the exploits of Schuyler King, an Arizona rancher who flew to adventure in his plane, the *Songbird*. Sky was accompanied on his adventures by his niece, Penny, and his nephew, Clipper. In later programs, they were often joined by Sky's ranch foreman, Jim Bell. Several different actors played Sky, with Roy Engel the first and Earl Nightingale perhaps the best known. Penny was played by Beryl Vaughn and Clipper was played by Jack Bivens and Johnny Coons; Cliff Soubier played Jim Bell. Long-time television newscaster Mike Wallace was the announcer. A television version of the program was seen from 1951 to 1954 (and in re-runs from 1959 to 1966), with Kirby Grant as Sky.

SLOANE, EVERETT (1909–1965). Born in New York City, Sloane made his acting debut as a youngster in a Greenwich Village show. He left acting for a job on Wall Street, but turned to radio during the Depression. His first radio job was in a supporting role on a local New York program, which led to continuing parts on such programs as *Bulldog Drummond*, *The Shadow*, *The Goldbergs*, *This Is Nora Drake*, *Pretty Kitty Kelly*, and *Twenty-First Precinct*. In 1938, Sloane joined **Orson Welles** and his *Mercury Theatre on the Air* and followed Welles to Hollywood, where he acted in such Welles movies as *Citizen Kane* (1941), *Journey into Fear* (1942), and *The Lady from Shanghai* (1947). Sloane also worked on Broadway and in television during his long acting career.

SMALL, MARY. Mary Small was a child singer who was only 11 years old when her program first appeared on the network in 1934, but she had been appearing as a guest artist on **music programs** for several years previously. Her voice was remarkably mature at an early age, leading many listeners to believe that she was an adult. She hosted several programs heard from 1934 to 1946, with an interruption from 1937 to 1941. Her first program was called *Little Miss Bab-O's Surprise Party* (named for the sponsor) and her 1944 to 1946 programs were called *The Mary Small Revue*.

SMART, J. SCOTT (1902–1960). Jack Smart is remembered best as the heavy private detective, Brad Runyon, on *The Fat Man*. At the time the program was aired, Smart actually outweighed his fat fictional counterpart by more than 30 pounds. The deep-voiced Scott started out his acting career specializing in dialect parts on such programs as *Gasoline Alley* and *The March of Time*. He later acted on many other radio programs, including *Big Town*, *The Cavalcade of America*, *Columbia Presents Corwin*, *The Fred Allen Show*, *Town Hall Tonight*, and *Theatre Guild on the Air*. Smart also starred in *The Fat Man*, a 1951 movie based on the radio show.

SMILIN' ED'S BUSTER BROWN GANG. A 30-minute Saturday morning program for children heard from 1944 to 1953, this program was sponsored by Buster Brown Shoes and is sometimes confused with an earlier program, a juvenile serial drama called *The Buster Brown Gang*, with the same sponsor. Buster Brown was a little boy who lived in a shoe with his dog Tige; they were the trademark of Buster Brown Shoes. Smilin' Ed was an ex-vaudeville performer who sang silly songs, carried on imaginary dialogues with a cast of imaginary characters, and told adventure stories that were dramatized with music and sound effects. One of the best-remembered characters was Froggy, who spoke with a croaking voice and was ordinarily invisible, although he could plunk his "magic twanger" to become visible and harass the other imaginary characters. A television version of the program began in 1950. Before beginning his **children's program**, Smilin' Ed also hosted a long series of light music programs for adults from 1932 to 1941, often listed as *The Smilin' Ed McConnell Show*.

SMYTHE, J. ANTHONY (1885–1966). Smythe found his career role when he was cast in 1932 as Henry Barbour, the father on radio's *One Man's Family*. He played the part for the entire run of the program, 27 years. Smythe had appeared previously on other network programs, including *Carefree Carnival*, which he also wrote and directed. A bachelor, Smythe played the head of the popular radio family with great conviction. He was not cast in the role, however, when the program moved to television.

SNOW VILLAGE SKETCHES. There were at least three different versions of this program, appearing in 1936, 1943, and 1946, all of them **situation comedies** featuring Arthur Allen and **Parker Fennelly** as rustic New Englanders living on farms or in small towns. In the 1946 version both of them were farmers who doubled in other roles, Allen as a game warden and Fennelly as a truant officer. From 1928 to 1946, Allen and Fennelly appeared in several other programs of the same general character, including *Soconyland Sketches*, *Uncle Abe and David*, *Gibbs and Finney*, *General Delivery*, *The Simpson Boys of Sprucehead Bay*, and *The Stebbins Boys*.

SOAP OPERA. Although daytime radio programming included all manner of programs, it was dominated by a type of adult serial drama usually called "soap opera," a term that came to be applied to dramatic programs directed primarily at a female audience and characterized by stock characters and situations, sentimentality, and melodrama. Most were 15-minute daytime programs with continuing plot lines that moved very slowly; the emphasis was on the relationship between the characters rather than the plot. The term Soap Opera stems from the fact that many of these programs were sponsored by makers of facial or laundry soap.

Considered by many to be the first of the genre, ***Painted Dreams*** was first heard on WGN Chicago in 1930. Written by **Irna Phillips**, it was the story of a kindly older woman and her grown children.

At about the same time that *Painted Dreams* was appearing on WGN, Frank Hummert, a young advertising executive in Chicago, noticed that the serial fiction stories appearing in women's magazines were very popular and it occurred to him that it might be possible to do the same sort of thing with daytime radio drama. He induced a young writer, **Robert Hardy Andrews**, to write a serial drama for radio and Andrews eventually produced the script for ***Betty and Bob***, which first appeared in 1932. **Frank and Anne Hummert** soon developed a new technique for the rapid production of similar programs and between 1937 and 1942 introduced 22 new serial dramas to the networks.

Soap opera programming continued to grow until, by 1941, there was no time period between 10:00 A.M. and 5:30 P.M. during which there was not at least one soap opera appearing on some network. There were times during the day when the only network programs on the air were soap operas; in fact, nine of every 10 sponsored daytime network programs were soap operas.

On some programs, the same characters were played by the same performers for so many years that they almost did not need a script; just knowing the general direction of the plot would allow them to ad-lib dialogue appropriate to their character. On *Ma Perkins*, for example, **Virginia Payne** played the lead character for 27 years and Malcolm Forbes played her husband for the same period. Similar situations existed on a few other long-running programs: *Stella Dallas* was played by Anne Elstner for 17 years, Arthur Hughes played *Just Plain Bill* for 22 years, and J. Anthony Smythe played Henry Barbour for 27 years on *One Man's Family*.

Soap operas began to appear on television in 1950 and the number of soaps on radio diminished steadily, as did all radio network programming. The soaps hung on longer than many other types of programs, but they continued to move to television. By 1959, only seven were left on radio. On 25 November 1960, the last soaps still on a network schedule left the air. Although the plots were terminated in such a way as to allow resumption of the programs later, none ever returned.

"SORRY, WRONG NUMBER." *See SUSPENSE.*

SOTHERN, ANN (1909–2001). Born Harriette Arlene Lake, Ann Sothern began her film career as an extra in silent films. She changed her name to Ann Sothern at the request of a movie executive and in 1939 made the first of a series of nine romantic comedies based on the adventures of a sassy Brooklyn girl named Maisie. The movie series led to two radio series based on the same character: *Maisie*, a CBS program that aired from 1945 to 1947; and *The Adventures of Maisie*, a syndicated version that aired from 1949 to 1952. On television she starred on *Private Secretary* and *The Ann Sothern Show*. She and her second husband, actor Robert Sterling, had a daughter, Tisha Sterling, who also became an actress. Sothern has two stars on the Hollywood Walk of Fame, one for television and one for motion pictures.

SOULE, OLAN (1909–1994). Soule began his acting career with a touring stock company in the 1920s and in the early 1930s began working at WGN Chicago. After appearing as the Chinese cook on *Little Orphan Annie*, he went on to featured roles on *Bachelor's Children*, *The First Nighter*, and *Jack Armstrong, The All-American Boy*. When *The First Nighter* moved to Hollywood in 1947, he moved with it and began working in motion pictures and on television. On TV he appeared on *My Three Sons*, *Arnie*, and *Captain Midnight*; he also provided the voice of Batman on several Saturday morning cartoon series in the 1960s and 1970s.

SPACE PATROL. *Space Patrol* was a 30-minute **juvenile adventure program** that was heard from 1950 to 1955, running concurrently on radio and television with many of the same performers on both programs. Set in the 30th century, it featured the adventures of Buzz Corey, commander of the Space Patrol, and his companion, Cadet Happy, noted for his catchphrase when surprised: "Smokin' rockets!" The program offered many **premiums**, including rings, binoculars, cardboard spaceship cockpits, and once even a full-sized clubhouse shaped like a rocket. Commander Corey was played by Ed Kemmer and Cadet Happy was played by Lyn Osborn. Archvillian Mr. Proteus was played by **Marvin Miller**.

SPIKE JONES SHOW (THE). A 30-minute program aired from 1945 to 1949, this program was heard under several different names, beginning as a summer version of *The Chase and Sanborn Show*, then broadcast as *Spike's at the Troc* and *The Spotlight Revue*. On the latter show, Jones shared billing with Dorothy Shay, before the program became *The Spike Jones Show* in 1949. Jones was a drummer with a genius for comic invention and his band played on cowbells, kitchen utensils, and other unusual objects, as well as on regular instruments. In addition to their radio work and headlining a popular touring show called "The Musical Depreciation Review," Jones and his band made several very successful records, having seven major hits from 1942 to 1949. One of these, a parody ridiculing the Axis powers, was called "Der Fuehrer's Face" and was so popular that it was said to have been heard by Adolph Hitler himself.

SPIVAK, LAWRENCE E. (1900–1994). Co-founder (with Martha Rountree) of the long-running radio and television program *Meet the Press*, Spivak was a successful magazine publisher when he came to radio. He helped found both *Ellery Queen's Mystery Magazine* and *The Magazine of Fantasy and Science Fiction* and was editor/publisher of the literary magazine *American Mercury* when *Meet the Press* began on radio. He served as a regular panelist on the program and was known for his tenacity in grilling the guests. The program also was seen on television, beginning in 1947, and is now the longest-running show in TV history. In the 1950s, Spivak appeared on two other TV public affairs programs, *Keep Posted* and *The Big Issue*.

SPORTS BROADCASTS. Boxing and baseball were among the earliest sporting events to be broadcast on radio, and pioneering station **KDKA** Pittsburgh was active in both, broadcasting the description of a boxing match as early as April of 1921 and following up with a description of a Pirates–Phillies baseball game in August of the same year. Soon thereafter, KDKA also experimented with the broadcast of football and tennis, and other stations, particularly those in New York, soon followed suit. **Harold Arlin**, who may have been the first salaried announcer in broadcast radio, handled many of the early sporting events broadcasts for KDKA and **Graham McNamee**, working for station WEAF New York and later for NBC, soon became the best-known name in sports announcing, covering boxing, baseball, and football, among other things.

After Arlin and McNamee, there was a long series of pioneering announcers, all very prominent because it was a time when networks did not employ an entire stable of announcers, instead having one "star" announcer handle many different sporting events. Red Barber and Ted Husing were among the first of these, although Barber became known primarily as a baseball announcer and Husing for football. Clem McCarthy was noted for his rapid-fire description of horse races and boxing events. Eventually, there came to be a sort of farm system for sports announcers, with announcers beginning in small towns, broadcasting local sporting events over local stations, the more successful gradually moving up to larger cities and eventually, to the networks. This system produced **Bill Stern**, who was possibly the most controversial sports broadcaster during the period of old time radio, noted for being colorful rather than accurate.

The other controversial sports personality of the era was not a product of this system and was in some ways not a sports broadcaster at all. **Gordon McLendon** perfected the art of re-creating baseball games from the bare-bones pitch-to-pitch information furnished to stations on ticker tape. He furnished sound effects and fictitious "color" comments, and was phenomenally successful for a time, parlaying his re-creations into an entire short-lived network, *The Liberty Network*.

STAFFORD, HANLEY (1900–1968). Born Alfred John Austin in Hanley, Staffordshire, England, Stafford took his stage name from his birthplace. He came to radio at KFI Los Angeles in 1930 and later was featured on such network programs as *The Baby Snooks Show* (as "Daddy" Higgins), *Blondie* (as Dagwood's boss, J. C. Dithers), *Fu Manchu*, and *John's Other Wife*. Stafford was married to radio actress Veola Vonn who appeared with him on several programs, including *Blondie*.

STARS OVER HOLLYWOOD. A long-running 30-minute **drama anthology** heard from 1941 to 1954 in an unusual Saturday morning time slot, *Stars over Hollywood* presented light romances or comedies performed by major Hollywood stars, who had to appear at 9:30 A.M. local time to do the live program. Produced and directed by Paul Pierce for many years, it was later directed by Les Mitchel and a series of guest directors. The show was casual and relaxed, and the budget was small, but the performances were very professional. Music was provided by Ivan Ditmar, who played the organ as well as the harp and the violin.

STELLA DALLAS. A 15-minute daily **soap opera** heard from 1938 to 1955, *Stella Dallas* was remarkably stable in several respects, appearing in the same time slot for the entire run, as well as having the same performer in the lead role and keeping the same sponsor. It was produced by **Frank and Anne Hummert** and was partially based on a 1937 motion picture of the same name, which was in turn based on the 1923 novel by Olive Higgins Prouty. Stella was a seamstress who lived in a Boston rooming house. She and all of her friends were working-class people, but her daughter had been raised by a wealthy ex-husband and had grown up to marry in her own social class, creating clashes between her world and that of her mother. **Anne Elstner** played Stella for the entire run and was said to have missed only one performance in the more than 17 years that the program was on the air. In a 1966 interview, Elstner said that she played the role without ever having read the novel or seen either of the two motion pictures based on it. Stella's daughter Laurel, called "Lolly-Baby," was first played by Joy Hathaway, but Vivian Smolen held the role for most of the run.

STEPMOTHER. Listed in some sources as *Kay Fairchild, Stepmother*, this 15-minute **soap opera** was heard from 1938 to 1942. Although billed as the story of Kay Fairchild's efforts to raise the children of John Fairchild, the widower whom she had married, it was at least as devoted to more traditional soap opera concerns, such as marital discord, infidelity, politics, and even murder. The plot was very complex and became more so as the series continued. John lost his job at the bank as a result of his attraction to a scheming divorcee in the small Midwestern town where the Fairchilds lived, and Kay was forced to open a dress shop to support the family. John later disappeared because he became convinced that Kay was in love with another man. His grown daughter married a man who also ran away, leaving her pregnant, and leaving Kay to deal with all of these problems and more to follow. Kay was played by three different actresses, including Sunda Love, Janet Logan, and Charlotte Manson. Several different actors played the part of John, and the cast became very large as the plot became more complex and involved more characters.

STERN, BILL (1907–1971). Sportscaster Stern made his radio debut over WHAM Rochester in 1925. He hosted his own radio programs beginning in 1937 with *Carnival of Champions*. His long-running program that featured dramatizations of sporting events, *Colgate Sports Newsreel*, aired from 1939 to 1956. Although the stories presented were not always accurate, the program was melodramatic and entertaining. Stern broadcast the first televised sporting event, a college baseball game, in 1939; and he was featured on a number of TV programs in the 1950s. He was inducted into the Radio Hall of Fame in 1988. *See also* SPORTS BROADCASTS.

STONE, EZRA (1918–1994). Stone is best remembered today for his portrayal of Henry Aldrich on the popular radio program *The*

Aldrich Family, which aired from 1939 to 1953. He originated the role of Henry on the Broadway stage, and played the part for most of the radio show's long run. A product of The American Academy of Dramatic Arts, Stone began his radio career doing recitations over station WCAU Philadelphia. After *The Aldrich Family* ended on radio, he spent his later years as a producer and director on both radio and television.

STOOPNAGLE AND BUDD. Lemuel Q. Stoopnagle and Budd were comedic characters created by Frederick Chase Taylor and Wilbur Budd Hulick. Taylor was Colonel Stoopnagle, a name given him on impulse by Hulick when they were quite accidentally thrown together and asked to fill some time on a local station. They were among the first to produce the type of unscripted satiric dialogue later brought to perfection by **Bob and Ray** and were featured on a long series of programs from 1931 to 1937, sometimes as headliners, sometimes as part of a variety program. There were almost as many titles as there were programs and included *The Gloomchasers*, *The Ivory Soap Program*, *The Pontiac Program*, **The Camel Caravan**, *The Schlitz Spotlight Revue*, *The Gulf Headliners*, and *The Minute Men*—as well as two separate appearances on *Town Hall Tonight* as summer replacements for **Fred Allen**. They ended their partnership in 1937 and Hulick became the host of a game show, *What's My Name*, while Taylor later hosted several programs, including *Quixie Doodles*, *Lemuel Stoopnagle's Stooperoos*, and the *Colonel Stoopnagle Show*.

STOP THE MUSIC. A 60-minute **quiz program** heard from 1948 to 1952, *Stop the Music* was created by Lewis G. Cowan and hosted by **Bert Parks** (with music by the Harry Saltar orchestra). The format was in some ways similar to *Pot O' Gold*, a program that had appeared some years earlier: telephone numbers were called at random and when the telephone was answered Parks would shout "Stop the music!" and ask the person on the telephone to name the song that the orchestra had been playing. A correct answer won a very substantial prize and a chance to compete for the jackpot prize, which averaged over $20,000 in value. The initial questions were very easy to answer if the person had been listening to the program, although the "Mystery Melody" that had to be identified to win the jackpot was much more difficult. The program was placed opposite both

The Fred Allen Show and *The Edgar Bergen–Charlie McCarthy Show* on the schedule and was so popular that it drove both of them off the air.

STORY OF MARY MARLIN (THE). A 15-minute **soap opera** heard from 1935 to 1945, and again in 1951–1952, *The Story of Mary Marlin* was not set in a small town, as were most soap operas. Part of the action was in Washington, D.C., where Mary Marlin had been appointed U.S. senator from Iowa by the governor, after the disappearance and long absence of her senator husband Joe in a plane crash. For many years, the story moved back and forth between the daily happenings on the political scene in Washington and remote settings in Asia, where Joe was wandering in search of his identity, afflicted by amnesia that had resulted from the crash. He was sought by a private detective hired by Mary, named *Never Fail Hendricks*, and did eventually return, although his return caused more complications, including dealing with the romantic designs of a Washington socialite. The lead role was played by six different actresses during the run, of whom Joan Blaine was first. Joe was played by Robert Griffin and Never Fail Hendricks by Frank Dane and William A. Lee.

STRAIGHT ARROW. A 30-minute **juvenile adventure program** heard during 1948-1951, *Straight Arrow* featured Steve Adams, owner of the Broken Bow ranch, who had a secret identity as a Comanche warrior named Straight Arrow. Straight Arrow fought for justice riding a golden palomino named Fury, who was kept in a hidden cavern on his ranch. Steve's sidekick was Packy McCloud, who was the only person who knew of his secret identity. Howard Culver played the part of Steve, altering his voice when he changed from rancher to warrior; Packy was played by Fred Howard. The sound effects were dramatic, with drumbeats, Indian music, and the flight of arrows simulated by a tremolo played on the organ. Many **premiums** were offered, including feathered headbands, drums, and rings. For a time, Nabisco, which sponsored the program, printed "Injun-uity Cards," which contained information on Indian lore and customs and were placed in boxes of their Shredded Wheat.

STRANGE ROMANCE OF EVELYN WINTERS (THE). A 15-minute daily **soap opera** produced by **Frank and Anne Hummert** and heard from 1944 to 1948, *The Strange Romance of Evelyn Winters* was the story of a 23-year-old woman who lived with her guardian, Gary Bennett, a successful playwright who was 15 years older than she. She had been left in his care by her father, an army colonel who had been Bennett's commander during the war and had been killed in action. Gary and Evelyn fell in love, but tried to deny it to themselves and later to conceal it from others because of the difference in their ages. After revealing their feelings for each other, they had to deal with the reactions, both positive and negative, that the revelation caused among other people. Toni Darnay played the part of Evelyn; Gary was played by **Karl Weber** and Martin Blaine. The original program was sponsored by Sweetheart soap, but some of the episodes were repeated in a 1951–1952 version sponsored by Phillip Morris cigarettes.

STRIKE IT RICH. A 30-minute quiz program heard from 1947 to 1957, *Strike It Rich* was really more a giveaway program than a quiz program. Contestants were asked to tell why they needed money and their stories were the most important part of the program, often involving the need for medical treatment or help for relatives or friends who were in dire straits. The questions asked in the quiz were extremely simple and even if the contestant could not answer them, he or she was always rewarded in some way. There was a special telephone onstage where listeners could call in and donate cash or merchandise to the contestant. Originally heard weekly, it became a daily daytime program in 1950. It was hosted by Todd Russell for the first year and by **Warren Hull** thereafter.

STRIKER, FRAN (1903–1962). Striker first worked in radio as an announcer for station WEBR Buffalo, and wrote for local programs until he sold some scripts to station WXYZ in Detroit. He wrote the scripts for several WXYZ programs, but is best known today as the scriptwriter for *The Lone Ranger*, *The Green Hornet*, and *Sergeant Preston of the Yukon*, three of station WXYZ's most famous programs. Although many of the features of *The Lone Ranger* were created by committee, Striker was a major contributor, responsible for the introduction of silver bullets and the creation of Tonto. He worked on the program for its entire run. In addition to radio scripts, Striker wrote novels, movie serials, and comic strips about the characters he helped create. In the late 1930s, it was estimated that he wrote 60,000 words a week. He was inducted into the Radio Hall of Fame in 1988.

STUDEBAKER, HUGH (1900–1978). Studebaker began his career in the early 1920s as a singer in a male quartet, and then had a song and piano act, which led to work as an announcer and piano player at station KMBC Kansas City in 1929. He moved to Chicago in the early 1930s, began acting, and joined *Fibber McGee and Molly* as McGee's unpaid houseboy, Silly Watson, during the program's first season. Other acting roles followed, including that of Dr. Bob Graham on *Bachelor's Children* in 1936. Studebaker later was featured on such popular programs as *Captain Midnight*, *The Guiding Light*, *The Right to Happiness*, *Showboat*, *Vic and Sade*, and *Woman in White*.

SULLIVAN, ED (1901–1974). Sullivan was originally a theater columnist for the *New York Daily News*. His column concentrated on Broadway shows and gossip, and he continued writing for the *Daily News* throughout his radio/TV broadcasting career. His first radio program, the *Ed Sullivan Show*, was a talk and interview program that ran for only one year in 1932. It was on this program that Sullivan introduced such entertainment greats as **Jack Benny** and **Jack Pearl** to radio audiences. Sullivan returned to radio with *Ed Sullivan Variety* in 1941, which became *Ed Sullivan Entertains* during 1943–1944. He then starred on *Ed Sullivan's Pipelines* in 1946. In 1948, CBS hired him to do a weekly Sunday night television variety show, *Toast of the Town* (later called *The Ed Sullivan Show*), which was seen until 1971. Sullivan himself had little acting ability; his mannerisms on camera were somewhat awkward and often caricatured by comedians. Despite his manner, Sullivan became the most famous **variety show** host in the history of television. In 1971, the National Academy of TV Arts and Sciences presented him with a special Emmy Award.

SUSPENSE. One of the great **drama anthologies** of radio, *Suspense* was a 30-minute program heard from 1942 to 1962. There were many distinguished producers and directors during the long run, including William Spier, **Norman Macdonnell**, and **Elliott Lewis**. The types of material presented varied slightly with each director, but with the exception of an occasional science fiction story, the programs were generally realistic rather than fantastic. One of the most famous programs of old-time radio was "Sorry, Wrong Number" starring **Agnes Moorehead**. It was the story of an invalid woman who accidentally overheard the telephone conversation of two men plotting to murder a bedridden woman. She was unable to get telephone operators or law-enforcement people to give her story serious attention and she became increasingly hysterical, finally realizing to her horror that she was the intended victim of the murder plot. The episode won many awards and was repeated seven times over the course of the program's long run. Over 900 episodes of *Suspense* are available for listening today.

SWING, RAYMOND GRAM (1887–1968). A foreign correspondent, newspaper journalist, and radio commentator, Raymond Swing added the name of his second wife, militant suffragette Betty Gram, and was known as Raymond Gram Swing for the rest of his life despite their later divorce. As early as 1931, Swing broadcast over NBC to the United States from Geneva and—as the National Socialist Party came to power in Germany—Swing's knowledge of German allowed him to translate and comment upon Adolph Hitler's speeches. Swing was considered to be both intellectual and liberal. By 1940, he was being heard almost daily on more than 100 stations. Swing's last on-air assignment was for the Voice of America under **Edward R. Murrow**, but he later wrote many of Murrow's newscasts and edited his *This I Believe* series.

SYNDICATED PROGRAMS. A syndicated program is one created by an independent producer for the purpose of sale to a network or to individual stations. Particularly during the early years of network broadcasting, networks often did not offer a full day of programming to their affiliates. Also, many stations were not affiliated with any network and sought to supplement their programming with affordable content that could be flexibly scheduled. To a producer, the advantage to selling to a network was that once a network picked up a show, it became a part of the network feed and was usually guaranteed to run on all of the network affiliates on the same day of the week and at the same time. The disadvantage was that the national networks were notoriously hard bargainers, often paying much less than would be paid by individual stations. Production companies would sometimes sell their shows to networks at a loss, or for very little profit, hoping that the series would succeed and that eventual off-network syndication would turn a profit for the show.

A syndicated program could be sold to stations outright, with the rights to insert ads at the station level or it could be given to stations without charge in order to have access to airtime, in which case the syndicators could insert the ads and get the ad revenue. Some shows were produced with the advertising material already inserted: a "turnkey" product that only required the individual station to play the recorded program, without announcer intervention or attention.

All syndicated programs were recorded because the networks controlled the landlines and transmission cables over which live broadcasts were transmitted. After the recording of programs became more common, networks would sometimes syndicate their own shows and sell them to individual markets for use as reruns. All of these practices are still common in radio and in television and some of the best-known programs in both media have been produced in syndication.

– T –

TAKE IT OR LEAVE IT. A 30-minute **quiz program** heard from 1940 to 1952, *Take It or Leave It* presented contestants with a series of questions, each worth double the amount of the previous question, up to a maximum of $64. After each correct answer, the contestant was offered a choice of taking the winnings or going on to the next question. If a question were missed, all previous winnings were forfeited. The program was so popular that the phrase "the 64 dollar question" became a part of everyday speech, referring to any particularly thorny or difficult question. The first host was Bob Hawk, but there were several others, including **Phil Baker**, **Garry Moore**, Jack Paar, and **Eddie Cantor**.

TALES OF THE TEXAS RANGERS. A 30-minute **crime program** heard from 1950 to 1952, *Tales of the Texas Rangers* dramatized true cases from the records of the Texas Rangers. The program starred

Joel McCrea as Ranger Jace Pearson and the cases were modern, taken from the records of 1928–1948. Jace moved about the state by automobile, although he towed a horse trailer containing his horse, Charcoal, and frequently had to pursue criminals on horseback. At the end of each program, the disposition of the case was announced, which was often a prison term in the Texas state penitentiary. McCrea then returned to relate some piece of Texas Ranger history before closing the show.

TALK AND INFORMATION PROGRAMS. Chatty, informal programs were popular on daytime radio, and one of the first programs ever to appear on network radio was one of these, the ***Betty Crocker Magazine of the Air***. Beginning as a local program in 1924, before any networks existed, it moved to NBC in 1926 and remained on the air for 27 years, dispensing recipes, cooking tips, and other information for homemakers. ***Mary Margaret McBride*** usually appeared at noon or in the early afternoon, and was often referred to as a female Arthur Godfrey. She did have a casual personality similar to Godfrey's, but her program was very different, consisting almost entirely of interviews and chat.

Several programs invited the listener to join a well-informed couple for breakfast. The first of these, ***The Fitzgeralds***, featured Ed and Pegeen Fitzgerald discussing books, beauty, fashion, and current events, all without a script or any rehearsal. ***Breakfast with Dorothy and Dick*** was primarily a local New York program, but it was widely heard on many stations of the Mutual network, and featured the breakfast conversation of newspaper columnist **Dorothy Kilgallen** and her husband **Richard Kollmar**, as well as the chirping of their canary in the background. ***Tex and Jinx*** was a similar program, seldom heard on the network, but a staple on New York radio for many years and widely known nationwide.

TARZAN. There were several versions of this program, all of them **juvenile adventure programs** based on the Edgar Rice Burroughs novels, telling the story of a child of English descent who had been raised among the apes after being left an orphan. The first was a syndicated 15-minute program heard from 1932 to 1934 with James Pierce as Tarzan and Joan Burroughs, his wife (and the daughter of Edgar Rice Burroughs), as Jane. Although not a network program, it was very popular in the Northeast and is often cited as the first major syndicated serial. From 1934 to 1936, Burroughs assumed more control of the program and a new version was produced, starring Carlton KaDell as Tarzan. This version was also syndicated, but was widely distributed and was heard on many major outlets. Another syndicated version was produced in 1950, with Lamont Johnson as Tarzan, and was heard on CBS during 1952–1953.

TAYLOR, DEEMS (1885–1966). Taylor was the composer of the first American opera to be heard on radio, and he narrated a broadcast of the opera to inaugurate the opening of the CBS network. He served as co-commentator with **Milton Cross** during the first season of Metropolitan Opera broadcasts in 1931–1932, which led to his own radio program, *The Deems Taylor Music Series*, in 1932. Taylor provided commentary on many radio **music programs**, and hosted several others, including *Coronet on the Air*, *The Kraft Music Hall*, *Music America Loves Best*, *The Opera Guild*, *The Prudential Family Hour*, and *The Radio Hall of Fame*. Beginning in 1941, he was a frequent guest panelist on *Information Please*, the popular radio quiz program. He is today perhaps best remembered as the host and narrator of the Disney film *Fantasia*.

TELEPHONE HOUR (THE). Also known as *The Bell Telephone Hour*, this prestigious 30-minute **concert music** series was heard from 1940 to 1958, originally starring James Melton and Francia White as vocalists and presenting a wide variety of popular and semi-classical music. It changed to a great artists series in 1942, presenting guest artists from opera and other classical music venues. Over the years, many of the greatest names in classical music were heard, some of them many times. There were occasional programs featuring popular music, and in 1946 the program also began to feature new or unknown talent. **Donald Voorhees** conducted the music for the entire run.

TEMPLETON, ALEC (1910–1963). A blind pianist, Templeton was born in Cardiff, South Wales. He came to the United States in 1935 and appeared on such programs as *The Kraft Music Hall*, *The National Barn Dance*, and *The Rudy Vallee Show*. He had his own **music program**, *Alec Templeton Time*, from 1939 to 1941, in 1943, and again in 1946–1947. After his radio career, he hosted *It's Alec Templeton Time* on television. Templeton had studied at London's Royal Academy and was also a composer, creating many piano and orchestral pieces.

TENNESSEE JED. A 15-minute **juvenile adventure program** heard from 1945 to 1947, *Tennessee Jed* was set on the frontier just after the Civil War. Jed was a frontiersman who rode a horse named Smoky and carried two six-guns, but his primary expertise was with a rifle, with which he always hit his target "dead center." The program had a country flavor, with the theme song sung by country star Elton Britt and the instrumental breaks done by harmonica, guitar, and accordion. Jed himself was cut from the Lone Ranger mold, largely humorless, always grammatically correct, and of spotless character. He eventually became an agent for the federal government, working directly for the president of the United States. Jed was played originally by Johnny Thomas and later by Don MacLaughlin.

TERRY AND THE PIRATES. A 15-minute **juvenile adventure program** first heard during 1937–1939 and then again from 1943 to 1948, *Terry and the Pirates* was based on the comic strip of the same name by Milton Caniff. In the first version, Terry, two-fisted journalist Pat Ryan, and their associates battled pirates, smugglers, and villains of various kinds in the Far East. The Japanese were fighting in China at the time and were never directly identified, but were referred to as "the enemy" or "the invaders." When the program returned in 1943, after being off the air for four years, it was a war story, with Terry and his friends battling both the Japanese and the many German agents who had been sent to the Far East to oversee operations there. His old enemy, The Dragon Lady, had become a guerrilla fighter for China and they sometimes worked together to defeat the Japanese and Germans. After the war, The Dragon Lady returned to being a pirate leader, and Terry returned to struggling against the various types of evil found in the area. **Jackie Kelk** and Cliff Carpenter played Terry in the early series with Owen Jordan in the role in the 1943–1948 version.

TETLEY, WALTER (1915–1975). Tetley was a child performer who began his acting career in vaudeville, imitating Sir Harry Lauder.

On radio, Tetley appeared on hundreds of programs, including *The Children's Hour*, *Coast-to-Coast on a Bus*, *The Fred Allen Show*, and *Let's Pretend*. For his long-running roles on *The Great Gildersleeve* and *The Phil Harris–Alice Faye Show*, however, he is best remembered today. On the former, he played Leroy, Gildersleeve's nephew; on the latter, he was delivery boy Julius Abbruzio. In the early 1960s, Tetley provided the voice of Sherman on television's *The Bullwinkle Show*, a popular cartoon series.

TEX AND JINX. Tex and Jinx were Tex McCrary and Jinx Falkenburg, a husband-and-wife team who had a breakfast-time program heard on a network only in 1947–1948, but appearing on New York radio for many years. Unlike the other breakfast-hour programs, they did not pretend to eat, nor to engage in domestic chat. Instead, they interviewed well-known figures and discussed important issues of the day. McCrary was a publicist and journalist who had worked with **Walter Winchell**, and who was later credited with having coined the "I Like Ike" slogan for Dwight D. Eisenhower's presidential campaign of 1952. Jinx was a famous model and actress who, although not well educated, was an excellent interviewer, particularly skilled at encouraging guests to couch their answers in terms understandable to the housewives who were a large part of their listening audience. *See also* TALK AND INFORMATION PROGRAMS.

TEXACO STAR THEATER (THE). A generic title applied to series of programs sponsored by Texaco and heard from 1938 to 1949, *The Texaco Star Theater* was first heard as a 60-minute **variety program** hosted by Adolph Menjou, then by John Barrymore and **Ken Murray**. It featured well-known vocalists **Jane Froman**, **Frances Langford**, and **Kenny Baker**, as well as comedic episodes and a 20-minute dramatic skit each week. In 1940, comedian **Fred Allen** became the star and the program from that period is often listed as *The Fred Allen Show*. In 1944, the program again became a variety program, now headed by tenor James Melton, but Melton left after the 1946 season and Tony Martin and Evelyn Knight hosted the program until Gordon MacRae replaced Tony Martin in 1948. In the fall of that year, the program featured comedian **Milton Berle** and was also known as *The Milton Berle Show*. A television version of the program made Berle a major star and was seen until 1956.

THEATRE GUILD ON THE AIR. A 60-minute **drama anthology** heard from 1945 to 1954, *Theatre Guild on the Air* was sponsored by United States Steel and was often billed as *The United States Steel Hour*. The purpose of the program was to present radio adaptations of the best American plays of the last thirty years, using the original casts when possible. Many of the plays were written by guild members, although that was not a criterion for selection. Outstanding novels were occasionally dramatized. Because the Broadway stage was much more uninhibited and explicit than radio, many adaptations also had those characteristics and *Theatre Guild* was one of the first programs to present adult topics and situations on the air. The program migrated to television in 1953.

THIRD MAN (THE). A 30-minute **adventure program**, *The Third Man* featured Harry Lime, the character from the Graham Green novel and the motion picture of the same name. Lime was a likable international scoundrel who moved from country to country, always skirting the law, but always kind to those who were worse off than he. He also usually victimized characters who were richly deserving of such treatment. As in the movie, Lime was played by **Orson Welles**. The program was produced in syndication by the BBC and was heard on American radio in 1952. The music was the same that the movie had made famous: *The Third Man Theme*, played on a zither by Anton Karas, who was also the composer.

THIS IS MY BEST. A 30-minute prestige **drama anthology**, *This Is My Best* was based on a book of the same name, in which modern authors chose what they felt to be their best works, not all of which were well known. Heard from 1944 to 1946, the program changed format in 1945 when **Orson Welles** became the director, narrator, and star. He changed the content to more classical stories, but had a more or less constant battle with the network and the sponsor and was fired after only a few weeks. When the program returned in the fall, it was directed by Don Clark and had changed again, presenting motion picture scripts that had not previously been produced.

THIS IS NORA DRAKE. A 15-minute **soap opera** heard from 1947 to 1949, *Nora Drake* was the story of a woman who fell in love with a doctor, Ken Martinson. Ken was as flawed as many male romantic characters in radio soap operas and married another woman before realizing that he truly loved Nora. When he asked his wife for a divorce, she refused and—after a furious confrontation with Nora—drove away recklessly, becoming involved in an accident that left her a dependent cripple. Ken then felt unable to leave her and the story grew more complicated as Nora's long lost father appeared and proved to be unstable and impulsive, eventually going to prison for shooting a gambler. Nora was played by Charlotte Holland, Joan Tompkins, and **Mary Jane Higby**. Ken was played by Alan Hewitt.

THIS IS YOUR FBI. A 30-minute crime drama that dramatized true stories from the Federal Bureau of Investigation (FBI) files and was heard from 1945 to 1953, *This Is Your FBI* was similar in many ways to *The FBI in Peace and War*, although it was based on real case files while the stories in *The FBI in Peace and War* were fictitious. *This Is Your FBI* was endorsed by the FBI and director Jerry Devine had access to FBI files. He was allowed to dramatize any case history, only changing the names and places involved. The program originated in New York from 1945 to1947, and then moved to Hollywood. For the first year, the program presented cases of spies, saboteurs, and Nazi agents, each program taking place in a different FBI field office, with different lead characters. When production moved to Hollywood, the format changed and a fictitious agent, Jim Taylor, headlined each episode, dealing with all types of crimes. The stories were told by alternating the viewpoints of the agent and the criminals. Stacy Harris played Jim Taylor and Larry Keating was the announcer for the entire time the program was produced in Hollywood.

THIS IS YOUR LIFE. *This Is Your Life* was the creation of host **Ralph Edwards,** who was also the host of radio's popular *Truth or Consequences*. In a 1946 radio broadcast of the latter program, Edwards presented a capsule narrative of the past life of a disabled World War II veteran and received such positive feedback that he developed the formula for a separate program on which guests were surprised with a presentation of their past life in the form of a narrative read by Edwards and on-air appearances of childhood friends and important figures in the subject's life. Both celebrities and less well-known people were profiled and the subjects were often unaware that they were to be featured. The program was heard on radio from

1948 to 1950 and became a television program in 1952. *See also* AUDIENCE-PARTICIPATION PROGRAMS.

THOMAS, LOWELL (1892–1981). A news commentator and adventurer, Thomas had the longest continually operating newscast on radio, running from 1930 to 1976. He also broadcast the first televised news program in 1939. He later appeared in several TV series, including *High Adventure with Lowell Thomas* and *Lowell Thomas Remembers* for PBS. In 1979, he returned to radio with a daily syndicated series, *The Best Years*, about the accomplishments of famous people in their later years. As a businessman, he was chairman of the Cinerama Corporation, narrating its early exhibition films, and co-founder of Capital Cities Broadcasting Corporation. He was also a prolific author, writing 54 books including his autobiography, *Good Evening Everybody*, published in 1976. *See also* NEWS PROGRAMS.

THOMPSON, BILL (1913–1971). Thompson came from a vaudeville family and won a talent contest in 1934 with a routine in which he spoke in ten different dialects. He then performed on several radio shows and joined *Fibber McGee and Molly* in 1936. Thompson worked on their program for many years and played several unforgettable characters, among them The Old Timer ("That's pretty good, Johnny, but that ain't the way I hear-ed it"), Horatio K. Boomer ("And. . . a check for a short beer"), and Wallace Wimple ("Sweetie Face, my big old wife"). Thompson left the show to serve in the Navy during World War II, but rejoined the program in 1946. That same year, ABC starred him in his own **comedy program**. In addition to his radio work, Thompson supplied the voices for several Disney cartoon characters. In his spare time, he served as president of the Southern California Area Boy Scouts of America. When *Fibber McGee and Molly* left the air in 1957, Thompson retired from show business and went to work for the Union Oil Company.

THOSE WE LOVE. A 30-minute serial drama heard from 1938 to 1945 with many interruptions, *Those We Love* was the story of John Marshall, a lawyer who, after the death of his wife, raised twin children (Kathy and Kit) with the help of Aunt Emily Mayfield. Kit was interested primarily in aviation, but—after a near fatal crash—began a career in law. Kathy became the central character, with many romantic misadventures. Kit was the perfect brother, ready to listen and help if he could. Nan Grey played Kathy, with Richard Cromwell and Bill Henry as Kit. Several performers played John Marshall, but Pedro de Cordoba was the first. The program had a troubled history and was cancelled several times, but these cancellations always created a storm of protest letters from its many faithful listeners.

TIBBETT, LAWRENCE (1897–1960). Tibbett was a baritone who became a member of the Metropolitan Opera in the early 1920s and made regular appearances on a number of radio programs, including *The Voice of Firestone*, *Your Hit Parade*, and *The Packard Show*. As a singing actor, he had leads in such American operas as *Emperor Jones* and *The King's Henchman*. Tibbett had a brief Hollywood career, and in 1930 was nominated for an Academy Award for his very first film, *The Rogue Song*. His last Met appearance was in 1950, and his final Broadway role was in 1956. He was one of the founders of the **American Federation of Radio Artists (AFRA)** in 1937, and served as its president. Tibbett was later pictured on a set of United States postage stamps that celebrated opera singers.

TILTON, MARTHA (1915–2006). A popular big band singer, Martha Tilton was known at one time as "Liltin' Miss Tilton." She sang with several popular bands during the Big Band Era, including those of Jimmy Dorsey, Benny Goodman, and Artie Shaw. She appeared on radio with Goodman on *Benny Goodman's Swing School*, a version of *The Camel Caravan*, during the late 1930s and then was hired as vocalist with the Billy Mills Orchestra on the *Fibber McGee and Molly* program in 1941. She starred on her own 15-minute NBC program on Sunday afternoons, and was featured on several other radio programs, including *The Radio Hall of Fame* and *Your Hit Parade*. From 1949 to 1954, she co-starred on the *Curt Massey–Martha Tilton Program*. She appeared in a few Hollywood movies during the early 1940s and made hit recordings throughout the 1950s. Her sister Liz was also a band singer.

TODAY'S CHILDREN. A 15-minute daily **soap opera** heard from 1933 to 1937 and again from 1943 to 1950, *Today's Children* was written by **Irna Phillips** and was a thinly disguised copy of an earlier

Phillips program, **Painted Dreams**. Phillips had left the earlier program in a dispute with station management and re-created the show for NBC with different names for the characters, but still based in Chicago and featuring a kindly mother figure, Mother Moran, patterned after the writer's own mother. The program left the air after Phillip's mother died in 1937. It reappeared in 1943, but was now the story of the Schultz family; it appeared with two other Phillips serials as a part of *The General Mills Hour*. In the earlier version, Irna Phillips herself played the part of Mother Moran, with **Ireene Wicker** as her daughter. In the second version, **Virginia Payne** and Murray Forbes played the parts of Mama and Papa Schultz.

TOM CORBETT, SPACE CADET. A 30-minute **juvenile adventure program** heard on radio only in 1952, *Tom Corbett, Space Cadet* is better known as a television program, where it was seen from 1950 to 1956. There were also several Tom Corbett books, comic books, and a newspaper comic strip; but the setting was the same on all versions: Tom and his friends Roger Manning and Astro, a Venusian, were boys enrolled at the Space Academy, a military school located on Luna. While at the Academy, the boys were involved in a series of adventures with Captain Larry Strong of the Space Patrol. On radio, Tom was played by Frankie Thomas, Roger by Jan Merlin, Astro by Al Markim, and Captain Strong by Edward Bryce.

TOM MIX. A **juvenile adventure program** heard from 1933 to 1950, *Tom Mix*, sometimes listed as *The Tom Mix Ralston Straight Shooters*, was supposedly based on the life of the real Tom Mix, a cowboy motion picture star of the 1930s, although the actual events on the program were fictitious. On the first version, Tom lived on his TM-Bar ranch near Dobie Township, with his wonder horse, Tony, his two young wards, Jane and Jimmy, and his sidekick, "The Old Wrangler." Tom's friends were "Straight Shooters." Several performers played Tom, including Artells Dickson, Jack Holden, and Russell Thorson; Percy Henson was The Old Wrangler. **Joe "Curley" Bradley** played Pecos Williams, another Mix sidekick. The program was off the air from 1942 to 1944; when it returned, Bradley played Tom and The Old Wrangler was replaced by Sheriff Mike Shaw, played by **Harold Peary**, **Willard Waterman**, and Leo Curley. Don Gordon was the announcer and introduced the stories. In 1949, the program changed to a 30-minute format. Ralston-Purina was the sponsor throughout the entire long run and offered many **premiums**, some of which are quite valuable today.

TOMMY RIGGS AND BETTY LOU. Riggs was a voice actor who had a condition physicians called bi-vocalism. He could speak in his own baritone voice and in the voice of a seven-year-old girl he named Betty Lou. It was not a falsetto; he actually could produce the voice of a young girl. He was working as a singer and piano player at WCAE Pittsburgh, when the studio manager heard his little girl impression and insisted that it become part of Riggs' act. After appearing locally on several stations, he appeared on *The Rudy Vallee Show* in 1937 and was so successful that he was invited back several times and was eventually signed for 49 weeks. As a result of his success on this show, he headlined *The Quaker Party* in 1938 to 1940 and then reappeared in 1942–1943 with his own program, *Tommy Riggs and Betty Lou*. Riggs joined the Navy when this program ended and served until the end of World War II. He was heard again in 1946 as a summer substitute for *The Ginny Simms Show*. In the 1950s, Riggs returned to WCAE as a disc jockey and music director.

TONY WONS' SCRAPBOOK. A program of poetry, readings, folksy philosophy, and romantic dialogue, *Tony Wons' Scrapbook* was heard from 1930 to 1942, with several short interruptions. Tony's real name was Anthony Snow; he created his stage name by simply reversing the letters in his last name. Self-educated, he read widely and the program was patterned on an actual scrapbook that he had once constructed while in the hospital during a lengthy rehabilitation. His delivery was low-key and intimate, and most of the fan mail, of which there was a great deal, was from female listeners. His catchphrase was "Are ya listenin'?" In 1934–1935, he hosted a similar program called *The House by the Side of the Road*. He was the author of several "scrapbooks," which were collections of the items used on the program, along with similar material. There were several editions of the scrapbooks.

TOSCANINI, ARTURO (1867–1957). Toscanini was considered by many of his contemporaries to be the greatest conductor of his time. Born in Italy, he began his career as a conductor at age nineteen while

on tour with the orchestra of an opera company. Strongly opposed
to Italian and German fascism, he left Europe for the United States,
where in 1937 the NBC Symphony Orchestra was created for him.
On Christmas Night in 1937, he inaugurated the *NBC Symphony* radio broadcasts. These broadcasts were heard until 1954, although Toscanini himself conducted fewer than 20 concerts per season. Many
critics considered this program the highest level of orchestral performance reached up to that time. From 1943 to 1945, these broadcasts
were called *Symphony of the Air*. In 1949, he conducted the NBC
Symphony Orchestra on television, the first of such TV appearances,
thus becoming the first conducting superstar of modern mass media.
He retired at age 87. His daughter Wanda married Vladimir Horo-
witz, the world famous pianist.

TOWN CRIER (THE). The simple but memorable introduction of *The
Town Crier* consisted of the ringing of a bell and host Alexander
Woollcott crying "hear ye, hear ye" after the manner of medieval
town criers. It was a program of book reviews, literary criticism,
interviews, and commentary by Woollcott, who was for many years
the drama critic for the *New Times* as well as author of a column
called "Shouts and Murmurs" for the *New Yorker*. He was the model
for Sheridan Whiteside, the central character in *The Man Who Came
to Dinner*. Woollcott was first heard on radio in 1929, booked as *The
Early Bookworm*. The program appeared intermittently until 1933
when the name changed to *The Town Crier*; it was heard until 1943,
although with several breaks in continuity. Woollcott died in 1943,
collapsing while leading a panel discussion on a radio program called
People's Platform.

TREMAYNE, LES (1913–2003). Born in London, England, Lester
Tremayne was voted one of the three most famous voices in American radio in the early 1940s (along with President Franklin D. Roosevelt and singer **Bing Crosby**). At the same time, he was routinely
voted radio's top dramatic actor. Tremayne achieved this exceptional
popularity by starring on several important radio programs during
the golden age of the medium, including ***The First Nighter, Grand
Hotel, Betty and Bob, The Old Gold Program, The Thin Man***, and
The Falcon. When he was married to versatile actress Alice Reinheart, they worked together on programs such as ***One Man's Family***

and *The Woman in My House*. They also starred on *The Tremaynes*, a six-day-a-week breakfast talk show on WOR New York. Tremayne began on radio in 1930 after working in vaudeville and the theater. After radio, he worked in television, motion pictures, and on Broadway. In a radio career that spanned 60 years, he once estimated that he had appeared on more than 30,000 broadcasts. Tremayne was elected to the Radio Hall of Fame in 1995.

TRENDLE, GEORGE W. (1884–1972). Trendle, who had owned a chain of movie theaters, bought radio station WGHP Detroit in 1930 and changed the call letters to WXYZ ("the last word in radio"). The station was a CBS affiliate, but, in 1932, Trendle did not renew the contract with the network, deciding to become an independent station and to produce his own programs. With the help of key personnel at the station and writer **Fran Striker**, Trendle created *The Lone Ranger*, who became the best-known western hero ever heard on radio. Later, members of the same team created *The Green Hornet* and then *Challenge of the Yukon*, later known as *Sergeant Preston of the Yukon*. All three programs were major radio successes, and went on to be successful in most other media as well. Trendle sold his interest in his characters and their assets in 1957.

TRENT, SYBIL (1926–2000). An actress, singer, and dancer since early childhood, by age six, Trent was the host of her own radio show on station WHN New York, where she was billed as "Baby Sybil Elaine and her Kiddie Revue." She appeared on several radio programs during the 1940s and 1950s, including *Let's Pretend*, *We Love and Learn*, *Stella Dallas*, and *Under Arrest*. She also appeared in more than 25 short films as a member of the Warner Brothers stock company. She made her Broadway debut alongside **Jimmy Durante** in Billy Rose's "Jumbo" at the Hippodrome Theater. She was one of the 150 charter members of the **American Federation of Radio Artists (AFRA)**. After her radio career ended, she acted on television. When she retired from performing, she became a talent agent. From 1973 to 1994 she was the casting director at the Young & Rubicam advertising agency in Manhattan.

TROTTER, JOHN SCOTT (1908–1975). Trotter was musical arranger and conductor for **Bing Crosby** on Crosby's radio show for many years. During his period with Crosby, several of his band members became well-known personalities, including Jerry Colonna and **Spike Jones**. After his association with Crosby ended, Trotter was the orchestra leader for George Gobel's television show from 1954 to 1960 and he composed Gobel's distinctive TV theme song. In the 1960s, he also served as musical director for several TV specials.

TROUT, ROBERT (BOB) (1909–2000). Trout began his career as a radio reporter in 1931, working for station WJSV Washington, which became a CBS station the next year. While there, Trout covered John Philip Sousa's last public performance, the repeal of Prohibition, and the campaign speeches of Franklin D. Roosevelt. During Roosevelt's presidency, Trout was the first broadcaster to use the term "fireside chat" to describe Roosevelt's radio addresses to the nation, and usually introduced the president on these programs. On 13 March 1938, Trout went on the air to introduce CBS's 30-minute *World News Roundup* only two days after the German army marched into Austria, and he kept the country informed throughout World War II and for years afterward. He spent part of the war years in London, working with **Edward R. Murrow**, and hosting a program called *Transatlantic Call*, which placed long-distance calls from wives and sweethearts to their loved ones overseas in the armed forces. Trout was the announcer who told CBS listeners about the D-Day invasion in June 1944, at one point staying on the air for more than seven hours straight. He then reported on both V-E and V-J Days, these efforts earning him the nickname "The Iron Man of Radio." Trout continued to work in radio and on television, mostly for CBS, covering such events as Alan Shepard's space flight in 1961. His radio program, *Robert Trout with the News Till Now*, aired during 1946–1947, and then again in 1952–1953. Trout retired from full-time reporting in 1996, but continued to work as a commentator for NPR's *All Things Considered*. He received a **Peabody Award** in 1980. *See also* NEWS PROGRAMS.

TRUE DETECTIVE MYSTERIES. Several versions of *True Detective Mysteries* were heard from 1929 to 1958, all of them based on cases taken from *True Detective* magazine. The best-known version was heard from 1944 to 1958, with Richard Keith narrating the program, posing as John Shuttleworth, editor of the magazine. In a later version, the editor was unnamed and was played by John Griggs. Although often told from the criminal's perspective, the theme of the episodes was that crime does not pay, and at the end of every program descriptions were given of wanted criminals, with large cash rewards for information leading to their arrest. The program was sponsored for many years by Oh Henry! candy bars, which were referred to in commercials as "Public energy number one." *See also* CRIME PROGRAMS.

TRUTH OR CONSEQUENCES. Created and hosted by **Ralph Edwards**, *Truth or Consequences* was one of the two great stunt programs of old-time radio, along with *People Are Funny*. Based on an old parlor game, contestants were asked to answer an essentially impossible question and upon failure to do so were required to pay the "consequences," usually by performing some ridiculous or embarrassing stunt. The program was heard from 1940 to 1957, and some of the stunts were very elaborate and expensive, lasting several weeks. In addition to the stunts, one of the most popular features of the program was a contest to identify a mystery guest, whose recorded voice was heard each week. Clues to the identity were given on each program, with the cash prize building every week.

In 1950, Edwards announced that the 10th anniversary broadcast would be made from any town that chose to change its name to Truth or Consequences, and the town of Hot Springs, New Mexico, elected to do so. After the anniversary broadcast, Edwards visited the annual festival in the town every year for the next 50 years, and the Ralph Edwards Truth or Consequences Fiesta is still held in May of every year. The program was seen on television from 1950 to 1987, originally hosted by Edwards, but later with several other hosts. *See also* AUDIENCE-PARTICIPATION PROGRAMS.

TUTTLE, LURENE (1907–1986). Lurene Tuttle was born into a theatrical family and beginning in the mid-1930s, she appeared in important supporting roles on some of radio's most successful programs, including *The Adventures of Ozzie and Harriett*, *The Adventures of Sam Spade*, *Blondie*, *The Cass Daley Show*, *A Date with Judy*, *Dr. Christian*, *Duffy's Tavern*, *The Great Gildersleeve*, and *The Red Skelton Show*. On television, she appeared in many guest roles and was a featured actress on three different comedy series: *Life* with *Father*, *Father of the Bride*, and *Julia*. She was also active in union affairs, and at one time was president of the Los Angeles local of the **American Federation of Radio Artists (AFRA)**.

TWENTY-FIRST PRECINCT. After observing the success of *Dragnet*, CBS decided in 1953 to produce a similar program, using New York City as the venue and concentrating on the activities of a single precinct. Heard during 1953–1956, *Twenty-First Precinct* had the cooperation of the Patrolman's Benevolent Association of the New York City Police Department and as on *Dragnet*, actual cases were dramatized. Each program began with a call for assistance made to the precinct switchboard. The response to the call was followed through to the writing of the final report, and each program ended with another call to the switchboard, often suggesting the content of the next week's program, as well as making it clear that the work of the precinct went on around-the-clock, every day of the year. The precinct captain, Frank Kennelly, was also the narrator, and was played by **Everett Sloane**, James Gregory, and **Les Damon**. The actual title of the program was *21st Precinct* (with numerals), although the title was often spelled out in published broadcast schedules and is usually so listed in old-time radio sources.

TWENTY QUESTIONS. An outgrowth of an old parlor game, *Twenty Questions* was a 30-minute panel program on which the panel members were told only that an object was animal, vegetable, or mineral and then were allowed 20 true–false questions to determine its identity. It was heard from 1946 to 1954, hosted by Bill Slater, who had the sometimes-difficult job of deciding the correct answer to the questions posed by the panel members. The listening audience was told what the object was by a "mystery voice," speaking from offstage through a filtered microphone; the studio audience was shown the answer on a placard. The program was devised by Fred Van Deventer, a newsman at WOR New York; and he and his wife, Florence Rinard, appeared as panel members, along with their son, called Bobby McGuire. There was a rotating guest chair on the panel, which was sometimes filled by the Van Deventer's daughter, Nancy.

TWENTY THOUSAND YEARS IN SING-SING. One of the earliest of the radio crime dramas, *Twenty Thousand Years in Sing-Sing* was based on a book of the same name by Warden Lewis E. Lawes. The title derived from the fact that the average sentence of the 2,000 inmates was 10 years. With Lawes as the narrator, the program consisted primarily of human-interest stories based on prison life, and many were upbeat, concerned with the manner in which inmates changed their lives and left prison better people than they had been when they entered—although many death house stories were also dramatized. The program used no music, which made the stories presented seem particularly stark. In 1937, the title of the program was changed to *Behind Prison Bars* and the next year to *Criminal Case Histories*. A similar program called *Crime Cases of Warden Lawes* was heard on Mutual in 1946–1947.

– U –

UNCLE DON. A **children's program** that was heard for over 20 years on local radio in New York, *Uncle Don* only appeared on a national network for a year in 1939. Uncle Don Carney's real name was Howard Rice, and he had a vaudeville career as a trick pianist before beginning on radio in WOR, New York, where he remained for his entire career. His program was an unscripted collection of simple songs, stories for children, birthday announcements, and dialogue between characters he had invented. He read the funny papers on Sunday morning and headed a number of "clubs" for young listeners, giving club news and **premiums** for various sponsor-related products. For many years, the story persisted that he once said "There, I guess that'll hold the little bastards" when he thought the microphone had been turned off. The story was not true; however, the incident actually involved the host of another "Uncle" show in Philadelphia.

UNITED INDEPENDENT BROADCASTERS (UIB). In 1927, New York talent agent Arthur Judson headed a group of investors called the *United Independent Broadcasters* that opened a network of 47 independent stations, intended to compete with the newly formed **National Broadcasting Company (NBC)**. The network had financial difficulties and, in 1928, the Columbia Phonographic Manufacturing Company invested heavily in the network and it was renamed the Columbia Phonographic Broadcasting System. The next year, Columbia sold its interest in the company to **William S. Paley** and the company was renamed the **Columbia Broadcasting System (CBS)**.

UNIVERSITY OF CHICAGO ROUNDTABLE (THE). A 30-minute public affairs discussion heard from 1933 to 1955, *The Roundtable* was a panel program on which issues of the day were discussed by professors from the University of Chicago. There were no scripts, although there was an outline of the topics to be explored. The panel consisted of three professors and there were frequent guests, some of them quite prominent. Members were rotated each week, depending on the topic under discussion and their areas of expertise. The program won a **Peabody Award** in 1939.

– V –

VAGUE, VERA. Vera Vague was a comic character created by Barbara Jo Allen (1905–1974), who started out as a serious actress, and under her own name appeared on *One Man's Family* and other programs. When her acting career waned, Allen created Vera Vague, a man-hunting old maid. This characterization revived her career; as Vera Vague, she appeared on *The Bob Hope Show*, *The Edgar Bergen–Charlie McCarthy Show*, and *The Jimmy Durante Show*. She then hosted *The Vera Vague Show*, a 15-minute musical variety program on ABC in 1949. Allen also acted in several motion pictures during the 1940s and 1950s, billed under both her names.

VALLEE, RUDY (1901–1986). Hubert Prior Vallee was a saxophone player, orchestra leader, jazz-age crooner, recording artist, motion picture actor, TV host, and Broadway star. He changed his name to Rudy to honor the saxophonist Rudy Wiedoft. His 60-minute **variety program**, *The Fleishmann Yeast Hour*, aired from 1929 to 1936, and he then starred on *The Royal Gelatin Hour* during 1936–1939. In 1940, he hosted a show called *Vallee Varieties*, and after military service in World War II returned to radio in 1944 with a musical variety series called *Villa Vallee*. All of these programs are sometimes referred to as *The Rudy Vallee Show*. Vallee had a local disc jockey show on WOR New York during 1950–1951, and then returned to network radio in 1955 with a talk show sponsored by Kraft Foods.

During his radio career, Vallee introduced many famous names to broadcasting, including **Eddie Cantor**, **Alice Faye**, **Red Skelton**, and **Edgar Bergen**. Vallee wrote three autobiographical books; the last one, *Let the Chips Fall*, was published in 1975.

VALIANT LADY. A 15-minute daily **soap opera** heard from 1938 to 1946 and again during 1951–1952, *Valiant Lady* was the story of Joan Blake, an actress who gave up her career to care for her father when he was injured in an automobile accident. In addition to financial and legal problems, she fell in love with and married a surgeon, Dr. Truman Scott, whose nickname was Tubby. Tubby was not only insanely jealous, but as a result of an attack by street thugs developed a blood clot in his brain, which periodically transformed his personality and caused him to live a dual existence as both a kindly philanthropist and a greedy opportunist. He was later apparently killed in an accident in a mine, although his body was never found. Joan was first played by Joan Blaine, later by **Joan Banks** and Florence Freeman. Dr. Scott was played by Charles Carroll, Bartlett Robinson, and Martin Blaine.

VARIETY PROGRAMS. Many of the old-time radio programs that were referred to as variety programs were in fact either **comedy programs** with musical interludes, such as *The Bob Hope Show*, or **music programs** with comedic interludes, such as *The Bing Crosby Show*. It was difficult to produce a true variety program on radio because basically only monologues, skits, and music could be presented; dancers, tumblers, jugglers, contortionists, magicians, and many of the other staples of vaudeville could not be presented if they could not be seen. *The Rudy Vallee Show* is often referred to as a variety program, and it did present dramatic episodes as well as musicians and comedians, but his extremely popular program was actually very much like the other comedy/variety or music/variety programs.

The various amateur or talent-scout programs attempted to create true variety shows, although they were limited in the types of acts they could present. The best known was *Major Bowes' Original Amateur Hour*, which conducted auditions every week and presented untold thousands of different amateur acts over the course of its long run. *Arthur Godfrey's Talent Scouts* presented professional acts and many later famous performers appeared first on this program, including Pat Boone, the Chordettes, and the McGuire Sisters, all of whom later appeared on Godfrey's daytime program. The program appeared on both radio and television for many years.

Late in the period of old-time radio, NBC produced a high-budget 90-minute variety program called *The Big Show*, starring Tallulah Bankhead and a long list of comedy and music stars, but it never achieved high ratings. After the cancellation of *The Big Show*, NBC later produced the show that was perhaps the closest to being a true variety program: *Monitor*, a weekend magazine-format program that presented comedy, interviews, news, and music for more than 20 years—long after other old-time radio programs had left the air. *See also* COMEDY PROGRAMS; MUSIC PROGRAMS.

VIC AND SADE. A **comedy program** created and written by Paul Rhymer, *Vic and Sade* was heard from 1932 to 1946, most of the time as a 15-minute daily daytime program. At the height of its popularity, it was heard over all three networks and as many as six times a day. Vic and Sade were Mr. and Mrs. Victor Gook, who lived in a small town somewhere in Illinois with their adopted son, Rush. All of the action took place in the Gook's house and for many years, these were the only three characters heard on the program; all other characters existed only as people discussed by Vic, Sade, and Rush. Vic was played by Art Van Harvey, Sade by **Bernardine Flynn**, and Rush by **Bill Idelson**. In 1940, Uncle Fletcher, already well known from years of references to him, was added to the cast when Van Harvey had to be written out of the show temporarily for health reasons. When Van Harvey recovered, Uncle Fletcher, played by Clarence Hartzell, was retained, and became an important regular character. Idelson left to join the Navy during World War II and another son-figure, the orphaned nephew of a business associate, was added. The show left the air in 1944, returning briefly in 1945 as a series of skits alternating with songs by Jack Smith and in 1946 as a 30-minute evening **situation comedy**.

VICTOR BORGE SHOW (THE). Victor Borge was a Danish comedian and pianist who was very well known in Scandinavia before fleeing the German invasion in 1940 and coming to the United States. He spoke no English upon arrival but soon learned and became a popular guest on almost every radio **variety program** of the wartime years. He hosted a series of musical **comedy programs** under his own name from 1943 to 1947. The first was a 15-minute program on which he appeared alone, but the better-known versions were 30-minute programs heard in 1945, when he was supported by the Billy Mills orchestra, and 1946–1947, when his program included the Benny Goodman orchestra. Borge also appeared on a series of unusual five-minute filler programs in 1951.

VOICE OF EXPERIENCE (THE). A 15-minute program of advice to listeners heard from 1933 to 1939, *The Voice of Experience* was hosted by Marion Sayle Taylor. Taylor had some experience as a social worker, but had made his name as a lecturer on the Chautauqua circuit, which sent tent shows to small towns, featuring lecturers, musicians, and dramatic performances. Taylor's program was first heard locally over WOR New York in 1932 but it was picked up by the network the next year, where it was so popular that Taylor had to employ a staff of more than 30 to deal with the mail, at one time receiving more than 75,000 letters a month. He dealt primarily with marital issues, romantic problems, and difficulties in family relationships, although he received requests for advice on every conceivable subject.

VOICE OF FIRESTONE (THE). A prestige **music program** heard from 1928 to 1957, *The Voice of Firestone* was first called *The Firestone Hour* or *The Firestone Concert* and featured popular music and music from Broadway shows, starring soprano **Vaughn DeLeath** and tenor Franklyn Baur. When DeLeath and Baur left in 1931, the format changed to classical and operatic music and remained that way for the remainder of the long run. The best-known artists of the day appeared, many of them several times, and the program was simulcast on television beginning in 1949. The theme song for the program was written by Idabelle Firestone, the wife of Harvey Firestone, president of the sponsoring company.

VOLA, VICKI (1916–1985). Vicki Vola began on radio in 1933 working on KLZ Denver, moved to Hollywood, where she worked on *The Lux Radio Theatre*, and in 1938 settled in New York where she became a prominent New York radio personality. She appeared on many popular radio programs during the era of old-time radio, including *Buck Rogers*, *The Cisco Kid*, yours truly, *Johnny Dollar*, *The Fat Man*, and *Death Valley Days*. In addition, she had continuing roles on such popular programs as *Backstage Wife*, *Our Gal Sunday*, *The Road of Life*, and *Woman in Love*. She is best remembered as Miss Miller, secretary to the District Attorney on *Mr. District Attorney*, from 1939 to 1952.

VON ZELL, HARRY (1906–1981). Harry Von Zell began his radio career in 1927 as a singer, but became best known to radio listeners as an announcer on such shows as *Burns and Allen*, *The Eddie Cantor Show*, *Town Hall Tonight*, and *Stoopnagle and Budd*. Von Zell also acted on radio, with starring roles on *Chicken Every Sunday* and *The Smiths of Hollywood*. In the mid-1930s, he began acting in motion pictures, and made more than a score of films over the years, the last one in 1980. He followed *Burns and Allen* when they moved to television in the early 1950s, and appeared as himself on television programs starring George Burns until 1959. During 1959–1960, he was a regular on *The George Gobel Show*. He was also a writer, creating several scripts for television.

VOORHEES, DONALD (1903–1989). A composer and musical conductor, Voorhees began his radio career in 1925 conducting experimental concerts. When CBS was founded in 1927, he was joint house conductor with Howard Barlow and in the 1930s he conducted the orchestras on such programs as *The Fire Chief* and *Showboat*. From 1940 to 1953, he conducted on *The Cavalcade of America*, often composing some of the music used on the programs. Voorhees appeared on a wide variety of old-time radio programs, including *The Atwater Kent Radio Hour* and *The March of Time*, but he is best remembered for conducting the orchestras on *The Bell Telephone Hour* on both radio and television. His tenure on this program spanned nearly three decades, from 1940 to 1968. He won several awards for his musical work, including the Lowell Mason Award in 1955.

VOX POP. A 30-minute human-interest program featuring interviews with the man-in-the-street, *Vox Pop* was heard from 1935 to 1948. The program was first called *Sidewalk Interviews*, but in 1938 the name was changed to *Vox Pop*, taken from the Latin phrase "vox populi," meaning "voice of the people," and the program is sometimes listed by the Latin name. Parks Johnson and Jerry Belcher originated the program in Houston in 1932 and it was brought to New York in 1935. Wally Butterworth replaced Belcher in 1936 and was in turn replaced by Neal O'Malley in 1942. **Warren Hull** later became master of ceremonies and Johnson's wife, Louise, became a part of the program, shopping each week for hard-to-find items in the various locations from which the program originated.

VOYAGE OF THE SCARLET QUEEN (THE). A 30-minute weekly **adventure program** starring **Elliott Lewis**, *The Voyage of the Scarlet Queen* was heard during 1947–1948. Lewis played Philip Carney, captain of a schooner that cruised the South Pacific. The program opened with sounds of the sea, the cry of the lookout, and the reading of an entry in the ship's log, which introduced the episode, similar to the introduction used many years later by *Star Trek* on television. Each week, the ship visited a different exotic port, where Lewis would have an adventure, often one that involved extricating a crew member or passenger from serious trouble with the locals. The program signed off with a further entry into the log, "Ship secured for the night. Signed, Philip Carney, Master."

– W –

WALDO, JANET (1918–). Although she performed on many radio programs during radio's Golden Age, including ***One Man's Family***, Janet Waldo is best remembered as Corliss Archer, the breathless teenager on *Meet Corliss Archer*, a role she played for 10 years. She was Mel Torme's girlfriend on *The Mel Torme Show* and later costarred with Jimmy Lydon on *Young Love*. Waldo also played Emmy Lou on ***The Adventures of Ozzie and Harriet***, on both the radio and television versions of the program. Later in her career, she did voice work in television, especially on Saturday morning cartoon shows—including the voice of Judy Jetson on *The Jetsons* and of Josie on *Josie and the Pussycats*. She also played Libby Freeman on *Valentine's Day*, a TV situation comedy seen in the mid-1960s.

WALL, LUCILLE (1898–1986). In a long career on daytime radio, Lucille Wall played Belle on the long-running serial ***Lorenzo Jones***, and starred as lawyer Portia Blake Manning on *Portia Faces Life* for the entire run, thus appearing on two of radio's longest-running programs. She was also featured on *The Chase*, *The Court of Human Relations*, and *Your Family and Mine*. On television, she later played head nurse Lucille Marsh (1963–1976) on the highly successful ABC **soap opera**, *General Hospital*.

WALLINGTON, JIMMY (1907–1972). James S. Wallington joined station WGY Schenectady in the 1920s. By the early 1930s, he was one of the highest-paid staff members at NBC. He was the announcer on many network programs, including *Burns and Allen*, *Duffy's Tavern*, *The Eddie Cantor Show*, *The Life of Riley*, *The Martin and Lewis Show*, *The Mysterious Traveler*, *Stella Dallas*, and *Texaco Star Theater*. He was the narrator of *Stranger Than Fiction* from 1934 to 1939 and also starred with Harold Lloyd on the comedy-drama, *Comedy Theater*, in 1944–1945.

"WAR OF THE WORLDS." "War of the Worlds," possibly the best-known radio dramatic production in history, was performed by *Mercury Theatre on the Air* as a Halloween special on 30 October 1938. A story of a Martian invasion of earth, it was a radio adaptation of a novel by H. G. Wells, with the action transferred from England to contemporary New Jersey.

The program began with a short introduction and then continued as an apparently ordinary music show, only occasionally interrupted by news flashes, initially reporting strange explosions sighted on Mars. The news reports grew more frequent and increasingly ominous after a meteorite, later revealed as a Martian rocket, was reported to have landed in Grovers Mill, New Jersey. More Martian ships landed, and the Martians began a march toward New York City, destroying bridges and railroads, spraying a poison gas into the air and defeating military forces sent against them. The reporter who observed the attack from atop the CBS building reported the Martians invading New York City itself, then he, too, collapsed from the poison gas and a radio operator was heard asking if there was anyone on the air, but there was no reply.

The last portion of the broadcast was a dialogue with **Orson Welles** playing the part of an astronomer from a prominent university and offering informed commentary on the developing events of the invasion. The story ended with the Martians falling victim to earthly diseases, and following the conclusion of the play, Welles broke character to remind listeners that the play was only a Halloween concoction, the equivalent of dressing up in a sheet and saying "Boo." It has been estimated that six million people heard the broadcast, and that nearly two million believed it to be true, although reports of panic caused by the program were overblown. Howard Koch, who did the adaptation for radio, later wrote a book, *The Panic Broadcast*, that described the broadcast and its aftermath.

WARNOW, MARK (1902–1949). A violinist and conductor, Warnow was the musical director of *Your Hit Parade* from 1939 to 1947. He and his orchestra also appeared on many other radio programs, including *The Pursuit of Happiness* and *We, the People*. Orchestra leader Raymond Scott was his brother and succeeded him on *Your Hit Parade*.

WASHINGTON MERRY-GO-ROUND. A long-running and extremely popular news commentary program, *Washington Merry-Go-Round* was heard from 1935 to 1953 and was an outgrowth of a book by the same name published in 1931 by **Drew Pearson** and Robert S. Allen. The success of the book, essentially a collection of muckraking items about well-known Washington figures, led to another book the next year and the establishment of a syndicated newspaper column of the same name. The radio program originally featured both Allen and Pearson, but Allen left for military service during World War II and never returned to the show. Pearson subsequently became one of the most prominent and influential media personalities of his day. After his retirement in 1969, his newspaper column was assumed by Jack Anderson, who had been one of his assistants.

WATERMAN, WILLARD (1914–1995). Waterman began his acting career at the University of Wisconsin in the early 1930s. On radio, he appeared on many programs and was a regular cast member on *The Guiding Light*, *Girl Alone*, *The Halls of Ivy*, *The Road of Life*, and several others. He starred in *The Great Gildersleeve* after Harold Peary left the show in 1950 and, in the mid-1950s, again played Gildersleeve on the television version of the program. He was Mr. Quigley on TV's *Dennis the Menace* and also acted on the stage and in motion pictures.

WE LOVE AND LEARN. *We Love and Learn* was an outgrowth of an earlier program called *As the Twig Is Bent.* It was a 15-minute daytime **soap opera** heard from 1941 to 1944 and again from 1948 to 1951. In the first appearance, it was the story of Andrea Reynolds, a schoolteacher living in New York, her marriage to Bill Peters, and their struggles to deal with married life during the period when World War II was a significant feature of daily living. When the program reappeared in 1948, the focus was on another couple, Jim and Thelma Carlton, whose marriage was troubled by Jim's meddling mother. Many of the same scripts were used in a later soap opera, *The Story of Ruby Valentine*, although the setting was moved to a Harlem beauty parlor, and the cast was all African American.

WE THE PEOPLE. A human-interest program created by **Phillips H. Lord**, *We the People* was a vehicle for telling stories by a combination of interview and narrative. Heard from 1936 to 1951, the program presented all kinds of people, some famous, some unknown, some with an appeal for help, some to discuss current events, some with a strange story to tell. The stories told were sometimes so strange that they were candidates for *Believe It or Not*, a program that specialized in bizarre or unbelievable facts. There were several instances of hoaxes during the long run, and it became necessary to screen all stories very carefully before allowing them on the air. The program was scripted, and many of the people presented had difficulty reading the scripts, which gave some episodes an artificial quality; but the program remained popular for many years

WEBB, JACK (1920–1982). Webb began his radio career in the late 1930s on local radio in Los Angeles. In 1945, he moved to San Francisco and worked at station KGO, where he hosted a jazz program. He played the lead in *Pat Novak for Hire* on KGO, beginning in 1946, and then moved with the program when it joined the ABC network. He played other detectives in *Johnny Madero, Pier 23*, and *Jeff Regan, Investigator*, but it was *Dragnet*, beginning on NBC radio in 1949, that made him a major star on both radio and television. In the early 1960s, Webb hosted *G. E. True*, a television anthology series of stories from *True Magazine*; in 1970, he revived *Dragnet*, with himself again in the lead role. At one time, Webb was head of Warner TV and produced a number of new series, including *Adam-12* and

Emergency. He was also a movie actor and executive, producing and directing several films during the 1950s and 1960s, one of which was based on *Dragnet.* His first wife was actress–singer Julie London and he was instrumental in developing her career as a jazz singer.

WEBER, KARL (1916–1990). A versatile performer, Weber acted on the stage, on radio and television, and did considerable voiceover work. On radio, he appeared on many programs, with continuing roles on **soap operas**, such as *The Second Mrs. Burton, The Strange Romance of Evelyn Winters, When a Girl Marries,* and *Woman in White.* He starred on *Dr. Sixgun* and *Inspector Thorne.* On television in the mid-1950s, he played the role of Arthur Tate on the soap opera *Search for Tomorrow.*

WELCOME TRAVELERS. A human-interest program heard from 1947 to 1954, *Welcome Travelers* was an interview show hosted by Tommy Bartlett, on which travelers arriving in Chicago on trains or buses were interviewed. Originally Bartlett selected the travelers himself, but the program later moved to the Hotel Sherman; and "scouts" met the trains and buses, searching for travelers who looked interesting or unique. The studio audience also consisted of travelers, who obtained free tickets to the show from booths at airports and train stations.

WELLES, ORSON (1915–1985). George Orson Welles was the first radio performer to play *The Shadow.* He was one of the co-directors of **Mercury Theatre on the Air**, which became famous after its broadcast of H. G. Wells' **"War of the Worlds"** on 30 October 1938, when Welles was only 23 years old. On the basis of his radio work, Welles was invited to Hollywood, where he almost single-handedly created what many have called the greatest motion picture every made, *Citizen Kane.* Welles worked in almost all entertainment media, including other radio roles on **This Is My Best**, *The Black Museum*, and **The Third Man**, a syndicated adventure series. His later years were spent doing guest appearances and television commercials. In the mid-1940s, he was married to Rita Hayworth, at the time Hollywood's "Love Goddess" and a favorite pin-up girl of American servicemen. The former "boy genius" was elected to the Radio Hall of Fame in 1988.

WENDY WARREN AND THE NEWS. A 15-minute daily **soap opera** heard from 1947 to 1958, *Wendy Warren and the News* was heard at noon, the time when most stations were programming news, and it began with three minutes of genuine news of the day, read by respected newscaster Douglas Edwards. At the end of the news, Edwards introduced Wendy Warren, played by Florence Freeman, with "news for the ladies." After Wendy's brief report, there was a commercial break, after which the listener entered Wendy's private life, where she had to deal with two boyfriends and two scheming female enemies. With her career involving the media, it was necessary for the story to be at least somewhat related to current events and writers John Picard and Frank Provo provided scripts that many authorities thought to be among the best of all the daytime serial dramas. The cast was remarkably stable, with **Les Tremayne** as Gil Kendal and Lamont Johnson as Mark Douglas, Wendy's two love interests. No role was cast more than once during the entire run.

WESTERN PROGRAMS. Although there were western adventure programs on radio from the early years of the medium, most of the early westerns were aimed at a juvenile audience. Both *Gene Autry's Melody Ranch* and *The Roy Rogers Show* were rather more adult than other western programs—offering high-quality western music along with drama—and many adults listened to these programs, as well as to *The Lone Ranger*, and *The Cisco Kid*, but the truly adult western started much later in network radio.

Death Valley Days, an anthology program of true adventures, was one of the earliest adult westerns. This program later became *Death Valley Sheriff* (and still later *The Sheriff*) and remained on radio until it moved to television in 1952 as *Death Valley Days*. *Hawk Larabee* (originally titled *Hawk Durango*) began in 1946, starring veteran radio actors **Elliott Lewis** and **Barton Yarborough** as a saloon owner and his sidekick. With the title change came some cast changes as well, with Yarborough taking over the title role as owner of the Black Mesa ranch. Unquestionably the most successful adult western on radio was *Gunsmoke*, which began in 1952 and lasted until 1961, by which time the television version was on its way to becoming TV's longest-running western, although with a different cast than the radio version. During its eight years on radio, *Gunsmoke* won several awards and its success led to other adult western series. *Have Gun,*

Will Travel originated on television before migrating to radio, one of the few programs to do so. The radio version had a different cast than the television series, but the production was very similar. *Hopalong Cassidy* was also seen first on television before adding the radio version in 1952, with William Boyd starring in both versions.

In the 1950s, major Hollywood actors began to star on radio westerns. James Stewart played easygoing drifter Britt Ponset in *The Six Shooter*, whose plots were decidedly mature, often containing humor and resolving problems without gunfights or other violence. Joel McCrea was Ranger Jace Pearson in *Tales of the Texas Rangers*, in stories that were reenactments from the modern files of the real Texas Rangers, a Texas law enforcement agency. Raymond Burr starred in a program called *Fort Laramie*, which depicted the life of soldiers on the western frontier. *Frontier Gentleman* starred **John Dehner** and featured the western adventures of J. B. Kendall, an English journalist who traveled through the West in the 1870s and reported stories back to the *London Times*.

Several other western adventure programs made an appearance, but all were short-lived. Some authorities have suggested that the importance of scenery and visual action in western stories was responsible for the relatively small role that westerns played in radio drama, but it might have been simply that adult westerns got a late start on radio and that the creative efforts of writers and producers were by then concentrated on television. *See also* JUVENILE ADVENTURE PROGRAMS.

WHAT'S DOIN', LADIES? A daytime **audience-participation program** intended primarily for a female audience, *What's Doin' Ladies* was heard from 1943 to 1948 and was originally hosted by **Art Linkletter**. The program was first broadcast from the Hale Brothers Department Store in San Francisco, where Linkletter interviewed customers and involved them in small demonstrations, games, and other contests. The program moved to Hollywood in 1943 and Perry Ward became the host, later replaced by Jay Stewart.

WHAT'S MY LINE? A popular television panel program for 18 years, *What's My Line?* appeared briefly on radio during 1952–1953, with the same format: a panel attempted to guess the occupation of a guest and, if they took over 10 questions to do so, a modest cash prize was awarded to the guest. As on TV, the program was hosted by John Daly and regular panelists were **Arlene Francis**, **Dorothy Kilgallen**, Bennett Cerf, and Hal Block.

WHAT'S MY NAME? A 30-minute **quiz program** heard from 1938 to 1950, *What's My Name* was one of the first radio programs to give away cash. The amounts were modest, although the prizes grew larger over the years of the show's long run. Contestants were asked to identify a well-known person from a series of clues given by the hosts of the program, with the amount of award diminishing with the number of clues required to make the identification. **Arlene Francis** was the hostess throughout the run, with a long series of male co-hosts, the first of whom was Budd Hulick.

WHEN A GIRL MARRIES. A 15-minute daily **soap opera** written by **Elaine Carrington**, *When a Girl Marries* was heard from 1939 to 1957 and was, for many years, one of the most popular of the daytime serial dramas. It was the story of Joan and Harry Davis, she from a wealthy family, he a young lawyer from a poor family. The social class differences led to problems with families and neighbors in the small town of Stanwood; but in spite of Harry's insecurity, and occasional appearances of the usual soap opera devices in the plot, Joan and Harry remained basically true to each other and to their values. Noel Mills was the first Joan, but she was soon replaced by **Mary Jane Higby**, who played the role for the remainder of the run. Four different performers played Harry, and the cast grew very large over the course of the long run.

WHISPERING STREETS. An unusual romance drama, *Whispering Streets* was heard from 1952 to 1960, beginning as a 20-minute daily program with each story complete in one episode. In 1954, it became a 15-minute program with serialized stories, usually completed in five episodes. The program was narrated by a fictitious novelist, Hope Winslow, initially played by Gertrude Warner, later by **Cathy Lewis**, Bette Davis, and **Anne Seymour**.

WHISTLER (THE). A 30-minute mystery anthology, *The Whistler* actually appeared on network radio for only one season, 1947–1948, but it was a regular feature on the CBS West Coast regional network for many years, and is very well known to old-time radio fans, with over 450 recorded episodes still available. The program opened with echoing footsteps and a whistled melody that gradually grew louder until it blended with the orchestra and a spooky narrator called The Whistler introduced the story. The whistled melody was written for the program by **Wilbur Hatch** and was extremely difficult; it was once estimated that not one person in 20 could whistle it. The programs were murder mysteries, usually told from the point of the view of the murderer, and were performed by a stock company containing some of the finest radio performers on the West Coast. Bill Forman was The Whistler.

WHITEMAN, PAUL (1890–1967). Whiteman was a conductor and orchestra leader who at one time was referred to as the "Dean of Modern American Music." He began his radio career in the early 1920s on special broadcasts and, beginning in 1929, he and his orchestra appeared on a regular basis on such programs as *The Old Gold Show*, *The Kraft Music Hall*, *Chesterfield Presents*, and *Burns and Allen*. During 1947–1948, he starred on *The Paul Whiteman Club*, the first nationwide disc jockey program; in 1948, "Pops" Whiteman and his orchestra were featured on the inaugural telecast of the ABC television network. Several Whiteman TV programs followed, including *America's Greatest Bands* in 1955, which he hosted. He continued to conduct into the 1960s, often in tribute concerts for George Gershwin, an early Whiteman protégé. A biography by Thomas A. DeLong, *Pops: Paul Whiteman, King of Jazz*, was published in 1983.

WICKER, IREENE (1900–1987). Although she frequently appeared in **soap operas**, including *Painted Dreams* and *Today's Children*, Ireene Wicker is most famous in the history of radio as the star of *The Singing Story Lady*, which appeared on the NBC Blue Network from 1932 to 1941. Because of her work on this children's program, Wicker received a **Peabody Award** in 1958 for lifetime achievement. She also wrote several successful children's books, some of which are still in print today. She added the extra "e" to her first name on the advice of a numerologist, who told her that it would bring her success.

WILCOX, HARLOW (1900–1960). Wilcox usually is identified with *Fibber McGee and Molly*, for whom he did the Johnson Wax commercials from 1935 to 1952; but he also announced on several other network programs, including *Amos 'n' Andy*, *The Baby Snooks Show*, *The Ben Bernie Show*, *The Frank Morgan Show*, *Suspense*, and *Truth or Consequences*. Wilcox was from a family of musicians, and studied voice in his youth. His first radio work was at station WGES Chicago in 1930. In March 1932, he cut in on a remote band broadcast to announce the story of the Lindbergh baby's kidnapping. Subsequently, he was hired by NBC as a staff announcer. In the late 1940s, he headed the television department of Rocket Pictures, Inc.

WILD BILL HICKOK. A 30-minute **juvenile adventure program** heard from 1951 to 1956, *Wild Bill Hickok* starred the same characters as the television version: Guy Madison as Wild Bill and Andy Devine as his sidekick, Jingles. The show was standard juvenile western fare, with Wild Bill and his sidekick traveling about and encountering villains of various kinds. Hollywood radio performers appeared in supporting roles. The program was noted for offering many premiums, particularly during the time it was sponsored by Kellogg's cereals.

WILLSON, MEREDITH (1902–1984). Willson was born in Mason City, Iowa, and played the flute in John Philip Sousa's famous marching band from 1921 to 1923. He then joined the New York Philharmonic Orchestra and, in the early 1930s, moved to San Francisco, where he served as concert director for KFRC and as musical director at NBC in San Francisco. In the late 1930s, he moved to NBC Hollywood and subsequently appeared on many radio programs of that era, including *Burns and Allen*, *Good News of 1937–1940*, *Maxwell House Coffee Time*, and *Meredith Willson's Music Room*. During World War II, he served in the U.S. Army and was involved in the operation of the **Armed Forces Radio Service**. He wrote many songs, some of which have become standards, including "76 Trombones," "May the Good Lord Bless and Keep You," "You and I," and "Till There Was You." He is most famous today as the author–composer of the popular Broadway musical *The Music Man*.

WILSON, DON (1900–1982). Wilson was, for many years, associated with **Jack Benny**, both on radio and television, but he also worked as an announcer on other network radio programs, including *Command*

Performance, *The Packard Hour*, and ***Tommy Riggs and Betty Lou***. Born in Nebraska, he graduated from the University of Colorado and began his radio career in San Francisco, then moved to KFI Los Angeles, where he became chief announcer. His association with Benny began in the early 1930s and lasted until the mid-1960s, a total of 33 years.

WILSON, MARIE (1917–1972). Wilson, whose real name was Kathleen Elizabeth White, signed a motion picture contract at Warner Brothers when she was only 15. After her name change, she was featured in several movies, beginning in 1936 with *Satan Met a Lady*. Wilson appeared as a guest on a few radio programs during the 1940s and then, in 1947, was cast as the lead on ***My Friend Irma***, a part she performed until 1954. Wilson's role as the kooky secretary was very popular and led to a television series and two films based on her character. The TV series was seen from 1952 to 1954. A movie, *My Friend Irma* (1949), was very successful and introduced the comedy team of Dean Martin and Jerry Lewis. As late as 1970, Wilson supplied the voice of Penny McCoy on *Where's Huddles*, a TV animated cartoon series.

WINCHELL, WALTER (1897–1972). Walter Winchell quit school in the sixth grade to sing in vaudeville, and, at one time, he sang in a trio with **Eddie Cantor** and George Jessell. Although part of a song-and-dance act in the early 1920s, he collected show business gossip for backstage bulletin boards and trade journals, and New York's tabloid newspapers picked up his items. He was eventually hired by the *New York Daily Mirror*. His *Jergens Journal* was heard on radio from 1932 to 1948. He had other programs of gossip and news that ran until 1957, but during the period of his Jergens program, when he also had a syndicated newspaper column, he was considered the most influential reporter in the nation. After radio, he worked in television, hosting news, drama, and variety shows. He was also the staccato narrator on *The Untouchables*, the hugely successful hour-long TV crime program set in the Chicago of the 1930s. Winchell was elected to the Radio Hall of Fame in 2004.

WINKLER, BETTY (1915–2002). Betty Winkler began performing at age five, and acted on Chicago radio as a teenager. She was featured on several popular radio series, including ***Grand Hotel***, ***The First***

Nighter, and **Fibber McGee and Molly**, and at one time was said to have the "sweetest, most feminine voice on radio." She was also the winner of a reader's poll for best radio actress. She married Broadway star George Keane, and they worked together on the serial *Rosemary*. A back injury led her to the study of sensory awareness, and she spent her later years teaching her own individual approach to sensing. In 1979, she published the book *Sensing: Letting Yourself Live*.

WITCH'S TALE (THE). One of the earliest horror programs on radio, *The Witch's Tale* was heard from 1934 to 1937, after having been heard regionally in New York for several years previously. The show's narrator was Old Nancy, a witch, who would cackle and introduce the program, accompanied by some howling from her black cat, Satan. Adelaide Fitz-Allen was the first Old Nancy; when she died in 1935, she was replaced by **Miriam Wolfe**, who was only 13 years old at the time.

WOLFE, MIRIAM (1922–2000). Miriam Wolfe began her radio career at the age of four, reciting poems on WGBS New York. She then appeared on **The Children's Hour** before joining the cast of **Let's Pretend** in 1934. She performed on that program for the next 20 years, playing a variety of evil queens, wicked witches, and nasty step-mothers. An eerie cackle that she had learned as a child also won her the role of Old Nancy, the crone who narrated **The Witch's Tale** in the mid-1930s. Wolfe appeared on a variety of other radio programs until she moved to Canada in 1956, where she married and went to work as a radio writer and director for the Canadian Broadcasting Corporation. She later worked in Canadian television and did voice work in animated films and cartoons.

WOLFMAN JACK (1938–1995). Wolfman Jack was a disc jockey whose real name was Robert Smith. Although there is some disagreement about the exact date, he began his disc jockey career around 1960, during an era when many disc jockeys had a gimmick of one sort or another and utilized signature sound effects. Smith adapted some of his act from a previous disc jockey who had called himself "Moondog" and used a recorded how! to identify himself. Smith became well known on **border radio**, broadcasting from Ciudad Acuna from 1962 to 1964, and later from other "border blaster" stations.

His delivery was such that many listeners believed him to be African American, although he was not. He returned to work in New York City in 1973, but it was his appearance in *American Graffiti,* a motion picture produced that same year, that made him something of a cult figure and also gave him the financial security to work as he pleased. He was hosting a nationally syndicated weekly program from Planet Hollywood when he died of a heart attack at his home in Belvidere, North Carolina.

WOMAN IN MY HOUSE. A 15-minute daily **soap opera** heard from 1951 to 1959, *Woman in My House* was written by **Carlton E. Morse**, who also wrote *One Man's Family*. It was the story of James and Jessie Carter of Miami and their adult children. The plots generally pertained to the generation gap, with James very conservative and disapproving of the ways of modern youth and his wife more understanding and sympathetic. Some of the scripts were recycled from *One Man's Family* and the programs were seen as similar in many ways. Forrest Lewis and Janet Scott played James and Jessie, their grown son Jeff was played by **Les Tremayne**, and their grown daughter Virginia by Alice Reinheart.

WOMAN IN WHITE. A 15-minute daily **soap opera** written by **Irna Phillips**, *Woman in White* was first heard from 1938 to 1942 as the story of Karen Adams, a young nurse who dedicated her life to others, taking care of two younger siblings after the death of her parents. Karen spent much of her time counseling others, although she did find time to marry and experience some marital difficulties of her own. The program returned from 1944 to 1948 as the story of nurse Eileen Holmes and her romance with Dr. Paul Burton, with only a few characters remaining from the original version. During this later period, the program appeared as part of *The General Mills Hour*, along with two other Irna Phillips serials, *The Guiding Light* and *Today's Children*, and Phillips experimented with combining plots and moving characters among the three stories.

WOMAN OF AMERICA. An unusual 15-minute daytime serial drama heard from 1943 to 1946, *Woman of America* began as the story of pioneer woman Prudence Dane, who in 1865 took the Oregon Trail from Pennsylvania to Kansas, along with her three children. A great-granddaughter, Margaret, was the narrator and added a new story each day about her pioneering ancestor. **Anne Seymour** played both Prudence and Margaret. When the trip ended, action shifted to a modern setting and the story of another great-granddaughter, also named Prudence. The latter-day Prudence was a journalist and was played by Florence Freeman.

WOOLLEY, MONTY (1888–1963). Woolley's real name was Edgar Montillion Woolley, and he was primarily a stage and screen actor whose radio work was brief but memorable. He appeared with **Rudy Vallee** on *Villa Vallee* during 1944–1945, and he starred on *The Magnificent Montague* in 1950–1951. In this situation comedy, Montague belonged to a club of Shakespearean actors and spent much of his time trying to keep his fellow members from discovering that he was appearing as "Uncle Goodheart" on the radio. Woolley studied at both Yale and Harvard universities, and taught dramatics at the former. His most important role was his stage and screen interpretation of the title role in *The Man Who Came to Dinner*. He was nominated for two Oscars for his work in motion pictures and played himself in *Night and Day* (1946), the film biography of Cole Porter.

WYNN, ED (1886–1966). Although he was also a writer, director, and producer, Wynn (whose real name was Isaiah Edwin Leopold) was best known as a comedian. Billed as "The Perfect Fool," he was a successful vaudeville comic before he was 18 and appeared in several Ziegfeld Follies. He debuted on radio in 1932 as *The Fire Chief*, and after *The Fire Chief* left the air in 1935, had several other radio programs, including *Ed Wynn's Grab Bag*, *The Perfect Fool*, and a **situation comedy** called *Happy Island*. In the late 1940s and early 1950s, he was very successful on television, winning two Emmy Awards in 1949. Wynn began playing dramatic roles in the mid-1950s, and continued to be active on TV and in films until shortly before his death.

– X –

X MINUS ONE. An outgrowth of ***Dimension X***, a previous NBC program, *X Minus One* was a 30-minute science fiction anthology, heard in several different time-slots from 1955 to 1958. The stories included the very best material from the best science fiction writers of the day, often taken from *Galaxy Science Fiction* magazine. Although the sound effects and production were superior to *Dimension X*, the format was similar and some of the same stories were presented on both programs.

– Y –

YANKEE NETWORK (THE). A regional radio network founded in Boston in 1930 by radio pioneer John Shepard, the Yankee Network specialized in gathering and broadcasting news. The Yankee News Service was the most elaborate radio news operation in the United States during the mid-1930s. Beginning in 1934, they hired part-time reporters or "stringers" in each of the locations containing a network affiliate, and the stories submitted by these reporters were collated and edited at WNAC Boston, the flagship station of the network. The Yankee Network was also a pioneer in the area of FM broadcasting, establishing the first FM network as early as 1941, but the FM operation was driven out of business by political machinations of the major networks, who feared the competition. The network was purchased by General Tire and Rubber in 1943 and remained on the air until 1967.

YARBOROUGH, BARTON (1900–1951). Yarborough was a major radio star and played Clifford Barbour on *One Man's Family*, Doc Long on *I Love a Mystery* and *I Love Adventure*, and Sgt. Ben Romero on *Dragnet*. He also had featured roles on *The Adventures of Christopher London*, *The Halls of Ivy*, *Hawk Larabee*, and *Today's Children*. Yarborough moved to television with *Dragnet* in 1951, but died suddenly of a heart attack early in the show's first season. He also acted in motion pictures and is remembered today by horror fans as Dr. Kettering in the 1942 cult film *The Ghost of Frankenstein*. Yarborough's other films included the 1945–1946 series based on the *I Love a Mystery* radio show, in which he again was cast as Doc Long.

YOU ARE THERE. *You Are There* was an unusual 30-minute informative dramatic program heard from 1947 to 1950. Created by

Goodman Ace and originally called *CBS Is There*, the program asked the listener to believe that the CBS microphone was present at some great moment in history. Events were presented as if witnessed by newsmen, with news bulletins interspersed with on-the-spot interviews and analysis of the situation as it unfolded. The program was hosted by Don Hollenbeck and John Daly, who also served as reporters. Other prominent newsmen, including Guy Sorel, Ken Roberts, and Jackson Beck, participated in the reconstruction of events.

YOU BET YOUR LIFE. A **quiz program** in format, *You Bet Your Life* was primarily a vehicle for the ad-lib comedy of **Groucho Marx**. Heard from 1947 to 1956, and seen on television from 1950 to 1961, the program was the brainchild of John Guedel, and he and Marx were the co-owners of show. Contestants appeared in pairs, and each pair was given $20 to wager on a series of four questions, each of which would double the money if answered correctly. The couple with the largest winning total would have an opportunity to answer a jackpot question, with jackpots starting at $1,000 and increasing by $500 each week that the jackpot question was not answered. A common word was chosen as "The Secret Word" and if spoken by any contestant during the program, an immediate cash reward was paid. The program was taped and then edited to include only the more interesting and humorous segments. Jack Slattery was the first announcer, but was soon replaced by **George Fenneman**, who became Groucho's sidekick for the rest of the run on both radio and television.

YOUNG DR. MALONE. *Young Dr. Malone* was a 15-minute daily **soap opera** heard from 1939 to 1960. It was the story of Jerry Malone, a young physician who, during the course of the long run, progressed to mature practitioner and eventually medical director of a clinic. In addition to problems with his wife Ann and his daughter Jill, who grew to maturity during the program, Jerry was shot down in an airplane during World War II and was, for some time, presumed dead. After returning, he was stricken with a crippling disease, which he overcame with the aid of some high-risk medical interventions. All of the major characters were played by several performers during the long run, but Sandy Becker is the best-remembered Jerry, playing the role from 1947 to 1960. The program left the air on 25 November 1960, but a television version was seen from 1958 to 1963.

YOUNG WIDDER BROWN. One of the most successful of the many **soap operas** produced by **Frank and Anne Hummert**, *Young Widder Brown* was heard from 1938 to 1956. It was the story of widowed Ellen Brown, who ran a tea room to support her two fatherless children. Although courted by a number of eligible men, many obstacles to marriage appeared and the program was primarily the story of these difficulties. These difficulties included vicious gossip, a false accusation of murder, amnesia, and the opposition of her children. She never did marry on the program, although she did agree to marry long-time suitor Dr. Anthony Loring on the last episode, broadcast in June of 1956. Florence Freeman played Ellen for most of the program, although toward the end of the run she was replaced, first by Wendy Drew and then by Millicent Brower. Ned Wever played the part of Anthony Loring for nearly 20 years.

YOUNG, ALAN (1919–). Born Angus Young in England, Young grew up in Canada and was a professional performer at an early age. He was the summer replacement for **Eddie Cantor** in 1944 and subsequently was heard on other radio programs during the 1940s, including *The Jimmy Durante Show* and *Texaco Star Theater*. His own program, *The Alan Young Show*, included at times **Jim Backus** (as Hubert Updike, the 3rd) and Ed Begley (as Papa Dittenfeffer). On television, Young hosted his own variety program in the early 1950s, was a regular on *Saturday Night Revue* in 1954, and then became famous as Wilbur Post, the owner of a talking horse, on *Mr. Ed*, a part he played from 1961 until 1966. Young left show business in the late 1960s to do church work, but later returned to acting and did voice work for children's cartoons, including the voice of Scrooge McDuck in *Mickey's Christmas Carol* (1983). His autobiography, *There's No Business Like Show Business. . .Was*, appeared in 2006.

YOUNG, VICTOR (1900–1956). Young had a long career as a violinist, arranger, bandleader, popular songwriter, and composer from the 1930s until the year of his death. On radio, he appeared on *The*

Carnation Contented Hour, *The John Charles Thomas Show*, ***The Shell Chateau***, and ***Texaco Star Theater***. On television, he was the orchestra leader on *The Milton Berle Show* in the mid-1950s. In Hollywood, he worked on hundreds of motion pictures, including *Around the World in 80 Days* (1956), for which he received an Oscar posthumously.

YOUR HIT PARADE. A long-running **music program** that presented the most popular songs of the week, *Your Hit Parade* was heard from 1935 to 1959. The popularity rankings of the songs were widely accepted, although the actual method of computation remained at least murky, if not secret. The ratings were compiled by an agency that represented the American Tobacco Company, the show's sponsor, and were supposedly based on radio requests, sheet music sales, jukebox tabulations, and requests to orchestra leaders. The format of the program changed several times during the very long run, but in the best-remembered version, the top seven songs were played, with a countdown to the number one song, which was heralded by a fanfare. Over 50 singers appeared during the course of the run, including Frank Sinatra, **Lawrence Tibbett**, Andy Russell, and Joan Edwards. The later singers—**Snooky Lanson**, Dorothy Collins, and Gisele MacKenzie—were thought of primarily as television personalities, although the program was simulcast on radio from 1950 to 1959.

YOURS TRULY, JOHNNY DOLLAR. A detective drama featuring a freelance insurance investigator, each episode of *Yours Truly, Johnny Dollar* began and ended with a dictation of items to be posted to Dollar's expense account. Heard from 1949 to 1962, *Johnny Dollar* began as a 30-minute tough-guy detective drama starring Charles Russell, later featuring Edmund O'Brien and John Lund in the title role. It changed to a 15-minute nightly program beginning in 1955, with Bob Bailey as Dollar and five-part continuing stories, usually completed in one week. In 1956, it returned to a 30-minute weekly format, still with Bailey in the lead role, although he was replaced by Bob Readick in 1960 and by Mandel Kramer in 1961. The program had the distinction of being the last dramatic series to be heard on network radio during the medium's golden age, leaving the air on 30 September 1962.

– Z –

ZIEGFELD FOLLIES OF THE AIR (THE). A **variety program** produced by Florenz Ziegfeld, the famous producer of stage shows, *The Ziegfeld Follies of the Air* had two brief runs, the first as a 30-minute program in 1932 and the second as a 60-minute show in 1936. Ziegfeld himself appeared on the 1932 version and the program included many of the stars of Ziegfeld's previous stage productions, including Will Rogers, **Jack Pearl**, and **Fanny Brice**. Ziegfeld died soon after the first version left the air and the 1936 version was slightly different, although still composed of comedic skits and musical interludes. Brice introduced Baby Snooks on this program and then moved the character to the *Good News* program when the Follies ended after a run of only a few months.

ZIV, FREDERIC W. was the leading producer of **syndicated programs** during the period of old-time radio. His intention was to produce high-quality programs for local and regional advertisers, who often could not afford the high-priced programs produced by the networks. He was based in Cincinnati, and was so successful that he eventually became the primary source of programming outside of the networks. In 1948, Ziv branched into the television market, where he was also very successful, at one time producing more than 250 half-hour episodes annually. In 1959, he sold 80 percent of the company to a group of Wall Street investors. The next year, the entire company, including Ziv's remaining 20 percent was bought by United Artists.

Bibliography

The bibliography that follows is a listing of some of the book-length and other sources used in preparing this reference work. Many sources other than those listed here were used, of course, including hundreds of newspaper and magazine articles and many of the annual trade publications that were produced during the Golden Age of Radio. Most of the journals, weekly and monthly magazines, and annual publications devoted to radio are not listed because they are now out of print and many of the organizations that were responsible for their publication no longer exist. Although difficult to find, these sources sometimes are available in large public libraries and from dealers who specialize in old-time radio (OTR) materials. They include, among others, the *Broadcast Bibliophile's Booknotes*, *Broadcasting*, *Broadcasting Yearbook*, *Dimensions of Radio*, *Journal of Broadcasting*, *Mass Media Booknotes*, *Radio Broadcast*, *Radio Daily*, *Radio Directory*, *Radio Guide*, *Radio Life*, *Radio-TV Mirror*, *Radio Programming Profile*, *Radio Stars*, and *Variety*. *The Journal of Popular Culture*, begun in 1966 and still being published, was especially helpful. Also useful were the several nostalgia magazines that have been published since the 1970s, including *Memories*, *Remember When*, and *Reminisce*.

In addition, use was made of numerous program logs, newsletters, and other publications of OTR fans and clubs, including the following: *Collector's Corner* (Old Radio Warehouse, Yonkers, NY 10710), *The Golden Years of Radio & TV* (World of Yesterday, Waynesville, NC 28786), *Hello, Again* (Jay Hickerson, Hamden, CT 06514), *Hello Again, Radio* (Cincinnati, OH 45206), *Old Time Radio Digest* (Royal Promotions, Cincinnati, OH 45212), *The Sounds of Yesterday* (Paul Anderson, Laramie, WY 82070), *SPERDVAC Radiogram* (Society to Preserve and Encourage Radio Drama, Variety, and Comedy, Van Nuys, CA 91409), *The Illustrated Press* (The Old Time Radio Club, Buffalo, NY 14220), and *Memories* (annual magazine of The Old Time Radio

Club). *Radiohero*, a fanzine issued by Jim Harmon for three issues in 1963–1964, contains several articles of interest to OTR fans and collectors.

Of the commercially published books on old-time radio listed, the following four titles can be recommended for a basic library on the subject, each for a somewhat different reason:

1) Buxton and Owen's *Radio's Golden Age* (1966). Revised edition: *The Big Broadcast, 1920–1950* (Viking, 1972). The first attempt at a comprehensive reference work in the field. Particularly useful for its inclusion of information about producers, directors, and music directors.
2) Dunning's *On the Air: The Encyclopedia of Old-Time Radio* (Oxford University Press, 1998). A very readable coverage of many of the favorite programs of Radio's Golden Age. Provides extensive critical comments on programs.
3) Greenfield's *Radio: A Reference Guide* (Greenwood, 1989). A scholarly work on radio research materials, focusing on popular radio broadcasting. It provides historical overview of the medium from the late 1900s through the 1980s and is especially valuable for its listing of station histories.
4) Swartz and Reinehr's *Handbook of Old-Time Radio: A Comprehensive Guide to Golden Age Radio Listening and Collecting* (Scarecrow, 1993). Information on several thousand old-time radio programs of all types, divided into program category and program descriptive logs. A brief history of networks and broadcasting in the United States also is provided, along with other information for the fan and collector of OTR programs.

The number of public and private collections on radio materials is extremely large; there are useful collections located throughout the United States. The Washington, D.C., area may be the single best location for major library and printed archival collections, housing the Broadcast Pioneers Library (in the National Association of Broadcasters building), the National Museum of American History (featuring the Clark Collection in the museum's Archives Center), and the Motion Picture, Broadcasting, and Recorded Sound Division of the Library of Congress. The manuscript division of the Library of Congress is also an important resource, holding several good collections including the papers of Eric

Sevareid. Washington, D.C., also is home of the National Public Radio Library and Audio Archive.

The New York Public Library has a substantial collection of books and periodicals covering all aspects of radio. Three of the major networks also have their own official libraries and archives located in New York, but these are not research centers in the conventional sense. The Lincoln Center Performing Arts Research Center, the Museum of Broadcasting, and Columbia University's Butler Library (housing the Oral History Collection) also are in New York City. The David Sarnoff Library in Princeton, New Jersey, is a major source of information on the business aspects of early radio.

In the Midwest, the State Historical Society of Wisconsin's library in Madison is probably the best-known and most widely used resource for radio historians: it has collections on almost every aspect of radio. In Marquette, Michigan, is the Catalogue of Classical Radio Programs, located in the Speech Department of Northern Michigan University. The Museum of Broadcast Communications, Chicago, archives consist of the A. C. Nielsen, Jr. Online Research Center, with more than 4,000 radio programs, and the Radio Hall of Fame.

On the West Coast, some of the larger universities have developed important archives and libraries on radio and related fields. These include the National Academy of Television Arts and Sciences Television Library and the Theater Arts Library, both at the University of California at Los Angeles (UCLA). The North American Radio Archives Library has holdings in Seattle, Washington, and in the Los Angeles area. Among its holdings are more than 15,000 taped radio programs. The Mass Media Studies Program, University of San Francisco, is also a resource for the researcher in old-time radio. Other important sites around the country include the Yale Collection of Historical Sound Recordings (Sterling Memorial Library), and the George Foster Peabody Collection at the University of Georgia (School of Journalism and Mass Communications). Significant fan club libraries include those of SPERDVAC (Society to Preserve and Encourage Radio Drama, Variety, and Comedy (Van Nuys, California), Friends of Old-Time Radio (Hamden, Connecticut), Old Time Radio Club of Buffalo (Lancaster, New York), and Golden Radio Buffs (Baltimore, Maryland). For anyone seeking information on audio collections and radio archives, both Greenfield's *Radio: A Reference Guide* and Godfrey's *A Directory of Broadcast Archives* are highly recommended.

PUBLISHED BOOKS AND MONOGRAPHS

Ace, Goodman. *Ladies and Gentlemen—Easy Aces*. New York: Doubleday, 1970.

Adams, Douglas, and Geoffrey Perkins. *"The Hitchhiker's Guide to the Galaxy": The Original Radio Scripts*. NY: Harmony Books, 1985.

Allen, Fred. *Treadmill to Oblivion*. NY: Little, Brown, & Co., 1954.

Allen, Robert C. *Speaking of Soap Operas*. Chapel Hill, NC: University of North Carolina Press, 1985.

Allen, Steve. *The Funny Men*. NY: Simon and Schuster, 1956.

Anderson, Arthur. *Let's Pretend: A History of Radio's Best Loved Children's Show*. Jefferson, NC: McFarland, 1994.

Ansbro, George. *I Have a Lady in the Balcony: Memoirs of a Broadcaster in Radio and Television*. Jefferson, NC: McFarland, 2000.

Autry, Gene (with Mickey Herskowitz). *Back in the Saddle Again*. NY: Doubleday, 1978.

Backus, Jim. *Rocks on the Roof*. NY: G. P. Putnam's, 1958.

Bannerman, R. LeRoy. *On a Note of Triumph: Norman Corwin and the Golden Years of Radio*. NY: Lyle Stuart, 1986.

Barber, Red. *The Broadcasters*. NY: Dial Publishers, 1970.

Barfield, Ray. *Listening to Radio: 1920–1950*. NY: Praeger, 1996.

Barnouw, Erik. *A History of Broadcasting in the United States*. Volumes 1–3. NY: Oxford University Press, 1966–1970.

Baron, Michael (Ed.). *Flywheel, Shyster, and Flywheel*. NY: Pantheon Books, 1988.

Beal, William G., Alice Sapienza-Donnelly, and Richard J. Harris. *When Radio Was Young: Questions and Answers about Early Pittsburgh Radio*. Wilkinsburg, PA: The Wilkinsburg Commission, 1995.

Beaumont, Charles. *Remember? Remember?* NY: Macmillan, 1963.

Berle, Milton. *Milton Berle*. NY: Dell, 1975.

Boemer, Marilyn Lawrence. *The Children's Hour: Radio Programs for Children, 1929–1956*. Metuchen, NJ: Scarecrow, 1989.

Brown, Robert J. *Manipulating the Ether: The Power of Broadcast Radio in Thirties America*. Jefferson, NC: McFarland, 1998.

Burnham, Bob. *Listening Guide to Classic Radio Programs*. Redford, MI: BRC Productions, 1986.

Buxton, Frank, and Bill Owen. *The Big Broadcast, 1920–1950*. NY: Viking Press, 1972.

Campbell, Robert. *The Golden Years of Broadcasting: A Celebration of the First Fifty Years of Radio and TV on NBC*. NY: Charles Scribner's Sons, 1976.

Cantor, Muriel G., and Suzanne Pingree. *The Soap Opera*. Thousand Oaks, CA: Sage Publications, 1983.

Carey, Macdonald. *The Days of My Life*. NY: St. Martin's Press, 1991.

Charnley, Mitchell. *News by Radio*. NY: Macmillan, 1948.

Chase, Francis, Jr. *Sound and Fury: An Informal History of Broadcasting*. NY: Harper and Row, 1942.

Chase, Gilbert. *Music in Radio Broadcasting*. NY: McGraw-Hill, 1946.

Christman, Trent. *Brass Button Broadcasters*. Paducah, KY: Turner Publishing, 1992.

Columbia Broadcasting System. *Serious Music on the Columbia Broadcasting System: A Survey of Series, Soloists, and Special Performances, 1927–1938*. NY: CBS, 1938.

Corwin, Norman. *Thirteen by Corwin*. NY: Henry Holt, 1942.

———. *More by Corwin: Sixteen Radio Dramas*. NY: Henry Holt, 1944.

Cox, Jim. *Frank and Anne Hummert's Radio Factory: The Programs and Personalities of Broadcasting's Most Prolific Producers*. Jefferson, NC: McFarland, 2003.

———. *The Great Radio Audience Participation Shows: Seventeen Programs from the 1940s and 1950s*. Jefferson, NC: McFarland, 2001.

———. *The Great Radio Soap Operas*. Jefferson, NC: McFarland, 1999.

———. *Historical Dictionary of American Radio Soap Operas*. Lanham, MD: Scarecrow, 2005.

———. *Radio Crime Fighters*. Jefferson, NC: McFarland, 2002.

DeLong, Thomas A. *The Mighty Music Box: The Golden Age of Musical Radio*. Los Angeles, CA: Amber Crest Books, 1980.

———. *Quiz Craze: America's Infatuation with Game Shows*. NY: Praeger, 1991.

———. *Radio Stars: An Illustrated Biographical Dictionary of 953 Performers, 1920 through 1960*. Jefferson, NC: McFarland, 1996.

Douglas, George H. *The Early Days of Radio Broadcasting*. Metuchen, NJ: Scarecrow, 1987.

Drew, Bernard A. *Jingle of the Silver Spurs: The Hopalong Cassidy Radio Program*. Boalsburg, PA: Bear Manor Media, 2005.

Dunning, John. *Tune in Yesterday: The Ultimate Encyclopedia of Old-Time Radio 1925–1976*. Englewood Cliffs, NJ: Prentice-Hall, 1976.

———. *On the Air: The Encyclopedia of Old-Time Radio*. NY: Oxford University Press, 1998.

Edmiston, Fred W. *The Coon-Sanders Nighthawks*. Jefferson, NC: McFarland, 2003.

Edmondson, Madeleine, and David Rounds. *The Soaps: Daytime Serials of Radio And TV*. NY: Stein and Day, 1973.

Eichberg, Robert. *Radio Stars of Today: or, Behind the Scenes in Broadcasting*. Boston, MA: L. C. Page, 1937.

Erickson, Hal. *Religious Radio and Television in the United States, 1921–1991*. Jefferson, NC: McFarland, 1992.

Fang, Irving E. *Those Radio Commentators!* Ames, IA: The Iowa State University Press, 1977.

Feldman, Ruth D. *Whatever Happened to the Quiz Kids?* Chicago, IL: Chicago Review Press, 1982.

Finkelstein, Norman H. *Sounds in the Air*. NY: Atheneum, 1993.

Flynn, Bess. *Bachelor's Children*. Chicago, IL: Old Dutch Cleanser, 1939.

Fowler, Gene, and Bill Crawford. *Border Radio*. Austin, TX: Texas Monthly Press, 1987.

French, Jack. *Private Eyelashes: Radio's Lady Detectives*. Boalsburg, PA: Bear Manor Media, 2004.

Garay, Ronald. *Gordon McLendon: The Maverick of Radio*. Westport, CT: Greenwood Press, 1992.

Gaver, Jack, and Dave Stanley. *There's Laughter in the Air! Radio's Top Comedians and Their Best Shows*. NY: Greenberg Press, 1945.

Gibson, Walter (with Anthony Tollin). *The Shadow Scrapbook*. San Diego, CA: Harcourt Brace-Jovanovich, 1979.

Godfrey, Donald G. *A Directory of Broadcast Archives*. Washington, DC: Broadcast Education Association, 1983.

Godfrey, Donald G., and Frederic A. Leigh (Eds.). *Historical Dictionary of American Radio*. Westport, CT: Greenwood Press, 1998.

Goldin, J. David. *The Golden Age of Radio*. Sandy Hook, CT: Yesteryear Press, 1998.

Golenpaul, Dan. *Information, Please!* NY: Random House, 1940.

Gordon, George N., and Irving A. Falk. *On the Spot Reporting: Radio Records History*. NY: Julian Messner, 1967.

Grams, Martin, Jr. *Information Please*. Boalsburg, PA: Bear Manor Media, 2003.

———. *Radio Drama: A Comprehensive Chronicle of American Network Programs, 1932–1962*. Jefferson, NC: McFarland, 2000.

———. *Suspense: Twenty Years of Thrills and Chills*. Kearney, NE: Morris Publishing, 1997.

Green, Abel, and Joe Laurie Jr. *Show Biz: From Vaude to Video*. Garden City, NY: Garden City Books, 1952.

Greenfield, Thomas Allen. *Radio: A Reference Guide*. Westport, CT: Greenwood Press, 1989.

Gross, Ben. *I Looked and I Listened*. NY: Random House, 1954.

Harmon, Jim. *The Great Radio Comedians*. Garden City, NY: Doubleday, 1970.

———. *The Great Radio Heroes*. Garden City, NY: Doubleday, 1967.

———. *The Great Radio Heroes, Revised Edition*. Jefferson, NC: McFarland, 2001.

———. *Radio & TV Premiums*. Iola, WI: Krause, 1997.

———. *Radio Mystery and Adventure and Its Appearances in Film, Television and Other Media*. Jefferson, NC: McFarland, 1992.

——— (Ed.). *It's That Time Again 2!* Boalsburg, PA: Bear Manor Media, 2004.

——— (Ed.). *It's That Time Again 3!* Boalsburg, PA: Bear Manor Media, 2006.

Henderson, Amy. *On the Air: Pioneers of American Broadcasting*. Washington, DC: Smithsonian Institution Press, 1988.

Hickerson, Jay. *The 3rd Revised Ultimate History of Network Radio Programming and Guide to All Circulating Shows*. Hamden, CT: J. Hickerson, 2005.

Higby, Mary Jane. *Tune in Tomorrow*. NY: Cowles, 1965.

Hill, George, and Lenwood Davis. *Religious Broadcasting, 1920–1983*. NY: Garland Publishing, 1984.

Hilmes, Michele. *Radio Voices: American Broadcasting, 1922–1952*. Minneapolis, MN: University of Minnesota Press, 1997.

Jaker, Bill, Frank Sulek, and Peter Kanze. *The Airwaves of New York*. Jefferson, NC: McFarland, 1998.

Journal of Popular Culture. In-Depth Radio. Bowling Green, OH: Bowling Green State University, Fall 1978 (Vol. XII, No. 2).

Julian, Joseph. *This Was Radio: A Personal Memoir*. NY: Viking, 1975.

Kallis, Stephen A., Jr. *Radio's Captain Midnight: The Wartime Biography*. Jefferson, NC: McFarland, 2000.

Kaltenborn, H. V. *H. V. Kaltenborn, Fifty Fabulous Years*. NY: G. P. Putnam's Sons, 1950.

King, Stephen. *Danse Macabre*. NY: Everest House, 1981.

Kirby, Edward M., and Jack W. Harris. *Star-Spangled Radio*. NY: Ziff-Davis, 1948.

Knight, Ruth. *Stand By for the Ladies! The Distaff Side of Radio*. NY: Coward-McCann, 1939.

Lackmann, Ron. *Same Time . . . Same Station: An A-Z Guide to Radio from Jack Benny to Howard Stern*. NY: Facts on File, 1996.

———. *The Encyclopedia of American Radio*. NY: Facts on File, 2000.

Lamparski, Richard. *Whatever Became Of . . . ?* NY: Crown, 1967–1989.

Landry, Robert. *This Fascinating Radio Business*. NY: Bobbs-Merrill, 1946.

Langguth, A. J. (Ed.). *Norman Corwin's Letters*. NY: Barricade Books, 1994.

LaPrade, Ernest. *Broadcasting Music*. NY: Rinehart and Company, 1947.

Lawrence, Jerome (Ed). *Off Mike: Radio Writing by the Nation's Top Radio Writers*. NY: Essential Books, 1944.

Lewis, Tom. *Empire of the Air. The Men Who Made Radio*. NY: Edward Burlingame Books, 1991.

Lichty, Lawrence, and Malachi Topping (Eds.). *American Broadcasting: A Sourcebook on the History of Radio and Television*. NY: Hastings House, 1975.

Lieberman, Philip A. *Radio's Morning Show Personalities*. Jefferson, NC: McFarland, 1996.

MacDonald, J. Fred. *Don't Touch That Dial!* Chicago, IL: Nelson-Hall, 1979.

McBride, Mary Margaret. *Out of the Air*. NY: Doubleday, 1960.

McCavitt, William. *Radio and Television: A Selected Annotated Bibliography*. Metuchen, NJ: Scarecrow Press, 1978; *Supplement One: 1977–1981*. Scarecrow Press, 1982; Pringle, Peter K., and Helen H. Clinton. *Supplement Two: 1982–1986*. Scarecrow Press, 1989.

McNeil, Alex. *Total Television: The Comprehensive Guide to Programming from 1948 to the Present, Fourth Edition*. NY: Penguin Books, 1996.

Macy, Marianne. *WOR Radio 1922–1982: The First Sixty Years*. New York, WOR: 1982.

Maltin, Leonard. *The Great American Broadcast: A Celebration of Radio's Golden Age*. New York, Dutton, 1997.

Marco, Guy A. (Ed.). *Encyclopedia of Recorded Sound in the United States*. NY: Garland, 1993.

Mitchell, Curtis. *Cavalcade of Broadcasting*. NY: Follett, 1970.

Morgan, Henry. *Here's Morgan!* NY: Barricade Books, 1994.

Morse, Carlton E. *The One Man's Family Album*. Woodside, CA: Seven Stones Press, 1988.

Mott, Robert L. *Radio Sound Effects*. Jefferson, NC: McFarland, 1992.

———. *Radio Live! Televsion Live!* Jefferson, NC: McFarland, 2000.

Murrow, Edward R. *In Search of Light, The Broadcasts of Edward R. Murrow, 1938-1965*. NY: Knopf, 1967.

Mutual Broadcasting System, Inc. *Ten Telling Years*. Chicago, IL: Mutual, 1944.

Nachman, Gerald. *Raised on Radio*. Berkeley, CA: University of California Press, 2000.

Nevins, Francis M., and Ray Stanich. *The Sound of Detection*. Madison, IN: Brownstone Books, 1983.

Newsome, Iris. *Wonderful Inventions*. Washington, DC: Library of Congress, 1985.

Oboler, Arch. *Oboler Omnibus*. NY: Duell, Sloan and Pearce, 1945.

Ohmart, Ben (Ed.). *It's That Time Again!* Boalsburg, PA: Bear Manor Media, 2002.

Ohmart, Ben, and Charles Stumpf. *Walter Tetley: For Corn's Sake*. Boalsburg, PA: Bear Manor Media, 2003.

O'Neill, Ellen (Ed.). *Jack Benny: The Radio and Television Work*. NY: Harper Perennial Publishers, 1991.

Osgood, Dick. *WYXIE Wonderland: An Unauthorized 50 Year Diary of WXYZ Detroit*. Bowling Green, OH: Popular Press, 1981.

Paper, Lewis J. *Empire: William S. Paley and the Making of CBS*. NY: St. Martin's Press, 1987.

Perry, Dick. *Not Just a Sound*. NY: Prentice-Hall, 1971.

Pitts, Michael R. *Radio Soundtracks: A Reference Guide, Second Edition*. Metuchen, NJ: Scarecrow Press, 1986.

Poindexter, Ray. *Golden Throats and Silver Tongues: The Radio Announcers*. Conway, AR: River Road Press, 1978.

Poteet, G. Howard. *Published Radio, Television, and Film Scripts: A Bibliography*. Troy, NY: Whitston, 1975.

————. *Radio!* Dayton, OH: Pflaum, 1975.

Radio Foto Log for 1940 and 41. Newark, NJ: National Union Radio Corporation, 1941.

Rapp, Philip. *The Baby Snooks Show Scripts*. Boalsburg, PA. Bear Manor, 2003.

————. *The Bickersons Scripts*. Boalsurg, PA: Bear Manor Media, 2002.

Robeson, Kenneth (Lester Dent). *The Incredible Radio Exploits of Doc Savage: Volume 1, The Green Ghost*. Greenwood, MA: Odyssey, 1982.

Rockwell, Don (Ed.). *Radio Personalities: A Pictorial and Biographical Annual*. NY: Press Bureau, 1935.

Rogers, Will. *Radio Broadcasts of Will Rogers*. Claremore, OK: Will Rogers Heritage Trust, Inc. n.d.

Rose, Oscar (Ed.). *Radio Broadcasting and Television: An Annotated Bibliography*. NY: H. W. Wilson, 1947.

Schemering, Christopher. *Guiding Light: A 50th Anniversary Celebration*. NY: Ballantine Books, 1987.

Sennett, Ted (Ed.). *The Old-Time Radio Book*. NY: Pyramid Books, 1976.

Settel, Irving. *A Pictorial History of Radio* (Second edition). NY: Grosset and Dunlap, 1967.

Shurick, E. P. J. *The First Quarter-Century of American Broadcasting*. Kansas City, MO: Midland, 1946.

Sies, Leora M., and Luther R. Sies. *Encyclopedia of Women in Radio*. Jefferson, NC: McFarland, 2003.

Sies, Luther. *Encyclopedia of American Radio, 1920–1960*. Jefferson, NC: McFarland, 2000.

Slide, Anthony. *Great Radio Personalities*. Vestal, NY: The Vestal Press, 1982.

————. (Ed.). *Selected Radio and Television Criticism*. Metuchen, NJ: Scarecrow Press, 1987.

Smart, James R. *Radio Broadcasts in the Library of Congress*. Washington, DC: Library of Congress, 1982.

Soares, Manuela. *The Soap Opera Book*. NY: Harmony, 1978.

Sperber, A. M. *Murrow: His Life and Times*. NY: Freundlich Books, 1986.

Stedman, Raymond. *The Serials*. Norman, OK: University of Oklahoma Press, 1972.

Sterling, Christopher H., and John M. Kittross. *Stay Tuned: A Concise History of American Broadcasting*. Belmont, CA: Wadsworth, 1978.

Stumpf, Charles K. *Ma Perkins, Little Orphan Annie, and Heigh Yo, Silver! Second Edition*. Waynesville, NC: World of Yesterday, 1986.

Stumpf, Charles K., and Tom Price. *Heavenly Days!* Waynesville, NC: The World of Yesterday, 1987.

Summers, Harrison B. *A Thirty-Year History of Programs Carried on National Radio Networks in the U.S., 1926–1956*. NY: Arno Press, 1971.

Swartz, Jon D., and Robert C. Reinehr. *Handbook of Old-Time Radio: A Comprehensive Guide to Golden Age Radio Listening and Collecting*. Lanham, MD: Scarecrow Press, 1993.

———. "Radio Program Recordings." In *Encyclopedia of Recorded Sound in the United States*, Guy A. Marco ed. NY: Garland, 1993 [pages 563–567].

Swing, Raymond Gram. *Preview of History*. NY: Doubleday, Doran and Co., 1943

Tarshish, Jacob. *Little Journeys with the Lamplighter*. Columbus, OH: F. J. Heer, 1935.

Taylor, Robert. *Fred Allen: His Life and Wit*. NY: Little, Brown, 1989.

Terrace, Vincent. *Radio's Golden Years*. San Diego, CA: A. S. Barnes & Company, 1981.

———. *Radio Program Openings and Closings, 1931–1972*. Jefferson, NC: McFarland, 2003.

———. *Radio Programs, 1924–1984: A Catalog of Over 1800 Shows*. Jefferson, NC: McFarland, 1999.

Tranberg, Charles. *I Love the Illusion: The Life And Career of Agnes Moorehead*. Boalsburg, PA: Bear Manor Media, 2005.

Variety Radio Directory. NY: Variety, 1937–1941.

Walker, Leo. *The Big Band Almanac*. Cambridge, MA: Da Capo Press, 1989.

Waller, Judith C. *Radio: The Fifth Estate*. NY: Houghton Mifflin, 1950.

Wertheim, Arthur Frank. *Radio Comedy*. NY: Oxford University Press, 1979.

White, Llewellyn. *The American Radio*. Chicago, IL: University of Chicago Press, 1947. (Reprinted by Arno Press in 1971).

Widner, James F., and Meade Frierson III. *Science Fiction on Radio: A Revised Look at 1950–1975*. Birmingham, AL: A.F.A.B., 1996.

Wons, Anthony. *Tony's Scrap Book, 1941–42 Edition*. Chicago, IL: Reilly & Lee, 1941.

Yagoda, Ben. *Will Rogers*. NY: Alfred A. Knopf, 1993.

Young, Jordan R. *The Laugh Crafters: Comedy Writing in Radio and TV's Golden Age*. Beverly Hills, CA: Past Times, 1999.

PUBLISHED ARTICLES AND REPORTS

Beaumont, Charles. "Requiem for Radio." *Playboy* (May 1960): 84.

Culbert, David. "The Armed Forces Radio Service's Education Unit in World War II: An Interview with Eric Barnouw." *Journal of Popular Culture* 12, no. 2 (Fall 1979): 275–284.

Heinze, Catharine. "Women Radio Pioneers." *Journal of Popular Culture* 12, no. 2 (Fall 1979): 304–314.

Shultz, Gary. "Radio Pioneer Gordon McLendon Dies." *Dallas Times Herald* (September 15, 1986).

UNPUBLISHED/PRIVATELY PUBLISHED WORKS

Boggs, Redd. "I Remember Buck Rogers." *Radiohero*, Volume 1, No. 2 (1963): 33–37.

Delay, Theodore S. *An Historical Study of the Armed Forces Radio Service to 1946*. Los Angeles, CA: University of Southern California, 1951.

Frierson, Meade, and Penny Frierson. *Science Fiction on Radio (Revised)*. Birmingham. AL: Authors, 1976.

Grams, Martin, Jr. *The History of the Cavalcade of America*. Author, 1999.

———. *Inner Sanctum Mysteries: Beyond the Creaking Door*. Churchville, MD: OTR Publishing, 2002.

———. *The I Love a Mystery Companion*. Churchville, MD: OTR Publishing, 2003.

Harmon, Jim. "Johnny Dollar: Radio's Last Hero." *Radiohero*, Volume 1, No. 1 (1963): 15–17.

King, Fred L. *The Jack Armstrong Encyclopedia*. Macon, MO: Author, 1986.

Kressley, David. *The Frederick W. Ziv Company*. Author, 1983.

Neily, Robert E. "Soap Suds." *Radiohero*, Volume II, No. 1 (1964): 16–19.

Pomeroy, Owens L. *The Other Side of the Microphone, Second Edition*. Baltimore, MD: Golden Radio Buffs of Maryland, 1986.

Price, Tom. *Radio Program Timelines, 1920–1980*. Salinas, CA: Author, nd.

Sabis, Bill. *Adventures in Time and Space on NBC Radio's Dimension X and X Minus One*. Gainesville, FL: Author, 1978.

Salomonson, Terry. *The Lone Ranger Log*. St. Charles, MO: Author, 1985.

Who's Who on the Air. NY: Ludwig Baumann, 1932.

INTERNET SOURCES AND CDS

There are hundreds of old-time radio (OTR)-related sites on the internet, some of them information-only sites presenting historical information on almost every conceivable aspect of OTR, many of them offering recordings of old-time radio programs for sale. A few of these latter are well-established commercial operations, but many are operated by hobbyists or other OTR fans and they come in and out of existence too frequently to make it practical to list them by name. Entering "OTR" in a Google search engine will yield hundreds of sites of interest. The quality of service varies, but prices for recordings of OTR programs have become very reasonable, and it is possible to own hundreds of recordings with only a very small investment.

This is a period of transition for all providers of OTR recordings, whether commercial or otherwise. A few recordings are still available on cassette tape, usually at extremely low prices, but the vast majority of OTR recordings are now provided on CD. The use of conventional CD's is also declining rapidly in favor of MP3. If you are not familiar with MP3, you need not concern yourself with the technical details, only make certain that you have a CD player that will play disks recorded in MP3 format. Most recently manufactured CD players do so as do many players in late model cars, but you do need to be certain that you have a player that is so designed.

MP3 has several advantages, allowing programs to be downloaded directly from provider sites, as well as allowing them to be stored and played on a computer or on the very compact little MP3 players that are now popular with music fans, but for users of compact discs, MP3 is simply a method of recording that allows vastly more information to be recorded on a disc than would be the case with conventional recording. A conventional CD holds as much as 74 or 80 minutes of recorded material, for example, or two episodes of most OTR programs. A disc recorded in MP3 format might hold upwards of 100 programs.

ABOUT THE AUTHORS

Robert C. Reinehr (Ph.D., Texas, 1965) is emeritus professor of psychology, Southwestern University, Georgetown, Texas, where he taught from 1981 until his retirement in 1999. Previously, he taught at Austin Community College and at the University of Texas at Austin, Extension Division. He has also served as chief psychologist, Austin State Hospital, and as director of program analysis, Texas Department of Mental Health-Mental Retardation, Austin, Texas.

Jon D. Swartz (Ph.D., Texas, 1969) was chief of psychological services, Central Counties Center for Mental Health-Mental Retardation, Temple, Texas, from 1990 until his retirement in 1999. From 1978 to 1990, he was affiliated with Southwestern University, where he was associate dean and Brown Professor of Education and Psychology. He has also taught at two of the campuses of the University of Texas (Austin, Odessa), the National University of Mexico, and the University of Central Texas.

Reinehr and Swartz have worked together in several capacities since the early 1960s, collaborating on several books and monographs, the last of which was *Holtzman Inkblot Technique: Research Guide and Bibliography* (The Hogg Foundation for Mental Health, 1999). Their combined publications and papers total in the hundreds. They grew up listening to old-time radio (OTR) and have been fans and collectors of OTR programs, premiums, and other radio-related memorabilia for many years. They authored the chapter, "Radio Program Recordings," in the *Encyclopedia of Recorded Sound in the United States* (1993) and the reference work, *Handbook of Old-Time Radio: A Comprehensive Guide to Golden Age Radio Listening and Collecting* (Scarecrow Press, 1993).